LIMITEDS, LOCALS, AND EXPRESSES IN INDIANA, 1838–1971

Railroads Past and Present
Series editor: George M. Smerk

Limiteds, Locals, and Expresses in Indiana, 1838–1971

Craig Sanders

INDIANA
University Press
Bloomington & Indianapolis

This book is a publication of

INDIANA UNIVERSITY PRESS
601 North Morton Street
Bloomington, Indiana 47404-3797 USA

http://iupress.indiana.edu

Telephone orders   800-842-6796
Fax orders   812-855-7931
Orders by e-mail   iuporder@indiana.edu

The paper used in this publication meets the minimum requirements of American National Standard for Information Sciences—Permanence of Paper for Printed Library Materials, ANSI Z39.48-1984.

Manufactured in the United States of America

Library of Congress Cataloging-in-Publication Data

Sanders, Craig, date
   Limiteds, locals, and expresses in Indiana, 1838–1971 /
Craig Sanders.
      p. cm. — (Railroads past and present)
   Includes bibliographical references and index.
   ISBN 0-253-34216-3 (cloth : alk. paper)
   1. Railroads—Indiana—History. I. Title. II. Series.
   385'.22'09772—dc 21
                                        2002014180

1 2 3 4 5 08 07 06 05 04 03

CONTENTS

PREFACE

The passenger train has long held a special place in the imagination of Americans. Although people traveled by train to get from one place to another, the journey itself was often special because of exquisite service, Pullmans, diners, and parlor cars. For stay-at-homes, the train was a summons to imagine what it might be like to travel to faraway places. The train also brought students home from school, reunited families, and carried soldiers off to war.

Indiana was a bustling railroad crossroads. All trains between Chicago, St. Louis, and the East, as well as many between Chicago and the South, passed through Indiana. Hoosiers had their pick of some of the finest passenger trains in the land. Indiana also was home to numerous local passenger trains that traversed the many branch and secondary lines that laced the state. Indianapolis was a vital railroad hub with routes fanning out to all corners of the state.

The development of all-weather highways coupled with the speed of air travel siphoned travelers away from the train. The automobile offered travelers the freedom to set their own schedules. Airplanes made it possible to travel long distances in hours rather than days.

The decline of the passenger train was slow and often agonizing. Some railroads made it clear that they no longer wanted to carry passengers and stripped their trains of dining, lounge, and observation cars, turning trains into virtual ghosts of their former selves. Yet a few railroads maintained high-quality service until the end.

There are many reasons why railroad passenger service diminished in America. But as much as anything, the decline of the passenger train was due to cultural changes in how people viewed time, distance, and convenience.

Limiteds, Locals, and Expresses chronicles the development, operation, and decline of passenger service on Indiana's railroads between 1838 and 1971. Much has been written about such famous trains as the Pennsylvania Railroad's *Broadway Limited*, the New York Central's *Twentieth Century Limited*, and the Baltimore & Ohio's *Capitol Limited*. The history of these trains is told here, but this book is just as much the story of the countless locals, accommodation trains, and secondary expresses that Hoosiers patronized during the Golden Age of the passenger train. Some of these trains had colorful names or nicknames including *Brazil and Mudlavia Express*, *Indian Springs Express*, "Old Nellie," "Abe Martin Special," and *Indiana Arrow*. Most of them have been forgotten.

Much of the information presented here was found in *The Official Guide of the Railways* and its predecessor, the *Traveler's Official Railway Guide* (the name changed with the June 1900 issue). I relied extensively on the *Official Guide* collection of the John W. Barriger III

National Railroad Library of the St. Louis Mercantile Library at the University of Missouri–St. Louis. I wish to thank curator Gregory Ames for helping me find my way around the Barriger collection, which is one of the finest of its kind.

I also relied upon numerous books and magazine articles, all of which are shown in the references at the end of the book. Many of these sources I borrowed through an intralibrary loan program known as Ohiolink, which is made up of college libraries within the state of Ohio. I offer my thanks to the staff of the libraries of John Carroll University (where I taught when I began this book) and Cleveland State University (where I taught when I finished this book) for their help.

This book would not have been possible without the pioneering efforts of Richard S. Simons and Francis H. Parker, authors of *Railroads of Indiana*. Not only was their book instrumental in identifying the history of Indiana's railroads, it also inspired me to create a similar book focused on passenger service. Mr. Simons and Mr. Parker also provided advice and encouragement. Similarly, the work of the late Elmer Sulzer, author of *Ghost Railroads of Indiana*, was helpful in providing information on early Indiana railroads.

Several individuals provided photographs for use in this book. I'd like to thank John Fuller, Ron Stuckey, Jay Williams, Dave McKay, John B. Corns, M. D. McCarter, Bob Liljestrand, Richard S. Simons, the Chesapeake & Ohio Railroad Historical Society, and the Louisville, New Albany & Corydon Railroad. Stephen Fletcher and the staff of the Indiana Historical Society were particularly helpful in directing me to the photographs from the Society's holdings that are used in this book.

Several individuals provided information, guidance, and encouragement during the course of this project. I'd like to thank William D. Middleton, Carol Sulanke, Bill Stephens, Harold Schreiber, Randy West, and Richard Pearson. A special thank-you goes to graphic artist Joel Downey, who created the maps used in this book. Roberta Diehl and George Smerk provided much-needed comments and guidance as this book wound its way to completion, and I'd like to also offer them a special thank-you.

Finally, I offer my hearty thanks to my wife, Mary Ann Whitley, who copyedited the manuscript, served as co–photo editor, and offered many helpful suggestions. Mary Ann also provided inspiration and encouragement along the way when I needed it most, beginning with the day I came home in August 1998 from a steam train trip in Indiana with the idea that evolved into this book. I can't thank her enough.

The responsibility for any errors or omissions is, of course, mine.

LIMITEDS, LOCALS, AND EXPRESSES IN INDIANA, 1838–1971

Amtrak

To Grand Rapids

To Detroit

To Chicago

Gary

South Bend

I-80

I-69

To Cleveland, Buffalo

To Akron, Pittsburgh

To Pittsburgh

Fort Wayne

To Chicago

I-65

Logansport

Marion

Lafayette

I-74

Richmond

Indianapolis

To Columbus, Pittsburgh

Terre Haute

I-70

To Cincinnati

To St. Louis

I-74

To Cincinnati

Columbus

To Cincinnati

Bloomington

I-65

I-64

Louisville

Evansville

To Nashville

| In service | ┝┼┼┼┥ |
| Former routes | - - - - |

CHAPTER 1

LIFE AND TIMES OF THE PASSENGER TRAIN

The completion of a railroad in the 19th century was cause for celebration, greeted with booming cannons, ringing church bells, and exquisite oratory. Most of Indianapolis turned out on October 1, 1847, to hail the arrival of the Madison & Indianapolis, Indiana's first intercity railroad. Many had never seen a locomotive, and few could have predicted the degree of mobility that the railroad would offer them.

America's railroad age had dawned on a clear and unseasonably cool July 4, 1828, in Baltimore. With the thrust of a silver-plated shovel, Maryland patriarch Charles Carroll, last surviving signer of the Declaration of Independence, launched the Baltimore & Ohio Railroad, America's first common carrier. At that time, the United States had two railroads. Pennsylvania's 9-mile Mauch Chunk railway used gravity, horses, and mules to haul coal to the Lehigh River. The Massachusetts & Quincy used horses to haul granite blocks from a quarry to nearby Boston Harbor. The B&O was expected to carry freight *and* passengers over a 340-mile double-track route ending at the Ohio River at Wheeling, W.Va. Using horse-drawn carriages, the B&O carried its first revenue passengers on May 24, 1830, between Baltimore and Elicott's Mills, a distance of 13 miles. The round-trip fare was 75 cents.

Indiana's Transportation Challenge

Travel in pioneer Indiana was laborious. The 86-mile stagecoach trip between Indianapolis and Madison took 2 to 5 days. The ride was rough, and the wheels might splinter or become mired in mud. People didn't travel so much as move from place to place. A modern transportation network was critical if Indiana was to become part of the regional and national economy. The state's two dozen highways were merely cleared trails that were impassable in the muddy spring and fall. Boat travel was slow, and navigable rivers did not reach much of the state. Railroads were cheaper to build and could reach places that canals could not.

The state chartered eight railroads in 1832, but none developed, although later railroads followed some of the proposed routes. The Lawrenceburg & Indianapolis opened a 1.25-mile demonstration railroad, Indiana's first, near Shelbyville on July 4, 1834, using a horse-drawn carriage on wooden rails.

Although pioneer Hoosiers were Jeffersonians who believed in individual responsibility and limited government, they expected the state and federal governments to develop a transportation network. The Internal Improvements Act, signed by Gov. Noah Noble on January 27, 1836, funded three canals, two highways, and a railroad between Madison and Lafayette via Indianapolis. An internal improvements board was authorized to borrow $10 million, a daring move considering annual state revenue was less than $75,000.

An 1837 depression pushed Indiana into bankruptcy and torpedoed the internal improvements program. A constitutional provision that prohibited the state from going into debt precluded Indiana from financing railroads. Local governments, seeing railroads as essential to their future, financed railroad development, which after the Civil War was done with a combination of private capital and local bond issues.

Construction of the Madison & Indianapolis began in 1837. Gov. David Wallace rode Indiana's first steam train 15 miles from North Madison to Graham's Ford on November 29, 1838. Two years after the 1847 completion of the M&I, Indiana had 100 miles of railroad.

A burst of construction in the 1850s increased the state's rail mileage to 240 miles by March 1851 and 1,400 miles by 1854, with lines linking Indianapolis with Richmond, Peru, Terre Haute, Union City, Madison, Jeffersonville, Lawrenceburg, and Lafayette.

The first railroads to extend beyond Indiana, the Michigan Central and the Michigan Southern, reached Chicago in 1852. Completion of the Ohio & Indiana to Fort Wayne in 1854 created the state's first rail link to the East. Nearly 2,000 miles were built in the 1850s, and Indiana ranked fifth nationally in railroad mileage. On the eve of the Civil War, 71 of Indiana's 92 counties had a railroad. Seven routes crossed the Illinois border, and eight crossed the Ohio border.

Railroads triggered the demise of the canal and the decline of some river ports. Indianapolis quadrupled in population as railroads transformed the city from a landlocked somnolent outpost into the state's center of commerce and a regional crossroads.

Early railroads were neither integrated nor efficient. Built to serve local interests, most were less than 200 miles in length. Making connections often required a change of stations. The use of 11 different gauges, including four in Indiana, discouraged the interchange of cars.

Indianapolis, however, benefited from the foresight of those who formed the Indianapolis Union Railway in 1850 to promote interchange among the city's railroads. That same year, work began on a joint passenger depot on Louisiana Street. America's first union station opened September 28, 1853.

Indiana's rail mileage grew from 2,163 miles in 1860 to 3,177 miles in 1870 to 4,454 miles in 1880. Railroad development culminated in the first decade of the 20th century, with few lines built after 1911. The state's rail network peaked in 1920 at 7,426 miles, most of which hosted passenger service.

A Primitive Conveyance

Early passenger trains were primitive, and travel was boring, uncomfortable, and dangerous. Rails were wooden stringers with an iron strap fastened to the top. Locomotives and cars could cause the strap to bend upward causing a "snakehead" that could puncture a passenger car, killing or maiming its occupants. Although eventually replaced by iron T-rail, some strap rail remained until the late 1860s. Trains traveled a maximum of 15 mph, which was faster than a stagecoach or steamboat but considered by some to be reckless or contrary to how God had intended man to travel.

The first passenger cars were modified stagecoaches or boxcars with wooden benches. The standard passenger coach was built of wood and accommodated 50 to 60 passengers.

_____

(*Facing page*)   Pioneer railroads used posters to advertise their service. This poster for the Madison & Indianapolis, dated June 1, 1852, showed one train between its namesake cities. The fare was $2.50. Indiana Historical Society, Bass photo collection, negative A100.

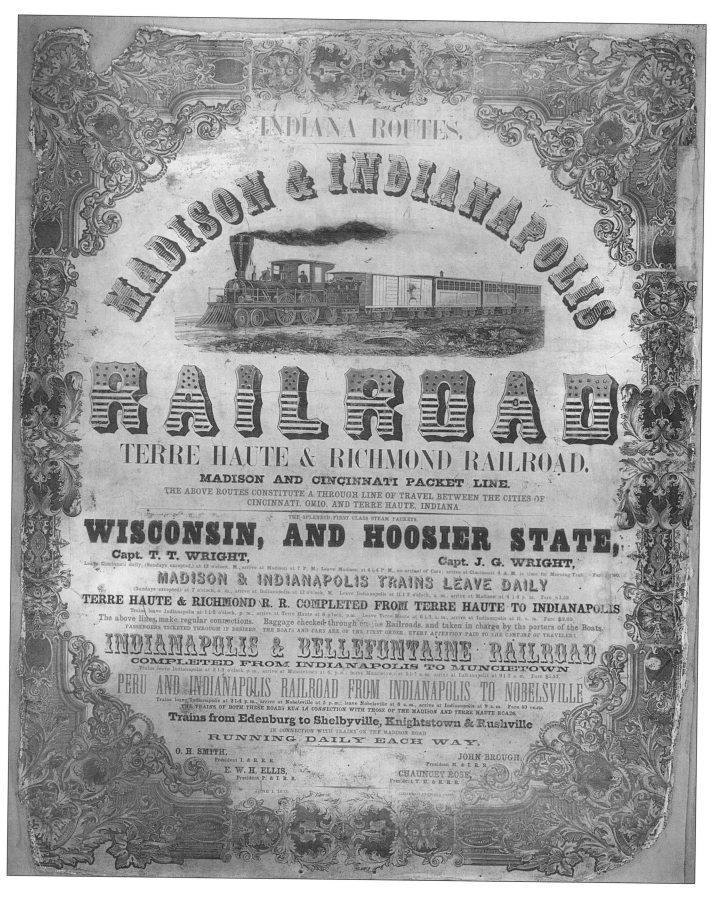

INDIANA ROUTES,

MADISON & INDIANAPOLIS

RAILROAD,

TERRE HAUTE & RICHMOND RAILROAD,

MADISON AND CINCINNATI PACKET LINE.

THE ABOVE ROUTES CONSTITUTE A THROUGH LINE OF TRAVEL BETWEEN THE CITIES OF
CINCINNATI, OHIO, AND TERRE HAUTE, INDIANA.

THE SPLENDID FIRST CLASS STEAM PACKETS,

WISCONSIN, AND HOOSIER STATE,

Capt. T. T. WRIGHT,   **Capt. J. G. WRIGHT,**

Leave Cincinnati daily, (Sundays excepted,) at 12 o'clock, M., arrive at Madison at 7 P. M.; Leave Madison at 4 1-4 P. M., on arrival of Cars; arrive at Cincinnati 4 A. M. in time for Morning Train.—Fare $0.60.

MADISON & INDIANAPOLIS TRAINS LEAVE DAILY

(Sundays excepted) at 7 o'clock, a. m., arrive at Indianapolis at 12 o'clock, M. Leave Indianapolis at 11 1-2 o'clock, a. m. arrive at Madison at 4 1-4 p. m. Fare $1.53.

TERRE HAUTE & RICHMOND R. R. COMPLETED FROM TERRE HAUTE TO INDIANAPOLIS

Train leave Indianapolis at 1 1-2 o'clock, p. m., arrive at Terre Haute at 6 o'clock, p. m. Leave Terre Haute at 6 1-2, a. m., arrive at Indianapolis at 11, a. m. Fare $2.00.

The above lines, make regular connections.   Baggage checked through on the Railroads, and taken in charge by the porters of the Boats.

PASSENGERS TICKETED THROUGH IF DESIRED.   THE BOATS AND CARS ARE OF THE FIRST ORDER. EVERY ATTENTION PAID TO THE COMFORT OF TRAVELERS

INDIANAPOLIS & BELLEFONTAINE RAILROAD

COMPLETED FROM INDIANAPOLIS TO MUNCIETOWN

Trains leave Indianapolis at 2 1-2 o'clock p. m., arrive at Muncietown at 6, p. m.; leave Muncietown at 5 1-2 a. m. arrive at Indianapolis at 9 1-2 a. m. Fare $1.57.

PERU AND INDIANAPOLIS RAILROAD FROM INDIANAPOLIS TO NOBELSVILLE

Trains leave Indianapolis at 2 1-4 p. m., arrive at Nobelsville at 5 p. m.; leave Nobelsville at 6 a. m., arrive at Indianapolis at 9 a. m. Fare 50 cents.

THE TRAINS OF BOTH THESE ROADS RUN IN CONNECTION WITH THOSE OF THE MADISON AND TERRE HAUTE ROADS.

Trains from Edenburg to Shelbyville, Knightstown & Rushville

IN CONNECTION WITH TRAINS ON THE MADISON ROAD

RUNNING DAILY EACH WAY.

O. H. SMITH,   JOHN BROUGH,
President I. & B. R. R.   President M. & I. R. R.

E. W. H. ELLIS,   CHAUNCEY ROSE,
President P. & I. R. R.   President T. H. & R. R. R.

JUNE 1, 1852.

3

Railroad development in
Indianapolis was nearly
complete by the 1870s when
this photo of a Panhandle
passenger train at Irvington
on the city's east side was
made. The Panhandle later
became part of the
Pennsylvania Railroad.
Indiana Historical Society,
negative C5630.

Two rows of wooden benches, some partly upholstered in leather, were separated by an
aisle. The better coaches had a corner toilet, which was nothing more than a rolling out-
house, and a water tank with a hand pump.

Cold in the winter and hot in the summer, the coaches bounced on lightly anchored roadbeds. Passengers endured smoke, dust, and sparks from the locomotive. Coaches were il-
luminated with candles or overhead lamps that burned lard oil and constantly smoked due
to the motion of the train. Wood stoves secured to the end walls provided heat. Derailments
were frequent, and there was the danger of an overturned stove starting a fire. Even if no
one was injured, a derailment might cause a lengthy delay while the crew re-railed the train
by whatever means necessary, there being no wreck trains to come to the rescue.

Passenger trains were labor-intensive, employing an engineer, fireman, baggageman,
conductor, two brakemen, and a train boy who tended the stove and lamps and brought
water from a barrel in the baggage car. On some trains, the train boy brought fruit baskets
and newspapers. Otherwise passengers ate whatever they could find during station stops.

Operating conditions made on-time performance problematic. Trains did not operate
at night (too dangerous) or on Sunday (too immoral), but these operating limitations had
largely ended by 1860. Although stations sold tickets, many passengers preferred to pay on
the train, much to the consternation of the conductor who had to deal with different forms
of currency, which at the time was issued by banks. Fares ranged from 5 to 3.5 cents per
mile and usually fell as competition increased.

Complaints about service were common. Indianapolis newspapers grumbled that the Madison & Indianapolis depot, located on South Street between Pennsylvania and Delaware Streets, was too far from the center of town, the morning train left too early, and derailments and locomotive failures were too frequent. M&I president Samuel Merrill responded that the passenger train had to leave early to get ahead of a freight train and that equipment failures were a fact of life on every railroad. That was true. Pioneer railroads had poor quality track and bridges, they engaged in reckless operating procedures, and maintenance was shoddy. Railroad accidents killed 234 people and seriously injured 496 in 1853.

Although people flocked to watch the arrival and departure of trains, most people traveled only out of necessity. To promote leisure travel, railroads operated excursions, often over newly built routes. Lavish picnics or political gatherings sometimes accompanied these trips.

Modern Trains Emerge

Labor unions, passengers, federal law, and the need to keep up with the competition pressured railroads into making travel safer and more comfortable by the late 19th century. Padded seats became widespread following the Civil War. Hot water heaters began replacing wood or coal stoves in 1868. Block signals based on a closed electrical circuit were developed in 1871. Six-wheel trucks introduced in the mid-1870s provided a more comfortable ride. Steam from the locomotive to heat cars was introduced in 1881. Gas lights replaced kerosene lamps, and many trains featured electric lights by 1887. The vestibule, developed in 1887, prevented icy blasts from entering a car. Vestibules and strengthened car ends reduced the risk of telescoping during collisions. The Railroad Safety Act of 1893 required automatic couplers and air brakes. Cars of all-steel construction became widespread by 1916, but some passengers feared electrocution during thunderstorms.

Railroads coordinated schedules, built union stations, and published schedules in the *Traveler's Official Railway Guide*, which began monthly publication in June 1868. Hub and spoke networks emanated from Chicago, St. Louis, Louisville, Cincinnati, Detroit, and Indianapolis. Passengers had to change trains, but a growing number of through sleepers, coaches, or entire trains were interchanged at major connecting points.

Once trains had become safer, more comfortable, and more reliable and the railroad network more integrated, a business travel market developed. Schedules were established to enable businessmen to put in a full day and get a night's rest traveling in a sleeping car.

Pioneer railroads were not built for speed. The locomotives of the era were not powerful enough to maintain swift running. And passenger comfort declined as speed increased. For trains to be able to average 60 mph in regular service, railroads needed better roadbeds that were well maintained.

Railroads were a risky financial proposition and bankruptcies, reorganizations, and mergers were commonplace. Before the Civil War, consolidations were local or regional in scope. Cornelius Vanderbilt, who controlled the New York Central, created the first trunk railroad when he gained control of the Lake Shore & Michigan Southern in 1869. Most Indiana railroads had been absorbed by trunk systems by 1893. As the New York Central and Pennsylvania gobbled up much of the state's rails, the *Indianapolis Journal* commented in early 1873, "The transportation of our people is at the mercy of men who never see us, who know nothing of us, and care nothing for us."

The small locomotives and freight cars dictated the amount of freight that pioneer railroads could handle. Passenger revenue was a fourth to a third of a railroad's total revenue. By the 1850s, though, the freight business had become economically more important than the passenger business. Both grew substantially in the late 19th century, but freight revenue grew far more than passenger receipts despite the stranglehold that railroads had on intercity travel. Passenger revenue was a fifth of total revenue at most railroads by the early 20th century.

Some railroad executives viewed the passenger business with contempt and disdain. James J. Hill, who founded and built the Great Northern, reportedly described passenger trains as "like the male teat—neither useful nor ornamental." Asked in 1882 if passenger trains made money, New York Central president William Vanderbilt replied, "No, not a bit of it. We only run it because we are forced to do so by the actions of the Pennsylvania. . . . We would abandon it if it was not for our competition keeping its trains on."

Economist Gregory Thompson said railroads viewed passenger service as a way to promote their freight business. Shippers traveled by train and, presumably, equated the quality of freight service with the quality of passenger service. On competitive routes, if one railroad invested in a new train, others followed suit even if the service was not profitable. Consequently, railroads neglected to invest in more promising passenger routes, Thompson said.

The Gilded Era

Construction of an elevated train shed at Indianapolis Union Station was well under way in 1920 when this photo was taken. The view is looking east. The track at right was used by the Illinois Central. Indiana Historical Society, Bass photo collection, negative 69857F.

By 1880 everyone except the poor took for granted the mobility that railroads had brought to American society. The average person purchased five to six railroad tickets a year. Passenger miles increased from 5 billion in 1870 to 12 billion (1890) to 35 billion in 1916. Through 1910, passenger trains carried 95 percent of the intercity travel market.

Most routes saw two to eight trains per day. Trains were designated mail, express, or accommodation, an indication of how fast the train traveled, how many stops it made, and the quality of service. By the beginning of the 20th century, trains on major routes carried 6 to 10 cars including sleeping, dining, and parlor cars.

Baltimore and Ohio Railroad

1933   G 11663

PASS   ***Mr. J. A. McDermott***
Vice-President & General Manage[r]
Artemus-Jellico R.R.
-Over All Lines-

UNTIL DECEMBER 31ST, UNLESS OTHERWISE ORDERED

Not good on Trains 1, 2, 5, and 6 West of
Washington, D. C., and Trains 27 and 28

VALID WHEN COUNTERSIGNED BY T. M. JONES

COUNTERSIGNED

Vice-President

1931   MONON ROUTE   No. 9077

CHICAGO, INDIANAPOLIS & LOUISVILLE RAILWAY

PASS   --J. A. McDermott--

Vice-Pres. & Gen. Mgr.
Artemus-Jellico Railroad Co.

OVER ALL LINES
UNTIL DECEMBER 31ST, 1931

VALID WHEN COUNTERSIGNED BY
V. A. HEWITT OR R. C. KEISTER.

PRESIDENT.

THE PENNSYLVANIA RAILROAD

NOT GOOD ON
LONG ISLAND R.R.   **1934**   WC 4857

Pass   - J. A. McDermott, -
Vice President & General Manager
Artemus-Jellico R. R. Co.

OVER ENTIRE SYSTEM

UNTIL DECEMBER 31ST, 1934, unless otherwise ordered
when countersigned by L. C. DOUGLASS, W. T. SCHIEL or E. A. THORNE
NOT GOOD ON TRAINS 28 AND 29

COUNTERSIGNATURE

THIS PASS ACCEPTED BY ME FOR USE
SUBJECT TO CONDITIONS ON BACK

VICE-PRESIDENT

LOUISVILLE & NASHVILLE

RAILROAD COMPANY

1934   NOT GOOD ON TRAINS 37, 38, 98, 99, 198 & 199.   No. 9204

PASS   J.A. McDermott---

ACCOUNT   Vice President & General Manage[r]
Artemus-Jellico RR Co.

OVER ENTIRE SYSTEM

UNTIL DEC. 31, 1934, UNLESS OTHERWISE ORDERED AND
TO CONDITIONS ON BACK.

VALID ONLY WHEN COUNTERSIGNED BY C.J. WEIS, OR A.M. TOON

COUNTERSIGNED BY

GENERAL

LOUISVILLE & NASHVILLE

RAILROAD COMPANY

1944   NOT GOOD ON TRAINS 11, 12. 15, 16, 37, 38, 98, 99, 198 & 199
   No. 4412

PASS   Ralph B. Martin---

ACCOUNT   General Superintendent,
Artemus-Jellico Railroad Co.

OVER ENTIRE SYSTEM

UNTIL DECEMBER 31, 1944, UNLESS OTHERWISE ORDERED AND
SUBJECT TO CONDITIONS ON BACK

VALID ONLY WHEN COUNTERSIGNED BY C. J. WEIS OR A. M. TOON

COUNTERSIGNED BY

Vice President and General Manager

LOUISVILLE & NASHVILLE

RAILROAD COMPANY

1933   NOT GOOD ON TRAINS 37, 38, 98, 99, 198 & 199.   No. 8855

PASS   -- J. A. McDermott --

ACCOUNT   Vice President & General Manager,
Artemus-Jellico Railroad Co.

OVER ENTIRE SYSTEM

UNTIL DEC. 31, 1933, UNLESS OTHERWISE ORDERED AND SUBJECT
TO CONDITIONS ON BACK

VALID ONLY WHEN COUNTERSIGNED BY C.J. WEIS, OR A.M. TOON.

COUNTERSIGNED BY

GENERAL MANAGER

Passes enabled the bearer to ride passenger trains for free, although some trains were exempt. The Pennsylvania Railroad pass shown here was not good on the *Broadway Limited*. Richard S. Simons collection.

Use of the term "limited" to denote a train making limited stops became widespread in the 1890s. Limited also usually meant first-class. Western railroads had sold legions of tickets, often at discounted prices, and a "very promiscuous class of travel" was overcrowding the trains. The wealthy demanded trains offering a level of service only they could afford.

Railroads built palatial passenger terminals in major cities. The lavishness and size of a terminal often reflected a railroad's attitude toward passenger service. Having outgrown the first union terminal, the Indianapolis railroads decided in 1884 to build a new facility between Illinois and Meridian Streets north of the existing station. Indianapolis Union Station opened September 17, 1888, although some trains began using the train shed a few weeks earlier. The station featured a red brick and granite Romanesque three-story headhouse and 185-foot clock tower. Fifteen railroads and 150 trains a day used the station in 1900.

As traffic increased, so did whining that the station was inadequate. Trains backed up waiting for an open track at the station. The crossing at Meridian Street just beyond the east edge of the train shed created operational and safety headaches. Construction of a new train shed and elevation of the tracks began in 1915. Trains began using the elevated tracks on July 30, 1918. When the project was completed four years later, Union Station had 12 station tracks and 2 bypass tracks.

The passenger business continued to grow. Patronage rose from 492 million in 1890 to 577 million (1900) to 972 million (1910) to a record 1.2 billion in 1920. Passenger miles increased from 11.8 billion in 1890 to a record 47.4 billion in 1920. The passenger car fleet peaked in 1920 at 56,102 cars. Fares declined from 2.19 cents per mile in 1890 to 1.93 cents per mile in 1909. Passengers expected trains to adhere to their published schedules.

Most limited passenger trains served Indiana tangentially, stopping only to change crews or to serve such urban centers as Evansville, Fort Wayne, South Bend, and Indianapolis. Their schedules were dictated by traffic patterns in Chicago, St. Louis, Detroit, Cincinnati, and the major urban centers of the East. Another web of trains served Indianapolis, and a third level consisted of numerous locals that linked neighboring communities.

The Interurban Challenge

The interurban, an electric railway operating between city centers, provided the first serious challenge to the steam railroads' dominance of the intercity passenger trade. By the end of World War I, 10,000 interurban cars operated over 18,000 miles of track. Indiana's interurban network, which peaked at 1,825 miles in 1914, reached 62 counties and every large town except Bloomington, Bedford, Madison, and Vincennes. Indiana's interurban mileage was second only to Ohio's 2,800 miles.

Indiana's first interurban, the South Bend & Mishawaka, opened June 19, 1890. The Union Traction Company, which opened January 1, 1898, between Anderson and Alexandria, was Indiana's first interurban that was not an extended streetcar line.

Built to lighter standards than steam railroads, interurbans were cheaper, cleaner, and more flexible to operate. They offered lower fares and more frequent service, and they went right down Main Street. Steam railroads had made intercity travel affordable, but interurbans made it practical.

The interurban came to Indianapolis on January 1, 1900, with the opening of the Indianapolis, Greenwood & Franklin. Interurban railway development in Indianapolis followed the pattern set earlier by steam railroads. The Indianapolis Traction and Terminal Company built a union terminal on Market Street a block east of the state capitol. Opened on September 12, 1904, the station had a nine-track train shed that could accommodate 36 passenger cars. The station handled 462 trains a day and 7.2 million passengers in 1916.

Even in their best years, interurbans had a rate of return of 3 percent, about two-thirds of what steam railroads earned. Their reliance on short-haul business made interurbans vulnerable as automobile use increased. Declining patronage and the ravages of the Depression forced most Indiana interurban lines to drop their wires by 1935. Interurban mileage nationally had fallen below 10,000 miles, a decline of 6,000 miles in 10 years.

The South Shore, which opened in 1908 between South Bend and Hammond, was the nation's last interurban railway by the 1960s. It survived because it had a sizable freight business. The Indiana General Assembly in 1977 authorized creation of the Northwest Indiana Commuter Transportation District, which preserved the South Shore's passenger operations.

Era of Transition

Even as rail passenger service reached its zenith in 1920, the forces that would trigger its decay were in place. Many accounts have credited development of the automobile as central to the downfall of the passenger train. There is much to recommend that theory. When Congress in 1916 authorized grants for highway construction, there were 3.3 million registered automobiles in the United States. Automotive registrations had mushroomed to 23 million by 1929. Intercity travel increased from 42 billion miles to 198 billion miles over the same period, three-quarters of it by automobile.

Railroad patronage declined from 1.2 billion in 1920 to 708 million in 1930 while passenger miles dropped from 47.4 billion to 26.9 billion, a 43 percent drop. Ticket sales fell by 44 percent and passenger revenue by 42 percent. Much of the decrease occurred in short-distance travel, a market that began collapsing as early as 1912, due to savage competition from interurban railways and the automobile. The passenger train by 1920 was becoming a specialized form of business travel. Some railroad executives blamed their woes on long-distance telephone service, saying that people who once traveled by train to visit with friends and relatives now visited by telephone.

Although railroads discontinued scores of local trains, most routes still hosted passenger service, and rail terminals were still busy places. In 1920 Indianapolis Union Station served 64,343 trains, an average of 176 a day. A decade later the station served 58,976 trains, an average of 162 trains a day.

The rise of the automobile notwithstanding, other forces also undermined the passenger train. Thompson argues that railroad managers misunderstood the cost of operating passenger trains, erroneously believing most costs were fixed and that adding additional cars would not appreciably increase the cost of fuel, wages, and maintenance. Railroads treated costs and revenues as independent variables. This favored trains that earned high gross revenues but whose high costs made them unprofitable. Railroads viewed luxury trains as a form of brand promotion. The all-Pullman limiteds that were popular in the 1920s required elaborate servicing facilities, higher switching charges, and a cumbersome reservations system.

Railroads responded to rising costs by raising fares in the belief that traffic declines would be minimal. For a while this worked, and passenger revenue covered operating expense. But traffic began falling during a 1921 recession and did not bounce back once the downturn had ended. By 1929, passenger revenue barely covered operating expense. Saddled with high fixed costs, even a small drop in passenger volume could adversely affect net revenue, which frequently happened after 1930 as many companies cut employee expense accounts and business travelers gave up traveling by Pullman in favor of driving.

Rail travel plummeted to 435 million passengers in 1933, a decline of 39 percent from 1930. Recognizing that their earlier practices had led to fares that were now too high, railroads won regulatory approval to lower fares. This stimulated increased gross revenue, but increased costs by nearly as much. The costs of operating some passenger trains were so high that, even if every seat had been filled, the train still would have lost money.

Railroad executives hoped their passenger deficits would diminish with the end of the Depression. The deficits stabilized after 1935 but did not disappear. Passenger trains covered about three-fourths of the nation's 233,000-mile rail network and captured 65 percent of the commercial intercity traffic.

Railroads during the 1930s introduced streamlined trains, taking advantage of such technological advances as the internal combustion engine (which replaced the steam locomotive), air conditioning, sealed windows, and "shot-welding," a construction process that produced stainless steel cars without the thousands of rivets found on heavyweight cars. Streamliners could cruise at 80–90 mph, whereas other passenger trains were held to 60–70 mph. The late 1930s also saw the introduction of deluxe streamlined all-coach long-distance trains with dining and lounge cars, services that previously had been restricted largely to first-class passengers.

Historians have given mixed reviews to how well railroads responded to the challenges that sapped the vitality of passenger trains. Donald Itzkoff, author of *Off the Track*, said streamlining gave passenger service a shot in the arm but was a cosmetic Band-Aid approach that glossed over the need for change. Thompson said streamlining worked for a while in attracting the public's attention and boosting rail travel, but the streamliner designs were inappropriate and railroads' investment in them was wasteful.

World War II boosted patronage and passenger revenue to levels not seen in two decades. Passenger deficits turned into profits overnight. Passenger miles zoomed to 95 billion by 1944, twice that of 1920 and greater than that recorded between 1931 and 1935. Railroads handled 92 percent of military personnel who traveled in groups. Consequently, many trains were standing-room-only and railroads asked the public to defer nonessential travel. The railroads put into service everything they had, including coaches that had not been used for years.

A similar boom had occurred during World War I, but whereas the average trip in 1918 had been 39 miles, in 1944 it was 105 miles. Railroads carried more than 1 billion revenue passengers in 1918 versus 910 million in 1944—the peak of World War II travel—but the longer distances traveled meant that revenue during World War II was substantially higher than during the earlier war.

Although retaining the war-level traffic volume was unlikely, railroads hoped that marketing campaigns and new equipment would stabilize postwar traffic at levels above those recorded in the 1930s. Even before the guns had fallen silent, railroads were ordering much-needed new equipment. They spent $750 million on more than 4,000 new passenger cars. Rail car manufacturers were so inundated with orders that the backlog was not worked off until the early 1950s.

Railroads created more streamlined trains following the war, and by 1949 more than 30 percent of the nation's rail passengers rode the more than 250 streamliners, many of them pulled by diesel locomotives. Some railroad executives expected tough competition from the automobile and the emerging airline industry, but a 1947 American Association of Railroads study expressed guarded optimism about the future of rail passenger service.

Who Shot the Passenger Train?

Railroad executives soon began questioning their postwar optimism as passenger service plunged into the red by $140 million in 1946, $425 million in 1947, $649 million in 1949, and $705 million in 1953. Passenger miles fell by a third, and the railroads' share of the intercity common carrier market fell to 46 percent.

Railroads experimented with lightweight trains with a low center of gravity in the mid-1950s that supposedly were faster and cheaper to operate and maintain than conventional trains. Some had tilt mechanisms that allowed the train to take curves at higher speeds. But the experimental trains proved only marginally faster than the trains they were designed to replace. They were rushed into service with little testing and proved to be rougher riding and less comfortable than conventional trains. The experimental trains attracted much interest but were quietly retired without having lived up to their billing as trains of tomorrow.

The Interstate Commerce Commission defined passenger expenses as "the sum of the operating expenses directly assignable to the passenger service, and an apportionment of the expenses common to both freight and passenger service." Critics contended the ICC formula overstated losses by prorating costs between freight and passenger service on a per-mile basis. Many expenses, critics argued, would remain even if passenger service disappeared. Critics also accused railroads of disproportionately charging expenses to passenger service. Raymond Hannon described the passenger train deficit as a sheer fiction, arguing that if only direct and allied services were counted as passenger train expenses, then passenger service was profitable.

Others argued that the ICC formula understated passenger losses by not taking into account such things as terminal facilities and mainline tracks maintained primarily or solely for the benefit of passenger service. Using a formula of avoidable costs, one study determined that railroads lost $708 million on passenger service in 1955, $232 million more than the deficit arrived at using the ICC formula. Even using the direct costs formula, passenger service ceased covering its direct costs in 1953, losing $113.6 million in 1957 and $140 million in 1958. By the late 1950s the debate largely had shifted from whether passenger trains lost money to how much money was being lost.

Patronage fell from 556.7 million in 1949 to 353.6 million in 1959. Train miles fell from 35 million to 22 million. Railroads had 29 percent of the common carrier intercity business and a mere 3 percent of all intercity travel by 1959. Critics accused railroads of discouraging patronage by allowing trains to deteriorate in quality and sharply reducing marketing of passenger service. Railroads retorted that passengers had deserted the train for the point-to-point convenience of the automobile and the swiftness of the airplane over long distances. Railroad executives also blasted government policies that lavished millions on airport and highway construction. Economist George Hilton contends that passenger trains were dying the natural death that could be expected in any industry whose service declines at an increasing rate.

Howard Hosmer, an ICC examiner, was directed to study ways to reduce the passenger deficit. His 79-page report, issued on September 18, 1958, used a study of traffic and economic data for the period 1947–57 to conclude that Pullman and parlor service would cease by 1965 and coach travel would be gone by 1970. Hosmer argued that the railroads' share of intercity travel was so small that the need for continuing passenger service was minimal. None of the proposed remedies, including lower labor costs, restructuring of fares, or lower taxes, held much promise for significantly lowering the deficit.

One of the sharpest critics of the Hosmer report was David P. Morgan, who tirelessly used his bully pulpit as editor of *Trains* magazine to campaign for passenger service. Morgan criticized Hosmer for focusing too much on the ills of passenger service and not enough on remedies. Morgan believed Hosmer had cast passenger service in an unduly pessimistic light, thus feeding the perception that passenger service would inevitably die. Morgan produced his own 36-page report in the April 1959 issue of *Trains* under the heading "Who Shot the Passenger Train?" Morgan agreed with Hosmer that the passenger train was a dying business and was losing a lot of money. "But the passenger train is not dying of old age. It was shot in the back," Morgan wrote.

As for who pulled the trigger, Morgan rounded up and discussed the usual suspects. These including labor unions that refused to give ground on work rules, government policies that favored highways and airways, recalcitrant regulators who forced railroads to continue money-losing passenger trains, railroad managers lacking in imagination or the will to tackle the problem, and intransigent cost structures. Morgan said passenger trains were not being killed by technological obsolescence, the jet, the automobile, or uncaring railroad executives. Morgan suggested that few fully understood the complexity of the passenger dilemma because "the problem has more facets than an armadillo has plates, and it may be insolvable." Among his suggestions for saving passenger service was separating freight and passenger operations into separate businesses.

An Accelerated Decline

The ICC was intricately involved in all facets of railroad regulation, but it lacked authority in regard to passenger train discontinuance. That was the province of state regulatory bodies, which often took months to decide discontinuance cases. Some regulators adamantly refused to let trains die regardless of how much money was being lost, particularly if it was the last train on the route.

The Transportation Act of 1958 amended the Interstate Commerce Act to enable the ICC to review passenger train discontinuances. Railroads could remove a train 30 days after notifying the ICC unless the Commission ordered an investigation, which delayed the discontinuance for four months. If the Commission determined that continued service would serve the public necessity and convenience, it could order the train to remain in service for up to a year. However, if the Commission found the train was not needed, it could be discontinued 10 days after the Commission gave notice that it had ended its investigation.

The pace of passenger train removal accelerated after 1958. But the ICC vacillated between contradictory doctrines. It decided early on that it would not allow unprofitable trains to be kept indefinitely simply because the railroad was profitable. Yet in response to the Hosmer report, the Commission had decided that allowing rail passenger service to end was not in the public interest. "The Commission found itself contrasting a reasonably definite set of costs with an extremely vague concept of public interest," wrote Hilton.

The Commissioners were inconsistent in determining what constituted substantial enough use of a train to justify continuance. They ordered trains continued that carried fewer than 35 passengers per day while approving the discontinuance of trains averaging more than 100 patrons a day. They tended to favor discontinuance of trains operated by financially distressed companies, while nitpicking about what financially healthy railroads could have done to cut costs or stimulate demand. Yet distressed and healthy railroads alike sometimes had to go to the ICC more than once before convincing Commissioners that a train's losses were unlikely to be reversed.

Throughout the 1960s, critics accused railroads of implementing tactics designed to exacerbate losses to bolster the case for removal. Trains were rescheduled to miss connections, passenger equipment and facilities were allowed to deteriorate, and dining, lounge, and sleeping cars were eliminated. Donald Itzkoff said railroads instructed ticket agents to lie about schedules, conceal reservations information, take the phone off the hook, and try to talk would-be passengers into taking the bus. Some conductors, waiters, and porters behaved in a surly manner.

One particularly effective stratagem was truncating a train's route, sometimes using the "Ohio strategy." The State of Ohio allowed railroads to discontinue a train within that state without regulatory review so long as it was not the last passenger train on the route. Ending one portion of the route weakened a train's performance by depriving it of connections or popular destinations.

The degree to which railroads actively sought to discourage business during the 1960s is open to debate. Some railroad executives openly loathed having to provide passenger service while others reduced service with reluctance and regret. But even passenger-friendly railroads could not ignore the red ink gushing from their ledgers. Author Fred W. Frailey found that so long as a train covered its direct costs, a railroad usually kept it going. But when direct costs exceeded revenue, the train got the hook, although some railroads gave it faster and more ruthlessly than others.

The year 1967 was a pivotal one for the passenger train. The U.S. Post Office Department removed most of the remaining railway post office cars, which Frailey said ended a source of revenue that had propped up many trains. Railroads still carried a lot of storage mail, but increasingly diverted it to freight trains, some of which they created expressly to carry mail. As the passenger fleet shrank to a hard core, the ICC began taking a harder line toward ending the last train on a route. Passenger train advocates increasingly turned to the courts to try to keep service going.

The Road to Amtrak

Discontinuance notices were pending in early 1968 for 108 of the nation's 650 intercity passenger trains with more likely to follow. The passenger train problem had become the passenger train crisis. Support was growing to save intercity passenger service, but no consensus had emerged as to how. The American Association of Railroads in February 1969 endorsed federal funding of intercity passenger service and a government-operated equipment pool. Several plans were introduced in Congress, and both chambers held hearings, but none of the proposals came to a vote.

On May 4, 1969, Federal Railroad Administration Manager Reginald Whitman outlined a plan called "Railpax" that was modeled after the Corporation for Public Broadcasting. Railpax would operate a national railroad passenger system with financing from the railroads in return for their being allowed to exit the passenger train business. The Railpax plan languished until March 1970, when Penn Central announced plans to discontinue nearly all passenger service west of Harrisburg, Pa., and Buffalo, N.Y. The Senate Commerce Committee that month approved a bill sponsored by Indiana's Vance Hartke to provide federal funding to railroads operating passenger trains. That prompted the Department of Transportation to release its own Railpax plan, which Hartke agreed to substitute for his direct funding bill. The Senate approved it on May 6.

After Penn Central sought bankruptcy protection on June 23, 1970, Railpax found a fast track through Congress. On October 14, the House adopted a more generous version of Railpax, and the Senate concurred. President Richard Nixon signed the Rail Passenger Service Act without ceremony on October 30. The law froze the nation's intercity rail passenger network into place until Railpax could begin operating. The Railpax structure had five Indiana routes, three via Indianapolis. The Railpax system of 23,000 miles and 221 trains was far less than the 53,000 miles and 547 trains operated before its creation.

In April 1971, Railpax became Amtrak, a derivative of the words *American* and *track*. Congress gave Amtrak $40 million in grants and $100 million in loan guarantees for equipment and improved facilities. Twenty railroads paid a collective $197 million buy-in fee, agreed to provide operating crews, and allowed Amtrak to use their tracks and facilities. All Indiana railroads that still had passenger trains joined Amtrak. Several eleventh-hour efforts to delay Amtrak in hopes of forcing its expansion failed, and Amtrak began on schedule on May 1, 1971.

Monon

CHAPTER 2

MONON

Many railroads served Indiana, but the Monon was Indiana's own, celebrating its heritage by naming its flagship passenger train the *Hoosier*, featuring traditional Indiana cooking in its dining cars, and offering homespun service. Humorist George Ade observed that to see Indiana, you had to ride the Monon. However, the modest passenger offerings of "The Hoosier Line" received little recognition beyond Indiana.

Although *Monon* was a Potawatomi word thought to mean "swift running," the Monon was not built for high-speed operation. If the Monon's diminutive size was a handicap in competing against larger, wealthier rivals, it also was the source of its charm.

The first passenger operation on the New Albany & Salem Rail Road, chartered July 31, 1847, was a three-mile excursion at New Albany on July 4, 1849. Passenger service to Salem in Washington County began in January 1851. That same year the Crawfordsville & Wabash began building from Lafayette southward. The NA&S reached Orleans in northern Orange County in January 1852, Bedford in April 1853, Bloomington in November 1853, and Gosport in northeast Owen County in January 1854.

With financial help from the Michigan Central, the NA&S purchased the C&W on June 17, 1852, and built between Michigan City and Lafayette and between Gosport and Crawfordsville. The NA&S became the first railroad to span Indiana north to south when the last spike was driven on June 24, 1854, 7 miles south of Greencastle. The first passenger train to operate the length of the line left Michigan City on July 3, 1854, at 5 a.m. and arrived in New Albany 16 hours later.

In the mid-1850s, the NA&S operated pairings between New Albany and Michigan City, Lafayette and Greencastle, and Lafayette and Michigan City. In conjunction with the Michigan Central and the Indianapolis & Cincinnati railroads (both later New York Central), the NA&S offered Chicago–Cincinnati service.

Forced into receivership in 1858, the NA&S emerged on October 24, 1859, as the Louisville, New Albany & Chicago. The fiscal struggles continued, and on November 1, 1860, the LNA&C turned over its Michigan City–Lafayette passenger service to the Michigan Central for the next two years.

LNA&C passenger service in the late 1860s consisted of New Albany–Lafayette and Greencastle–Lafayette round trips and two Lafayette–Michigan City round trips. By early 1870, in conjunction with the Michigan Central at Michigan City, the LNA&C had begun offering sleepers between New Albany and Chicago.

LNA&C president R. H. Veach described the post–Civil War LNA&C as "a line starting at no place and ending nowhere, without a place or habitation in any of the great cities." The 1881 purchase of the Chicago & Indianapolis Air Line enabled the LNA&C to reach Chicago. The Air Line and LNA&C crossed in northwest White County at Bradford, renamed Monon in 1879. The first known use of the Monon Route moniker was on a map issued in November 1882.

The Air Line developed in piecemeal fashion. Its forerunner was the narrow-gauge Indianapolis, Delphi & Chicago, which began passenger service on February 14, 1878, between Bradford and Rensselaer. Mixed train service began August 14, 1878, between Rensselaer and Monticello in southeast White County. A year later, service began to Delphi in western Carroll County, which the ID&C had reached on September 4, 1879. After the ID&C faltered in 1880, control of the company passed to its builder, S. N. Yeoman. Believing it unlikely that a narrow-gauge railroad would be allowed to enter Chicago, Yeoman converted the railroad, since renamed the Chicago & Indianapolis Air Line, to standard gauge.

After completion of a bridge over the Kankakee River near Shelby in southern Lake County, the Air Line was ready to serve Chicago using the Panhandle (later Pennsylvania) west of Dyer. Service began January 9, 1882, with a single Chicago–Louisville round trip. The Air Line later switched to the Chicago & Western Indiana, of which it was a part owner, between Chicago and Hammond. The Monon used a depot at 12th and State Streets in Chicago until the 1885 opening of Dearborn Station, which the Monon used for the duration of scheduled passenger service.

The first passenger train on the Air Line south of Delphi was an excursion to Frankfort on October 22, 1882. That same month, the Air Line reached Indianapolis, although passenger service did not begin until March 24, 1883. Initially operating two accommodation trains to the Lake Erie & Western (later Nickel Plate) freight station, passenger service between Chicago and Indianapolis began in May 1883. The Monon moved to Indianapolis Union Station that November.

The failure of Monon predecessor NA&S to terminate on the banks of the Ohio River at New Albany had enabled the Jeffersonville, Madison & Indianapolis (later Pennsylvania) to gain the upper hand in the Louisville passenger business. In 1882, the Monon negotiated use of the JM&I and the Louisville Bridge and Depot Company facilities. The Monon was a part owner of the Kentucky & Indiana Bridge Company, which completed a bridge across the Ohio River in 1910 that the Monon used along with Louisville Union Station for the duration of scheduled passenger service.

The Monon usually assigned its finest passenger equipment to its Chicago–Indianapolis trains. At 183 miles, the Monon route was 10 miles shorter than the New York Central and

In a quintessential 19th century scene, a Monon local passenger train unloads passengers and express freight at Lowell. Indiana Historical Society, negative C16.

19 miles shorter than the Pennsylvania Railroad. But slow running, particularly on the Chicago & Western Indiana, kept the Monon from being the fastest Chicago route. The Monon's best time of 4 hours could not beat the New York Central. The Monon only beat the Pennsylvania because the latter's trains reversed direction at Logansport.

The Monon could not match the frequency of service of the New York Central, which in 1949 operated six round trips versus two for the Monon. However, in 1922, the Monon opened Boulevard Station on 38th Street in Indianapolis, adjacent to the Indiana State Fairgrounds and the city's affluent northside neighborhoods. Until November 1944, Boulevard Station had a Chicago setout sleeper conveyed by the *Midnight Special*. On the Louisville line, numerous sharp curves and steep grades, combined with street running in Lafayette, Bedford, and New Albany, ensured that the Monon could not outrun the Pennsylvania to Chicago.

Mainline service in 1885 was two Chicago–Louisville expresses, two Indianapolis–Monon round trips, which conveyed Chicago cars, a Frankfort–Indianapolis accommodation train, and locals operating Mitchell to Lafayette and Greencastle to Louisville. A year later there were two Chicago–Indianapolis expresses, the Frankfort accommodation trains and three Chicago–Louisville expresses. By the following January, Chicago–Louisville service had fallen to two round trips.

The decade also saw the naming of most expresses. Between Chicago and Louisville, Nos. 3/4 were the *Louisville Limited/Chicago Express*. Nos. 5/6 were the *Fast Mail*. Between Chicago and Indianapolis, Nos. 1/2 were the *Indianapolis Night Express/Chicago Day Express*. Nos. 11/12 were the *Fast Mail*. No. 10 was the *Chicago Express*.

The Monon instituted Chicago–Lafayette and Bloomington–Louisville accommodation trains in 1887. A Lafayette–Bedford local joined the schedule in 1890, although by 1892 this train had begun terminating in Bloomington. On the Indianapolis line, the Monon increased service to four pairs of trains in 1890, two operating Chicago–Indianapolis and two operating Indianapolis–Monon. One of the latter pairings had begun operating to Chicago by 1896. Chicago–Indianapolis service increased to five round trips on September 15, 1896, spelling the end of the Indianapolis–Monon locals. By the end of the year, though, Chicago–Indianapolis service had fallen to four round trips.

By 1892 there were two pairs of Bloomington–Louisville locals and locals operating Louisville to Lafayette, Chicago to Bloomington, Lafayette to Monon, and Lafayette to Rensselaer. Within a year local service had settled into a pattern of single pairings operating Chicago–Monon, Chicago–Lafayette, and Lafayette–Bloomington. There were two Bloomington–Louisville round trips. This schedule pattern remained throughout much of the 1890s.

In the mid-1880s, the Monon and the Cincinnati, Hamilton & Dayton (later Baltimore & Ohio) launched Chicago–Cincinnati service. Some cars carried the heralds of both railroads. All Chicago–Indianapolis trains carried Cincinnati cars, interchanged with the CH&D at Indianapolis. One pair of Louisville trains interchanged Cincinnati cars with the CH&D at Roachdale in northern Putnam County.

The two roads purchased two five-car train sets of vestibule equipment from Pullman in 1889. The *Velvet Train* operated on a day schedule, the *Electric* on an overnight schedule. The two roads claimed to have the only dining car service between Chicago and Cincinnati, a parlor-diner-observation car featuring Pintsch gas lamps and carved oak seats with embossed green leather. Ohmer Restaurant Co. of Cincinnati catered the meals.

Never a major player in through car arrangements between Chicago and the South, the Monon in the early 1890s advertised through car service between Chicago and New Orleans, Memphis, Jacksonville, Fla., and Knoxville, Tenn. Through service began in March 1890 with New Orleans, Memphis, and Jacksonville cars interchanged with the Louisville & Nashville Railroad in Louisville. Two months later, the Monon began interchanging cars to the same three cities at Cincinnati with the L&N and the Queen & Crescent Route (later Southern). By year's end, all of the Jacksonville cars were interchanged at Cincinnati.

Chicago–Knoxville cars continued to interchange at Louisville. The Knoxville cars were gone by March 1891. The Jacksonville, New Orleans, and Memphis through cars continued until February 1894. The Monon in 1896 advertised a 36-hour Chicago–Florida service named the *Florida Flyer*.

In early 1901, the Monon hosted the *Chicago and Florida Special*, which operated on alternating days between Chicago and Cincinnati on the Monon/CH&D, the Big Four (later New York Central), and the Pennsylvania. The Chicago–St. Augustine train used the Monon for just one winter season. A Chicago–Florida sleeper that briefly operated in 1908 was the Monon's last through car between Chicago and the South.

Monon passenger operations peaked in the early 20th century with ridership cresting at 2.1 million in 1917, train miles hitting a high of 116 million in 1920, and passenger revenue topping out at $3.2 million a year later. The Monon offered three Chicago–Indianapolis expresses, all carrying Cincinnati cars. The *Fast Mail* was the only named Monon train on the Indianapolis line. A fourth pairing operated Chicago to Indianapolis and Indianapolis to Monon. The schedule also showed two Chicago–Louisville round trips and locals operating Louisville–Bloomington (two pairings), Bloomington–Lafayette, Lafayette–Chicago, Monon to Hammond, and Monon to Lafayette. Nos. 5/6 between Chicago and Louisville operated as the *Day Express*.

Chicago–Indianapolis service increased to four round trips on July 6, 1901, with all trains carrying Cincinnati cars. Chicago–Louisville trains Nos. 3/4 interchanged Cincinnati cars with the CH&D at Roachdale. One pair of Bloomington–Louisville locals was curtailed to New Albany by 1901 and soon disappeared.

The Monon in 1903 and 1907 received new cars built in Jeffersonville by American Car and Foundry, formerly the Ohio Falls Car Manufacturing Company. Assigned to Cincinnati service, the cars were green with gold trim. Pullman introduced new parlor cars on the Monon on February 13, 1913.

Birth of a Legend

In the face of fierce competition with the Big Four for Chicago–Indianapolis traffic, Monon president Fairfax Harrison sought an edge by creating a new luxury train in 1911. Inaugurated on August 27, the *Hoosier Limited* had new cars built by Barney and Smith that featured the train name on the letter board. The new service, though, received mixed reviews. "Railroad men here [Cincinnati] say that the business originating in Indianapolis is not large enough to warrant this train," reported the *New York Times*.

But the *Hoosier*, its name shortened in April 1914, persevered as the Monon's standard-bearer until its discontinuance in 1959. Featuring a more polished interior design than other Monon trains, the *Hoosier* offered diner-lounge and parlor-observation cars for most of its life. It wasn't just elegant service and convenient schedules that made the train special. The *Hoosier* was "more than a train; it was an institution and a tradition in Indiana. It had that family atmosphere which develops on an ocean cruise after the second day out," wrote *Indianapolis Times* columnist John W. Hillman in 1945. The *Indianapolis Star* observed that "acquaintances between the train's family, from engineer to chef to brakeman and the passengers, were as common as on branch lines."

The *Hoosier* celebrated traditional Indiana culture with menu covers featuring images of an Indian cooking over an open fire and the train rolling through Indiana farmland at night. Menus also featured a drawing by *Chicago Tribune* cartoonist John T. McCutcheon, a native Hoosier, of a barefoot farmboy exchanging waves with passengers on the observation car platform, and a tribute from George Ade: "My first dream was to ride the Monon." Travelers left work early to catch the "5 o'clock Monon," as the *Hoosier* came to be known, relaxing in the diner and enjoying a steak dinner or the round-robin meal, both just $1.50. Also on the menu were broiled whitefish, omelet with preserves, broiled shad

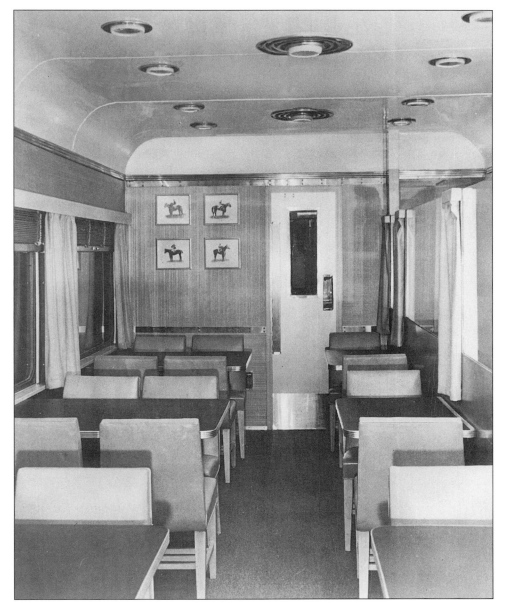

Nothing was finer, or lost more money, than the dining car. Railroads shrugged off the losses as the cost of doing business. The diner was a showpiece for the railroad's service. Shown is a Monon diner-bar lounge of the late 1940s. Indiana Historical Society, negative C8882.

roe with bacon, tenderloin steak, grilled roast beef au jus, fried spring chicken, new potatoes in cream, green beans, and strawberry or apple pie that had been baked on board.

The practice of leaving Chicago and Indianapolis at 5 P.M., which gave the *Hoosier* its nickname, did not begin until 1930. In its early years, the *Hoosier* operated on a number of schedules, including one that left Indianapolis at 7:30 A.M.

All Indianapolis line expresses had names by 1906. In addition to the *Fast Mail*, there was the *Day Express*, the *Flyer*, and the *Cincinnati Limited/Chicago Limited* (northbound). By 1911, the *Day Express* had become the *Monon Special*, and the *Cincinnati Limited* and *Chicago Limited* names shortened to the *Limited*, which later became the *Hoosier Limited*.

The *Monon Special* became the *Daylight Limited* in 1912, and the *Fast Mail* became the *Midday Special* in May 1914. The Monon dropped all train names during World War I except the *Hoosier*. Naming resumed in June 1920 when the overnight Chicago–Indianapolis trains became the *Midnight Special*.

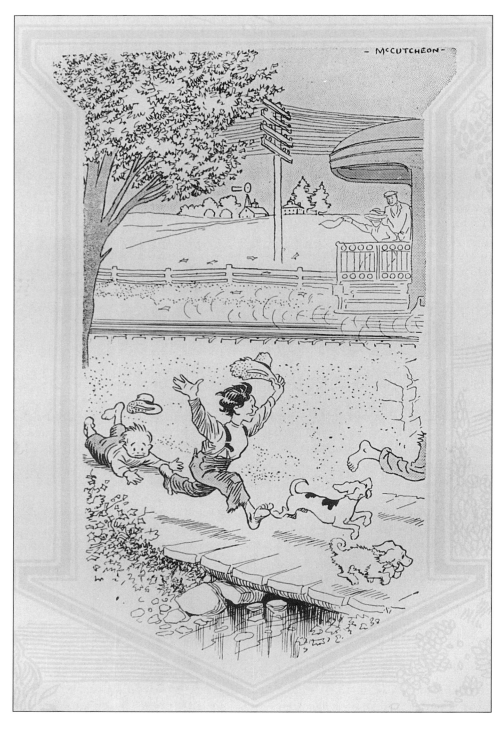

Monon dining car menus featured folksy scenes drawn by Hoosier native and *Chicago Tribune* cartoonist John T. McCutcheon. Indiana Historical Society.

All Chicago–Indianapolis trains again had names by December 1923: the *Hoosier*, *Midnight Special*, *Tippecanoe*, and *Daylight Limited/Chicago Limited* (northbound). The latter became the *Daylight Limited* in May 1930. On April 30, 1939, the northbound *Tippecanoe* was renamed the *Executive*.

Gradual Decline

Due to wartime travel restrictions, Chicago–Indianapolis service fell to three round trips in August 1918 and Cincinnati service was suspended. Service increased to four round trips in May 1919, and Cincinnati service resumed in August 1920. Chicago–Indianapolis service reached its zenith in August 1920 with the addition of a fifth round trip that lasted less than four months, ending on November 28.

The Bloomington–Lafayette locals ended August 2, 1925, the Lafayette–Chicago locals ended May 6, 1928, and the Bloomington–Louisville locals ended March 30, 1930. The latter were the last passenger trains to use the original mainline via Smithville in southern Monroe County. Other trains ran on a 9.4-mile route via Harrodsburg that opened September 1, 1899, and featured gentler grades. The last Louisville line locals were a pair of mixed trains operating between Orleans and Borden in Clark County that ended in December 1934.

Retrenchment on the Indianapolis line began August 2, 1925, when the Monon–Indianapolis locals ended. The *Daylight Limited* made its final runs on July 9, 1932, reducing Chicago–Indianapolis service to three round trips. Shortly before the discontinuance of the *Daylight Limited*, the Monon had removed Cincinnati cars from the southbound *Daylight Limited* and northbound *Tippecanoe*. With the demise of the *Daylight Limited*, the northbound *Tippecanoe* regained Cincinnati coaches. The Cincinnati cars came off the southbound *Tippecanoe* in April 1936 and the northbound *Tippecanoe* a month later. The Monon's last Cincinnati through coaches and sleepers operated on the *Midnight Special* until April 1938.

The Monon seldom operated full-length dining cars on its Louisville trains, usually assigning a diner-coach or parlor-diner. In the mid-1930s, a café car replaced the parlor-diner cars on Nos. 5/6. By July 1939, dining on Nos. 5/6 was a diner-lounge operating between Lafayette and Bloomington. It was removed a month later.

A 1923 order of four all-steel coaches and the air conditioning of its cars in 1938 were among the few significant improvements the Monon made to its passenger service. The Monon went into receivership in late 1933, citing 1931 passenger losses of $250,000. Patronage dropped to 173,362 in 1932, but rebounded to more than 200,000 in 1933 and 1934.

Rock-Bottom Service

Although most Class I railroads set revenue and traffic records during World War II, the Monon's traffic was just two-thirds of its previous best performance. The Office of Defense Transportation in early 1945 ordered discontinuance of trains that in November 1944 had averaged less than 35 percent occupancy. Only the *Hoosier* met this criterion, but the government allowed Chicago–Louisville Nos. 3/4 to remain.

Chicago–Louisville Nos. 5/6 ended March 4, 1945. By August, the sleepers on Nos. 3/4 were gone, and on August 27, 1945, these trains were consolidated with the *Hoosier* between Chicago and Monon, putting Nos. 3/4 on a daylight schedule. The assignment of a restaurant-lounge returned full dining service to the Louisville trains for the first time in more than two decades.

On the Indianapolis line, the *Tippecanoe* and the *Executive* made their final runs on August 17, 1940. The war-related discontinuance of the *Midnight Special* on March 4, 1945, left the *Hoosier* as the sole Chicago–Indianapolis train. Idled Monon passenger equipment was sent elsewhere for troop train use, including on the Southern Pacific in California.

Monon patronage fell from 424,000 in 1944 to 261,082 in 1945. The passenger car fleet dropped from 99 to 55 as the Monon cannibalized itself to keep its aging equipment on the rails. Understanding the need for wartime sacrifices, Hoosiers stoically accepted the slippage in Monon passenger service. But a public outcry greeted the February 24, 1945, rescheduling of the *Hoosier* to depart Chicago at 8:15 A.M. and Indianapolis at 2:10 P.M., enabling the train to operate with one set of equipment. It made sense from a logistics viewpoint but didn't sit well with sentimental Hoosiers. The *Indianapolis Star* wrote that many felt "the real *Hoosier* will be just history." John Hillman called for a campaign to restore the 5 o'clock Monon.

Widespread criticism of the 1945 service changes prompted the Indiana Public Service Commission to hold hearings. The end of World War II did not bring significant service improvements. The Monon's trustees insisted that the railroad could not become profitable if the 1945 passenger service cuts were restored.

The Barriger Renaissance

Upon emerging from receivership on May 1, 1946, the Monon promised "up-to-date, modern railroad service" and appointed as president 46-year-old John Walker Barriger III, an unabashed passenger train optimist. "[Our] passenger potential is one of the bright spots on the Monon horizon," he said in 1947. But the Monon's passenger service was an embarrassment. Barriger knocked down cobwebs with his hand in one depot and asked for a broom to sweep out the dust. The weary locomotive fleet was prone to breakdowns. The passenger car fleet was equally decrepit with some coaches and baggage cars having been in service since the late 19th century. *Trains* magazine editor David P. Morgan observed that the postwar Monon was physically and spiritually bankrupt.

The U.S. Army had a fleet of surplus hospital cars. Built in 1944–45, these cars were similar to postwar streamlined equipment except that their six-axle trucks and carbon steel

The Monon spent $1 million to rebuild 28 World War II U.S. Army Hospital cars into modern streamlined equipment. This equipment display was at the Indiana State Fairgrounds in Indianapolis in 1954. Photo by Ron Stuckey; John Fuller collection.

construction made them nearly as heavy as traditional heavyweight equipment. The Monon purchased 28 hospital cars, which began arriving in January 1947 at the Lafayette shops to be rebuilt into streamlined equipment. Industrial designer Raymond Loewy fashioned a bold look for the cars, which gave the Monon a much-needed new image, including a herald emblazoned with the slogan "The Hoosier Line."

Parlor and lounge cars had a horse-racing motif. Parlor cars featured large, overstuffed chairs that angled slightly inward. Most coaches had high-density seating, reflecting the expectation that the coach business would be short-haul. Observation cars had flat ends with train names featured prominently above the coupler. The exteriors featured two shades of gray separated by a band of red accented with white striping edged in gold. Trainman uniforms were designed in these tones, which were the colors of Indiana University and Wabash College.

The first set of streamlined equipment was released in July 1947 and sent on a publicity tour. The Lafayette shops finished rebuilding the hospital cars in late 1948. The project, including the purchase price of the cars, had cost $1 million and produced eight coaches, six deluxe coaches, five grill-coaches, three dining-bar-lounges, two parlor-observations, and two baggage-mail cars.

The first diesel locomotive assigned to Monon passenger service was an Alco General Electric RS-2 road switcher. Nicknamed the *Hoosier Belle*, it began service February 15, 1947, on the French Lick branch. The Monon ordered eight passenger F3A units from the Electro-Motive Division of General Motors. These began arriving in May 1947 and entered service on Louisville trains. The Monon later purchased an F3 A-B-A demonstrator set.

The Monon restored twice-daily Chicago–Indianapolis service on July 21, 1946. Initially shown in *The Official Guide of the Railways* as the *Morning Hoosier/Afternoon Hoosier*, the Monon revived the *Tippecanoe* name for the morning trains. The *Hoosier* resumed its storied role as the 5 o'clock Monon, although it departed Indianapolis at 5:15 P.M.

The *Hoosier* and *Tippecanoe* operated with heavyweight coaches, parlor cars, and diners until the first set of streamlined equipment arrived. Mrs. Emil Schramm, wife of the Indiana-born president of the New York Stock Exchange, christened the new equipment with a bottle of champagne on August 17, 1947, at Indianapolis Union Station. The equipment entered service on the *Tippecanoe*. That afternoon, *Chicago Tribune* cartoonist McCutcheon christened the same equipment at Dearborn Station before it departed on the *Hoosier*. A second set of equipment entered service in November to complete the streamlining of the Indianapolis trains.

The Louisville trains resumed independent operation July 21, 1946, as Nos. 5/6, departing both terminals in the morning. The next month, Nos. 5/6 were named *Day Express* and assigned a heavyweight diner that operated between Chicago and Bainbridge in northern Putnam County. The diner's operation changed to Chicago–Crawfordsville on August 17, 1947. The Monon arranged with Pullman for heavyweight sleepers for a revival of overnight Chicago–Louisville service, which began September 29, 1946, as the *Night Express*. The *Day Express* was assigned a lounge car, but it was removed on December 12, 1947.

The Louisville trains began sporting a more modern look in 1947. The first revenue service run of the Monon's new F3A diesels occurred on May 18, 1947, on the southbound *Day Express*. Subsequently, diesels were assigned to the southbound *Night Express* and northbound *Day Express*. The superior accelerating ability of the F3A units over the Alco Brooks K5A Pacific 4-6-2 steam locomotives that they replaced enabled the Monon to shave 50 minutes off the running time of the northbound *Day Express*.

The Monon assigned five streamlined coaches to the *Day Express* on February 15, 1948, and renamed it the *Thoroughbred*. In a further tribute to the route's southern terminus, the *Night Express* became the *Bluegrass*. By July, streamlined dining-lounge-observation cars had replaced the *Thoroughbred*'s heavyweight diner.

Barriger's renewal of passenger service succeeded in bolstering the Monon's downtrodden image by rebuilding public confidence in the railroad. But goodwill and positive

Twisting curves and steep grades ruled the Monon in Southern Indiana. The Chicago–Louisville *Day Express* is south of Bloomington in the mid-1940s. Indiana Historical Society, negative C4412.

publicity could not stem the red ink. Patronage reached 307,000 in 1948, but by 1949 it had begun a steady descent, with the Monon losing $85,000 a month on passenger service.

Although ridership and revenue on the *Bluegrass* steadily improved through October 1948, by mid-1949, the train and its French Lick connecting trains were losing $40,000 a month. They made their final runs on September 24, 1949. The same month, grill coaches replaced the *Tippecanoe*'s parlor-observation cars. Dining-parlor-observation cars later removed from the *Thoroughbred* were reassigned to the *Tippecanoe*, although they were not advertised as observation cars.

The Monon board of directors declined to implement a Barriger-suggested Bloomington–Monon train that would have connected with the Chicago–Indianapolis trains. Instead, the northbound *Thoroughbred* began operating 2.5 hours earlier. Two other Barriger

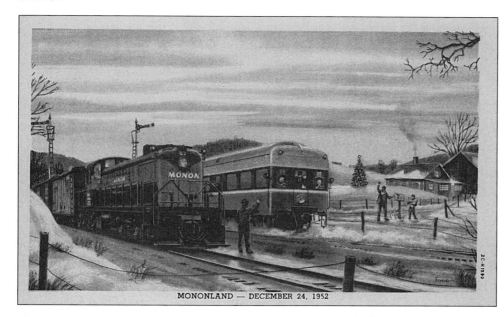

MONONLAND — DECEMBER 24, 1952

For several decades, railroads used postcards as promotional tools. The Monon commissioned this idyllic Christmas scene in 1952. The observation car belongs to the *Hoosier*, the Monon's flagship Chicago–Indianapolis passenger train. Author's collection.

ideas that failed to come to fruition included establishing through service with the Southern or L&N at Louisville and reviving Chicago–Cincinnati through service. Barriger wanted to rebuild the Indianapolis line for 100 mph operation, which would have cut the Chicago–Indianapolis running time from 4 hours to 2.5. He proposed trimming the Chicago–Louisville travel time from 8 hours to 5. But his vision was more than the Monon could afford.

Nonetheless, the early 1950s were a time of experimentation. The Monon served several colleges including St. Joseph (Rensselaer), Purdue (West Lafayette), Wabash (Crawfordsville), DePauw (Greencastle), and Indiana University (Bloomington). To tap the college market, the Monon on January 6, 1950, launched the *Varsity*, which departed Bloomington on Friday evening and returned on Sunday evening. The *Varsity*, which carried coaches and a grill coach, made its final run on June 18, 1950. Revived in early 1953, it ended for good on May 29, 1953.

A Budd Rail Diesel Car began experimental service on April 1, 1950, departing Bloomington in the morning for Monon where it connected with the *Tippecanoe*. The car then departed for Bedford and returned to Monon for connections with the *Hoosier*, before returning to Bloomington. Although described as "another step toward Monon's Service Goal," the Monon never seriously considered purchasing the car. The trial service lasted 15 days.

Requiem for a Hoosier

Barriger resigned in late 1952 to become a vice president at the New Haven Railroad. His successor, Warren W. Brown, was not as optimistic about passenger service. Management discussions at the Monon increasingly focused on how to reduce the growing passenger deficit. After patronage had fallen from 245,000 in 1949 to 172,000 in 1952, the Monon considered ending passenger service south of Bloomington.

The 1950s saw a steady diminishing of service. In September 1951, the Monon replaced diner-lounge-observation cars on the *Thoroughbred* with grill-parlor cars. Two months later these were downgraded to grill coaches, which were further downgraded in October 1956 to refreshment coaches. A year later, food service was sandwiches and drinks sold by an employee who boarded at Greencastle.

The Monon had counted heavily on first-class passengers to make the streamlined *Hoosier* a success. But fewer business travelers were still riding the rails, and demand for

A troop train splits the semaphore signals adjacent to the State Fairgrounds just north of Boulevard Station in Indianapolis in the mid-1950s. Photo by Ron Stuckey; John Fuller collection.

parlor seats, meals, and drinks diminished faster than the demand for coach seats. The *Tippecanoe* and the *Hoosier* began sharing equipment sets in 1956. The southbound *Tippecanoe* and northbound *Hoosier* carried coaches and a former *Thoroughbred* dining-parlor-observation car. The northbound *Tippecanoe* and southbound *Hoosier* carried coaches, a dining-bar-lounge, and a parlor-observation. Dining and parlor service ended on both trains in September 1957 in favor of waiters (still wearing their dining car uniforms) selling sandwiches and snacks from baskets.

Monon management had concluded by 1955 that passenger service had to end in order to remove a serious drain on the railroad's earnings. The next year the Monon earned $1.8 million in passenger revenue that had cost $3 million to provide. Curtailing dining and parlor service had helped to shave the passenger deficit, but by the Interstate Commerce Commission's calculations, the Monon lost $622,948 on passenger service in 1957.

On April 26, 1958, the Monon sought Indiana Public Service Commission approval to discontinue all three passenger trains. The Commission held hearings and announced on March 31, 1959, that the Monon could end service to Indianapolis. Noting the Monon had lost $4 million on passenger service since 1951, the Commission wrote, "To insist that these losses be continued would be to jeopardize the [Monon's] freight service." The *Thoroughbred* sometimes earned enough mail and express revenue to cover its direct costs, so the commission ordered it continued.

The *Hoosier* and *Tippecanoe* made their final runs on April 9, 1959. The *Indianapolis Star* reported that the final day of Monon passenger service to Indianapolis occurred without ceremony, an official farewell, or unusually large crowds. The *Tippecanoe* left Indianapolis Union Station under overcast skies with 15 passengers aboard a four-car train. The *Indianapolis News* reported that "a few solemn-faced Monon employees watched [and] waved a half-hearted good-bye."

Over the next five years, Indianapolis officials lobbied the Monon to restore passenger service to Chicago. Those efforts seemed to have paid off when Monon president William

C. Coleman announced on February 17, 1964, that Chicago–Indianapolis service would be revived if it could generate sufficient mail and express business and the ICC would agree to view the service as experimental. Citing an Indianapolis Chamber of Commerce survey showing demand for fast, daily passenger train service to Chicago, Coleman said the trains would operate on a 3.5-hour schedule. But the proposal never moved beyond the talking stage.

The Long Good-bye

The *Thoroughbred* continued to race up and down the Monon for another nine years with few notable changes. One of those, though, was its outward appearance. By the early 1960s, the Monon had begun repainting its passenger equipment in the black and gold livery (the colors of DePauw and Purdue Universities) that had long adorned Monon freight locomotives.

The Monon conducted a passenger survey in 1964 with an eye toward restructuring the *Thoroughbred*'s schedule. The resulting changes effectively wrote off travel south of Bloomington, where ridership already was slight. Effective October 25, 1964, No. 5 began departing Chicago 7 hours later at 5:25 P.M., arriving in Louisville at 2:10 A.M. No. 6 departed Louisville at 6:30 A.M., arriving in Chicago at 1:05 P.M. This enabled the *Thoroughbred* to operate with one set of equipment. Although described as part of a long-range improvement plan, little had changed except the schedule.

In August 1966, the Monon took delivery of two Alco C-420 locomotives with steam boilers. Purchased with the idea that they also could be used for freight service, the Monon was, nevertheless, one of the last railroads to buy new passenger locomotives.

On December 31, 1965, the U.S. Post Office withdrew the Monon's railway post office (RPO), depriving the railroad of $140,000 in annual mail revenue. RPO and bulk mail had accounted for two-thirds of the *Thoroughbred*'s revenue. The *Thoroughbred* still carried

A porter uses a baggage cart to load luggage as the northbound *Thoroughbred* pauses at Bloomington in 1962. Photo by Ron Stuckey; John Fuller collection.

pouch mail, but mail revenue dropped from $307,243 in 1965 to $167,571 in 1966. In an effort to boost revenue, the *Thoroughbred* began handling express cars bound for off-line stations. Indiana's full-crew law required longer train consists to have larger crews, and the increased labor costs negated the revenue gains. Railway Express Agency refused to negotiate a more favorable rate, and by February 1967, when the service ended, the Monon was losing $6,000 a month on this business.

The *Thoroughbred*'s losses ballooned from $174,021 in 1965 to $321,958 in 1967. Monon management had seen enough and notified the ICC on March 27, 1967, of its plans to discontinue the *Thoroughbred* on May 8. The commission held hearings in Chicago, Rensselaer, Lafayette, Crawfordsville, Greencastle, Bloomington, and Louisville. Although ridership had fallen from 50,476 in 1962 to 42,914 in 1965, it rebounded in 1966 to 45,168. "Generally, the passenger witnesses testified that the equipment was satisfactory, the employees helpful, and their trips comfortable," the ICC reported.

All 16 stations served by the *Thoroughbred* had bus service, but many of the 80 who protested the train's removal said alternative transportation was not as suitable as the train. Witnesses criticized the Monon for dirty stations, inadequate food service, and closing ticket offices in the evening. The *Thoroughbred*'s patronage had been heaviest on weekends and when colleges were beginning or ending a term. The ICC considered ordering the *Thoroughbred* continued as a triweekly Chicago–Bloomington train. Although this would have sliced the yearly operating costs by a projected $240,000, the ICC said the losses the Monon would continue to incur would have been a "substantial and severely cumbersome burden."

The ICC described the Monon as a marginal railroad that had paid no cash dividends between 1958 and 1965. It could not afford to continue absorbing passenger losses. The Monon agreed to operate the *Thoroughbred* through the end of September to accommodate students returning to college. In its final years, the *Thoroughbred* sometimes carried a single coach. The last Monon public timetable was a mimeographed sheet dated April 30, 1967. Sandwiches, coffee, and soft drinks were available between Chicago and Crawfordsville.

The *Thoroughbred* made its final southbound run on September 29, 1967, departing Dearborn Station with Alco C-420 No. 502, former RPO-Express No. 10, express-baggage No. 102, coach No. 42, coach No. 25, and business car No. 3. No. 6 left Louisville the next day with 75 people aboard. Despite the early hour, a high school band serenaded the train at New Albany. By the time No. 6 had departed Salem, it was standing room only. A man played taps at each stop. Another high school band greeted the train at Lowell in southern Lake County. The *Indianapolis Star* reported that "people greeted [the last run] with mixed emotions of sadness and cheer, many of them climbing aboard if only for a ride to the next station."

Led by Alco C-420 No. 501, the Monon's Louisville to Chicago *Thoroughbred* basks in the early morning sun at Bedford on May 28, 1967. The Monon's last scheduled passenger train ended four months later. Photo by Dave McKay.

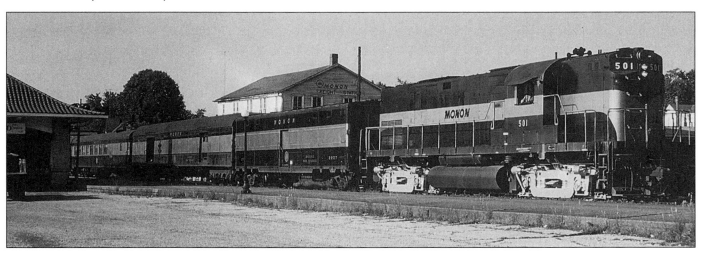

Monon's Five Branch Lines

French Lick Branch

The 17-mile Orleans–French Lick branch had the most extensive passenger operations of the Monon's five branch lines. Much of the line's passenger traffic was bound for the Orange County resort communities of French Lick and West Baden. Founded in the mid-19th century, the resorts featured artesian mineral springs and casino gambling. At French Lick, Pullmans often filled the two house tracks that extended to the hotel's front door.

Organized in 1885 as the Orleans, Paoli & Jasper, the Monon purchased the company in 1886. Construction began in July 1886 and reached French Lick in 1887. Passenger service began that August. Initially three round trips, service fluctuated between two and four round trips during the 1890s. French Lick cars usually were conveyed by Louisville trains and cut out at Orleans, Bloomington, or Bedford. Sleepers, parlor cars, and coaches originated at Chicago, Indianapolis, Michigan City, Lafayette, and Louisville. Off-line sleepers originated at New York, Boston, and St. Louis.

The all-Pullman *Red Devil*, a name inspired by the label of a brand of Pluto Water bottled at French Lick, began operating March 3, 1912, between Chicago and French Lick. The train carried New York sleepers conveyed to Indiana by the New York Central on a semiweekly schedule in the spring and fall. By 1908, the Pennsylvania had begun conveying coaches and a diner-parlor car between Indianapolis and Gosport, where the cars interchanged with the Monon. The *French Lick New Yorker*, a New York–French Lick service, began in September 1925 as an extension of an existing Indianapolis–French Lick service via the Pennsylvania. The New York service ended that December, but a coach and parlor car serving Indianapolis continued until July 19, 1931.

Kentucky Derby weekend was a busy time on the French Lick branch. Pullmans and private cars would arrive on Friday with their occupants spending the night drinking and gambling. On Derby Day, the Monon took the cars to Louisville. Passengers returned Saturday night for more partying before leaving on Sunday afternoon.

By 1908 the Monon operated six daily round trips between Orleans and French Lick, a pattern that remained through the late 1920s. Some of these trains originated at Mitchell (B&O connection), Monon, and Lafayette. Effective August 12, 1928, French Lick branch service was reduced to four round trips. That dwindled to three with the discontinuance of Indianapolis service in 1931. The Monon curtailed French Lick service to a single round trip on November 22, 1931. World War II service reductions ended scheduled service on March 4, 1945. Scheduled service resumed September 26, 1946. The cars, including a Chicago–French Lick sleeper, were conveyed by the *Night Express* to Bloomington and interchanged to a connecting train.

Barriger proposed reinstating sleeper service between French Lick and the East. The Pennsylvania Railroad was amenable to granting the Monon passenger service trackage rights between Gosport Junction and Indianapolis, but the idea was shelved. Unfortunately for the Monon, restoration of French Lick service had occurred as the clandestine gambling that long had flourished there was ending. Even in its best years, French Lick passenger service had been marginally profitable. The last scheduled trains on the French Lick branch made their final runs on September 24, 1949. Specials and Kentucky Derby trains continued to operate to French Lick for several more years.

Bedford–Switz City

In 1886, the Monon purchased the narrow-gauge Bedford & Bloomfield, which operated a 41-mile branch between Bedford and Switz City in central Greene County. Built between 1874 and 1877, the B&B was in poor condition and derailments were frequent. Initially, the Monon operated a single round trip, but within a year this had become two round trips, both mixed trains. Shortly thereafter, a Bedford–Bloomfield pairing was introduced, which brought the line up to three pairs of passenger trains. One Bedford–Switz City pairing was discontinued in 1894, and it wasn't long before the Bloomfield trains were also gone. By the end of the 1890s, though, the second round trip had been reinstated and trains operated between Bedford and Switz City and between Bloomfield and Switz City. The latter ended July 3, 1900, and service never again increased above one round trip.

An agreement reached September 30, 1902, with the Indianapolis Southern (later Illinois Central) enabled the Monon to operate passenger service between Bedford and Linton in western Greene County, primarily to take coal miners to work. Monon passenger service to Linton ended May 21, 1911, and the train resumed Bedford–Switz City operation. B&B branch passenger trains were affectionately known as "Old Nellie," a name still remembered decades after the service ended August 2, 1925.

Wallace Junction–Victoria

In 1906, the Monon began constructing a route from Wallace Junction in northern Owen County on the Louisville line toward the southwestern Indiana coal fields. Passenger service to Victoria in northwestern Greene County began following completion of the 47-mile line on October 1, 1907, with one daily round trip. Service was cut back to Vicksburg, also in Greene County, on March 30, 1919. Passenger service on the branch ended on August 2, 1925.

McCoysburg–Dinwiddie

On March 15, 1914, the Monon purchased the 40-mile Chicago & Wabash Valley between McCoysburg, on the Chicago line in southeast Jasper County, and Dinwiddie in southern Lake County. Organized on September 10, 1898, the line was completed by July 1, 1899, between Zadoc and Comer. It was extended to Kersey by 1900 and in 1901 was extended southward to connect with the Monon at McCoysburg. The line reached Dinwiddie in 1906.

Named the Onion Belt after one of its major commodities, the Monon offered three round trips between McCoysburg and Kersey with irregular service to Dinwiddie. This fell to one daily-except-Sunday round trip on December 12, 1920. Service became triweekly in March 1932 and ended in August 1933.

Michigan City Branch

Although the New Albany & Salem was built to link Michigan City and New Albany, passenger operations between the two cities did not last long. By the mid-1860s, passenger trains on the Michigan City line terminated at Monon or Lafayette. The proliferation of railroads serving northwest Indiana sharply reduced the connecting business on the Michigan City line. Increasingly, much of the line's passenger traffic was bound for Indianapolis.

Through the late 1880s, the Monon operated an Indianapolis–Michigan City round trip. During much of the 1890s the Michigan City line hosted three round trips, all terminating at Monon until mid-1897, when Lafayette became the southern terminus. In 1900, the Monon had three round trips on the Michigan City line, two of which terminated at Monon. Service fell to two round trips on May 10, 1903, and one on December 20, 1903. By 1910, service had increased to two round trips, one of which carried French Lick coaches.

Service fell to one round trip during World War I. The second round trip returned on March 30, 1919, but on August 2, 1925, the Monon discontinued Nos. 1/2. Passenger service was discontinued north of Medaryville in western Pulaski County on May 6, 1928. Passenger service ended on July 31, 1931. Although Barriger thought that rail diesel cars might be suitable for a revival of passenger service on the Michigan City line, service was never restored.

CHAPTER 3

BALTIMORE & OHIO

A majestic royal blue livery, trains bearing such stately names as *Capitol Limited, National Limited,* and the *Diplomat,* and impeccable service made the Baltimore & Ohio a monarch of the rails. As America's first railroad to carry revenue passengers, the B&O was richer in tradition than in financial resources.

Safety, comfort, courtesy, on-time performance, cleanliness, and exemplary dining were more attainable for the B&O than speed and state-of-the-art equipment. The B&O's post–World War II 500-car passenger fleet included just 67 lightweight streamlined cars. B&O diners featured such delicacies as crab imperial, oyster pie, chicken with corn fritters, and Smithfield ham. Dinners came with a generous "help yourself salad bowl" and Deer Park bottled spring water. Meals were served on blue china with heavy-plated silverware and gold linen napkins.

The B&O made headlines for a rearguard attempt to resuscitate passenger service in the 1960s. Those efforts failed, but not before the B&O had tried such innovations as reduced fares for midweek travel, auto train service, and on-board movies.

As Indiana's sixth largest railroad, the B&O's 585 miles made up 7.8 percent of the state's peak rail mileage.

Chicago Line

Following the Civil War, B&O president John W. Garrett concluded that to compete with the Pennsylvania, Erie, and New York Central for western traffic, the B&O needed to serve Chicago. A subsidiary company (the Baltimore, Pittsburgh & Chicago Railroad) began construction in 1873 between Chicago and Chicago Junction (later Willard, Ohio) located on the B&O-owned Central Ohio Railroad (Sandusky–Bellaire, Ohio).

Built across Indiana in 1874, the 263-mile Chicago Division featured over 240 miles of tangent track and grades of less than 0.5 percent. The B&O entered Chicago on the Illinois Central. The B&O bragged of having built the line during a depression and paying cash for the $7.8 million project. But the *Traveler's Official Railway Guide* noted the top speed on the Chicago Division was 20 mph.

The Chicago line opened on November 23, 1874, with two round trips between Chicago and Chicago Junction, where passengers connected with Baltimore and Washington trains. Service expanded a year later to three round trips and a Chicago to Garrett local that

Baltimore and Ohio

later became a mixed train terminating at South Chicago, Ill. Locals also operated between Garrett and Chicago Junction.

B&O trains began operating between Chicago and Wheeling, W.Va., in 1880. Another round trip operated between Garrett and Wheeling. Mixed trains operated South Chicago–Garrett and Garrett–Chicago Junction. Calling itself the "great national highway," the B&O instituted through sleeping cars between Chicago and Baltimore.

B&O service to New York began in the 1870s using the Philadelphia, Wilmington & Baltimore (later Pennsylvania Railroad) to Philadelphia, and the Pennsy to Jersey City, N.J. The B&O opened its own line between Baltimore and Philadelphia on September 19, 1886, and used the Reading and the Jersey Central Railroads to reach Jersey City. Until the May 25, 1873, opening of the Metropolitan branch between Washington and Point of Rocks, Md., trains had arrived in Baltimore and then run southward to Washington.

To demonstrate its superiority, the B&O in June 1884 had a special train make the 784-mile trip from Chicago to Washington in a record 22.5 hours, scampering 6 miles in less than 4 minutes at one point. Robert Garrett, who had succeeded his father as B&O president, was so impressed that he ordered a general speedup of B&O passenger trains.

In the late 1880s, the B&O operated four Chicago–Wheeling round trips, one of which was a Philadelphia train. Sleepers operated between Chicago and Philadelphia, Washington, Baltimore, and Columbus, Ohio. In 1890–91, the B&O extended the Chicago line to Akron, Ohio, and purchased the Pittsburgh & Western between Pittsburgh and Akron via New Castle, Pa. Service between Chicago and Pittsburgh via Akron began August 9, 1891, with two round trips. In the early 1890s, the B&O operated four Chicago–Wheeling round trips, one of which was a Pittsburgh train via Washington, Pa. Pittsburgh service via Akron was three round trips, usually operated in combination with Wheeling trains between Chicago and Chicago Junction.

The B&O switched to the Rock Island to enter Chicago and built a passenger station at Harrison and Well Streets. B&O moved to Grand Central Station when it opened on December 1, 1891. The B&O double-tracked 125 miles of its Chicago Division between 1901 and 1904.

The B&O's best Chicago–New York time in the early 20th century was 25 hours, 55 minutes, several hours slower than the New York Central and Pennsylvania Railroads. Therefore, the B&O emphasized stopovers in Washington.

On the eve of the 20th century, the B&O had two Chicago–New York round trips, one via Akron, one via Wheeling. Local service included Chicago–Walkerton (in southwest St. Joseph County), Garrett–Wheeling, Chicago Junction to Walkerton, and Walkerton to Newark, Ohio. Two years later, the Walkerton trains had begun operating to Chicago, boosting Chicago service to four arrivals and five departures, a schedule pattern that remained through 1910. Indiana locals operated between Garrett and Rock Island Junction (Chicago) by 1906. All four Chicago–New York trains were named in 1910. Nos. 5/6 were the *New York and Chicago Limited/Chicago and New York Limited*, and Nos. 7/8 were the *New York–Chicago Special/ Chicago–New York Special.*

The Willard Era

The appointment of Daniel Willard as president on January 15, 1910, signaled a new direction for B&O passenger service. Willard immediately canceled his railroad's passenger service advertisements, explaining, "I will not advertise a service unworthy of the name of the railroad."

During Willard's presidency, which lasted until June 1, 1941, the B&O spent $139 million to rebuild its mainlines, including double-tracking the Chicago–Philadelphia route. By 1917, three-fourths of the B&O passenger fleet was all-steel cars. Willard insisted on six-wheel trucks for safety and comfort.

By the mid-1920s, the B&O had the high-quality passenger trains that Willard desired. The fleet leader was the all-Pullman *Capitol Limited* (Chicago–New York), which featured lounge cars, train secretary, valet, maid, manicure, and shower bath. The B&O took great pride in the *Capitol Limited*, yet during a conference about Pullman service, Willard remarked, "We are spending too much time on the problem of the Pullman passenger. Eighty percent of our patrons ride in the day coaches, yet we barely give them 20 percent of our attention."

Willard urged B&O employees in 1923 to emphasize safety, comfort, and on-time performance. He rejected faster schedules for fear that faster trains would be less comfortable. Willard demanded that the B&O be known for smooth starts and stops.

The B&O earned its reputation for excellent dining in the Willard era. Headquartered near the Maryland tidewater, the B&O served a great deal of fresh seafood. If Willard liked a meal, he sent the chef a note and autographed photograph. Every B&O chef coveted a photo of Willard as evidence of his culinary skills.

In the 1920s, the B&O spent 50 cents per patron before it spent a penny for food. E. V. Baugh, manager of dining and commissary services, defended the expense. "The one big reason that we have a dining car department is because we want to be hospitable to our patrons in all respects—to make them feel the comfort and convenience and homelike atmosphere of our accommodations as soon as they step on our trains."

The devotion to comfort paid off in 1936 when a survey by *Sales Management* magazine of frequent travelers ranked the B&O as the top railroad in the East and third nationally for service behind Union Pacific and Santa Fe. But such accolades could not stop passenger traffic from declining. Willard predicted in the early 1930s that railroads would never regain business lost to the automobile.

Chicago Service Matures

The 1912 addition of the eastbound *Chicago–Wheeling Night Express* and the westbound *Night Express* between the same points increased Chicago service to 10 trains. Among the new names in the timetable were *Chicago Express, Chicago, Pittsburgh, Washington and New York Express, New York, Pittsburgh and Chicago Express, Chicago, Pittsburgh and New York Express*, and *Interstate Express*.

The B&O favored the Akron route for Chicago–East Coast service by 1914. The *Chicago Express* briefly operated via Wheeling in 1915, and a Chicago–Newark, Ohio, train began terminating at Chicago Junction. The following year, a new Pittsburgh to Chicago train increased Chicago service to six arrivals and five departures. Also added in 1916 was a Garrett–Wheeling local.

All Chicago–New York trains operated through Akron by January 1918. The B&O had four Chicago–Pittsburgh round trips, and locals operating Chicago to Garrett, Chicago Junction to Chicago, Garrett to Chicago Junction, and Garrett–Gary. Several names had changed by early 1918. Nos. 5/6 were now the *Washington–Chicago Limited/Chicago–Washington Limited*. No. 7 was the *Chicago Special*, and No. 8 was the *Washington Special*. Nos. 9/10 were the *Pittsburgh and Chicago Express/Chicago and Pittsburgh Express*. No. 15 had become the *Middle West Express*, and No. 16 was the *Washington Express*. One Chicago–Pittsburgh train ended in 1918, and Chicago–Wheeling Nos. 45/46 began combining with Nos. 10/16 between Chicago and Chicago Junction. No. 45 became the *Chicago Night Express*, and No. 46 was the *Wheeling Night Express*.

The United States Railway Administration, which controlled the nation's railroads during World War I, ordered the Pennsylvania Railroad in April 1918 to allow the B&O to use New York Penn Station. However, the B&O suspended Chicago–New York service until mid-1919.

After USRA control ended on March 1, 1920, Willard negotiated a five-year extension of the use of Penn Station. The Pennsylvania soon regretted it and said the B&O could not use Penn Station after the agreement expired. Willard wrangled an extension until September 1, 1926, when the B&O went back to its previous Jersey City route via the Reading and the Central of New Jersey. Buses whisked passengers between the platform at Jersey City and Manhattan or Brooklyn (via ferry). Luggage was transferred to the traveler's hotel.

Through the early 1920s, Chicago service remained four round trips via Pittsburgh, one of which conveyed the Wheeling trains between Chicago and Willard, Ohio. Locals operated Chicago to Garrett, Garrett to Willard, Willard to Chicago, and Gary to Garrett. Nos. 7/8 were renamed the *New York–Chicago Special/Chicago–Washington–New York Special*. Nos. 5/6 became the *New York–Chicago Limited/Chicago–Washington–New York Limited*. No. 10 became the *Chicago–Pittsburgh–Washington Express*. The longest name belonged to No. 16, the *Chicago–Pittsburgh–Washington–Baltimore Express*.

A Capitol Idea

The B&O created the *Capitol Limited* with the idea that it would be a peer of the New York Central's *Twentieth Century Limited* and the Pennsylvania Railroad's *Broadway Limited*. But due to financial constraints, new equipment was out of the question. The mountainous profile of the B&O west of Cumberland, Md., and the roundabout route into New York made matching the travel times of the *Century* and *Broadway* impossible. The B&O hoped that sumptuous service would cause travelers to disregard the speed advantage of the *Century* or *Broadway*.

The B&O renamed Nos. 5/6 the *Capitol Limited*, assigned it refurbished equipment, and sent it out on May 13, 1923, as the first Chicago–Baltimore all-Pullman luxury liner. The *Capitol Limited* sought dominance of the Chicago–Baltimore/Washington market, and soon it was the train of choice among government and business officials.

William F. Howes Jr., who supervised B&O passenger service in the late 1960s, described the personality of the *Capitol Limited* as genteel decorum that mixed easily with southern hospitality. Howes, who rode the *Capitol Limited* more than 115 times, commented, "You were likely to become engaged in table conversation with a politician, Hollywood personality, labor leader, or captain of industry over one of B&O's fabled Chesapeake Bay dining car recipes. And there was an air of mystery behind the closed doors in the Pullmans where celebrities took meals in the privacy of their rooms."

The *Capitol Limited* straddled the fault line between North and South, and its dining car reflected the heritage of the two regions. Entrees had a decidedly Maryland flavor with seafood and chicken prepared in the ways favored by Baltimore and Maryland's Eastern Shore. But a southern flavor also was apparent with such morsels as hush puppies, cornbread pie, and spoon bread.

Although billed as a Chicago–New York train, the *Capitol Limited* terminated in Baltimore. The Pennsylvania conveyed the New York sleepers north of Washington until it evicted the B&O from New York Penn Station in 1926. Thenceforth, New York cars of the *Capitol Limited* and other B&O long-distance trains were detached at Washington and conveyed by Royal Blue line trains to Jersey City.

The Pennsylvania responded to the launch of the *Capitol Limited* by creating a Washington section of the *Broadway Limited*. In September 1925 the Pennsylvania established its own elite Chicago–Baltimore/Washington train, the *Liberty Limited*, which was slightly faster than the *Capitol Limited* despite a circuitous route.

The B&O responded by upgrading the equipment of the *Capitol Limited* and shaving time off the schedule by (beginning in 1929) bypassing Pittsburgh to avoid a backup move at the B&O terminal. In 1934, the B&O negotiated trackage rights over the Pittsburgh & Lake Erie between McKeesport and New Castle, Pa. This gave the *Capitol Limited* a faster route and enabled it to serve the P&LE station across the Monongahela River from Pittsburgh's Golden Triangle. The P&LE became the preferred route through Pittsburgh for most B&O long-distance passenger trains.

The *Middle West Express* was renamed the *Washingtonian* in June 1923. The Gary–Garrett local was extended to South Chicago, which it served until the train ended in June 1928. Chicago–Wheeling trains resumed independent operation between Chicago and Willard under the names *Chicago–Wheeling Night Express/Wheeling–Chicago Night Express*. The Wheeling trains consolidated with Nos. 15/16 between Chicago and Willard in 1925 and resumed their former names of *Chicago Night Express/Wheeling Night Express*.

The B&O inaugurated another all-Pullman train in June 1927: the Chicago–Pittsburgh *Fort Pitt Limited*. However, passengers paid no extra fare. That same month, the *Washingtonian* became the *Western Express*. Chicago–Pittsburgh service expanded to five round trips in 1928: *Capitol Limited, Fort Pitt Limited, Chicago–Pittsburgh–Washington–Baltimore Express, New York–Chicago Special, Chicago–Washington–New York Special, Pittsburgh and Chicago Express, Chicago–Pittsburgh–Washington Express,* and the *Western Express.*

The Garrett–Willard local now operated to Pittsburgh. Adventurous passengers who rode the distance endured a prolonged ride. No. 67 left Pittsburgh at 4:15 A.M. and arrived at Garrett at 3:55 P.M. No. 68 departed Garrett at 8:40 A.M. and arrived in Pittsburgh at 7:55 P.M. The trains ended on July 13, 1930.

Capitol Limited's *New Look*

Although passenger traffic declined by more than a quarter in the 1920s, the B&O continued to invest in passenger service, purchasing 20 Pacific 4-6-2 locomotives from Baldwin in 1927. These locomotives, mainstays of B&O mainline passenger service until dieselization, were named for U.S. presidents.

The branch between Louisville and North Vernon was a heavy passenger carrier through the 1950s. In this 1956 scene at North Vernon, steam locomotive No. 5206 is making one of its last appearances. Soon GP9 diesels would take over. Photo by Ron Stuckey; John Fuller collection.

B&O stock plunged from $145 a share in 1929 to less than $4 a share in 1932, but the company continued to improve passenger service, installing reclining seats in many day coaches and air-conditioning its trains in 1930. The *Capitol Limited* on May 22, 1932, became the first Chicago line train to be air-conditioned. With the traveling public increasingly demanding private rooms rather than berths, B&O president Willard talked the Pullman Company into assigning additional sleepers with private rooms to the *Capitol Limited*.

The B&O purchased one of the first diesel-electric road engines built by the Electro-Motive Corporation and in May 1937 received the first EMC E-unit, an A-B set. Initially assigned to the Jersey City–Washington *Royal Blue*, the diesels were soon transferred to the *Capitol Limited*. The purchase of a second A-B set enabled the *Capitol Limited* to operate as the first dieselized train between Chicago and the East. Steam locomotives pulled B&O trains north of Washington until after World War II.

Willard had always favored heavyweight equipment. He hired industrial designer Otto Kuhler to streamline the *Capitol Limited*, using the B&O's existing stock of heavyweight cars. Kuhler gave the exteriors a striking livery of blue and gray accented by gold striping and lettering. Cars received full diaphragms and skirts, tight-lock couplers, rounded roofs, and improved trucks. The interiors received indirect lighting and an array of bright colors. Pullman rebuilt 19 cars for the *Capitol Limited*, all sleepers except for two baggage-dormitory-buffet lounges. The newly streamlined *Capitol Limited* entered service in 1938, making it the first diesel-powered streamliner in the East.

The Pennsylvania countered by assigning new lightweight Pullmans and stainless steel diners to the *Liberty Limited*. By now, though, the *Capitol Limited* was the dominant Chicago–Washington train.

The B&O discontinued the *New York–Chicago Special/Chicago–Washington–New York Special* (Nos. 7/8) in 1931, but reinstated both two years later. No. 7 assumed its former name, but No. 8 went unnamed until 1934 when it became the *Fort Pitt Limited* and No. 7 became the *Western States Limited*. The later name was replaced in May 1937 by *Fort Pitt Limited*.

The *Blue Ridge Limited* name appeared on No. 16 in 1934. Its counterpart, No. 15, was named the *Blue Ridge Limited* in May 1937. At the same time, Nos. 9/10 became the *Shenandoah*, which catered to those who could not afford the *Capitol Limited*. Overnight from Washington to Pittsburgh, its midafternoon arrival in Chicago gave the *Shenandoah* the most convenient connections with late afternoon western trains. The eastbound *Shenandoah* departed Chicago late at night, was a day train through the mountains, and arrived in Washington in late afternoon.

The *Blue Ridge Limited* was a high-status train in its early years. When the eastbound *Blue Ridge Limited* was discontinued west of Pittsburgh in September 1938, mail train No. 32 began handling passengers to Chicago to fill the void. The *Blue Ridge Limited* usually left Washington a couple of hours ahead of the *Shenandoah* and had a slower schedule due to the numerous head-end cars that it conveyed. It was steam-powered until well after World War II, carrying a Washington to Chicago sleeper and, west of Pittsburgh, a diner.

In the late 1930s there were six trains from Chicago to Pittsburgh, but this ended with the September 1938 discontinuance of the eastbound *Blue Ridge Limited*. The B&O had five Chicago–Pittsburgh round trips into the 1940s. The August 4, 1940, assignment of coaches to the *Capitol Limited* temporarily ended its all-Pullman status.

The Columbian *Debuts*

Encouraged by the success of the New York Central's *Pacemaker* and the Pennsylvania's *Trail Blazer*, all-coach Chicago–New York trains, the B&O created the all-coach *Columbian*. Unable to afford new lightweight streamlined equipment, which Willard didn't like anyway, the B&O shops modernized and streamlined existing heavyweight coaches, diners, and observation lounge cars. Offering many of the services and amenities of the *Capitol*

Limited, most notably dining and lounge service, the *Columbian* was priced for budget-minded travelers seeking a fast dusk-to-dawn journey in a coach seat between Chicago and the East.

The coaches had larger women's lounges because, the B&O discovered, many women disliked traveling overnight by coach because of the small washrooms in traditional heavy-weight coaches. To further appeal to women, the B&O assigned stewardess-nurses to the *Columbian,* a service begun on the *Capitol Limited* in 1937.

The *Columbian* debuted on December 19, 1941. Although advertised as a Chicago–New York train, the *Columbian*'s Chicago–Jersey City coach was conveyed with the Jersey City cars of the *Capitol Limited* north of Washington. The *Columbian* departed 5 to 10 minutes behind the *Capitol Limited* and arrived in Chicago and Washington 30 to 45 minutes later than its diesel-powered running mate, which had reverted to all-Pullman status. The *Columbian* was an immediate success, and during World War II it ran with as many as 14 cars.

Other 1940 changes included the discontinuance of the *Fort Pitt Limited* on September 3. The former eastbound *Fort Pitt Express* between Chicago and Willard became the *West Virginia Night Express.* The *Chicago Night Express* began operating independently west of Willard. By early 1941, the *Chicago Night Express* had been consolidated with No. 9 between Chicago and Willard. The net effect was five trains to Chicago and four trains from Chicago until inauguration of the *Columbian* increased the schedule to six trains to Chicago and five from Chicago.

The B&O won regulatory approval in 1940 to cut fares. Passenger revenue had fallen more than 40 percent from $18.5 million in 1930 to $10.6 million in 1940. The B&O earned $14 million in passenger revenue in 1941 and operated 748 million passenger miles. In 1942 this rose to $27 million in revenue and 1.2 billion passenger miles. Passenger revenue and passenger miles peaked in 1944 at $51 million and 2.7 billion, respectively.

The *Capitol Limited* received its first lightweight streamlined Pullmans, as well as its first roomette cars, on January 15, 1941. The Pennsylvania's *Liberty Limited* had similar equipment, and the B&O feared that unless it offered private single rooms it would lose the patronage of the political and business leaders who frequented the *Capitol Limited.*

The *Capitol Limited* of the early 1940s usually operated with seven sleepers, three lounge cars (one doubling as a baggage car and crew dormitory), and a diner. The westbound *Capitol Limited* picked up a sleeper in Pittsburgh that returned on the *Shenandoah.* The *Capitol Limited* was crowded during World War II, but rarely operated in more than one section because the B&O did not have enough equipment for a second luxury train. It was difficult for those other than top political officials and key military personnel and defense contractors to book space.

The *Columbian* lost its observation-lounge cars, and the *New York–Pittsburgh–Chicago Express/Chicago–Pittsburgh–New York Express* ceased operating north of Washington in 1943, although the train names were not adjusted accordingly until 1945. The *Columbian* became diesel powered between Chicago and Washington in 1945. With thousands of military personnel returning home after the war, the *Capitol Limited* remained one of the toughest tickets in town. The B&O increased capacity somewhat by adding additional heavyweight sleepers.

Postwar Makeovers

With the nation returning to peacetime, the B&O on December 2, 1945, cut the running time of the *Capitol Limited* and *Columbian* by 25 minutes and the *Shenandoah* by 15 minutes. The *Chicago Night Express* resumed independent operation between Chicago and Willard, Ohio, which increased Chicago line service through Indiana to 10 Chicago–Pittsburgh trains and 2 Chicago–Wheeling trains.

The B&O ordered 18 E7A diesel locomotives from the Electro-Motive Division of General Motors in 1945. The *New York–Pittsburgh–Chicago Express/Chicago–Pittsburgh–New*

York Express received diesels later that year, and all Chicago–Washington trains were diesel powered by 1947. Knowing the New York Central and Pennsylvania Railroads had ordered new equipment for their all-coach trains, the B&O upgraded the *Columbian* to a lightweight streamlined train, ordering new equipment from Pullman-Standard in December 1945. But due to a postwar backlog, the cars were not delivered until 1949.

A typical *Columbian* consist was a baggage–dormitory–coffee shop, dining car, observation-tavern-lounge, and four chair cars, each named after a city on the route. The train was pulled by an A-B-A set of F3 diesel locomotives. The new equipment entered service May 5, 1949. The *Columbian*'s dining service was less lavish than that of the *Capitol Limited,* but still featured blue and white china, heavy silverware, and white tablecloths. Patrons enjoyed a complimentary morning cup of coffee.

The *Columbian* featured the first dome cars built by Pullman-Standard. Called Strata-Domes by the B&O, the cars featured two lounges under the dome, 18 coach seats forward, and 24 seats aft. In the dome, the 24 seats had low backs to provide better visibility. Unlike domes built by Budd, Pullman-Standard used flat instead of curved glass. Because of tight overhead clearances in eastern terminal areas, B&O dome cars had a lower profile, 21 inches above the roofline as opposed to 28 inches for domes operated by western railroads.

The B&O purchased three sleeper-domes from C&O in December 1950. Two of them, *Starlight Dome* and *Sunlight Dome,* were assigned to the *Capitol Limited* on December 20, 1950. The third, *Moonlight Dome,* was assigned to the *Shenandoah.* The *Columbian* dome cars, *High Dome* and *Sky Dome,* featured a speedometer, altimeter, barometer, clock, radio, wire-recorded music, a public address system, venetian blinds, and a stewardess-nurse. Because its dome cars traveled at night, the B&O in 1952 equipped them with four floodlights on each side just in front of the dome section. The lights, which used 250-watt locomotive headlights, were aimed at different angles and produced what *Railway Age* described as "a diffused beam, somewhat stronger than moonlight." The lights were turned off when a train passed through a town.

The B&O considered placing the *Columbian* on a daylight schedule, but this would have meant early morning departures and late night arrivals. Most passengers preferred to travel at night even if it meant missing some of the best scenery in the East.

The B&O could not afford new lightweight equipment in large batches, so the remake of the *Capitol Limited* occurred gradually. Some "new" lightweight equipment was purchased used. This included two C&O bedroom buffet-lounge-observation cars that B&O named *Dana* and *Metcalf.* The *Capitol Limited* of 1951 typically carried eight lightweight cars and five heavyweight cars. It would be 1955 before it became an all-lightweight train.

The *Capitol Limited* carried lightweight sleepers interchanged with the Santa Fe in transcontinental sleeping car service. The first of these (Washington–Los Angeles) began in July 1946 and interchanged with the *Chief.* This involved a cumbersome switching move in Chicago between Grand Central Station and Dearborn Station, used by the Santa Fe. The sleeper began operating to San Diego on March 15, 1951, and was transferred to the *Shenandoah* on January 10, 1954, because of its better connections with the Santa Fe's *Super Chief,* which now was conveying the transcontinental sleepers. The eastbound car continued to operate on the *Capitol Limited.* The Santa Fe curtailed operation of the sleeper to Los Angeles on April 24, 1954. The transcontinental cars ended on January 11, 1958, because of low patronage and high terminal expenses in Chicago.

Although B&O management viewed the *Shenandoah* as its second most important train, it did not have the same priority as the *Capitol Limited* or *Columbian* for new streamlined equipment. Consequently, the *Shenandoah* was primarily a heavyweight train for much of its life. Nonetheless, it had some of the fleet's best reclining seat coaches, several sleepers, a diner, and coach and first-class lounges. A stewardess-nurse was assigned in 1941, by which time the *Shenandoah* was diesel powered between Chicago and Washington. With its railway post office, numerous mail and express cars, and healthy passenger loads, the *Shenandoah* was a cash cow. The *Shenandoah* lost some of its intermediate setout sleepers during World War II, but once these cars returned, the *Shenandoah* had much the same appearance as it had before the war.

Concurrent with the inauguration of Washington–Los Angeles transcontinental sleeper service was the debut of a Washington–San Francisco sleeper on the *Shenandoah* interchanged with the Chicago & North Western's *Gold Coast.* The Union Pacific handled the car between Omaha, Neb., and Ogden, Utah, and the Southern Pacific conveyed it between Ogden and Oakland, Calif. It was a long, slow journey because the *Gold Coast* made every conditional stop. The San Francisco sleeper ended on April 28, 1948.

The *Shenandoah*'s coach lounge served light meals, but this ended on September 25, 1949. Hungry passengers could still find meals in the diner. The first lightweight sleeper was assigned to the *Shenandoah* on April 13, 1950, between Chicago and Pittsburgh. The dome-sleeper on the *Shenandoah* went west one day, east the next. When a dome-sleeper on the *Capitol Limited* was removed for service, the *Shenandoah*'s dome-sleeper usually replaced it, so the *Shenandoah* sometimes went without its dome car for several months.

The *Blue Ridge Limited* had a consist worthy of a first-class train including reclining seat coaches, a lounge with sleeping accommodations, a sleeper, and a combine coach. A diner added at Pittsburgh served breakfast and lunch. The lounge car began February 15, 1946, between Washington and Akron in a bid to boost overnight business. The car was extended to Chicago in June 1947 so that it could be used to provide Pullman lounge service on the eastbound *Chicago–Washington Express.* With postwar traffic sagging and the B&O providing four other evening trains out of Washington, there was little need for the *Blue Ridge Limited.* Discontinued on February 20, 1949, most of its equipment was shifted to the *Washington–Chicago Express.*

No. 32 had been the fifth train from Chicago to Pittsburgh since the discontinuance of the eastbound *Blue Ridge Limited* in 1938. Primarily a mail and express train to Jersey City, No. 32 carried passengers as far as Cumberland, Md., and was the only Chicago train still using the Pittsburgh & Western route between New Castle, Pa., and Pittsburgh and the downtown Pittsburgh B&O station. All other Chicago trains used the P&LE station. No. 32 departed Chicago 10 minutes after the *Shenandoah* and handled local traffic in Indiana and Ohio. Passenger service aboard No. 32 ended on February 20, 1949. Coupled with the discontinuance of the westbound *Blue Ridge Limited,* this reduced Chicago–Pittsburgh service to four round trips.

The other Chicago–Washington trains were the *Washington–Pittsburgh–Chicago Express* (No. 9) and the *Chicago–Pittsburgh–Washington Express* (No. 10). Both carried numerous mail and express cars. No. 9 was the first arrival in Chicago, at 7 A.M., and carried an Akron setout sleeper. No. 10 was the first departure from Chicago at 10:40 A.M., and operated as a local in Indiana, making 12 stops, more than any other B&O train. No. 9 offered a diner until April 1957, but due to its early arrival in Chicago there were few patrons. After April 26, 1953, the diner was open only between Cumberland, Md., and Pittsburgh. The *Washington–Pittsburgh–Chicago Express* carried sleepers originating at Washington, Akron, and Wheeling.

The *Chicago–Pittsburgh–Washington Express* earned more passenger and mail revenue because it carried an RPO. No. 10 handled the San Francisco to Washington sleeper between June 1, 1946, and April 28, 1948. Generally, the B&O assigned better coaches to No. 10. The Chicago to Jersey City coach conveyed by No. 10 was gone by 1949. Aside from occasional changes in the sleeping car equipment, Nos. 9/10 saw few changes through 1958. Both were dieselized in late 1945.

Awash in Red Ink

From a 1944 peak of $51 million, B&O passenger revenue had fallen to $22 million by 1949. Passenger train miles also steadily declined, bottoming out at 704 million in 1950. There was an uptick during the Korean War (800 million passenger miles in 1951), but passenger miles had fallen to 679 million in 1953.

Passenger revenue in 1950 was 5 percent of the B&O's total revenue, but the passenger deficit was 47.5 percent of net freight income, the highest percentage among major eastern railroads. Comparable figures were 45 percent at the New York Central, 38 percent at the Pennsylvania, and 21 percent at the C&O. The B&O had lost money on passenger service every year since the 1930s except during World War II.

Howard Simpson, who became B&O president in 1953, was reluctant to give up on passenger service, making every effort to keep as many trains as possible. The B&O aggressively and creatively wooed passengers. In spring 1947, it instituted "serva-seat service," providing inexpensive meals to coach passengers. It also began accepting credit cards for ticket purchases.

But Simpson was a realist who approved ending a train when revenue fell far below out-of-pocket costs. From 185 passenger trains in 1948, the B&O had 98 trains by July 1956. Its operating ratio (cost compared to income) was 173.26 percent in 1954 and 180.77 percent in 1955, one of the worst in the industry. The passenger deficit was $33 million by 1957. The B&O lost $13 million in 1959 and teetered on the brink of bankruptcy. Awash in $31 million in red ink by 1961, the B&O found a savior in the Chesapeake & Ohio. The two merged on February 4, 1963.

An aggressive cost-containment strategy helped the B&O slice out-of-pocket losses on passenger service from $12 million in 1958 to $5 million in 1961. The boldest move was ending all passenger service north of Baltimore on April 26, 1958, which the B&O expected would save $6.5 million a year. Five of the six Washington–Jersey City round trips were extensions of long-distance trains serving Chicago and St. Louis.

Withdrawal from the New York market had a ripple effect in lost traffic, but the consequences were relatively minimal because travel to Philadelphia and New York had made only a marginal, incremental contribution to the balance sheet. The B&O's strength was Chicago–Washington/Baltimore, where in the mid-1950s the *Capitol Limited* had 77.4 percent of the Pullman market in competition with the Pennsylvania and the C&O.

The *Columbian* and the Detroit–Baltimore *Ambassador* were consolidated on January 10, 1954, between Washington and Willard, Ohio, although during heavy travel periods, particularly between early April and Labor Day, the two often operated separately. The two trains continued to carry their own diners, a practice that ended on December 1, 1957, when operation of the *Columbian*'s diner was curtailed to Chicago–Willard.

The *Columbian-Ambassador* was combined with the *Capitol Limited* between Washington and Baltimore on April 27, 1958. At the same time, the *Columbian* received two Slumbercoaches. For the price of a coach ticket plus a $6 room charge, passengers had a private room. The Slumbercoaches were so popular that the B&O had to assign heavy-weight modernized sleepers to accommodate the business.

The consolidation of the *Columbian* and *Capitol Limited* between Chicago and Willard on October 26, 1958, effectively ended the *Capitol Limited*'s stature as an all-Pullman train. The *Columbian* and *Capitol Limited* ran independently during busy travel periods, but by 1960 this rarely occurred. The *Columbian* and *Capitol Limited* were consolidated all the way between Chicago and Baltimore on October 25, 1959. The *Columbian* name remained in B&O timetables until April 26, 1964.

The *Shenandoah* on October 30, 1960, lost its buffet-solarium lounge cars, the only heavyweight cars of their kind on a mainline passenger train in the country. Also ending were the stewardess-nurse and dining service west of Akron (eastbound) and Pittsburgh (westbound). The *Shenandoah* began terminating at Washington in fall 1962. The discontinuance of mail and express No. 32 shifted more head-end traffic to the *Shenandoah*. This improved the train's financial performance, but made it difficult to stay on time even with additional time built into the schedule. The *Shenandoah* lost its dome-sleeper on October 27, 1963, and its baggage-buffet-lounge on April 26, 1964.

Nos. 9/10 became the *Washington–Chicago Express/Chicago–Washington Express* in November 1959, then the *Washington–Chicago Express* in both directions in 1960 and later the *Washington Express* (eastbound) and *Chicago Express* (westbound). Operations of the *Chicago Night Express* and *Wheeling Night Express* changed little during the 1940s. Each had two or three head-end cars, an RPO-baggage car, a coach, and a sleeper. A diner operated between Wheeling and Newark, Ohio.

The *Chicago Night Express* operated west of Willard primarily as a mail train, its Wheeling–Chicago coach and sleeper transferred to the *Washington–Pittsburgh–Chicago Express* at Willard. It stopped in Indiana at Albion, Wawasee, Syracuse, Nappanee, Bremen, La Paz, Walkerton, Kingsbury, and Wellsboro, stations bypassed by many B&O trains. The *Wheeling Night Express* made the same Indiana stops, but conveyed its Wheeling cars the entire distance. During World War II, a lunch-counter coach between Chicago and Wheeling replaced the Wheeling–Newark diner, which returned in June 1947 as a diner-parlor car. The *Chicago Night Express* and *West Virginia Night Express* were dieselized in 1956.

Although losing $400,000 a year in the mid-1950s, B&O management for political reasons kept the Wheeling trains running east of Willard. They still had much head-end business, which west of Willard could be handled by the *Washington–Pittsburgh–Chicago Express* and mail train No. 31. The B&O sought Indiana and Ohio regulatory approval in August 1956 to end the *Chicago Night Express*/*West Virginia Night Express* between Chicago and Willard on October 28. Regulatory officials did not act in time for that to occur, but the B&O removed the Chicago–Wheeling coach on that day.

Sleeping car patronage between Wheeling and Chicago was still strong, and the B&O planned to continue it through a connection at Willard. The *Chicago Night Express*/*West Virginia Night Express* made their final runs west of Willard on December 1, 1956. By the late 1950s, patronage of the Chicago–Wheeling sleepers had diminished. The discontinuance of these cars on July 2, 1961, ended B&O passenger service between Chicago and Wheeling.

Making a Last Stand

B&O president Jervis Langdon Jr. said in 1962 that the railroad might end passenger service. But Langdon had a change of heart and authorized the nation's most far-reaching effort to revive passenger service. In January 1964, he asked a 31-year-old B&O executive how the railroad could cut expenses and boost revenue enough to cover the direct cost of passenger service. Two days later, Paul Reistrup had a two-year plan and, on February 1, a new title, director of passenger services. Answering only to the president, Reistrup was given wide latitude to revamp passenger service. And if Reistrup's plan didn't work? "We'll get rid of 'em," Langdon said.

Although the B&O's out-of-pocket passenger loss in 1963 had been nearly $2.4 million, the Chicago–Washington trains had covered their direct costs and earned $1 million. The *Capitol Limited* still carried solid loads, but in mid-1962 Langdon had ordered a slowdown because "the train traveled so fast through the Alleghenies that I found it difficult to shave, much less keep my coffee in its cup."

Some changes were cosmetic. The *Capitol Limited* briefly became the *Capitol*. The *Shenandoah* was renamed the *Diplomat*, a name used for decades on the St. Louis line. Most changes involved fares and on-board service. "Red circle day" fares reduced midweek Pullman fares by 31 percent, a plan later extended to coach travel.

In time for the 1964 Christmas travel season, the B&O leased projectors from In-Flight Motion Pictures and began showing first-run movies on board the *Capitol*. To boost beverage sales, passengers were given salty snacks. Surveys found 99 percent of passengers liked the movies.

The B&O launched "Take Your Auto Service" on the *Washington–Chicago Express* in summer 1965. A double auto-rack attached to the rear of the train carried a passenger's automobile between Chicago and Washington. The program generated $12,500 and extensive media coverage, but only averaged one auto per day in each direction. The program ended that fall.

One Baltimore & Ohio effort to boost passenger traffic was the "Take Your Auto Service," which began on the *Washington–Chicago Express* in summer 1965. A double auto-rack attached to the rear of the train carried a passenger's automobile between Chicago and Washington. C&O Railway Photo, courtesy Chesapeake & Ohio Historical Society Collection.

The *Capitol Limited* was the train of choice between Chicago and Washington/Baltimore, featuring service akin to that of a fine hotel. The eastbound *Capitol Limited* is at Gary on May 28, 1967. Photo by Dave McKay.

To reduce the $74,000-a-month dining department deficit, the B&O introduced frozen precooked meals. By late 1967, food-bar coaches had replaced diners on all trains except the *Capitol Limited*.

A July 1966 strike that shut down most air service between the Midwest and East gave the B&O an unexpected opportunity. It put everything it had on the rails and reaped a windfall in increased ridership. The *Capitol Limited* routinely operated with 18 to 22 cars. Passengers gave the B&O high marks, and the company nearly broke even on passenger service. But when the strike ended more than a month later, many travelers returned to the airways.

Even before the strike, Reistrup had begun to doubt that the B&O's bootstrap campaign would work. In a March 15, 1966, memorandum to B&O/C&O president Gregory DeVine, Reistrup recommended phasing out passenger service. Out-of-pocket passenger losses had fallen from nearly $4 million in 1965 to $2.7 million in 1966, but patronage was also falling after a brief increase. The B&O was unable to reduce many of its fixed costs, particularly terminal charges, which ran as high as $59 per car at St. Louis.

Langdon was not surprised that the effort to revive passenger service didn't work. "I never thought it would work," he told Fred Frailey, author of *Twilight of the Great Trains*, 28 years later. "But I wanted to make a last stand." Added Reistrup, who left the B&O/C&O in 1967, "I thought we could pull it off—we really tried hard."

The *Capitol Limited* lost its dome sleepers on October 1, 1965, and in October 1966 began terminating at Washington instead of Baltimore. One of its two sleepers came off on September 11, 1967, and 4 days later the railway post office was gone. Lightweight diners designated Chessie Tavern Service replaced the twin-unit diners in October. The onboard movies on the *Capitol Limited* also ended that fall. The B&O said the movies, which had cost $150,000 a year, provided no discernible increase in patronage.

The sleepers on the *Chicago Express* and eastbound *Diplomat* were curtailed to Chicago–Pittsburgh on June 10, 1966, and eliminated on September 9, 1967. Food-bar coaches replaced diners on the *Diplomat* and *Washington Express/Chicago Express* in September 1966. A Cornell University survey found most coach passengers preferred the food-bar coach because the formal-looking dining car was intimidating and they feared high prices. B&O food-bar coaches offered higher-quality service than similar cars at some railroads, serving hot entrees and a wide selection of sandwiches.

Sleeping car service on the *Washington Express* and westbound *Diplomat* ended on May 3, 1968. The *Capitol Limited*'s dome-lounges were rebuilt to provide a food bar called the Iron Horse Tavern. Dining operations were streamlined, and the Chessie Tavern Service menu was trimmed to four entrees and two special items.

The B&O had not discontinued a passenger train since 1964, but that would soon end, spurred by a 1967 decision of the U.S. Post Office and the Railway Express Agency to implement a wholesale removal of business from the railroads. By the end of October, the railway post offices were gone and much of the storage mail of the three Chicago–Washington trains had been diverted to trucks and airlines. Mail and express had made these trains marginally profitable, but without this business the red ink began gushing.

Using an Ohio law that allowed a railroad to discontinue a passenger train within the Buckeye state so long as it was not the last train on the route, the B&O on November 5, 1967, discontinued the *Chicago Express* and eastbound *Diplomat*. The remnants of these trains continued to run between Gary and Garrett until Indiana regulatory authorities allowed their removal on December 31, 1967.

The *Washington Express* was discontinued east of Pittsburgh on July 15, 1968, and renamed the *Gateway*. The observation-lounge-sleepers came off the *Capitol Limited* on September 9, 1968. About a month later, a lunch counter–tavern–observation car replaced the diners. By 1969 the *Gateway* and *Diplomat* operated with one coach, a food-bar coach, and two or more head-end cars.

In summer 1968 the *Capitol Limited*'s dome cars had shifted to the *Cincinnatian* (Detroit–Cincinnati), resulting in the consolidation of all of the *Capitol Limited*'s dining and lounge services into one car. The *Capitol Limited* typically carried two head-end cars, two coaches, a Slumbercoach, a sleeping car, and a tavern-lounge-diner.

Even as it retreated from the passenger business, the B&O launched several marketing strategies. In August 1967, B&O/C&O began the "Chessie Loves Passengers" campaign, which featured equipment displays at major stations, television and newspaper advertisements, and (for two weeks) round-trip fares at one-way prices.

The blue and yellow fares implemented on May 19, 1968, were billed as "one of the boldest efforts of any U.S. transportation company to modernize passenger prices." Modeled after Canadian National's red, white, and blue fares, the yellow fares offered an off-peak 10 percent discount on coach tickets for trips over 100 miles. The blue fare was 5 percent higher during peak travel times for journeys of less than 100 miles.

Taking a cue from Eurailpass, B&O/C&O instituted a Chessie pass, which allowed 28 days of travel for $185. The B&O/C&O also offered discounted multiple-ride tickets. The blue and yellow fare program was an effort to shear $1 million off the 1967 passenger deficit of $13 million. B&O patronage had declined from 1.5 million in 1962 to 875,000 in 1967.

The Chessie Starlight Sleeper plan, begun in January 1969, gave first-class passengers complimentary meals as part of their fare. However, the only sleeper left on the B&O was a 10 roomette, six double bedroom car on the *Capitol Limited.* The Slumbercoaches were removed in November 1968.

Grand Central Station was the Baltimore & Ohio's Chicago home until it closed on November 7, 1969. The *Capitol Limited* prepares for its 4 P.M. departure, circa 1964. Train to the right is the Chesapeake & Ohio's *Pere Marquette* to Grand Rapids, Mich. C&O Railway Photo, courtesy Chesapeake & Ohio Historical Society Collection.

The dome cars returned to the *Capitol Limited* on May 27, 1969, although only one equipment set had a dome until late June. After September 8, the dome cars operated 4 days a week until transferred in January 1970 to the Washington–Akron *Shenandoah*. To increase bedroom accommodations, the *Capitol Limited* got its observation-lounge-sleepers back in November 1969. The car was placed in the middle of the train in order to provide sandwich, snack, and beverage service to coach passengers. The free meals for first-class passengers ended on October 5, 1970.

With the closing of Chicago Grand Central Station on November 7, 1969, B&O passenger trains moved to the Chicago & North Western Terminal, which resulted in a circuitous journey within the Windy City.

The B&O announced on August 11, 1969, that it would discontinue the *Diplomat/Gateway* west of Akron a month later, saying the trains were losing $195,000 a year. B&O said Nos. 7/10 averaged fewer than eight passengers per day west of Akron. The B&O told the Interstate Commerce Commission it could not compete with Penn Central, which had a faster, more direct Chicago–Pittsburgh route.

The ICC approved the discontinuance on January 6, 1970, citing low patronage. The commission said most of those who had opposed the removal of Nos. 7/10 could be accommodated by the *Capitol Limited*, which would begin making additional stops. Indiana joined with the city of Chicago and others in asking the ICC to reconsider its decision. The petitioners argued the ICC had overstated the trains' yearly deficit by about $20,000. But the ICC turned the appeal aside.

Amtrak did not pick up any B&O trains, so the *Capitol Limited* began its final runs on April 30, 1971. For the last eastbound trip, the B&O attached additional cars, placed a lighted drumhead on the rear, and printed commemorative tickets and dining car menus. The *Capitol Limited* continued to Baltimore, ending its journey near the place the B&O had begun passenger train service more than a century earlier.

St. Louis Line

The oldest B&O predecessor in Indiana was the Ohio & Mississippi, a 6-foot broadgauge line built in the 1850s between East St. Louis, Ill., and Cincinnati. Indiana's only broad-gauge railroad, its charter (granted on February 14, 1848) called for a direct route between Lawrenceburg in Dearborn County and Vincennes. The first Indiana trackage was completed between Cincinnati and Lawrenceburg in 1854. The road opened between East St. Louis and Vincennes on July 11, 1855.

The O&M needed financial assistance from the city of Cincinnati to complete the line between Mitchell in Lawrence County and Vincennes in early 1857. Passenger service between Cincinnati and East St. Louis began on May 4, 1857, with two daily expresses each way. An accommodation train operated between Cincinnati and Cochran in Dearborn County.

The O&M was part of the American Central Route, which included the B&O (Baltimore–Grafton, W.Va.), Northwestern Virginia (Grafton–Parkersburg, W.Va.), and Marietta & Cincinnati (Marietta, Ohio–Cincinnati). Although travelers took a nine-hour boat ride on the Ohio River between Parkersburg and Marietta, the American Central Route was 52 miles shorter than any other rail route between St. Louis and the East.

The O&M served sparsely populated areas of Illinois and Indiana that did not produce much traffic, and it endured several receiverships following the Civil War. The O&M converted to standard gauge on July 13, 1871, and was rebuilt in 1899 and 1901. The 1874 opening of Eads Bridge across the Mississippi River enabled the O&M to serve St. Louis. Consolidated in 1893 with the Baltimore & Ohio Southwestern, of which the B&O was a major stockholder, the O&M operated as a separate entity until July 1, 1900.

In its early years, the O&M typically operated two East St. Louis–Cincinnati round trips and a Cincinnati local that terminated at Osgood in Ripley County or at Seymour. East St. Louis–Cincinnati service had increased to three round trips by 1871. Locals operated Cincinnati–Seymour and Cincinnati–North Vernon.

By the 1880s, through sleepers operated between St. Louis and Baltimore, Washington and Louisville. A through train operated from St. Louis to Baltimore. In January 1885, the O&M had three St. Louis–Cincinnati round trips, a Cincinnati to St. Louis accommodation train, and locals operating Cincinnati–North Vernon, Cincinnati–Osgood, and Vincennes to Cincinnati. St. Louis–Cincinnati service had increased to four round trips by 1888, with locals operating Cincinnati–Osgood and Cincinnati–Cochran.

The premier train was the *Vestibuled Limited* between St. Louis and the East. For most of the 1890s, the B&O Southwestern had four St. Louis–Cincinnati round trips. By 1897 the *Vestibuled Limited* had become the *Royal Blue Flyer*. Nos. 3/4 were the *New York Express*, and Nos. 5/6 were the *St. Louis Express/Cincinnati Express*. A St. Louis–Vincennes local had begun by the early 1890s. The Cincinnati–Cochran local was gone by 1892. A Cincinnati–Vincennes train had begun terminating at Mitchell by 1896 and at Osgood in 1897 before ending in 1898.

On the eve of the 20th century, all three St. Louis–Cincinnati round trips carried New York sleepers. Nos. 3/4 were the *Cincinnati and New York Limited/Washington and New York Limited*. The *Royal Blue Limited* was the line's flagship train. The third express was the *Fast Mail*.

The St. Louis–Vincennes locals resumed July 27, 1902, after a six-year hiatus. Within two years these trains were operating between St. Louis and Flora, Ill. A Sunday-only train operated between St. Louis and Washington in Daviess County where the B&O had a division headquarters. Daily St. Louis–Vincennes operation resumed in 1905. The Sunday service, which had also included a Vincennes–St. Louis train, was gone.

St. Louis–Cincinnati service increased to five round trips in 1903 including the *Cincinnati and St. Louis Express/St. Louis, Cincinnati, and New York Express*, the *Fast Mail*, and the *Metropolitan Express*. Four of the 10 St. Louis–Cincinnati trains carried New York cars. Seven trains carried Washington and Baltimore cars. Named trains by 1905 included *Royal Blue Limited* (Nos. 1/2), *St. Louis Express* (No. 3), *Fast Mail* (Nos. 4/5), *Metropolitan Express* (No. 12), *Queen City Limited* (No. 6), and *Mound City Limited* (No. 11).

The *Royal Blue Limited* became the *St. Louis and New York Limited/New York and St. Louis Limited* in 1910. The name changed in 1913 to *St. Louis–Cincinnati–New York Limited–Cincinnati–St. Louis Limited*. The *Metropolitan Express* became the *Metropolitan Special* in 1917.

Nos. 21/22 (St. Louis–Vincennes) began operating to Washington, Ind., in 1906 when a Sunday-only St. Louis–Vincennes round trip began. Within a year Nos. 21/22 again operated St. Louis–Vincennes. Another local began operating between Vincennes and Flora, Ill., but was replaced in 1915 by mixed trains operating Washington–Bridgeport, Ill., and Bridgeport–Vincennes. The Bridgeport to Washington train ended in 1916, and its westbound counterpart began originating at Seymour. The Vincennes–Bridgeport trains were replaced on January 27, 1918, by a Vincennes–North Vernon train. The Washington–Bridgeport trains resumed operating in both directions.

World War I travel restrictions prompted cancellation of two St. Louis–Cincinnati round trips and all St. Louis–New York cars on January 27, 1918. A third round trip was shortened to St. Louis–Vincennes. This left four St. Louis–Cincinnati expresses: *Washington–Cincinnati–St. Louis Limited*, *St. Louis–Cincinnati–Washington Limited*, *New York–Washington–Cincinnati–St. Louis Express*, and *St. Louis–Cincinnati Express* (formerly the *Metropolitan Special*). St. Louis–Cincinnati service increased to three round trips in 1919, and the St. Louis–New York cars were reinstated. The *Metropolitan Special* name returned to St. Louis–Cincinnati No. 12 in 1924.

The *National Limited* was the premier Baltimore & Ohio passenger train to St. Louis. Passengers rode in style in the observation car "Capitol Escort," shown at North Vernon on July 17, 1946. Photo by M. D. McCarter.

A New National Priority

The B&O launched a new St. Louis–Washington luxury train on April 26, 1925. The all-Pullman *National Limited* featured lounge cars, secretary, valet, maid, manicure, and shower bath. It also carried New York sleepers.

St. Louis–Cincinnati service fell to three round trips in 1926. Although the Vincennes–North Vernon locals had ended, St. Louis–Vincennes service rose to two round trips. The Washington–Bridgeport locals and one St. Louis–Vincennes round trip ended on April 3, 1927, but the Vincennes–North Vernon locals were reinstated. The Vincennes–North Vernon trains ended and the St. Louis–Vincennes trains began operating St. Louis–Cincinnati on April 28, 1929.

Although still a formidable train in the mid-1960s, Baltimore & Ohio management gave up on the *National Limited,* shown here at Mitchell. The train ceased operating west of Cincinnati in September 1965. Photo by Ron Stuckey; John Fuller collection.

The *New York–Cincinnati–St. Louis Special/St. Louis–Cincinnati–New York Special* carried overnight coaches and sleepers between St. Louis and Washington. Briefly named the *Chesapeake Limited,* the trains were renamed the *Diplomat* in 1930. The *Diplomat* ran in the shadow of the *National Limited,* accommodating the latter's overflow business. Yet the *Diplomat* was just as fast and usually ran a few hours behind the *National Limited.* The other St. Louis–Cincinnati trains of the early 1930s were the eastbound *Metropolitan Special,* westbound *New York–Cincinnati–St. Louis Express,* and Nos. 61/62.

The *National Limited* became the B&O's first air-conditioned long-distance train on April 23, 1932, but later that year lost its all-Pullman status. The

New York–Cincinnati–St. Louis Express became the Metropolitan Special in 1937. An over-night train between St. Louis and Cincinnati, the Metropolitan Special carried numerous head-end cars.

St. Louis–Cincinnati service crested in February 1939 when a fifth round trip, Nos. 29/30, began operation. Nos. 61/62 ended west of Vincennes in July and was curtailed to Cincinnati–Washington, Ind., in October. The National Limited received a makeover in 1939 with sleepers and coaches rebuilt into heavyweight streamliners. The National Limited and the Diplomat had been assigned diesel locomotives by January 1942.

St. Louis line trains of the 1940s included the National Limited, the Diplomat, the Metropolitan Special, Nos. 29/30, and Nos. 61/62 (Cincinnati–Washington, Ind.). The National Limited and Diplomat carried New York sleepers, coaches, and diners. The Metropolitan Special had New York sleepers, but its coaches terminated at Washington. No. 29 originated at Jersey City, but handled passengers only between Cumberland, Md., and St. Louis. Operating overnight from Cincinnati to St. Louis, No. 29 stopped accepting passengers west of Cincinnati on November 12, 1944.

The National Limited received its first lightweight cars, a 10 roomette, five double bed-room sleeper, in 1945. A second section of the National Limited, Nos. 121/122, began in June 1945. War-related travel restrictions forced the temporary removal of St. Louis–Louisville and St. Louis–Cincinnati sleepers from the Metropolitan Special. The debut of the Cincinnatian between Cincinnati and Baltimore on January 17, 1947, prompted the discontinuance of Nos. 121/122 east of Cincinnati. The trains ended west of Cincinnati on April 27, 1947.

Southwestern Trails

The most far-reaching postwar change was the commencement of interline service at St. Louis between Washington and the Southwest on July 7, 1946. Washington–Houston sleepers ran on the National Limited and the Missouri Pacific's Texan (westbound) and Sunshine Special (eastbound). These trains also conveyed a Washington–Fort Worth coach.

Washington–Oklahoma City sleepers operated on the Diplomat (westbound) and National Limited (eastbound) and the St. Louis–San Francisco Railway's (Frisco) Meteor. Washington–San Antonio sleepers operated on the Diplomat (westbound) and National Limited (eastbound) and the Texas Special, operated jointly by the Frisco and Missouri–Kansas–Texas (Katy). The Washington–Oklahoma City sleepers and Fort Worth coaches soon began originating at Jersey City.

Although originally a St. Louis train, the Baltimore & Ohio revived the name Diplomat in 1964 and applied it to Chicago–Washington Nos. 7 and 8, formerly the Shenandoah. No. 7 is at Sterling, Ohio, on December 17, 1966. Photo by Dave McKay.

Sleepers used in interline service were heavyweights from the Pullman pool. Lightweight sleepers began operating to Oklahoma City, San Antonio, and Fort Worth in 1948. All four railroads contributed cars adorned in their respective liveries.

Patronage of the interline services was disappointing. The Fort Worth coach ended in February 1947, the Houston sleeper ended in April 1948, and the Oklahoma sleeper ended in November 1949. The San Antonio sleeper began terminating at Dallas on July 6, 1955, after the Katy discontinued the *Texas Special* south of there. The Frisco's discontinuance of its leg of the *Texas Special* (St. Louis–Vinita, Okla.) on October 6, 1957, ended the Dallas sleeper. The Baltimore–Fort Worth sleepers began their final runs on July 16, 1962.

The B&O and Missouri Pacific began Slumbercoach service between Baltimore and San Antonio in September 1959, the only interline Slumbercoach service in the country. This also turned out to be the last interline service at St. Louis, operating on the *National Limited* and MoPac's *Texas Eagle*. The cars left for the last time from Baltimore on May 15, 1964, and from San Antonio on May 17.

The westbound schedule of the *National Limited* was trimmed in September 1949 from 25 hours, 14 minutes to 24 hours. The eastbound *National Limited* was 25 minutes slower because it handled more mail and express. A typical consist was a railway post office, baggage-dorm-buffet-lounge, three coaches, a diner, five sleepers, and a sunroom lounge-sleeper.

The B&O purchased three lightweight observation sleepers from the New York Central in the early 1950s. Named for rivers, including the Wabash, the cars were assigned to the *National Limited* on March 13, 1954.

The *Metropolitan Special* was steam powered until 1950, and some of its assigned cars did not wear the B&O's blue and gray livery. The coaches lacked reclining seats, and the diner did not operate west of Cincinnati. The St. Louis Cardinals and Cincinnati Reds baseball teams often rode the *Metropolitan Special*. The Reds were regular patrons until 1959. Gradually, the B&O spiffed up the *Metropolitan Special*, assigning a lunch-counter coach and reclining seat coaches in July 1949. Typically, the *Metropolitan Special* received equipment that was available because the marquee trains had received new equipment.

No. 30 from St. Louis to Cumberland, Md., carried no passengers from Cincinnati to Parkersburg, W.Va. Operating overnight from St. Louis to Cincinnati, No. 30's fortunes fell as its mail and express business declined. It ended on October 27, 1957. Nos. 61/62 were steam-powered locals that departed Washington, Ind., at 8 A.M. and arrived in Cincinnati at 2:30 P.M. The 40 intermediate stops included 34 in Indiana, most of them flag stops. The return train left Cincinnati at 5:30 P.M. and arrived in Washington 39 stations later at 9:35 P.M. Nos. 61/62 made their last trips on January 8, 1950.

No Diplomatic Immunity

The *Diplomat* of the late 1940s had three coaches, a diner, and two heavyweight sleepers. By the early 1950s, this had dwindled to two coaches except on weekends. Lacking enough business to support two trains with schedules a few hours apart, B&O management considered combining the *Diplomat* and *National Limited*.

Following the 1957 holidays, the B&O removed the stewardess-nurse from the *Diplomat*. By now the train's head-end business had declined, and promotional fares introduced in the early 1960s failed to stimulate patronage. The *Diplomat* ended between Baltimore and Cincinnati on September 18, 1960, saving the B&O $1.2 million. The train continued between St. Louis and Cincinnati with its stately name, diner-lounge, baggage-lounge, and a coach until its demise on April 30, 1961.

The *Metropolitan Special* soldiered on largely unchanged in the 1950s, needing 24 hours, 30 minutes to rumble between St. Louis and Washington. A typical consist included a St. Louis–Washington coach, a St. Louis–Cincinnati lunch-counter coach and sleeper, and a St. Louis–Jersey City sleeper.

The *Metropolitan Special* acquired additional head-end cars and en route switching duties as other trains ended. After consolidating with Mail and Express No. 29 west of Cincinnati in 1957, the *Metropolitan Special*'s head-end business swelled to 10 cars. Truncated to St. Louis–Baltimore on April 28, 1958, the *Metropolitan Special* was assigned its first lightweight car, a sleeper. But the heavy volume of mail and express made it difficult for the *Metropolitan Special* to meet its schedule.

Removal of the lunch-counter coaches on May 20, 1962, ended food service west of Cincinnati. That fall the train began terminating at Washington. With the *Metropolitan Special* no longer special, the B&O removed the train's name on April 26, 1964, and added a timetable notice that Nos. 11/12 were "primarily mail and express trains." Nos. 11/12 were renamed the *Metropolitan* in October. The St. Louis–Cincinnati sleepers ended on April 25, 1965.

Despite its Spartan passenger accommodations, the *Metropolitan* was profitable. In March 1967, it earned a $80,000 profit. For the first quarter of 1967, the *Metropolitan* netted $200,000. When the Post Office Department began in earnest to remove mail from passenger trains in October 1967, it was a stab in the heart of the *Metropolitan*. Mail had accounted for 55 percent of the B&O's passenger revenue. Removal of most storage mail and all but two railway post offices that month cost the B&O $1.9 million in mail revenue.

The *Metropolitan*'s St. Louis–Cincinnati RPO ran for the last time on April 5, 1968. The *Metropolitan* went from handling 10 to 12 head-end cars to a baggage car and one storage mail car. In less than a year, the *Metropolitan* had lost more than $1.5 million in mail and express revenue.

In August 1968, the B&O told the Interstate Commerce Commission that it would discontinue the *Metropolitan* between Cincinnati and St. Louis on September 12. The *Metropolitan* was the last passenger train to follow an all-B&O routing between St. Louis and Washington. In its final months, the *Metropolitan* typically operated with one St. Louis–Washington coach, often a Chesapeake & Ohio lightweight car.

The *National Limited* began terminating at Baltimore on April 28, 1958, when the B&O ended passenger service to Jersey City. It received Slumbercoaches on May 29, 1959. A detour of five-months' duration in West Virginia in 1963 while a tunnel was being enlarged lengthened the running time by 3 hours, and patronage fell. The *National Limited* was barely covering its direct costs, so the drop in business plunged the train into the red. Revenue fell $150,000 below operating costs in 1964.

The *National Limited* of the early 1960s was a mix of lightweight and modernized heavyweight equipment. The *River* series observation cars, removed in July 1962, were replaced in December by leased Missouri Pacific bedroom buffet-lounge cars. Most of the marketing tactics used on the Chicago line, including the showing of on-board movies, were applied to the *National Limited*, whose name was shortened to the *National* in October 1964. The *River* series observation cars were restored on April 26, 1964.

A typical consist for the *National* was a mail storage car, RPO (St. Louis–Cincinnati), baggage-dorm-buffet-lounge, three coaches, diner, Slumbercoach, sleeper, and *River* series observation-lounge. Additional coaches were assigned on Fridays and during the summer. The *River* series observation-lounges were removed again on June 29, 1965.

Although business between Washington and St. Louis and Cincinnati was fair, there was little intermediate traffic between Washington and Cincinnati. The *National* was not responding to the B&O's marketing efforts, and management had concluded by 1965 that the train had little hope of covering its direct costs.

Let George Do It

Believing most of the *National*'s patronage could be preserved, the St. Louis–Baltimore cars were shifted to the C&O's *George Washington* between Washington and Cincinnati on September 7, 1965. Although 40 minutes slower than the *National*, the *George Washington* served a higher population base and covered its direct costs. The *National* was re-

After discontinuing the *National Limited* west of Cincinnati on September 7, 1965, the Baltimore & Ohio created a St. Louis–Cincinnati section of the *George Washington*, the Chesapeake & Ohio's Cincinnati–Washington, D.C., standard-bearer. The train, a mixture of B&O and C&O equipment, saunters by JO Tower in Seymour in 1969. Photo by John Fuller.

named the *George Washington* between St. Louis and Cincinnati and became an all-lightweight streamlined train, a mixture of B&O and C&O cars whose liveries did not match. The St. Louis–Baltimore cars began terminating at Washington on October 31, 1965. A typical *George Washington* consist between St. Louis and Cincinnati in the mid-1960s was two coaches, a diner, a Slumbercoach, and a 10 roomette, six double bedroom sleeper.

By now, though, the B&O's connecting business at St. Louis had nearly vanished. Five trains connected with the *National Limited* in 1963: the Rock Island–Burlington Route *Zephyr Rocket* (from Minneapolis), Missouri Pacific's *Missourian* (from Kansas City) and *Texas Eagle* (from Laredo, Texas), the Frisco's *Meteor* (from Oklahoma City), and a Wabash local from Council Bluffs, Iowa. By 1970, only the *Texas Eagle* remained.

A diner-lounge replaced the diner in early 1966, enabling the B&O to eliminate a dining car steward and a waiter-in-charge. The Slumbercoach stopped running west of Cincinnati on April 24, 1966. The diner-lounge was replaced by a baggage–coffee shop–lounge in early 1967.

The St. Louis section of the *George Washington* lost all head-end business except two storage mail cars in October 1967. The sleeper stopped operating west of Cincinnati on May 21, 1968. The consist had shrunk to an E8A locomotive, baggage-lounge, and two coaches. The coffee shop–lounge was curtailed to Cincinnati–Vincennes in November 1969 and ended in September 1970 in favor of an attendant selling sandwiches and snacks. The St. Louis *George Washington* section began its final runs on April 30, 1971.

Louisville Branch

The Ohio & Mississippi constructed a branch between North Vernon in Jennings County on the St. Louis line and Jeffersonville in 1869. Through the early 1870s, the O&M typically operated a daily mixed train on the branch and used the Louisville & Jeffersonville Bridge (Big Four Bridge) to reach Louisville. By the 1880s, the Louisville branch was hosting 10 passenger trains a day, of which two were mixed trains. Two pairings carried St. Louis cars. Seven trains carried Cincinnati cars.

The O&M constructed an 8-mile line in 1887 between Watson and New Albany to reach the Kentucky & Indiana Bridge, of which the O&M was a part owner. This gave the O&M two routes into Louisville, both of which hosted passenger trains.

By the early 1890s the B&O Southwestern operated three Louisville–Cincinnati and two Louisville–St. Louis round trips. In the mid-1890s, through service began between Cincinnati and New Orleans, the cars interchanging with the Illinois Central at Louisville Central Station. Two of the five North Vernon–Louisville round trips operated via Jeffersonville. The B&O Southwestern, IC, and Southern Pacific launched a weekly Cincinnati–San Francisco sleeper in 1899. The car interchanged with the SP at New Orleans and departed Cincinnati on Tuesday, San Francisco on Monday.

In the early 20th century, the branch hosted 16 daily passenger trains including four trains of the Big Four (later New York Central), which had trackage rights between North Vernon and Louisville. B&O service was five North Vernon–Louisville round trips and a Louisville to North Vernon mixed train. New Albany–Jeffersonville shuttle service began in 1903 with four trains to Jeffersonville and five trains to New Albany.

North Vernon–Louisville service increased to six round trips in 1909, four of them serving Cincinnati. North Vernon–Louisville service fell to five round trips in 1914 and the Jeffersonville shuttle had diminished to two trains to Jeffersonville and one to New Albany. By 1917, just one pair of trains served Jeffersonville. Service to Jeffersonville ended on January 27, 1918. That same day, North Vernon–Louisville service fell to four round trips, three of them Cincinnati trains. Previously, five trains had operated to Louisville and six to North Vernon, one of the latter having ended in 1917.

World War I travel restrictions eliminated the Cincinnati–New Orleans sleepers, but they resumed in June 1921. North Vernon–Louisville service was four round trips through the early 1920s, all of them Cincinnati trains. Service increased to five round trips, four of them Cincinnati trains, on December 23, 1922. During the 1930s, North Vernon–Louisville service usually was four trains to Louisville and five trains to North Vernon.

The Cincinnati–New Orleans sleeper ended in July 1933, but returned in April 1938. The New Orleans sleeper began originating in Jersey City in May 1939, conveyed by the *Diplomat*. In September this sleeper was curtailed to Cincinnati–New Orleans and a Louisville–New York sleeper began.

North Vernon–Louisville service evened out at five round trips in 1941, two of them Cincinnati pairings. During the mid-1940s, all three St. Louis–Cincinnati expresses had Louisville cars. The *Metropolitan* handled Louisville–St. Louis sleepers, the *National Limited* carried Louisville–New York sleepers, and the *Diplomat* conveyed Cincinnati coaches.

The Cincinnati trains carried parlor-diners or diners and Louisville–Detroit sleepers and coaches. The Cincinnati–New Orleans sleepers interchanged with the Illinois Central's *Irvin S. Cobb*. Steam power, usually a 4-6-2, handled Louisville trains until 1956 when GP9 diesel locomotives with steam generators arrived.

Louisville branch service increased to six round trips in 1945, three of them Cincinnati trains. Trains made the trip over the 58-mile single-track, unsignaled line in just over an hour. Service fell back to five round trips on April 27, 1947. That same day the Cincinnati–New Orleans sleeper began terminating at Memphis and a Cincinnati–Memphis coach began, alternately an IC or B&O heavyweight.

The Cincinnati–Memphis cars ended in January 1952. The St. Louis–Louisville sleepers ended in September 1954. Pittsburgh–Cincinnati Nos. 233/238 (via Wheeling) were consolidated with Cincinnati–Louisville Nos. 63/64, enabling the B&O to eliminate one equipment set. Few passengers connected at North Vernon with the *Metropolitan* and its connecting trains were discontinued on May 24, 1955. The discontinuance by the Illinois Central of the *Irvin S. Cobb* on January 30, 1957, ended connections in Louisville to the South.

The Louisville–Pittsburgh trains were discontinued east of Cincinnati on July 22, 1956. Louisville branch service fell to three round trips with the October 28, 1956, removal of the connecting trains serving the westbound *National Limited* and eastbound *Diplomat.* Nos. 63/64 lost their food service cars in October 1957 and were rescheduled to connect in Cincinnati with the *Cincinnatian* (Detroit–Cincinnati). The February 1958 discontinuance of Nos. 63/64 left the Louisville branch with two round trips, Nos. 57/58 (Louisville–Cincinnati), which carried the Louisville–Detroit cars, and a North Vernon–Louisville shuttle that connected with the westbound *Diplomat* and eastbound *National Limited.*

When the North Vernon–Louisville shuttle trains ended on October 26, 1958, Nos. 57/58 began handling the Baltimore–Louisville sleepers and a snack lounge car that offered breakfast and light dinners. The trains were named the *Night Express* on October 25, 1959. The Louisville–Baltimore sleepers ended in October 1960. Nos. 57/58 operated to Louisville for the final time on January 3, 1961.

Indianapolis Line

The 321-mile route between Hamilton, Ohio, and Springfield, Ill., began with the organization of the Cincinnati & Indianapolis Junction, which reached Connersville in Fayette County in 1862 but stalled until after the Civil War. In 1868 the company operated two Cincinnati–New Castle round trips and one round trip between Connersville and Morristown in Shelby County.

Completed to Indianapolis in 1869, passenger service was three Indianapolis–Cincinnati round trips and an Indianapolis–Connersville accommodation train. The Cincinnati, Hamilton & Indianapolis acquired the C&IJ in December 1872. The New Castle–Connersville line later became part of the Lake Erie & Western (later Nickel Plate).

Development west of Indianapolis began with the July 1869 formation of the Indianapolis, Decatur & Springfield, which opened on August 10, 1873, between Decatur, Ill., and Montezuma in Parke County. Passenger service was four trains a day, two of them mixed trains. Operations remained unchanged over the next five years.

The line opened to Bruin in Parke County on September 1, 1878, to Russellville in northeast Putnam County on November 9, 1879, and to Indianapolis in 1880. In the mid-1880s, the Indiana, Bloomington & Western (later Peoria & Eastern) leased the ID&S. Service was three Indianapolis–Decatur round trips, and a commuter train between Indianapolis and Moorfield on the west side of Indianapolis.

Subsequently, the line became the Indianapolis, Decatur & Western (December 1887) and the Indiana, Decatur & Western (May 1894). In 1902, it merged with the Cincinnati, Hamilton & Indianapolis to form the Cincinnati, Indianapolis & Western, which was leased by the Cincinnati, Hamilton & Dayton. The CH&D had operated the CH&I since 1886.

The CH&D was part of the short-lived Great Central Route, which collapsed in 1905. The Indianapolis line was sold on July 9, 1915, and reorganized as the Cincinnati, Indianapolis & Western, which began operating on December 1, 1915. The B&O purchased 96 percent of the capital stock of the CI&W in 1926 and absorbed it a year later.

In the mid-1880s, the Cincinnati, Hamilton & Dayton and the Monon launched Chicago–Cincinnati service via Indianapolis, although some cars interchanged at Roachdale in northern Putnam County. In the late 1880s, the Indianapolis, Decatur & Western operated through cars between Indianapolis and Keokuk, Iowa, interchanging with the Decatur & Springfield Railway at Decatur and the Wabash at Springfield. By 1890 these cars had begun originating at Cincinnati. Cincinnati–St. Louis service began in the early 1890s with parlor cars and sleepers interchanged with the Vandalia (later Pennsylvania) at Indianapolis. This service ended in 1897.

The Cincinnati–Keokuk cars were curtailed to Jacksonville, Ill., in 1894, but extended to Hannibal, Mo., in 1897 as the *Cincinnati–Hannibal Special,* scheduled to connect with

Wabash Kansas City trains. Also in 1897 the CH&D became part of a Chicago–Baltimore sleeper service involving the Monon (Chicago–Indianapolis) and the B&O (Cincinnati–Baltimore). Named the *Chicago–Baltimore Special*, this service lasted about two years. The Hannibal cars began terminating at Quincy, Ill., in May 1900. This service ended in June 1901. For the 1904 Louisiana Purchase Exposition in St. Louis, the CH&D and Wabash operated Cincinnati–St. Louis through cars via Decatur. The trains stopped at the Wabash fairground station and operated from June through November.

For much of the 1880s, the Indianapolis line hosted three Indianapolis–Cincinnati round trips, which had increased to five round trips by 1890. This remained until late in the decade when service increased to six round trips, many of them carrying Chicago through cars. West of Indianapolis, service during the 1890s was typically two Indianapolis–Decatur round trips, a round trip between Indianapolis and Tuscola, Ill., and a round trip between Tuscola and Moorfield (Indianapolis). By 1896 the latter trains had begun operating between Indianapolis and Roachdale.

In January 1900, the Cincinnati, Hamilton & Dayton operated six Cincinnati–Indianapolis round trips. Sleepers and coaches operated between Cincinnati and Springfield, Ill., via the ID&W and Wabash. The ID&W scheduled two Indianapolis–Decatur round trips and one Indianapolis–Tuscola round trip. The ID&W began operating its own passenger trains to Springfield on August 13, 1902.

After the ID&W and CH&D consolidated operations on November 2, 1902, ID&W trains began terminating at Cincinnati rather than Indianapolis. One Indianapolis–Decatur round trip ended, leaving three pairs of trains operating west of Indianapolis. East of Indianapolis, there remained six Indianapolis–Cincinnati round trips, two of which terminated at Indianapolis.

Service west of Indianapolis expanded to four round trips in 1903: Cincinnati–Springfield (two round trips), Cincinnati–Roachdale, and Cincinnati–Tuscola. During the heyday of the Great Central Route, the CH&D had seven Cincinnati–Indianapolis round trips, of which two terminated at Springfield, one at Decatur, and one at Roachdale. The demise of the Great Central Route led to the discontinuance of the Cincinnati–Roachdale trains and one Cincinnati–Springfield round trip. Cincinnati–Indianapolis service fell to four round trips, although it increased to six round trips in 1910.

A Cincinnati–Indianapolis round trip was curtailed to Cincinnati–Connersville on July 7, 1912. The Cincinnati–Springfield trains were discontinued on April 11, 1915, and the Cincinnati–Decatur trains began terminating at Indianapolis. The Cincinnati–Connersville trains ended, and a Sunday-only Cincinnati–Decatur train began. After the Indianapolis line was severed from the CH&D in December 1915, service became an Indianapolis–Decatur round trip and an Indianapolis–Springfield round trip. Cincinnati–Indianapolis service was five round trips.

Indianapolis–Cincinnati service declined during World War I, falling to four round trips on July 29, 1917, and three round trips on July 10, 1918. Chicago–Cincinnati service was suspended the next month. An Indianapolis–Hamilton, Ohio, round trip began December 10, 1918, but ended on April 20, 1919. West of Indianapolis, service remained at four trains, but the endpoints varied, with trains terminating at Decatur, Springfield, and Hume, Ill.

Cincinnati–Indianapolis service expanded to four round trips on December 28, 1919, and the Indianapolis–Hume trains began operating to Decatur. Earlier, the CI&W had added an Indianapolis–Hamilton train that connected at Hamilton with a Cincinnati–Toledo, Ohio, train. The addition of two Indianapolis–Decatur round trips increased service west of Indianapolis to eight trains.

Service west of Indianapolis reverted to four trains on November 28, 1920, Indianapolis–Decatur and Indianapolis–Springfield. The Indianapolis–Hamilton trains were discontinued on July 24, 1921. The CI&W in early 1922 assigned a diner to the Indianapolis–Springfield train. A Decatur–Montezuma round trip was added on November 2, 1921, but removed on

January 15, 1922. Later that year the Indianapolis–Springfield dining car was replaced by a parlor car, which was gone by spring 1923. Indianapolis–Cincinnati service fell to three round trips on March 11, 1923, and the Indianapolis–Decatur trains ended, leaving just one round trip (Indianapolis–Springfield) west of Indianapolis.

The CI&W revived Indianapolis–Decatur service on April 29, 1923, with two round trips. Both were discontinued on November 1, 1923, only to be reinstated on a Sunday-only schedule on May 1, 1924. The service resumed daily operation on September 28, 1924, when the CI&W began Cincinnati–Kansas City through cars via an interchange with the Chicago & Alton (later Gulf, Mobile & Ohio) at Springfield. Within a year, the CI&W again had upgraded the Springfield trains, which operated on a daytime schedule, with café-parlor cars. Indianapolis–Decatur service fell to one round trip on November 1, 1924, and the Cincinnati–Kansas City cars ended in September 1926.

After taking over the Indianapolis line, the B&O revamped service. The Indianapolis–Springfield trains were extended to Cincinnati on December 1, 1927, and assigned café-parlor cars and a sleeper that operated between Springfield and Washington, D.C. The Indianapolis–Decatur trains began operating between Indianapolis and Tuscola. These trains had operated with a motor car since September 30, 1928.

The westbound Springfield sleeper was conveyed by the *National Limited*. By early 1930, the eastbound Springfield sleeper operated to Jersey City, conveyed by the *St. Louis–Washington–New York Express*. A parlor-diner had replaced the café-parlor, and an observation-parlor-diner operated between Indianapolis and Cincinnati. Later that year the eastbound Springfield sleeper began terminating at Washington and switched to the *National Limited*.

One of the three Cincinnati–Indianapolis round trips ended on January 19, 1930. The Indianapolis–Decatur motor car train ended in July 1931. The Cincinnati–Springfield trains were curtailed to Indianapolis on September 30, 1934, and the Springfield–Washington sleeper began originating at Indianapolis. The Indianapolis–Springfield trains were rescheduled on September 29, 1935, to provide better connections with B&O trains at Indianapolis. This lasted until September 26, 1937, when the Springfield train began departing Indianapolis in late morning. That same month, the Indianapolis–Washington sleepers ended.

Parlor and dining service ended in April 1938 as did the Chicago–Cincinnati through car arrangement with the Monon. Citing high operating losses, the B&O pared Cincinnati–Indianapolis service to one round trip on June 4. This train changed to Indianapolis–Hamilton operation on September 24, 1939, and was assigned a motor car, at the time the only non-steam train at Indianapolis Union Station.

The B&O discontinued passenger service west of Decatur in July 1940. The Decatur and Hamilton trains arrived at Indianapolis in late morning and departed 10 minutes apart in late afternoon. This schedule remained largely unchanged through 1949. By the end of World War II, both trains had motor cars. A December 2, 1945, restructuring provided better connections from Indianapolis at Cincinnati with the *Diplomat* and *National Limited*.

The B&O removed the motor car from the Decatur train in December 1949 and discontinued the train west of Dana in Vermillion County in February 1950. The Indianapolis–Dana train continued until April 30, 1950. The Indianapolis–Hamilton trains, which operated until December 1950, were the last Indiana motor car trains.

Bedford Branch

The Cincinnati & Bedford, a subsidiary of the Ohio & Mississippi, built an 11-mile branch in Lawrence County between Rivervale on the Cincinnati–St. Louis line and Bedford. The first 6 miles opened in 1890. The line was extended 1.42 miles to Mitchell Hollow in May 1891 and completed to Bedford in September 1893.

Built to serve limestone quarries, a typical train had a baggage-coach, a merchandise car, and at least five cars carrying blocks of stone pulled by locomotive No. 86, a 4-4-0 built by Brooks. Scheduled passenger service never exceeded two round trips per day. The trains usually operated in shuttle fashion, starting at Rivervale in the morning. Few connections were available at Rivervale because most mainline trains did not stop there. The first Bedford station was north of 16th Street. In 1897 the line was extended to near 13th Street between I and J Streets in downtown Bedford. Miners' trains of the Bedford Belt Railroad also used this station.

Scheduled service fell to one round trip on January 27, 1918. Traffic was light and in 1922 the branch carried 176 passengers. When there were no passengers, the crews sometimes stopped and went hunting. In the final years, light Consolidateds pulled the trains with a Ten-Wheeler and a 2-6-0 locomotive making brief appearances. The ICC gave permission on December 3, 1923, to abandon the line. The last train left Bedford on January 31, 1924.

Chesapeake & Ohio

CHAPTER 4

CHESAPEAKE & OHIO/ PERE MARQUETTE

Thanks to a sleepy kitten named Chessie, the Chesapeake & Ohio was known as a passenger railroad even though it had only three long-distance passenger trains. Coal was the C&O's raison d'être with passenger revenue insignificant by comparison. Introduced in 1933 to sell Pullman berths, Chessie invited travelers to "sleep like a kitten" en route to their destination. Chessie's phenomenal success made her the most famous railroad symbol in America, and for decades she graced C&O timetables, calendars, and advertisements.

The C&O had a minor passenger presence in Indiana. Service on its Chicago–Cincinnati route ended in 1949. C&O forerunner Pere Marquette served just one Indiana station, Michigan City, after 1926 on its Chicago–Grand Rapids, Mich., route.

Chicago–Cincinnati

The Chicago–Cincinnati route dates to the March 23, 1900, formation of the Cincinnati, Richmond & Muncie by W. A. Bradford Jr. and H. A. Christy. Construction began

For most of its passenger service history, the C&O of Indiana hosted slow, all-stops locals. Hammond to Cincinnati No. 18 takes on passengers at Peru on April 1, 1940. Bob's Photo.

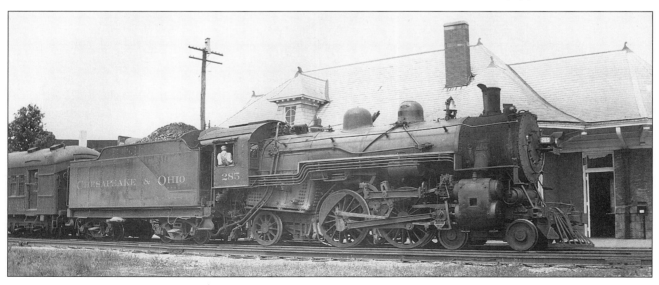

59

June 4, 1900, at Cottage Grove in Union County. Passenger service began February 28, 1901, with a round trip between Cottage Grove and Richmond. By year's end the road had three pairs of trains: two between Cottage Grove and Peru, and one between Cottage Grove and Marion. After opening to North Judson on May 18, 1902, two pairs of trains operated between there and Cottage Grove. Another pair operated Peru–Cottage Grove.

Two subsidiaries, the Chicago & Cincinnati, and the Cincinnati & Western Indiana, were formed to complete the railroad to Chicago and Cincinnati, respectively. A merger of these companies created the Chicago, Cincinnati & Louisville on June 1, 1903.

Service expanded to 10 trains on April 16, 1903, with trains originating and terminating at Cottage Grove, North Judson, Peru, Richmond, and Beatrice in Porter County. By early 1904, passenger operations had shrunk to three pairs operating Peru–Cottage Grove, Cottage Grove–North Judson, and triweekly service between North Judson and Beatrice. Passenger service began to Cincinnati on February 7, 1904, but the CC&L failed to obtain approval to use the Chicago Terminal Transfer Railroad (later Baltimore & Ohio). Cincinnati trains terminated at Peru. Another pair operated between Peru and Griffith in Lake County.

The Panic of 1903 weakened the CC&L, and in July 1904 it agreed to be controlled by the Cincinnati, Hamilton & Dayton (later B&O), which also controlled the Pere Marquette. The three companies made up the Great Central Route, a name displayed on passenger car letter boards. During the Great Central Route era, most CC&L passenger trains operated on the CH&D between Cottage Grove and Cincinnati through Hamilton, Ohio. A Cincinnati–Peru local used the CC&L route through Cheviot, Ohio. The Great Central Route collapsed in 1905 after the Pere Marquette and the CH&D went bankrupt. After the two companies renounced their obligations to the CC&L, a court awarded Bradford control of the railroad.

The CC&L constructed a track parallel to the Erie between Griffith and Hammond in 1906. A year later, the CC&L extended this route to Riverdale, Ill., to connect with the Illinois Central. During this period, the CC&L operated two pairs of passenger trains, Cincinnati–Griffith and Cincinnati–Peru. Passenger service between Chicago and Cincinnati began on April 7, 1907, with three round trips that used Chicago Central Station. The CC&L also operated a Richmond–Peru local. Sleepers operated between Chicago and Peru and Muncie.

After the Central Passenger Association refused to grant it membership, the CC&L retaliated by establishing a Chicago–Cincinnati fare of $5, undercutting other carriers by a dollar. In conjunction with the Union Traction Company, the CC&L offered a Chicago–Indianapolis round-trip fare of $2.50 via a connection at Peru. Calling itself "The Straight Line," the CC&L claimed to have the shortest Chicago–Cincinnati route. But the CC&L had the slowest route due to rolling terrain, tight curves, and steep grades south of Richmond, particularly on the climb out of Cincinnati through the Mill Creek Valley.

Just when the CC&L's future began to look auspicious, the Panic of 1907 triggered a dramatic drop in revenue. The CC&L defaulted on its mortgage bonds and entered receivership. One Chicago–Cincinnati round trip was discontinued on November 14, 1909. The CC&L offered buffet service on its remaining Chicago–Cincinnati trains and new Pullmans entered service between Chicago and Muncie. The third Chicago–Cincinnati round trip was reinstated on April 17, 1910.

As part of an effort to expand into the Midwest, the Chesapeake & Ohio purchased the CC&L on June 23, 1910, at a foreclosure sale in Richmond. The C&O thought the Midwest was a potentially better market for coal than the East. To avoid antitrust concerns, the C&O created a separate entity, the Chesapeake & Ohio of Indiana.

Passenger operations began changing with the December 1, 1910, move to Chicago's Dearborn Station. But Chicago–Cincinnati service fell to two round trips and the Richmond–Peru locals ended. Sleepers operated between Chicago and Richmond, and buffet parlors were assigned to day trains. Trains used Cincinnati's Fourth Street station.

The C&O extended the *Old Dominion Express* to Chicago on July 9, 1911, increasing Chicago–Cincinnati service to three round trips. Sleepers and coaches operated between Chicago and Old Point Comfort, Va., the site of a resort hotel and Fort Monroe in Virginia's Tidewater. The *Old Dominion Express* crossed Indiana during daylight hours, and a diner operated Huntington, W.Va., to Peru and Peru to Maysville, Ky.

Until now, the C&O and Big Four (later New York Central) offered through service between Chicago and Old Point Comfort via Indianapolis. In May 1889, C&O president Melville E. Ingalls, a former Big Four president, had suggested starting the Chicago–Old Point Comfort service in hopes of giving C&O passenger service a new image. C&O tweaked the service on January 7, 1912, by assigning parlor diners between Chicago and Old Point Comfort. Diner operation was changed to Chicago to Maysville and Russell, Ky., to Chicago on June 2, 1912.

Chicago–Cincinnati Nos. 3/8 received sleepers on November 24, 1912. At the same time, C&O renamed the Old Point Comfort trains the *Old Dominion Limited* and discontinued the third Chicago–Cincinnati round trip in favor of locals operating Chicago–Peru and Peru–Cincinnati. The locals subsequently became a Chicago–Cincinnati train on April 6, 1913.

Later in 1913, C&O shifted two of the Chicago–Cincinnati trains, including the *Old Dominion Limited*, to Cincinnati's Grand Union Station. One Chicago–Cincinnati pair still used Fourth Street station. Sleepers were removed from Nos. 3/8.

On April 12, 1914, the C&O began operating the Chicago–Washington, D.C., *C&O Limited* via the C&O of Indiana in place of the *Old Dominion Limited*. Although the *C&O Limited* carried the Old Point Comfort sleepers and coaches to Chicago, no sleepers operated between Chicago and Washington. Diners serving a la carte meals operated between Chicago and Cincinnati. This arrangement lasted just over a month. The *Old Dominion Limited* resumed operation to Chicago on May 24 with Old Point Comfort coaches and sleepers. The *C&O Limited* continued to operate through Indiana with coaches to Washington and sleepers to Old Point Comfort.

On January 3, 1915, the *Old Dominion Limited* to Chicago was again replaced by the *C&O Limited*, which continued to carry Chicago–Washington coaches and Chicago–Old Point Comfort sleepers. One Chicago–Cincinnati train was curtailed to La Crosse–Cincinnati, although it was extended to Griffith on December 10, 1916.

Operation of long-distance trains over the C&O of Indiana proved to be unsatisfactory, perhaps due to the route's lack of population density. On July 1, 1917, the C&O moved its Chicago–Tidewater and Chicago–Washington cars back to the Big Four through Indianapolis.

The *Old Dominion Express, Old Dominion Limited, and C&O Limited* were the only C&O express trains to use the C&O of Indiana. After July 1, 1917, service was two pairs of Chicago–Cincinnati trains. Nos. 7/8 operated on a daylight schedule and used Cincinnati's Fourth Street terminal. The overnight trains carried Chicago–Muncie sleepers and used Grand Union station.

The level of service remained unchanged through the mid-1920s. All trains began using Fourth Street station on January 1, 1924, and originating and terminating in Covington, Ky., across the Ohio River from Cincinnati. This continued until November 1, 1925, when the trains resumed terminating in Cincinnati. C&O of Indiana passenger trains returned to Chicago's Central Station on March 1, 1925. Nos. 7/8 began originating and terminating at Hammond on August 5, 1928.

Concerned about declining branch line patronage, the C&O purchased six Brill gas-electric motor cars in 1929 to replace costly steam power on local passenger trains, including the Hammond–Cincinnati trains in June 1929. The motor cars seated 16 in walkover seats upholstered in brown leather. Each car had a baggage and mail compartment and was powerful enough to pull a trailer coach. The Hammond–Cincinnati run was the longest motor train route in Indiana.

The motor cars did not reverse the declining fortunes of passenger service on the C&O of Indiana. Nos. 7/8 were truncated to Peru–Cincinnati on May 24, 1931, and discontinued on April 24, 1932. The overnight Chicago–Cincinnati trains were trimmed to Hammond–Cincinnati on June 11, 1933, rescheduled for day operation and the sleepers removed.

Usually, Nos. 19/20 departed Hammond and Cincinnati at about 9 A.M., arriving in Hammond just before 4 P.M. and in Cincinnati before 6 P.M. All stations except Griffith, North Judson, Peru, Marion, Muncie, Richmond, and Cheviot, Ohio, were flag stops. The South Shore, the Erie, and the Monon honored C&O tickets for travel between Chicago and Hammond. Atlantic-type 4-4-2 steam locomotives usually pulled Nos. 19/20, although in the final years the motive power was a Pacific-type locomotive. The usual consist was a combination baggage-coach and a coach.

Although the C&O in 1948 earned a record $355 million in operating revenue, freight earnings plunged in 1949 due to labor unrest in the coal fields. C&O president Walter J. Tuohy told employees the railroad was reviewing local passenger operations "with a view to eliminations." At a May 1949 workshop in Newport News, C&O management repeatedly emphasized the need to prune branch line passenger service.

Given this sense of urgency, it is not surprising that the Hammond–Cincinnati trains wound up on the chopping block. C&O said the trains lost $44,000 in the first five months of 1949. The railroad said Nos. 19/20 earned 41 cents per mile during that period, but cost $1.85 per mile to operate. They were discontinued on October 25, 1949. Their operation had changed little since 1933. The final schedule showed 22 intermediate stops compared with 39 stops in 1944.

Pere Marquette

The Pere Marquette was created by the January 1, 1900, merger of the Chicago & West Michigan, the Flint & Pere Marquette, and the Detroit, Grand Rapids & Western. All three roads had been built to serve Michigan's lumber industry and were no strangers to foreclosure and receivership. Named for a Jesuit priest who explored the Great Lakes region in the 1600s, most of the 1,700-mile Pere Marquette system was in Michigan.

A 1900 merger of the Chicago & West Michigan and two other Michigan railroads created the Pere Marquette. C&WM No. 22, a 4-4-0, is shown at Holland, Mich., in 1880, 2 years before the road opened to La Crosse, Ind. Photo courtesy Chesapeake & Ohio Historical Society Collection.

The Chicago & West Michigan Railroad completed a line between New Buffalo, Mich., and La Crosse, Ind., in November 1882. Passenger service began November 12 with two round trips between La Crosse and Grand Rapids.

As part of an effort to create a Chicago–Buffalo, N.Y., route, the Pere Marquette in 1903 formed a subsidiary, the Pere Marquette Railroad Company of Indiana, to build from New Buffalo to Hammond. Construction halted at Porter, Ind., in December 1903, and the railroad negotiated trackage rights between Porter and Pine (Gary) on the Lake Shore and Michigan Southern (later New York Central) and between Pine and Chicago's Grand Central Station on the Chicago Transfer Railroad (later B&O).

Passengers traveling between Chicago and Detroit could connect at Grand Rapids, but the circuitous route made the travel times longer than those of the Michigan Central or Grand Trunk Western. The Chicago–Grand Rapids route had four stations in Indiana, but service ceased at three of them in the 1920s. Service ended at Whiting in June 1925, at Porter on September 16, 1926, and at Indiana Harbor on June 28, 1929.

Oris P. and Mantis J. Van Sweringen, the Cleveland bachelor brothers who owned the C&O, began acquiring the Pere Marquette in 1924, which they saw as a potential market for C&O coal. Although the C&O purchased a controlling interest in the Pere Marquette in 1929, it operated as an independent company until June 6, 1947. For several years, the C&O treated the Pere Marquette as an autonomous district.

The Chicago & West Michigan began passenger service to Chicago on October 2, 1887, with three Chicago–Grand Rapids round trips via an interchange with the Michigan Central at Michigan City or New Buffalo, Mich. Service was four round trips by the late 1890s. The Michigan Central arrangement continued until the Pere Marquette began operating on its own to Chicago on December 15, 1903. Of the four round trips that the Pere Marquette initially offered, one originated at Grand Rapids, another at Traverse City, Mich., and two at Petoskey, Mich.

With congestion on the Chicago Terminal Transfer Railroad often delaying its passenger trains, the Pere Marquette negotiated agreements in June 1904 with the Pennsylvania and Chicago & Alton railroads for 12 miles of trackage rights between Clark Junction in Gary and 16th Street in Chicago. Pere Marquette continued to use the Chicago Terminal Transfer to reach Chicago Grand Central Station. The agreement also enabled Pere Marquette to increase Chicago–Grand Rapids service to five round trips.

Due to fierce competition and costly trackage rights fees, one round trip had been pared less than a year later, although it was restored in summer 1909. But after the *Resort Special* went into winter hibernation on September 25, 1910, Chicago–Grand Rapids operations again fell to four round trips. Chicago–Grand Rapids service fell to three round trips in June 1917. The level of service fluctuated between three and five round trips over the next two years before reverting to five again on June 22, 1919.

The Rebuilding Years

The Pere Marquette twice went into receivership in the early 20th century. When it emerged from the second receivership in April 1917, it finally had a management interested in rebuilding it. Pere Marquette ordered its first steel coaches, 12 cars from Standard Steel Car Co., in 1921. Two years later, it purchased two steel dining and parlor cars from Pullman.

Chicago–Grand Rapids trains received names in February 1920. Nos. 1/8 became the *Night Express*, Nos. 4/5 the *Furniture City Special*, No. 2 the *South Shore Express*, No. 3 the *Michigan Express*, No. 7 the *Grand Rapids Limited*, and No. 8 the *Chicago Limited*. Later, No. 16 became the *Chicago Local* and No. 17 the *Grand Rapids Local*. The latter trains were short-lived. Their discontinuance on November 27, 1921, reduced Grand Rapids service to four round trips.

Chicago–Grand Rapids service expanded on June 11, 1923, to six pairs of trains including the seasonal *Resort Special*. During the 1920s, Chicago–Grand Rapids service fluctu-

Still sporting Pere Marquette colors and styling, Chesapeake & Ohio No. 3 is ready to depart Grand Rapids, Mich., for Chicago in 1949. Photo courtesy Chesapeake & Ohio Historical Society Collection.

ated between four and five round trips. Resumption of the *Resort Special* in the summer usually increased service to six round trips.

Nos. 17/18 began operating on a seasonal basis in 1924, typically discontinued in the fall and restored in the summer. However, in 1927, Nos. 17/18 operated until January 22, 1928. The summer of 1929 was the last time the Pere Marquette offered six Chicago–Grand Rapids round trips. Service fell to four round trips on November 24, 1929.

The *Resort Special* resumed operation on June 22, 1930, but Nos. 17/18 did not. Grand Rapids Service fell to three round trips on May 22, 1932, with the discontinuance of the *Business Man's Special/East Coast Flyer*. Service increased to four round trips that summer when the *Resort Special* resumed service. This pattern continued throughout the 1930s.

The Pere Marquette placed into service in 1930 eight Imperial Salon coaches built by Pullman. The cars had 2-1 seating in the nonsmoking section and eight double seats in the smoking section. Every seat was opposite a window. These comfortable coaches helped boost ridership. Train names on the Chicago–Grand Rapids route came off all trains except the *Night Express* and *Resort Special*.

During the World War II years, the Pere Marquette had three scheduled Chicago–Grand Rapids round trips. The *Night Express* handled sleepers and coaches between Chicago and Grand Rapids, Traverse City, Muskegon, and Petoskey. Nos. 3, 5, 6, and 8 featured coaches, Pullman parlor cars, and diners. The Muskegon and Petoskey sleepers ended on July 16, 1945, and the Petoskey coaches shifted from the *Night Express* to Nos. 5/6. Parlor cars also began operating between Chicago and Petoskey. The Muskegon sleepers were restored on December 15, 1946.

As part of a plan to modernize its passenger fleet, the Pere Marquette ordered 14 lightweight passenger cars from Pullman in 1944. This equipment was delivered in June 1946.

In 1946 and 1947, the Pere Marquette took delivery of eight E7A diesel locomotives from the Electro-Motive Division (EMD) of General Motors. Painted enchantment blue and Venetian yellow, the new equipment began service on August 10, 1946, between Grand Rapids and Detroit under the name *Pere Marquette*. Billed as the nation's first postwar streamliners, each seven-car train had a railway post office baggage car, two coaches, a diner, and two squared-end coach-observation cars.

Second to None

The C&O was optimistic that the World War II rail travel boom would continue. Its board of directors adopted a resolution in 1944 vowing to offer "the safest and the most modern equipment that can be acquired . . . to the end that this company's passenger service should be second to none." The driving force behind the postwar bid to modernize and expand passenger service was C&O's gadfly chairman, Robert R. Young. He had reason to be optimistic. C&O passenger patronage in 1944 had been eight times higher than that of 1939. Young believed fast schedules and convenient service would enable railroads to maintain business built during the war.

Paramount to Young's plans was new lightweight streamlined equipment. In its 1946 annual report, C&O described its order of more than 300 passenger cars from Pullman Standard as "the largest single order for passenger-carrying equipment ever awarded to a single builder."

The C&O also initiated numerous innovative practices as part of its aggressive marketing campaign. The railroad put passenger service representatives aboard trains in 1947 to help patrons sort out travel problems. Booklets titled "Now If I Ran the Railroad" asked passengers to comment about ticketing practices, dining car service, on-board entertainment, train speed, seat reservations, and car lighting. A "pay-on-the-train" plan enabled passengers to make reservations and pay for tickets on the train. C&O also instituted on-board hostesses, a no-tipping policy in dining cars, and a central reservations bureau.

One result of the passenger polls was a schedule change on the Chicago–Grand Rapids route. On November 22, 1948, C&O increased the layover time in Chicago between the arrival of the morning train from Grand Rapids and the departure of the afternoon return train from 2.5 hours to 6.5 hours. The running time was cut to 3 hours, 55 minutes. The following month, ridership rose 30.8 percent.

The *Night Express* name disappeared from Nos. 2/7 in July 1947. But the train continued to offer sleepers between Chicago and Grand Rapids, Petoskey, and Muskegon and was the only Pere Marquette train stopping at Michigan City. Even then it was a flag stop. The seasonal *Resort Special* had been suspended during the war, but its 1946 return increased Chicago–Grand Rapids service to four round trips.

The same falling financial fortunes that caused the end of passenger service on the C&O of Indiana affected Pere Marquette District trains. Year-round service between Chicago and Petoskey and Muskegon ended on September 25, 1949. Two months later, on November 20, Chicago–Grand Rapids service shrank to two round trips. The day trains also began stopping at Michigan City, which was dropped from the schedule of the overnight trains. Nonetheless, Pere Marquette District passenger traffic held up reasonably well following World War II, showing that railroads could succeed in offering downtown-to-downtown passenger service over medium distances.

Robert Young's dream of making the C&O the nation's preeminent passenger carrier had its critics, who questioned the prudence of emphasizing passenger service at a railroad that was predominantly a coal carrier. Skeptics said the $78 million that the C&O spent between 1947 and 1948 to improve passenger service was out of line for a carrier that served few metropolitan areas. Passenger, mail, and baggage revenues were the C&O's smallest source of gross income. It was becoming clear to C&O management that despite their best efforts, passenger service was declining and the railroad had ordered more equipment than it needed. Most of the Pullman-Standard equipment order was cancelled or sold.

The sorry saga of the ill-fated streamliner called the *Chessie* illustrated the C&O's passenger predicament. Planned as a Washington–Cincinnati day train, the *Chessie* was to feature new equipment with every design innovation and amenity available. C&O ordered 46 cars from the Budd Company, enough to equip two 11-car train sets and two 4-car connecting trains.

But the *Chessie* never turned a wheel. Declining passenger revenues in 1947 doomed the luxurious streamliner. Much of the equipment intended for the *Chessie* went to the Pere Marquette District in 1948, enabling the C&O to inaugurate streamliner service between Chicago and Grand Rapids on November 21, 1948. The *Chessie* equipment was assigned to the day trains, and the Pere Marquette name was placed on the flanks of the cars. Equipment assignments for the overnight trains remained largely unchanged.

The *Chessie* cars assigned to the Pere Marquette District included a twin-unit diner, tavern lounge, and dome-observation cars. The latter operated on the Muskegon–Holland connecting trains until reassigned to Chicago–Grand Rapids service in spring 1949. This equipment operated on the Pere Marquette District until late 1949. The dome-observation cars were sold to the Denver & Rio Grande Western, and the twin-unit diner was sold to the Atlantic Coast Line.

Equipment from an ill-fated luxury streamliner, the *Chessie*, briefly operated on Pere Marquette District passenger trains between Chicago and Grand Rapids in 1948, the first streamlined equipment assigned to the route. The train is near St. Joseph, Mich. C&O Railway Photo, courtesy Chesapeake & Ohio Historical Society Collection.

The C&O took delivery of new coaches from Pullman-Standard in 1950 and sold the 1946 *Pere Marquettes* streamlined coaches to the Chicago & Eastern Illinois. The overnight Chicago–Grand Rapids trains received new Pullman 10 roomette, six double bedroom sleepers in 1950. C&O equipment was adorned in eye-catching enchantment blue and federal yellow, a livery inspired by the *Pere Marquettes*.

After the C&O had sold much of the equipment that it received from its 1940s order, heavyweight sleepers were reassigned to the overnight Grand Rapids trains. During the 1950s Chicago–Grand Rapids service remained at two round trips plus the seasonal *Resort Special*. The day trains had coaches, parlor cars, and a tavern diner.

Young left the C&O in 1954 to head the New York Central. His efforts to advance C&O passenger service had been on the cutting edge of passenger equipment technology and service, but the C&O lacked the traffic to support it.

The C&O continued to seek ways to woo passengers and cut costs, particularly dining car costs. On February 5, 1952, C&O introduced aboard Chicago–Grand Rapids trains precooked, flash-frozen meals on disposable aluminum plates that were heated in an electric oven. Dinners featured meat, fish, or poultry entrées with potatoes and vegetables. Completing the "Chessie-Tray" was a salad made on board, fresh rolls and butter, and chilled fruit or ice cream for dessert. Breakfast meals included Canadian bacon, glazed apples, hot sweet rolls, and sausage links. Ham and eggs were prepared on board. Two chefs, two servers, and a steward staffed the diner. Preprinted checks listed meal choices. C&O hoped the experiment would cut dining costs in half, which in turn would lower the cost of meals.

Early in 1958 on the Chicago–Grand Rapids route, the C&O introduced the Chessie American Plan Package. Passengers who traveled on Tuesday and Wednesday were given two free meals. The plan led to a 5 percent ridership increase, but failed to significantly lower dining car losses.

The C&O sold round-trip tickets for 150 percent of the one-way fare and offered a 20 percent discount on dining car meals to passengers purchasing a dining coupon. In 1961, C&O began offering sleeping car space between Chicago and Grand Rapids for the price of a coach ticket. That same year, C&O cut fares and introduced the "Chessie Discount Meal Plan."

The Chesapeake & Ohio pioneered the use of the Roadrailer, a truck trailer with rubber tires and steel wheels that was attached to the rear of a passenger train, shown here at Plymouth, Mich. The C&O began Roadrailer service in late 1959 to haul mail and express between Chicago and Grand Rapids, Mich. Bob's Photo.

C&O launched Roadrailer service between Chicago and Grand Rapids in late 1959. A Roadrailer was a truck trailer with rubber tires and steel wheels that could operate on rails. Attached to the rear of a passenger train, it carried mail and express. A more cosmetic change occurred in May 1965 when the *Pere Marquette* name was applied to all Chicago–Grand Rapids trains.

Letting Go of Its Heritage

By the Interstate Commerce Commission's fully allocated cost formula, the C&O lost $7.5 million on passenger service in 1964. But the C&O also had operating income of $51 million that year and continued to pay, on average, $4 a share in dividends. C&O president Walter J. Tuohy dismissed the passenger losses as insignificant, no more than a dime a share. But Fred W. Frailey, author of *Twilight of the Great Trains*, contends that Tuohy underestimated by a factor of eight the drain of passenger losses on the C&O's profitability. Passenger service was a source of pride at the C&O, and Tuohy did not have the heart to end it. Nor was his successor, Gregory DeVine, any more enthusiastic about discontinuing passenger trains.

The C&O had acquired control of the Baltimore & Ohio in 1963. Each railroad's passenger operations remained independent until early 1965, when C&O passenger service was brought under the supervision of Paul Reistrup, the B&O's director of passenger services. Reistrup recommended in March 1966 that C&O/B&O phase out passenger service, but DeVine was afraid of political upheavals and community and shipper ill will if he followed Reistrup's recommendation.

C&O launched its Red Circle Days campaign in early 1965. On Monday, Tuesday, and Wednesday, fares were cut by a third in coaches and sleepers. A year later, C&O and B&O began an advertising campaign built on the slogan: "Forget Highway Tensions and Take the Train." Another marketing campaign began in 1967, this one built on the slogan "Chessie Loves Passengers (and Needs a Lot More of Them)." But more importantly, C&O/B&O management decided it was time for an orderly retreat from the passenger business. The Chicago–Grand Rapids sleepers were reduced to triweekly operation in spring 1962 and discontinued in October 1967. Dining cars were removed in 1967 from the day trains in favor of a tavern lounge.

C&O sought ICC approval to discontinue the overnight Chicago–Grand Rapids trains on December 2, 1968. C&O cited the loss of mail and express business and said the trains averaged less than two revenue passengers for each crew member. The ICC quickly acquiesced, citing a lack of protests and the availability of other transportation alternatives including rail.

Although C&O now viewed passenger service as a proven money-loser, it refrained from operating trains with dirty or malfunctioning equipment as some railroads had done in an effort to discourage what little patronage remained. But patronage on the *Pere Marquettes* was not enough on some days to fill one luxury coach. By late 1970, the *Pere Marquettes* usually operated with an E8A unit and a solitary coach. The tavern lounge came off the Chicago–Grand Rapids *Pere Marquettes* in October 1970. The train had lost its railway post office contract in 1969.

The *Pere Marquettes* shifted to Chicago North Western Terminal on November 9, 1969, following the closure of Grand Central Station. The eastbound *Pere Marquette* was the last train to depart from Grand Central, which had opened on December 8, 1890.

In the final months, the *Pere Marquette* departed Grand Rapids at 8:25 A.M. and arrived in Chicago at 12:05 P.M. The return train departed at 2:25 P.M. and arrived in Grand Rapids just after 8 P.M. The running time was 4 hours, 40 minutes. The *Pere Marquettes* made their final runs on April 30, 1971. The last C&O train to Grand Rapids had three cars pulled by B&O EA No. 1435.

Resort Service

Resorts and summer cottages dotted northern Michigan with its abundant lakes, bays, and forests. As logging began to play out, the vacation travel market took on greater importance and became a profitable source of passengers. The Pere Marquette, which once used the slogan "To the Heart of Holidayland," faced formidable competition from the Grand Rapids & Indiana (later Pennsylvania) and its seasonal *Northern Limited* (later the *Northern Arrow*). For nearly 60 summers, the Pere Marquette and C&O offered seasonal service between Chicago and the resort region. Pere Marquette's best-known train was the *Resort Special*, which once carried sleepers from St. Louis, Detroit, Toledo, and Cincinnati. Summer service began June 21, 1903, when the Pere Marquette began conveying sleepers from Chicago and St. Louis to Harbor Springs and Bay View, Mich. On June 27, 1910, the Pere Marquette inaugurated the *Resort Special* between Chicago and Bay View on an overnight schedule. A diner operating Traverse City–Bay View served breakfast northbound and dinner southbound. Sleepers operated between Bay View and Chicago, St. Louis, and Cincinnati. Sleepers also operated triweekly between Chicago and Frankfort, Mich. The *Resort Special* ended its first year on September 24, 1910. The following year, daily operation ended on September 23, but weekend operation continued until October 1. The train also carried a short-lived Chicago–Ludington, Mich., sleeper.

During the 1920s, the *Resort Special* continued to offer sleepers between Bay View and Chicago, St. Louis, and Cincinnati, between Chicago and Frankfort, and between Chicago and Traverse City. Service began in mid-June and ended in mid-September. Sleepers between Chicago and Traverse City and Petoskey operated year-round on the *Night Express*.

The St. Louis–Bay View sleepers did not operate in 1930, resumed the following year, and operated for the final time in 1937. The *Resort Special* was suspended between 1943 and 1945, but resumed Chicago–Bay View service on June 23, 1946. However, it no longer stopped at Michigan City.

The *Resort Special* began terminating in Petoskey in 1947. It would operate daily for two more summers, going on a triweekly schedule in 1950. The next year it began operating weekly, leaving Chicago on Friday and returning on Sunday night. This operating pattern continued through 1957, the last year that the *Resort Special* operated. In 1958, the overnight Chicago–Grand Rapids trains and Grand Rapids–Petoskey Nos. 25/26 began conveying the seasonal Chicago–Petoskey sleepers.

Travel to Michigan's resort region is about to end for the season as No. 25 makes its way through Walhalla, Mich., on September 1, 1958. The Grand Rapids to Petoskey, Mich., train carried a sleeper from Chicago. Photo courtesy Chesapeake & Ohio Historical Society Collection.

The summer sleeper taking vacationers "up north" began operating in 1960 between Chicago and Traverse City on a triweekly schedule. When the Traverse City sleeper made its final trip on September 7, 1964, more than a half-century of service between Chicago and Michigan's resort region had ended.

New Buffalo–La Crosse

In the early years, passenger trains on the La Crosse branch operated to Grand Rapids. On August 8, 1886, a mixed train began operating from Holland, Mich., to La Crosse, but there was no return train. Nearly a year later, on July 3, 1887, one Grand Rapids–La Crosse pair was discontinued and the Holland mixed train began operating from New Buffalo to La Crosse.

Service peaked in October 1887 at two round trips between La Crosse and New Buffalo, a Grand Rapids express train, and a Holland mixed train. Less than three years later, service had shrunk to two La Crosse–New Buffalo round trips. For the duration of passenger service on the branch, service seldom extended beyond New Buffalo and did not exceed two round trips a day. Service dipped to one round trip on November 23, 1902, when a New Buffalo–La Crosse round trip was discontinued.

For a brief time in 1903, the train to La Crosse originated in Traverse City and the return train terminated in Grand Rapids. The second La Crosse–New Buffalo round trip was restored on May 14, 1905, but discontinued for good on April 28, 1907.

The opening of the Chicago line in December 1903 had little effect on La Crosse service. Although the train to New Buffalo connected with a Chicago to Petoskey train, the New Buffalo to La Crosse train lacked convenient connections. New Buffalo–La Crosse service remained relatively unchanged until June 21, 1925, when the trains were downgraded to mixed trains. This service continued for four more years before ending on March 17, 1929.

CHAPTER 5

NEW YORK CENTRAL

In the Golden Age of the passenger train, America's most important passenger route was Chicago–New York. A traveler who could afford a Pullman had a choice of 10 routes and seven railroads at Chicago. But for those of means there was but one choice: the *Twentieth Century Limited*. Writing in the *Christian Science Monitor* on November 1, 1928, Franklin Snow observed, "There are trains and trains but no train has ever reached such adulation as does the *Twentieth Century Limited* from all New York Central men. To them it symbolizes their railroad."

The Pennsylvania Railroad, the other major player in the Chicago–New York market, had the *Broadway Limited*, which matched the *Century* in speed and sumptuous service. But for nearly five decades the *Century* stood alone. "The prestige of the *Twentieth Century Limited* was simply impervious to competition," wrote historian Lucius Beebe.

Aside from the *Century* and a few other marquee trains, the Central's passenger service was good but indistinct. Historian Geoffrey Doughty noted the Central lacked exotic feature cars and had few parlor cars. Lounges and diners were elegant but less distinguished than those of other railroads. The Central had such a vast passenger fleet that it usually ordered equipment off the shelf and swapped cars among its trains. But the Central had its own touches, such as the cup of hot clam broth served with breakfast on the *New England States*.

The New York Central used the slogan "The Water Level Route — You Can Sleep" because its Chicago–New York mainline skirted the Great Lakes, paralleled the Erie Canal in upstate New York, and hugged the Hudson River between New York City and Albany. New York Central maps showed the Pennsylvania as a jagged line through its namesake state, a subtle intimation that the Central's flatter route offered a smoother ride. Yet the Pennsylvania had the more direct route and assured its patrons, "You Can Sleep *Restfully*."

The New York Central led Indiana railroads in mileage with 1,629 miles (22 percent of the state's total). The former Big Four, whose focal point was Indianapolis, constituted 68 percent of the Central's Indiana mileage.

Chicago Line

The state of Michigan's 1837 internal improvements program spawned the Michigan Southern, whose first train operated between Monroe and Adrian, Mich., on November

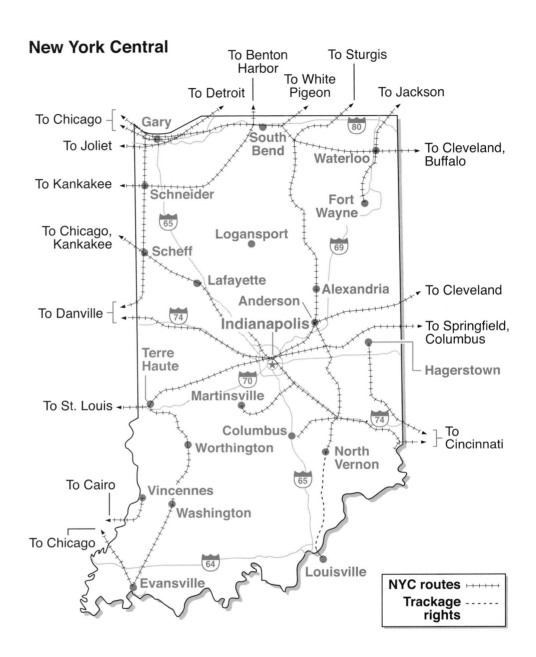

New York Central

To Chicago

Gary

To Joliet

To Kankakee

Schneider

To Chicago, Kankakee

Scheff

To Danville

Lafayette

Terre Haute

To St. Louis

Martinsville

To Cairo

To Chicago

Vincennes

Washington

Evansville

To Detroit

To Benton Harbor

To White Pigeon

To Sturgis

To Jackson

South Bend

Waterloo

To Cleveland, Buffalo

Fort Wayne

Logansport

Alexandria

To Cleveland

Anderson

Indianapolis

To Springfield, Columbus

Hagerstown

Columbus

Worthington

North Vernon

To Cincinnati

Louisville

NYC routes
Trackage rights

72

23, 1840. Created with the expectation that its western terminus would be New Buffalo, Mich., the Michigan Southern instead aimed for Chicago. Judge Thomas S. Stanfield built a line to connect South Bend with the Michigan Southern at White Pigeon, Mich. The first train reached South Bend on October 4, 1851.

A year earlier, the Michigan Southern had acquired the Northern Indiana Railroad, which was building from LaPorte to Elkhart. The MS (which merged with the Northern Indiana in 1855) reached Chicago on February 20, 1852, using a temporary station at 22d and Clark. Service between Toledo and Chicago began in May. Within weeks, the MS and its rival, the Michigan Central, were bringing 400 passengers a day to Chicago.

Several Ohio railroads formed a Toledo–Buffalo route in the mid-1850s, although travelers changed trains several times. Legrand Lockwood and Henry Keep gained control of the MS&NI and consolidated it with the Ohio lines in 1869 (most of which had merged in 1868 to form the Lake Shore Railway) to create the Lake Shore & Michigan Southern.

Cornelius "Commodore" Vanderbilt owned a New York shipping company and was nearly 70 when he began buying stock in the New York & Harlem and the Hudson River railroads. Vanderbilt purchased a few shares of the New York Central in 1863. The Central was an 1853 consolidation of 10 railroads operating between Albany and Buffalo, the earliest of which (Mohawk & Hudson) opened August 9, 1831. The roads began through service December 17, 1849. Vanderbilt became president of the New York Central in 1867 and two years later merged it with the Hudson River Railroad. He had little interest in expanding to Chicago, but at the urging of his son William, he began acquiring LS&MS stock.

An ill-fated attempt by Jay Gould and Jim Fisk to corner the gold market ruined Lockwood's brokerage firm. When the corner collapsed on September 24, 1869, Lockwood

The Lake Shore & Michigan Southern hosted the New York Central's fleet of fast Chicago–New York passenger trains. The location of this early-20th-century photo is unknown. Jay Williams collection.

needed cash and sold the LS&MS to Vanderbilt for $10 million, creating the nation's first trunk railroad. The Central absorbed the LS&MS on January 1, 1915.

Chicago–Toledo trains operated via Adrian, Mich., until the building of the Air Line Division in 1858 between Elkhart and Toledo, which was 9 miles shorter than the "Old Road" through Michigan. The Air Line featured 68.49 miles of tangent track between Butler in DeKalb County and Toledo. Following the Civil War, the LS&MS operated four Chicago–Toledo round trips, one via the Old Road. Another round trip operated between Elkhart and Toledo on the Air Line. Many trains operated to Cleveland or Buffalo. By the early 1870s, the Chicago line had nine trains a day, four via the Old Road.

The Chicago line hosted 14 trains by 1873. Ten operated Chicago–Cleveland, two Chicago–Buffalo, and two Chicago–Elkhart. By the mid-1870s, the LS&MS had two routes between Toledo and Cleveland: the original Lake Shore via Bellevue and Norwalk, and a route via Sandusky. The Sandusky route later became the primary route, but in the 1870s passenger traffic was split evenly between the two. Chicago line service had fallen to 8 trains by the late 1870s, but during the 1880s service was usually about 11 trains a day. By 1890, service had increased to 17 trains, including 4 accommodation trains between Elkhart and Goshen.

A New Train for a New Century

George Daniels was a former patent medicine salesman who became New York Central's general passenger agent in 1889. A born promoter, Daniels created red cap service in 1896, elaborate marketing booklets, and an on-board newsletter titled *Four-Track News*. But his greatest achievement was fast, luxurious trains.

The first of these, the New York–Buffalo *Empire State Express*, began in October 1891, partly to divert New York State local traffic from the *Chicago Limited*. The Central then launched the Chicago–New York *Exposition Flyer*, operating on a 20-hour schedule during the 1893 World's Columbian Exposition in Chicago. The *Flyer* ended after the fair closed, but its success had awakened the Central to the possibility of a year-round market for such a train. Besides, there was competition from the Pennsylvania's opulent *Pennsylvania Limited*. The Central rebuilt its track with the nation's first 6-inch steel rail, reduced grades, eliminated curves, and laid heavier ballast.

The June 1897 *Traveler's Official Railway Guide* announced the debut of the *Lake Shore Limited*, an extra-fare luxury train operating on a 24-hour Chicago–New York schedule and 26 hours between Chicago and Boston. Elkhart was the only Indiana stop. The *Lake Shore Limited*, which began on the LS&MS on May 30, 1897, featured sleepers, compartment cars, a buffet smoker, and a diner (all with vestibules) built by the Wagner Palace Car Company, the car supplier of the Central and LS&MS.

Daniels's masterpiece was the creation of the *Twentieth Century Limited*, a train that he wanted to run "like a bat out of hell." Historian Arthur Dubin described the name as a stroke of genius, capturing "the mood of passing from one century to another" and embodying "the growth of American mechanical superiority." Daniels suggested naming the train the *Twentieth Century*. It gained the *Limited* appendage five days after its June 15, 1902, debut. Central officials said this was done to compete with the *Pennsylvania Limited*, but some claimed it was the *Twentieth Century Limited* from the beginning.

The Pennsylvania's *Broadway Limited* (begun the same day as the *Century*, although initially called the *Pennsylvania Special*) was every inch a peer of the *Century*. The luxury trains of other railroads offered touches that the *Century* lacked. But none captured America's imagination quite like the *Century*. Beebe contends the *Century* gained its edge because of its association with the Vanderbilts, whose name was synonymous with "success, grandeur, and wealthy aloofness." The high-society clientele that patronized the *Century* made its reputation. "The personality of *The Century* for more than 50 years was constant; only its details were variable," Beebe wrote.

Throughout the 1890s, the LS&MS hosted 13 to 15 through trains, more than half of which used the Air Line. A gaggle of locals operated between Chicago and Toledo, terminating at Elkhart, Kendallville, or Waterloo, and at Wauseon, Ohio. On the eve of the 20th century, the LS&MS had 13 through trains, including 11 between Chicago and Buffalo. Six through trains used the Old Road, which also hosted four locals between Elkhart and White Pigeon, Mich. Locals operated Chicago–Elkhart, Elkhart–Kendallville, and Toledo–Kendallville.

The LS&MS had 21 through trains by 1905, 6 via the Old Road. Three locals used the Old Road between Toledo and Elkhart. Four locals operated between Toledo and Kendallville. Locals also operated between Chicago and Elkhart. Another local ran from Toledo to Elkhart via the Air Line. The Chicago–Elkhart locals briefly terminated at Chesterton in Porter County in 1907–1908.

The LS&MS had 24 through trains by 1910, 7 via the Old Road. Within two years, this had risen to 28 trains, 9 via the Old Road. Typically two through trains operated between Toledo and Cleveland via Norwalk. The New York Central carried 62 million passengers in 1914. During World War I, scheduled service fell to 21 trains, including 17 between Chicago and Buffalo. Four trains operated between Chicago and Cleveland, but by 1919 three of them were terminating at Toledo. Three locals operated between Chicago and Elkhart. Other locals operated Toledo–Elkhart and Kendallville–Elkhart.

Growth of a Legend

The *Twentieth Century Limited* made its maiden westbound run in 1902 with just 27 passengers aboard. Early consists included three sleepers, a buffet-library-smoking car (one named *Indiana*), and a diner. On-board services included a barbershop, valet, maid, and stenographer. A table d'hôte dinner cost one dollar. The equipment was a mixture of older Pullman and refurbished Wagner cars, all painted Pullman green.

Pullman delivered the first sleepers built for the *Century* in 1903. When the Central placed its order, it told Pullman it wanted equipment finer than what the Pennsylvania offered. All-steel cars began replacing wooden cars in 1910, and by 1912, when the train had been completely reequipped, the average consist had grown to seven cars. To promote its use of steel cars, the Central began calling its trains the Great Steel Fleet.

On June 21, 1905, four days after its running time was trimmed from 20 to 18 hours, the westbound *Century* derailed at 60 mph at Mentor, Ohio, killing 14 passengers and 5 crewmen. The accident raised concerns that the *Century* was too fast. The schedule varied between 18 and 19.5 hours until 1912 when the *Century* and the *Broadway Limited* were placed on 20-hour schedules.

The *Century* reached the pinnacle of its popularity in the 1920s. Shortly after World War I, the *Century* acquired a running mate, the *Advance Century*, which departed Chicago an hour earlier at 11:40 A.M. By 1926 the *Century* had a dedicated fleet of 122 cars and routinely operated in two or three sections, with six or seven sections for political conventions, football games, and other special events. The Central sought to keep all sections identical in makeup (usually 12 to 14 cars) and service.

No detail was too insignificant. Sleepers never turned at New York or Chicago, so that rooms faced the Hudson River between New York and Albany. Diners were positioned so that the kitchen was at the rear to keep the train's forward motion from causing odors to waft through the dining room. Management was obsessed with keeping the *Century* on time even if that meant running a snowplow train ahead of it during a heavy snowfall. Standby locomotives stood ready along the route in case of an engine failure. The daily on-time performance report was placed atop all other papers on the desk of New York Central president A. H. Smith.

The *Century* grossed $10 million in 1926. But more valuable than the fare box was the prestige of having the nation's acknowledged champion passenger train. The Pennsylvania's Penn Station was closer to Wall Street than the New York Central's Grand Central Terminal, but the *Century* was the train of choice for financial papers. Mailrooms stocked red, white, and blue tags stamped "via Twentieth Century." Some people made their final journey aboard the *Century*. The corpse was charged the regular tariff but was not assessed the extra fare that living passengers paid. The *Century* set a record for most passengers carried in a single day on January 7, 1929, when seven sections departed Chicago with 822 passengers, most of them bound for an automobile show in New York.

But for most Hoosiers the *Twentieth Century Limited* was merely a blur whose elegant service lived only in their imagination. The *Century's* only Indiana stop was Elkhart.

Chicago line service increased from 26 trains in 1920 to 30 by 1930. The *Century*, *Lake Shore Limited*, and eastbound *Fifth Avenue Special* were all-Pullman. Five trains typically operated via the Old Road, and one through train, the westbound *Western Express*, ran via Norwalk, Ohio. The *Chicago–Cleveland Special* (which operated between its namesake cities) had become all-Pullman by 1921. Its counterpart, the *Cleveland–Chicago Special*, did not become all-Pullman until the late 1920s. Both became the *Forest City* in 1928. Another all-Pullman train of the late 1920s was the westbound *Fast Mail*.

In late April 1929, the Central launched a new 21-hour New York–Chicago train, the *Iroquois*, and sped up the *Fast Mail*. The Chicago–Boston travel time was cut to 23.5 hours. Through cars operated between Chicago and Pittsburgh on the eastbound *Maumee* and westbound *Mohawk*. The cars reached Pittsburgh via New York Central subsidiary Pittsburgh & Lake Erie.

The Central launched a new 20-hour Chicago–New York train, the *Commodore Vanderbilt*, on September 29, 1929. All-Pullman and extra fare, the *Commodore Vanderbilt* featured club cars, diner, and observation sleepers, and was second in prestige only to the *Century*. The Central also began publishing the schedule of the *Advance Century* in the *Official Guide of the Railways*.

Cutbacks Begin

As the 1930s began, the New York Central scheduled 22 trains between Chicago and Buffalo, 4 between Chicago and Cleveland, and 5 between Chicago and Toledo. The all-Pullman trains were *Twentieth Century Limited*, *Advance Century*, *Commodore Vanderbilt*, *Lake Shore Limited*, the *Forest City*, the *Fast Mail*, *Fifth Avenue Special* (eastbound), and the *South Shore Express* (westbound). Five trains operated via the Old Road. A local operated from Chicago to Elkhart, and three locals operated between Elkhart and Toledo via the Air Line.

Within two years Chicago line service had fallen from 35 to 29 trains and diminished to 26 trains by 1934. Gone were the *Advance Century*, the *Western Express* (the last through train via Norwalk, Ohio), and the *Westerner* (the last westbound through train on the Old Road, which hosted a pair of Chicago–Toledo round trips).

The *Twentieth Century Limited* was air-conditioned in 1934, but operated with fewer extra sections because the Depression had dampened demand. Since 1927 the *Century* had been pulled by powerful Hudson locomotives, which enabled the *Century* to operate with longer consists. The Hudsons also enabled the *Century* to operate on an 18-hour schedule beginning in 1932.

The New York Central barely remained solvent during the Depression, and its passenger fleet began fraying around the edges. More than two-thirds of the cars and more than half of the locomotives were over 20 years old. On March 9, 1937, the New York Central and Pennsylvania announced plans to revamp their respective flagship trains, the *Twentieth Century Limited* and the *Broadway Limited*.

The Central had earlier retained industrial designer Henry Dreyfuss to design its first streamlined train, the Cleveland–Detroit *Mercury*. Dreyfuss gave the exterior of the *Century* two tones of gray with blue and silver stripes. Interior colors were rust, blue, tan, and gray in various tones and combinations. Dreyfuss redesigned everything about the *Century* including glassware, stationery, magazine binders, dishes, matchbook covers, and crew uniforms.

A handsome Hudson J3-a steam locomotive has the *Twentieth Century Limited* highstepping through Waterloo, Ind., en route to Chicago in April 1939. The *Century* is also showing off the new streamlined equipment it received in June 1938. Jay Williams collection.

The Central ordered 62 new cars from Pullman, 50 for the *Century* and 12 for the *Commodore Vanderbilt* and *Southwestern Limited* (a St. Louis–New York train). A standard *Century* consist was mail-baggage, lounge-baggage, eight sleepers, lounge, twin-unit diner, and observation car. By agreement the Pennsylvania and New York Central debuted their reequipped flagships on June 15, 1938, the 36th anniversary of each train. Both claimed to offer the first all-room train in America, as neither the *Century* nor *Broadway Limited* carried Pullman berths.

Dreyfuss streamlined 10 new Hudson locomotives that made it possible to cut the *Century*'s running time to a record 16 hours, or as the Central boasted in advertisements, "960 miles in 960 minutes." Unlike the *Broadway Limited*, which had refurbished heavyweight diners, all of the passenger cars on the *Century* were new. Other trains also were speeded up. The *Commodore Vanderbilt* went the distance in 17 hours.

The same day the *Century* was reequipped, the New York Central launched the Chicago–Boston *New England States*. For some 30 years the *Century* had had a Boston section that was virtually identical to the New York section. Inauguration of the *New England States* ended the practice of carrying Boston cars on the *Century*. The *New England States* was all-Pullman, but charged no extra fare and had heavyweight sleepers.

The New York Central and Pennsylvania launched all-coach Chicago–New York trains on July 28, 1939. The Central's *Pacemaker* and the Pennsy's *Trail Blazer* had similar consists, although the *Trail Blazer* featured an enclosed observation car whereas the *Pacemaker* had an open platform observation car. The *Pacemaker* was a success, but trailed the *Trail Blazer* in earnings and patronage.

For those who could not afford the *Century* or the *Commodore Vanderbilt*, there was the *Water Level Limited*. Begun in 1936, the *Water Level Limited* departed Chicago a half-hour after the *Century* and offered sleepers, coaches, and a diner. Although slower than the *Century*, the *Water Level Limited* was no slouch, stopping between Chicago and Toledo only at Englewood (in Chicago), South Bend, and Elkhart.

Postwar Optimism

Chicago line service increased from 27 trains in 1938 to 29 trains in 1940. The Central ordered additional lightweight cars from Pullman-Standard. New sleepers assigned to the

Century on October 25, 1940, bumped some of the 1938 *Century* order to the *Commodore Vanderbilt* and other trains.

World War II travel demands strained the capacity of the New York Central. The Central was unable to maintain its equipment as well as it did during peacetime. At the height of the war, the Chicago line handled 37 scheduled trains and numerous unpublished extras and troop trains. The *Commodore Vanderbilt* operated in two sections, the other named *Advance Commodore Vanderbilt*. An hour was added to the schedule of the *Century* and *Commodore Vanderbilt*. The *Century* no longer accepted passengers at Elkhart.

No railroad was more optimistic about passenger service following the war than the New York Central, which ordered 721 new cars in 1944–45, split among Pullman-Standard (354 cars), Budd (239 cars), and American Car and Foundry (128 cars). Equipment purchased between 1938 and 1940 was refurbished. The Central accepted its first passenger diesels, E7A units from the Electro-Motive Division of General Motors, in 1945. The *Century* received diesels in 1946.

The *Century*'s barbershop and secretaries had been suspended during the war, but were restored in February 1946. Also revived was the tradition begun in the 1920s of rolling out a red carpet for boarding at Grand Central Terminal. The carpet was 260 feet long and 6 feet wide and had the art deco *Century* logo woven into its Harvard red fabric.

The *Century*'s 16-hour running time was restored in April 1946 and shaved to 15.5 hours eastbound on April 1, 1947. Passengers were accepted only at Englewood, Albany, and Harmon, N.Y., where electric motors replaced diesels because steam and diesel locomotives were prohibited at Grand Central Terminal.

Dreyfuss redesigned the *Century* in the late 1940s. The overall décor changed little from his 1938 rendition, but the exterior was modified to provide dark gray above and below the windows with light gray accented with white stripes on the windowband. The reequipped *Twentieth Century Limited* debuted September 17, 1948. A typical consist included six sleepers with 10 roomettes and six double bedrooms, four sleepers with 13 double bedrooms, midtrain lounge, observation-lounge, and twin-unit diner.

New York Central was part of the proliferation of transcontinental sleepers that began March 31, 1946. The Central handled sleepers between New York and Los Angeles via three routes west of Chicago: the Santa Fe (via Albuquerque, N.M.), the Golden State Route (Rock Island–Southern Pacific via Phoenix), and the Overland Route (Chicago & North Western–Union Pacific via Omaha and Salt Lake City). Cars operated between New York and San Francisco (Oakland) via the Overland Route and via the *California Zephyr* Route (Burlington–Denver & Rio Grande–Western Pacific via Denver).

Old Road service fell to two trains on December 11, 1949, one of which was the Chicago to New York *Easterner*. The last through train on the Old Road ended September 28, 1952, in favor of an Elkhart to Toledo local.

A Turbulent Ride

William White became president of the New York Central in 1952 and ordered a track-rebuilding project designed to boost passenger train speeds. White wanted to knock a half-hour off the schedule of the *Twentieth Century Limited*. Although not accepting passengers between Englewood and Harmon, the *Century*'s schedule had edged up to 16.5 hours, a half-hour slower than its nemesis, the *Broadway Limited*. The Central had assigned diesel locomotives to all east-west streamlined trains by April 1952.

The Central also undertook what it termed "the most comprehensive analysis of its passenger operations ever attempted." Claiming to have spent more than any railroad on new passenger equipment ($80 million on more than 700 cars since 1944), the Central was losing money on passenger service. The Central slashed its $3 million dining department deficit to $1 million by sidetracking some 70 of its more than 240 dining cars. All but a handful of heavyweight cars (primarily diners and sleepers) were retired. The *Pacemaker* and *Advance Commodore Vanderbilt* were consolidated in 1949. Chicago line service was 29 trains.

Robert R. Young won a proxy fight and became New York Central's chairman in 1954. Young, who had headed the Chesapeake & Ohio, believed passenger service was hamstrung by antiquated work rules, excessive government regulation, and too much reliance on traditional practices. He established a passenger research bureau to find ways to make passenger service (which lost $13.6 million in 1954) more self-supporting. The bureau concluded the Central no longer met the needs of the market, which was travel of 100–500 miles in less than 12 hours. The bureau recommended mail and express be shifted to priority freight trains.

The bureau's "Travel Tailored Schedules" were implemented October 28, 1956. Departures were spread out over the day in five- to seven-car trains. Long-distance and overnight service became secondary. The *Commodore Vanderbilt* received coaches, and four trains ended: the eastbound *Lake Shore Limited*, westbound No. 5 (formerly the *Mohawk*), Chicago to Elkhart No. 708, and the eastbound *Interstate Express*. The Cleveland to Chicago *Prairie State* became the Albany to Chicago *Westerner*.

The Central also experimented with lightweight trains with low centers of gravity: *Xplorer* (built by Pullman-Standard) and *Aerotrain* (built by General Motors). Amid much hoopla, the *Aerotrain* began service July 15, 1956, between Chicago and Cleveland. The *Xplorer* began service that month between Cleveland and Cincinnati.

The all-coach *Aerotrain* had 10 cars that were 40-passenger bus bodies that had been widened 18 inches, mounted on two-axle welded steel frames, and given an air-ride suspension. *Aerotrain* featured angled windows and overhead reading lights and luggage bins. Food service came from a food cart called "Cruisin' Susan." The locomotive was half of an E unit. Unlike other experimental trains, *Aerotrain* was not articulated.

The westbound *Lake Shore Limited* ended west of Buffalo, and the *Great Lakes Aerotrain* operated on its schedule, departing Cleveland at 6:35 A.M., arriving in Chicago at midday, and returning at 4 P.M. No eastbound trains were discontinued.

Large crowds flocked to see the *Aerotrain* and *Xplorer*, but those who rode the trains gave them less than rave reviews. The experimental trains lacked the seat width and depth and the expansive lavatory facilities of conventional coaches. Nor did the experimental trains ride smoothly.

The *Great Lakes Aerotrain* made its final runs on October 27, 1956, and was sold to the Rock Island. The "Travel Tailored Schedules" had little chance to blossom. After the Central's superintendent of operations, Charles Clark, contended the plan would interfere with freight operations, president Alfred E. Perlman canceled it in July 1956.

The Central lost $48 million on passenger service in 1956, and when Perlman saw the first-quarter figures for 1957 (the passenger deficit reached $52 million that year), he commanded something be done to rein in the deficit. That wouldn't be easy, because passenger trains recorded 50 percent of the Central's train miles and Young had resisted the suggested wholesale abandonment of service.

Nonetheless, contraction became the order of the day. Passenger trains operated for the final time on the Old Road on November 19, 1956. The New York–San Francisco through sleepers ended in October 1957. The westbound *Pacemaker* and the eastbound *Forest City* (Chicago to Cleveland) ended October 27, 1957.

Perlman ordered the consolidation of the *Century* and *Commodore Limited* on August 4, 1957. The *Century* lost its barbershop and valet. The $5 extra fare charge ended. The *Century's* high-society coterie was outraged, and protests fell like rain on the Central's Lexington Avenue headquarters in New York. The *Century* reverted to its old self on Labor Day (September 3, 1957), but was losing its luster. The aristocracy whose loyal patronage had made the *Century* the nation's best-known train had begun forsaking it for the Pennsylvania's *Broadway Limited*. Others had quit rail travel altogether.

After a despondent Robert Young took his own life on January 25, 1958, Perlman seized the opportunity. A civil engineer by training, Perlman had not shared Young's enthusiasm for passenger service. In Perlman's view, shedding passenger trains was a matter of survival, for their cost was eating the New York Central alive. In less than a decade the Central had gone from the most bullish of eastern railroads in regard to passenger service to one of the most aggressive in seeking to end it.

The last transcontinental through sleepers, an interchange between the *Century* and the Santa Fe's *Super Chief* and between the *Commodore Vanderbilt* and the Union Pacific's *City of Los Angeles*, ended in April 1958. The *Century* and *Commodore Vanderbilt* permanently merged on April 27, 1958, although the *Vanderbilt* name lingered in timetables until October 30, 1960. The *Century* resumed taking passengers at Elkhart and began boarding them at Gary and South Bend.

But out the window went such amenities as the valet, barbershop, shower, radio-telephone service, and complimentary boutonnieres and corsages. The *Century* briefly regained all-sleeper status on October 25, 1959, when it received Budd-built sleepercoaches (known as Slumbercoaches elsewhere) and the coaches were reassigned to other trains. Sleepercoaches were also assigned to the *New England States*, which had carried coaches since summer 1949 and lost its observation car in 1956.

The *Century* regained coaches on April 24, 1960. A typical *Century* consist included three sleepers, a lounge car, a tavern lounge (summer operation only), twin-unit diner, reserved seat coaches, and observation lounge sleeper.

Not-So-Great Steel Fleet

As the 1950s closed, the New York Central had 18 Chicago line trains, 10 of which conveyed Chicago–New York sleepers and coaches. Even the *New England States* carried a New York sleeper and a Chicago–Clifton Forge, Va., sleeper interchanged with the C&O at Toledo. The *Fifth Avenue Special* merged December 6, 1958, with the *Cleveland Limited* (hitherto a Cleveland to New York train) and became the *Fifth Avenue–Cleveland Limited*. The New York to Chicago *South Shore* was reduced to an unnamed Buffalo to Chicago train on April 24, 1960.

To celebrate the 60th anniversary of the *Twentieth Century Limited*, the Central brought back the traditional complimentary boutonnieres and corsages. Dining and observation cars were refurbished and redecorated. Perlman boasted that the *Century* was the most profitable passenger train in the East, taking in $12 million while costing $7.5 million to operate.

But declining patronage had nudged the *Century* and what remained of the Great Steel Fleet into their twilight years. The eastbound *Pacemaker* was consolidated with the *New England States* on April 30, 1961, dropping Chicago line service to 16 trains. Four of these were Chicago–Elkhart commuter trains. One westbound commuter train ended in 1962 and the Central planned to end the remaining trains in November 1963. The Interstate Commerce Commission interceded and ordered an investigation.

The Central claimed the eastbound trains lost $31,000 apiece in 1962. The westbound train, which lost $8,429, carried an average of 248.6 passengers a day, most of them disembarking in Chicago. The eastbound trains averaged 132.7 and 127.2 a day, nearly all of them boarding at Chicago. Patronage had diminished by about 62 passengers in each direction since 1960, a 20 percent decline. The ICC cited this deteriorating performance and the existence of other commuter rail service in deciding on March 19, 1964, to allow the discontinuance. In the meantime Toledo to Chicago No. 289 had ended in February 1963. Chicago line service was 11 trains.

The *Fifth Avenue–Cleveland Limited* no longer carried Chicago to New York sleepers by 1965 and the *Forest City* had lost its Cleveland to Chicago sleeper and train name. The New York to Chicago *Iroquois* ceased operating west of Buffalo, and the eastbound *Chicagoan* lost its Chicago to New York sleeper on October 31, 1965. A New York to Chicago sleeper and coach conveyed by the *Empire State Express* was interchanged at Buffalo to No. 222, an arrangement that was short-lived. The coach-only *Pacemaker* (the sleepers had ended in 1963) began originating at Cleveland on April 24, 1966.

Perlman announced on July 26, 1966, the curtailment of long-distance business in favor of travel of less than 200 miles because this was where the demand was. But criticism from the New York State Public Service Commission kept the Central from taking action for a year. The Great Steel Fleet was in shabby condition, and management didn't care much what passengers thought about it.

Perlman said on July 27, 1967, that the Central would undertake a "sweeping appraisal" of its passenger service because the U.S. Post Office Department planned to remove railway post office cars from 44 of the 53 Central trains that still had them, depriving the railroad of $5 million in revenue. The Central lost $16 million on passenger service in 1966, and Perlman expected the deficit to grow in 1967 due to increased labor and overhead costs and declining patronage.

The Central would focus on service between New York and Buffalo while operating a handful of passenger trains west of Buffalo. The Central stripped every train name from the timetable except the Chicago–Cincinnati *James Whitcomb Riley* and tried to keep quiet the discontinuance of the *Twentieth Century Limited*.

On the eve of the December 3, 1967, restructuring, the Central had 10 Chicago line passenger trains. Only the *Century* had Chicago–New York sleepers. The *New England States* had the only Chicago–Boston cars. The *Fifth Avenue–Cleveland Limited* had Chicago–New York coaches and a diner lounge that operated to Buffalo and returned on the westbound *Chicagoan*, which had Chicago–New York coaches in both directions. The *Empire State Express* was shown operating from New York to Chicago, but did not list any through cars.

Nos. 57/96 was a bobtail operation between Chicago and Toledo that did not officially carry passengers east of Kendallville. No. 57 was the former *Cleveland Limited*, which had been extended to Chicago in 1966 in place of No. 201. No. 96 had replaced Chicago to Buffalo No. 222. Both were primarily mail and express trains that lost their RPO cars on July 1, 1967. The rest of their mail and express business was transferred to other trains in August 1967.

Discontinued in Ohio on September 9, 1967, they would have ended in Indiana on November 19 but for the intervention of the ICC. Each train had a coach and locomotive. No. 57 averaged 26.5 passengers per day during the first six months of 1967, and No. 96 averaged 3 per day. The Central said the trains lost more than $240,000 out of pocket, which was enough to persuade the ICC on March 12, 1968, to allow their removal.

Passengers in observation car "Sandy Creek" are just a few minutes out of Chicago as the *Twentieth Century Limited* momentarily halts at Gary on August 12, 1967. In less than four months, the nation's most famous passenger train would be only a memory. Photo by Dave McKay.

The *Century* and *New England States* were consolidated between Chicago and Buffalo on November 5, 1967. The *Century* began its final runs on December 2. Aside from the presence of a handful of reporters and rail enthusiasts, the *Century* went out without fanfare. The last *Century* arrived in Chicago 7 hours late following a detour in Ohio on the Nickel Plate due to a freight train derailment.

The former *New England States* (Nos. 27/28) was curtailed to Chicago–Buffalo, but conveyed sleepers, sleepercoaches, and coaches between Chicago and New York/Boston that interchanged at Buffalo and (in the case of the Boston cars) Albany. Nos. 27/28 also had a midtrain lounge and twin-unit diner. Nos. 63/64 operated between Chicago and New York and carried a diner lounge between Chicago and Buffalo. Nos. 51/98 were coaches-only Chicago–Buffalo trains.

The New York Central and Pennsylvania merged on February 1, 1968, to form Penn Central, which considered removing sleepers from former New York Central trains in October 1968. Otherwise Penn Central largely left the Chicago line alone, which was surprising considering how aggressively it sought to emasculate passenger service elsewhere in Indiana.

The diner lounge on Nos. 63/64 had become a grill diner by August 1970 and a snack coach in November. The Chicago–Boston sleepercoaches ended June 15, 1969. The Boston through sleepers and coaches ended October 26, 1969, forcing passengers to change trains at Albany.

Penn Central sought to end all six Chicago line trains with its March 10, 1970, petition to the Interstate Commerce Commission. Nos. 27/28 carried 84,361 revenue passengers in 1969, most of whom boarded or disembarked at stations east of Buffalo. Nos. 63/64 carried 40,379 passengers in 1969. Nos. 51/98 carried 28,701. Nos. 63/64 lost $957,680 in 1969. Nos. 27/28 lost $870,255. Nos. 51/98 lost $611,694. Nos. 27/28 had the highest patronage, so the ICC on September 22, 1970, ordered them to remain in operation for six months. The ICC also decided that the favorable schedule of Nos. 51/98 and the possibility of retaining their mail revenue justified keeping them. Nos. 63/64 could end on October 1.

A Pennsylvania federal court immediately stayed the ICC order. Passage of the Rail Passenger Service Act in October froze the nation's rail passenger network into place until Amtrak could begin operations.

In a controversial decision, Amtrak chose not to keep any of the six passenger trains on the former New York Central Chicago line. All six began their final runs on April 30, 1971. A few days later, the states along the route pledged funding for a second Chicago–New York Amtrak train. The *Lake Shore* began May 10 on a six-month trial basis.

St. Louis Line

The Indianapolis & Bellefontaine opened January 24, 1853, between Indianapolis and Union City (Randolph County), where it connected with the Bellefontaine & Indiana. The December 20, 1864, merger of the two roads created the Bellefontaine Railway, which merged with the Cleveland, Columbus & Cincinnati on May 16, 1868, to form the Cleveland, Columbus, Cincinnati & Indianapolis (Bee Line).

The Terre Haute & Alton opened between Terre Haute and the Mississippi River port of Alton, Ill., in March 1856. A consortium of railroads (including the Bee Line) created the Indianapolis & St. Louis, which opened August 28, 1867, between Indianapolis and Terre Haute. The June 1889 merger of the Bee Line, I&StL (lessor of the former TH&A) and the Cincinnati, Indianapolis, St. Louis & Chicago created the Cleveland, Cincinnati, Chicago & St. Louis (Big Four). The New York Central had stock control of the Big Four, but did not lease it until February 1, 1930.

The first passenger operation was from Indianapolis to Pendleton in southwest Madison County on December 11, 1850. Service expanded to Anderson on June 19, 1851, and to

Muncie on May 31, 1852. Following the Civil War, there were three Indianapolis–Cleveland round trips and trains operating Union City–Indianapolis and Union City–Cleveland. The TH&A had three round trips between Terre Haute and St. Louis.

The Cleveland, Columbus, Cincinnati & Indianapolis changed service to four round trips between Indianapolis and Crestline, Ohio. After the opening of the I&StL, service became three Indianapolis–St. Louis round trips and one round trip between Indianapolis and Mattoon, Ill. This remained the norm for the remainder of the 1870s. New York–St. Louis sleepers had begun by the late 1870s. The Bee Line typically had two Indianapolis–Cleveland round trips and locals operating Indianapolis–Muncie and Indianapolis–Union City. A local terminating at Union City originated at Cleveland or Galion, Ohio.

Big Four Reshapes Service

The Bee Line/I&StL offered St. Louis–New York sleepers and St. Louis–Cleveland coaches. By January 1883 this included sleepers between Indianapolis and Cleveland and Columbus, Ohio, and reclining-seat coaches between St. Louis and New York. Dining cars operated between Union City and Bellefontaine. Through trains began operating between St. Louis and Cleveland in 1885. This service included four St. Louis–Cleveland round trips, a Union City–St. Louis round trip, and trains operating Cleveland–Mattoon and Indianapolis–Cleveland. Three pairings operated between Indianapolis and Anderson.

The Big Four made several changes including the October 6, 1889, creation of a signature train, the *South-Western Limited*, which carried a café dining car between St. Louis and New York and sleepers between St. Louis and New York/Boston. Other trains handled coaches and sleepers between St. Louis and Cincinnati, a coach-sleeper combine between St. Louis and Columbus and coaches between St. Louis and Buffalo. The Big Four in conjunction with the C&O began through sleepers in 1892 between St. Louis and Washington (via Cincinnati).

No. 10 became the *Knickerbocker Special* on September 30, 1894. The *South-Western Limited* and *Knickerbocker Special* names lasted in modified form until St. Louis–Cleveland service ended in September 1967. In the mid-1890s the Big Four had three St. Louis–Cleveland round trips, a St. Louis–Indianapolis round trip, three Indianapolis–Anderson round trips, and trains operating Indianapolis–Terre Haute and Terre Haute–Cleveland.

St. Louis–Cleveland service had grown to four round trips by 1903 and five by 1907. The *Southwestern Limited* lost its hyphen. Single pairings operated between Indianapolis and Cleveland, St. Louis, Union City, Mattoon, Ill., and sometimes Muncie. Indianapolis–Anderson service varied between one and three round trips. One Indianapolis–St. Louis train used the original Terre Haute & Alton line through East Alton, Ill. Other trains used the more direct route between Hillsboro and Mitchell, Ill.

By 1910 the Big Four had 29 trains, including five St. Louis–Cleveland round trips, five trains between St. Louis and Indianapolis, and round trips operating Indianapolis–Mattoon, Indianapolis–Anderson (two pairings), and Union City–Bellefontaine. Trains also operated from Indianapolis to Cleveland, Galion to Union City, and Union City to Indianapolis. For a while in 1916 the Big Four had three Cleveland to St. Louis trains named Southwest: *Southwestern Limited, Southwest Mail,* and *Southwest Empire*.

Within five years, service had fallen to 24 trains, although St. Louis–Cleveland service was unchanged. During World War I, service sank to 15 trains: four St. Louis–Cleveland round trips, and round trips between Indianapolis and Mattoon, Cleveland, and Anderson. The *Toledo–Detroit Special* from Indianapolis to Bellefontaine and its counterpart, the *Detroit–Indianapolis Special,* carried through cars between Indianapolis and Detroit.

St. Louis–Cleveland service returned to five round trips in 1919. The premier trains were the westbound *Southwestern Limited* and eastbound *Knickerbocker Special*. Both conveyed sleepers between St. Louis and New York/Boston and charged extra fare. The *Knickerbocker Special* had a coach from St. Louis to Buffalo but did not handle local passengers. The

Southwestern Limited had a Cleveland to St. Louis coach. Both had St. Louis–New York club cars.

The *Southwestern Limited* became all-Pullman on April 26, 1925. The Central boasted the train had "equipment identical to the *Twentieth Century Limited*," including club cars, ladies' maid, valet, stenographer, stock market reports, and private room sleepers. For the first time since the late 1890s, the *Southwestern Limited* operated in both directions.

The Big Four had an Indianapolis–Cleveland local for much of the 1920s, but it was gone by late 1927. The Indianapolis–Mattoon local had become a motor train by the mid-1920s. St. Louis–Cleveland service was five round trips for much of the decade.

The New York Central in the early 20th century had a penchant for naming trains by their numbers. When St. Louis line service expanded to six St. Louis–Cleveland round trips in the late 1920s, the newcomers were named *Number Thirty-Nine/Number Forty*. They became the *Missourian* in February 1928.

Service Crests

St. Louis–Cleveland service crested in 1930 at seven round trips, falling to 11 trains within two years. The *Southwestern Limited* and *Knickerbocker* had a 23-hour St. Louis–New York schedule, and the *Knickerbocker* had a Cincinnati section. Cleveland–St. Louis service had evened out at five round trips by late 1933. During the 1930s, a Cleveland to Indianapolis train was named the *Indianapolis Special*. A Detroit to Indianapolis train was the *Indiana Special*.

The *Southwestern Limited* received coaches in the 1930s, initially from New York to St. Louis with the eastbound coaches originating at Buffalo. The westbound *Southwestern Limited* also had coaches that originated in Cincinnati. The *Southwestern Limited* conveyed the St. Louis–Washington sleepers interchanged with the C&O. The *Missourian* conveyed a St. Louis–Pittsburgh lounge-sleeper that reached Pittsburgh via the Erie (Cleveland–Youngstown, Ohio) and Pittsburgh & Lake Erie (Youngstown–Pittsburgh). These cars had ended by early 1935.

The *Cleveland–St. Louis Special* had a New York–St. Louis sleeper by early 1935, increasing to four the number of trains with St. Louis–New York sleepers. The only St. Louis–New York coaches went east on the *Knickerbocker* and returned on the *Southwestern Limited*. The *New York Special* offered sleepers from Indianapolis to New York, but there was no returning counterpart. The *Knickerbocker* began operating in both directions in 1936. There were 11 St. Louis–Cleveland trains during much of the 1930s.

By 1933, the St. Louis–Indianapolis local via East Alton had become a motor train that terminated at East St. Louis, Ill. The westbound leg became the *Mound City Special* in 1934, ending service from Indianapolis via the East Alton route. The *Mound City Special* began originating at Cleveland in 1935 and conveying the Washington to St. Louis sleeper. It ended in 1936. Between 1935 and 1938 the Big Four had two East St. Louis to Indianapolis locals via East Alton. One of these trains, No. 34, moved off the East Alton line in 1938 and began originating at St. Louis. The last train to Indianapolis via East Alton ended in 1939.

Into the 1940s, the New York Central had 11 St. Louis–Cleveland trains. Another train operated from St. Louis to Indianapolis. The Indianapolis to Cleveland *New York Special* had ended in 1939, leaving only the *Cleveland Special/Indianapolis Special* between Indianapolis and Cleveland. St. Louis to Indianapolis No. 34 had been extended to Galion. A motor car operated between Indianapolis and Terre Haute. The Indianapolis–Detroit overnight trains, the *Toledo–Detroit Express/Indianapolis Express*, resumed independent operation between Indianapolis and Bellefontaine in 1942, but the *Indianapolis Special* disappeared.

St. Louis–Cleveland service increased to 12 scheduled trains during World War II. The St. Louis to Galion local was extended to Cleveland. The eastbound *Southwestern Limited* began operating in two sections in 1944. The first section, which bypassed Cleveland, carried the New York/Boston sleepers and coaches. The second section terminated at Cleveland. The *Toledo–Detroit Express* operated independently from Indianapolis to Detroit, but the *Indianapolis Express* ran in combination with the *Knickerbocker* from Bellefontaine to Indianapolis. The *Cleveland Special* ran in combination with the *Toledo–Detroit Express* from Indianapolis to Bellefontaine. A Sunday-only local ran from Indianapolis to Galion.

Postwar Operations

The New York Central began interchanging through cars at St. Louis between the *Southwestern Limited* and three western trains on July 7, 1946. Sleepers between New York and San Antonio, Dallas, and Fort Worth and a New York–San Antonio coach interchanged with the *Texas Special* of the Frisco/Katy. A New York–Oklahoma City sleeper interchanged with the Frisco's *Meteor*. Sleepers between New York and Mexico City, Houston, and Fort Worth interchanged with the Missouri Pacific's *Sunshine Special*. A Washington–San Antonio sleeper (conveyed by the C&O between Washington and Cincinnati) interchanged with the *Sunshine Special*.

Rather than contribute new lightweight equipment to the Southwest through car pool, the Central quit the interchange in 1948 in favor of connecting service. The interchange with the *Texas Special* and the *Meteor* ended in May 1948, the same month that New York–Mexico City and Washington–San Antonio sleepers ended. Also discontinued was a westbound second section of the *Southwestern Limited* that had conveyed the through cars. The New York–Houston and New York–Fort Worth cars interchanged with the *Sunshine Special* continued until July 18, when the second eastbound section of the *Southwestern Limited* ended.

At its postwar apex in 1948, the New York Central operated 19 trains in Indiana on the St. Louis line, including 3 from St. Louis to New York and 2 from New York to St. Louis. The Pennsylvania with five St. Louis–New York round trips held the upper hand because it had a faster, more direct route. The Indianapolis–Terre Haute motor trains made 12 intermediate stops, many at stations bypassed by other trains. These trains ended August 9, 1948.

St. Louis–Cleveland service fell to 11 trains on December 5, 1948. The Indianapolis–Detroit trains were consolidated with the eastbound *Cleveland Express* and westbound *Knickerbocker* between Indianapolis and Bellefontaine. Further changes occurred December 11, 1949, with the discontinuance of the *St. Louis Express* (Cleveland to St. Louis) and the *Cleveland Express* east of Bellefontaine. The Indianapolis–Detroit trains resumed independent operation between Indianapolis and Bellefontaine. This left 8 trains operating west of Indianapolis and 10 trains east of Indianapolis.

The Central advertised the *Southwestern Limited*, *Knickerbocker*, and *Missourian* as diesel streamliners in 1949, but all had heavyweight sleepers until the early 1950s. St. Louis line passenger trains were diesel powered by 1952 except the *Cleveland–St. Louis Special*, the *Cleveland–Cincinnati Special*, and the Indianapolis–Detroit overnight trains. A second section of the *Missourian* that began operating in 1951 from St. Louis to Indianapolis became a second section of the *Cleveland–Cincinnati Special* and operated through late 1957.

The *Southwestern Limited* was second only to the *Twentieth Century Limited* in elegance and appointments. After the *Century* was reequipped in 1948, the *Southwestern Limited* received some streamlined equipment built for the *Century* a decade earlier. The *Southwestern Limited* received new lightweight equipment in the late 1940s, but it was 1953 before it was fully streamlined.

New equipment did little to boost patronage, and the *Southwestern Limited* was one of the poorest performers in the Great Steel Fleet. The St. Louis–Phoebus, Va., sleepers were gone by 1951, replaced by a St. Louis to Richmond sleeper. The *Southwestern Limited* had lost its observation-lounge cars and Boston to St. Louis coaches by 1955.

The *Southwestern Limited* hit rock bottom on October 28, 1956, when it became the *Southwestern*, a St. Louis–Cleveland train with coaches and a thrift grill. A rescheduling broke the connections to the *Texas Special* and *Texas Eagle* at St. Louis. The eastbound *Southwestern* had regained a St. Louis to New York sleeper and coach by early 1957. That April a New York to St. Louis coach returned to the westbound *Southwestern* along with a St. Louis to Boston sleeper for its eastbound counterpart.

The *Gateway* lost its Cleveland to St. Louis lounge-sleeper and sleeper in summer 1956. The St. Louis–Cincinnati sleepers (conveyed by the *Gateway* and the *Cleveland–Cincinnati Special*) also ended. The *Cleveland–St. Louis Special* was renamed *Missourian* on October 28, 1956, but lost its Indianapolis to St. Louis diner-lounge in 1957.

The Protracted Endgame

The New York Central wanted to abandon passenger service to St. Louis, notifying the Indiana Public Service Commission and the Illinois Commerce Commission on December 16, 1957, of its intent to eliminate passenger service west of Indianapolis. The Central claimed a 1956 out-of-pocket loss of $402,974 and expected to lose $1.2 million in 1957 on St. Louis service. Patronage had dropped 76 percent between 1946 and 1957. The overnight *Indianapolis Express/Detroit Express* made their final runs in May 1958. The *Missourian*, eastbound *Knickerbocker*, and westbound *Southwestern* ceased operating west of Indianapolis on August 17, 1958.

The *Missourian* became the *Indianapolis Special*, and its St. Louis to New York sleepers and coaches began originating at Indianapolis. The *Southwestern* name was dropped westbound, and its New York to St. Louis sleeper and coaches began terminating at Indianapolis. The eastbound *Southwestern* and westbound *Knickerbocker* each carried a lounge sleeper, two St. Louis–New York sleepers, St. Louis–Boston sleeper, St. Louis–New York coaches, and St. Louis–Cleveland diner.

The Central ended the eastbound *Knickerbocker* and No. 311 (former *Southwestern*) in Ohio on April 26, 1959, leaving an abridged train between Indianapolis and Muncie that operated in the evening. In March 1959, the Central sought Indiana Public Service Commission approval to discontinue these trains, claiming to have lost $126,312 in 1958. The Central said patronage averaged less than 1 passenger per day eastbound and 2.2 patrons per day westbound. The PSC approved the discontinuance on July 24, and the trains ended a week later.

Indiana public counselor George Dixon pleaded in vain for the public and political officials to attend PSC hearings and oppose removal of New York Central passenger trains on the St. Louis and Cincinnati lines. Describing attendance at some hearings as disappointing, Dixon asked the public to show evidence that discontinuances would cause hardship.

The *Knickerbocker*'s Detroit to St. Louis sleeper and coach ended April 26, 1959, and the diner on the *Knickerbocker/Southwestern* was curtailed to Indianapolis–Cleveland. Light meals were served west of Indianapolis in a lounge-sleeper. The St. Louis–Boston sleepers ended in October 1959. The *Gateway/Cleveland Special* ended west of Indianapolis on October 25, 1959. The *Gateway* had conveyed a Buffalo to St. Louis sleeper. The *Indianapolis Special* and *Gateway* names disappeared April 24, 1960, but the *Cleveland Special* name tarried until December 3, 1967.

The Central discontinued the *Indianapolis Special* east of Union City, Ind., on April 24, 1960. In the previous year, the train had lost its westbound New York, Buffalo, and Detroit sleepers and coaches. The Indianapolis to Cleveland sleeper made its final trip April 9. The *Indianapolis Special* ended between Indianapolis and Union City on January 6, 1961.

This left the St. Louis line with a pair of coaches-only Indianapolis–Cleveland trains and the *Knickerbocker/ Southwestern*, which offered an Indianapolis–New York sleeper and St. Louis–New York coaches and sleepers. The diner-lounge had resumed operating between St. Louis and Cleveland by mid-1961, but the lounge-sleeper was gone.

The *Knickerbocker/Southwestern* remained largely unchanged until October 27, 1963, when the Indianapolis–New York sleepers ended. The diner-lounge began operating be-

The New York–St. Louis *Southwestern Limited* was once second only to the *Twentieth Century Limited* in elegance and appointments. But by April 2, 1967, it had more head-end cars than passenger cars as it left St. Louis Union Station. Photo by Dave McKay.

tween Indianapolis and Cleveland in March 1965 and later that year became a buffet-lounge car serving beverages and light meals eastbound and breakfast westbound. The St. Louis–New York sleepers began terminating at Indianapolis in November 1966. The Central ended the *Knickerbocker/Southwestern* between Cleveland and Union City on September 6, 1967. Nos. 312/341 became unnamed trains with one coach pulled by a locomotive.

The Central notified the Interstate Commerce Commission on November 19, 1967, of its intent to end Nos. 312/341 a month later. Between September and the end of November, patronage had averaged 6.7 passengers per day eastbound and 7.6 westbound. Patronage had fallen steadily since 1965 when the trains averaged 14.6 per day eastbound and 12.4 westbound. Less than half of the 1967 passengers traveled between St. Louis and points east of Indianapolis.

Removal of the railway post office on August 5, 1967, deprived the trains of $304,094 in annual mail revenue. The bulk mail carried by Nos. 312/341 had been transferred to Nos. 315/316 (Indianapolis–Cleveland). The out-of-pocket losses for Nos. 312/341 grew from $519,801 in 1965 to $550,819 in 1966 to $282,329 in the first six months of 1967. The 13 witnesses who opposed removal of the trains criticized the Central for dirty coaches and late trains. The Central disputed the latter point, saying that the trains operated on time (within 30 minutes of schedule) on an average of 28 days a month.

Commissioner George M. Stafford swept aside the complaints as unsupported opinions. In approving discontinuance, Stafford noted that the decline in patronage probably was irreversible and crew wages in 1967 had been five times passenger revenue. Nos. 312/341 made their final trips on March 18, 1968.

Nos. 315/316 had survived principally because of their heavy mail business. No. 315 operated overnight from Cleveland to Indianapolis with No. 316 returning the next morning. They were among the 34 trains that Penn Central sought to end in its petition of March 10, 1970, to the Interstate Commerce Commission. No. 315 carried 1,921 passengers in 1969, an average of 5.3 per trip. No. 316 carried 2,815, an average of 7.7 per trip. Nearly 30 percent of the passengers rode the length of the route. Nos. 315/316 carried the least number of revenue passengers in 1969 of the 17 pairs of trains up for discontinuance.

The typical consist was a coach, baggage car, several Flexi-Vans (New York Central's name for a trailer on flatcar), and various mail storage cars. The trains earned 94 percent of their 1969 revenue of $665,452 from hauling mail. Passenger revenue was $39,484. Nos. 315/316 cost $962,731 to operate in 1969, producing an out-of-pocket loss of $297,630. Citing low patronage and high losses, the ICC approved the discontinuance, saying, "We find no real need for continuance of those trains." A legal challenge and the coming of Amtrak postponed discontinuance for several months. Nos. 315/316 began their final runs on April 30, 1971.

Cincinnati Line

The Indianapolis & Cincinnati operated its first train (Indianapolis to Lawrenceburg) on November 1, 1853. Until building its own line in 1863, the I&C used the Ohio & Mississippi (later B&O) to reach Cincinnati. The Lafayette & Indianapolis operated its first train between its namesake cities on December 16, 1852, and merged with the I&C on February 14, 1867, to form the Indianapolis, Cincinnati & Lafayette.

The Cincinnati, Lafayette & Chicago opened August 25, 1872, using 19 miles of the Lake Erie & Western (later Nickel Plate) between Lafayette and Templeton in southeast Benton County, 56 miles of its own track (Templeton–Kankakee, Ill.), and 54 miles of the Illinois Central (Kankakee–Chicago). The CL&C and the IC&L merged in March 1880 to form the Cincinnati, Indianapolis, St. Louis & Chicago (the first Big Four) and merged with the Bee Line in June 1889.

Following the Civil War, the IC&L had five trains between Cincinnati and Lafayette and trains operating Indianapolis–Lafayette, Indianapolis–Cincinnati (*St. Louis Express*), Fairland–Indianapolis, and Cincinnati–Newtown, Ind. The *St. Louis Express* had through cars for St. Louis, Kansas City, Chicago, and Omaha. After the Chicago extension opened in 1872, four trains operated between Lafayette and Kankakee and two between Lafayette and Templeton. The IC&L advertised a through Chicago–Cincinnati train. At the end of the 1870s, the IC&L had 10 trains, 6 of them between Cincinnati and Lafayette.

After the Big Four began, service changed to two Chicago–Cincinnati round trips and trains operating Cincinnati–Sheldon, Ill., and Cincinnati–Lafayette. Trains had sleepers and parlor cars, and the Big Four claimed to have the only solid Chicago–Cincinnati trains. Chicago–Cincinnati service remained two round trips during the 1880s. The route hosted 12 trains including an Indianapolis–Cincinnati pairing.

For the 1893 World's Columbian Exposition in Chicago, the Big Four spiffed up two trains and named them *World's Fair Express* and *North-western Limited*. Cincinnati line service had grown to 17 trains. Chicago–Cincinnati service expanded to three round trips with the August 30, 1896, inauguration of the *White City Special*, an all-vestibule train featuring buffet parlor cars.

Growth of Through Service

C&O president Melville Ingalls was a former Big Four president who suggested in 1889 interchanging at Cincinnati through sleepers between Chicago and Old Point Comfort in the Virginia Tidewater. By 1905, the Big Four had named a Chicago to Cincinnati train the *C&O Special*.

Chicago–Florida service began in January 1902. The *Chicago and Florida Special* alternated among three Chicago–Cincinnati routes, using the Big Four on Wednesday and

Saturday. The train also used the Southern (Cincinnati–Jacksonville, Fla.) and Florida East Coast (Jacksonville–St. Augustine). The *Chicago and Florida Special* operated just one season, but another seasonal train, the *Florida Special*, debuted January 7, 1907, with sleepers between Chicago and Jacksonville and St. Augustine. Chicago–Cincinnati service rose to four round trips with the inauguration of the *Queen City Special*.

The *Florida Special* operated as the *Florida Limited* when it resumed December 1, 1907. By 1910 it was the *Chicago Florida Limited* with Chicago–Jacksonville and Indianapolis–Jacksonville sleepers. It became the *Royal Palm* on November 2, 1913, a year-round all-steel train with Chicago–Jacksonville coaches and sleepers and Indianapolis–Jacksonville sleepers.

Chicago–Cincinnati service was 10 trains by 1915. Six other trains operated in Indiana: Indianapolis–Cincinnati, Indianapolis–Kankakee, and Indianapolis–Lawrenceburg Junction. The *Royal Palm* was suspended during World War I, and Chicago–Cincinnati service fell to six trains. Nine other trains also operated in Indiana.

The *Royal Palm* returned in 1919 and for about a year operated in combination with the *Chicago Night Special/Cincinnati Night Special*. The *Palm*'s through car assignments were the same as before the war, and it also had Chicago–Miami sleepers.

From 1911 to July 1, 1917, the Chicago cars interchanged with the C&O used the C&O's own line via Muncie. Following the war, the Chicago C&O sleepers began terminating at Clifton Forge, Va.

Eight trains operated between Chicago and Cincinnati. Indianapolis–Cincinnati service was four trains including the *Pivot City Limited/Queen City Limited*. Other service included Indianapolis–Lawrenceburg Junction locals and Kankakee to Indianapolis and Indianapolis to Chicago trains. The *Royal Palm* had resumed independent operation by January 1922, increasing Chicago–Cincinnati service to 10 trains. Also revived were St. Louis–Washington sleepers via the C&O. The *Pivot City Limited* became the *Indianapolis Limited*.

In June 1922, the Big Four launched the *Sycamore*, an all-steel Indianapolis–Chicago train featuring coaches, a diner-lounge, and an observation parlor. The northbound *Sycamore* began originating in Cincinnati in summer 1927. The southbound train was extended to Cincinnati on April 28, 1929.

The Big Four and the Southern began through sleepers between Chicago and Asheville, N.C., conveyed to Asheville by the *Carolina Special*. The C&O Chicago sleepers now operated to Richmond, Va. Chicago–St. Petersburg, Fla., sleepers began November 26, 1922, conveyed south of Cincinnati by the Southern's *Ohio Special*. The *Royal Palm*'s Indianapolis sleepers began operating to Miami. The *Palm* did not accept local passengers between Chicago and Cincinnati. The St. Petersburg sleepers were conveyed the next season by the Southern's *Suwanee River Special*, a seasonal train that began in November 1921 and carried these sleepers every winter through 1929.

The Indianapolis–Miami sleepers ended in 1923, but for the 1924–25 season sleepers operated between Indianapolis and Jacksonville. The next year, the Indianapolis sleepers were extended to Miami when the *Royal Palm* became all-Pullman. For the 1926–27 season, the *Royal Palm* carried sleepers between Chicago and Tampa/Sarasota, Fla. The Indianapolis–Miami sleepers were curtailed to Jacksonville for the 1929–30 and 1930–31 seasons. The *Royal Palm* did not carry sleepers originating in Indianapolis the following season.

A third Southern train that had Chicago–Florida cars was the seasonal *Ponce de Leon*, which began December 7, 1924, and carried Chicago–Miami sleepers. The next year the *Ponce de Leon* added sleepers between Chicago and Fort Myers. These cars did not return the next year, and for the remainder of the 1920s the *Ponce de Leon* carried only Chicago–Miami sleepers. The *Carolina Special* sleepers began terminating at Columbia, S.C., in 1925. The C&O Chicago sleepers were extended to Newport News, Va., in 1923.

In the late 1920s the Big Four operated 14 Chicago–Cincinnati trains and three Indianapolis–Cincinnati trains. Local service had virtually disappeared. The Indianapolis to

Lawrenceburg Junction local ended in 1927. Its counterpart ended in 1931. Also gone were the *Chicago Night Special/Cincinnati Night Special.* Chicago–Cincinnati service had fallen to nine trains by January 1934. Among the casualties was the northbound *Sycamore.*

The *Royal Palm* began operating in two sections south of Cincinnati in 1927. The second section was the seasonal all-Pullman *Royal Palm de Luxe,* later renamed *Royal Palm Special.* The year-round *Royal Palm* carried Chicago–Miami sleepers. The *Royal Palm Special* carried sleepers between Chicago and Miami/St. Petersburg, a Chicago–Miami observation-sleeper, and a Chicago–Jacksonville club lounge.

The discontinuance of the *Royal Palm Special* in 1932 left only the *Ponce de Leon* and *Royal Palm* with Chicago–Florida cars. The *Ponce de Leon* acquired a Chicago–St. Petersburg sleeper in 1933, but beginning in 1932 the only through cars on the *Royal Palm* on the Big Four were Chicago–Jacksonville sleepers.

The seasonal *Florida Sunbeam* began January 1, 1936, with sleepers, coaches, and a lounge-buffet sleeper between Chicago and Miami, and Chicago–St. Petersburg sleepers. The *Ponce de Leon* carried only Chicago–Jacksonville sleepers. The *Florida Sunbeam* was a solid train between Chicago and Cincinnati, becoming the *Royal Palm* during the summer. During the winter only the southbound *Royal Palm* operated on the Big Four. The C&O interchange expanded in the mid-1930s to include sleepers between Chicago and Washington/Old Point Comfort and between Indianapolis and Washington. The latter ended in 1936.

As the 1930s closed, the Cincinnati line hosted 10 Chicago–Cincinnati trains and a train from Indianapolis to Chicago. The top train, the Cincinnati to Chicago *Sycamore,* made the run in 5 hours, 55 minutes.

Birth of the Riley

Encouraged by the success of the Cleveland–Detroit and Chicago–Detroit *Mercury,* the New York Central created a third *Mercury* to operate between Chicago and Cincinnati. Using equipment rebuilt at the Central's Beech Grove shops in Indianapolis, the train

The *James Whitcomb Riley* has something old—steam locomotive No. 5441 and a heavyweight car—and something new—streamlined coaches. The train is being serviced at Lafayette in 1954. Photo by Ron Stuckey; John Fuller collection.

The Chicago–Cincinnati *James Whitcomb Riley* steams out of Greensburg, Ind., in 1955. Within a year, the steam locomotives would be retired and replaced by diesels. Photo by Charlie Preston; John Fuller collection.

began April 28, 1941, as the *James Whitcomb Riley* on a 5.5-hour schedule. Twenty-five minutes faster than the *Sycamore*, the *Riley* did not stop at Greensburg or Shelbyville.

The *Riley* had reserved seat coaches, observation-buffet-lounge, and a diner. The steam locomotives had streamlined shrouding, and the cars were red and gray. The Chicago-Cincinnati round-trip fare was $10.65. The New York Central now had 11 Chicago-Cincinnati trains with another pair between Indianapolis and Chicago.

The *Royal Palm* had Chicago-Jacksonville sleepers and coaches that operated year-round and seasonal Chicago-Miami sleepers. The all-Pullman *Florida Sunbeam* did not return in 1942 and remained suspended for the duration of World War II. The only Florida cars on the *Royal Palm* were Chicago–Jacksonville sleepers. During the war, Chicago–

Cincinnati service increased to 12 trains with another train from Chicago to Indianapolis. Through sleepers operated Chicago–Phoebus, Va. (C&O), and Chicago–Charleston, S.C. (Southern).

The *Florida Sunbeam* returned for the 1946–47 winter season with Chicago–Miami sleepers that operated southward through Indiana on the *Cincinnati Night Express* and northward on the *Royal Palm*, which also conveyed Chicago–Jacksonville sleepers. Chicago–Cincinnati service was 11 trains. A round trip operated between Chicago and Indianapolis, the southbound train being the *Indianapolis Mail.*

The *Florida Sunbeam* made its final run April 30, 1949. The *New Royal Palm* began December 17, 1949, with the Chicago–Miami sleepers previously assigned to the *Florida Sunbeam*. The *Royal Palm* ceased operating north of Cincinnati. The *James Whitcomb Riley* received new streamlined equipment in 1947, but the reequipping of the *Riley* was not completed until 1948.

Retrenchment Begins

As the 1950s began, there were 11 trains between Chicago and Cincinnati and a train from Chicago to Indianapolis. Through sleepers operated between Chicago and Asheville and Goldsboro, N.C., on the Southern's *Carolina Special*, a name also used for Chicago to Cincinnati No. 406 since 1943. C&O sleepers operated between Chicago and Clifton Forge and Phoebus. The *New Royal Palm* lost its Chicago–Jacksonville sleepers in May 1953. The seasonal Chicago–Miami sleepers continued until the *New Royal Palm* made its last trip on April 30, 1955.

The *White City Special* was curtailed to Indianapolis to Chicago on June 17, 1951, and the name was dropped. Chicago–Cincinnati service fell to eight trains on April 26, 1953, when the *Chicago Night Express/Cincinnati Night Express* consolidated with a pair of unnamed trains. All four trains had operated overnight. Another round trip operated between Chicago and Indianapolis.

The *James Whitcomb Riley* began stopping at Greensburg and Shelbyville in 1955. The *Riley*'s Cincinnati to Chicago running time rose to 6 hours, although the southbound *Riley* was 20 minutes faster. The New York Central downgraded the *Riley*'s diner to a thrift grill, but a year later brought back full dining service. The *Riley* was steam powered through 1956.

The St. Louis–Richmond and St. Louis–Washington sleepers via the C&O and a Chicago–Charleston, S.C., sleeper via the Southern ended in October 1956. The Central shuffled train names like cards in the late 1950s. The *Chicago Special/Cincinnati Special* became the *Booth Tarkington* on April 28, 1957, the second train named for a Hoosier author. The *Sycamore* and the southbound *Booth Tarkington* became the *Midwestern* on October 27, 1957. The *Carolina Special* became the *Cincinnati Special*, and the northbound *Midwestern* reverted to the *Sycamore* on April 27, 1958.

The *Booth Tarkington/Midwestern* ended in September 1958, dropping Chicago–Cincinnati service to six trains. The *Sycamore* yet again became the *Midwestern*. Seven months later the Central sought to end all passenger service between Chicago and Cincinnati, citing losses of $848,998 in 1958.

The Indiana Public Service Commission on February 26, 1959, gave the Central the green light to eliminate the overnight trains, but it had to keep the *James Whitcomb Riley* and the *Midwestern/Cincinnati Special*. Discontinued with the overnight trains were the Chicago–Asheville sleepers. The *Midwestern* was renamed the *Sycamore*.

Four years later, the PSC allowed the Central to discontinue the *Sycamore/Cincinnati Special* between Indianapolis and Cincinnati. In a decision announced August 2, 1963, the PSC cited low patronage and losses of $116,399 in 1961 and $128,000 in 1962. But the commission also chided the Central, saying if it put as much effort into marketing trains as it did trying to end them, they might become profitable.

The *Cincinnati Special* became the *Indianapolis Special* and through late 1966 had a tavern lounge. Penn Central announced in December 1968 it would end the former *Sycamore/Indianapolis Special* (the names were dropped December 3, 1967), citing low patronage and the loss of the railway post office and storage mail. Penn Central claimed the trains lost $120,261 in 1967. Nos. 302/305 operated for the final time on January 9, 1969. The former *Indianapolis Special* arrived on time at Indianapolis Union Station behind Illinois Central E7A No. 4012. The IC and NYC had pooled locomotive power on the Cincinnati line since 1956. Dale Wilson, director of the railroad division of the Indiana Public Service Commission, told the *Indianapolis News* he had urged a campaign to keep the service. But the public didn't seem to be interested.

The last C&O through cars (Chicago–Newport News sleepers) ended May 11, 1968. Penn Central cited the loss of these cars and removal of the RPO in July 1967 in seeking to end the *Riley* on July 20, 1969. The *Riley* had shrunk to a locomotive, baggage car, two coaches, and a diner. Two additional coaches were added between Chicago and Indianapolis on weekends and during the summer. The *Riley* averaged 96 passengers leaving Chicago in 1967 and 57 in 1969. The train arrived in Cincinnati with an average of 58 aboard in 1967 but only 25 in 1969. Corresponding figures for the northbound *Riley* were 74 on at Cincinnati in 1967 and 41 on in 1969, and 110 off at Chicago in 1967 and 77 off in 1969.

The ICC determined the *Riley* was profitable on the Illinois Central but lost money on the Penn Central, $346,205 in 1968. The commission concluded neither Penn Central nor Illinois Central had deliberately downgraded the *Riley*, but disagreed with the railroads' assertion that the public had left the train. Public hearings attracted 181 witnesses with all but three opposing removal of the *Riley*. Passengers and Penn Central crewmen described the *Riley* as dirty and unkempt. The *Riley* routinely operated late, often by more than a half-hour, due to slow orders (many for 30 mph) necessitated by poor track conditions over much of the Kankakee–Cincinnati route.

In a decision reached November 17, 1969, the ICC said the *Riley* would continue for another year, citing evidence of a strong demand for rail service in the Chicago–Indianapolis–Cincinnati corridor. The *Riley* did not materially improve. The dining car ended in May 1970 in favor of a snack bar coach that ended in October 1970. Amtrak rescued the *Riley* by incorporating it into its basic network.

Detroit Line

The Michigan Central opened in February 1838 between Detroit and Ypsilanti, Mich. After reaching New Buffalo, Mich., on April 23, 1849, the Michigan Central began serving Chicago via steamboat across Lake Michigan. The company reached Michigan City, Ind., on October 29, 1850, and paid the New Albany & Salem $500,000 to use its charter for legal authority to build across northwest Indiana. The Illinois Central built a spur from Kensington on Chicago's South Side to the Indiana border to connect with the Michigan Central, which on May 21, 1852, became the second railroad to reach Chicago from the east.

Through the late 1870s, the Michigan Central routed most of its eastern business over the Great Western, which opened January 17, 1854, between Windsor, Ontario, and Niagara Falls. Until a tunnel opened under the Detroit River in July 1910, through cars traveled by ferry between Detroit and Windsor. The Michigan Central was among the first railroads in Indiana to operate sleeping cars, placing into service in 1860 three sleepers that it converted from coaches.

Following the Civil War, the Michigan Central operated eight trains between Chicago and Detroit and a pair between Chicago and Michigan City. Within a year, the latter had been extended to Kalamazoo, Mich., although another train operated from Michigan City to Chicago. The frequency of Chicago–Detroit service remained stable in the 1870s, but service between Chicago and intermediate points gradually increased. Sleepers had begun operating between Chicago and New York by 1871. One Detroit to Chicago train was labeled an emigrant train in 1873.

The competition with the Lake Shore & Michigan Southern was brutal, and the Michigan Central feared financial ruin. Michigan Central chairman James F. Joy was a New York Central director. He approached Cornelius Vanderbilt about a merger, but Vanderbilt rejected Joy's price as too high. Vanderbilt began buying Michigan Central stock, which fell in value after an 1873 financial panic. Vanderbilt held stock control of the Michigan Central by 1876. He also acquired the bankrupt Canada Southern, which was building across Ontario parallel to the Great Western. The Michigan Central leased the Canada Southern in 1882.

Detroit Service Grows

Chicago–Detroit service increased to five round trips in 1880, six round trips by 1890, and seven round trips within another two years. One of the most heavily traveled New York Central routes, the Michigan Central dominated the Chicago–Detroit market. The frequency of Michigan Central service in Indiana rivaled that of the Lake Shore & Southern Michigan.

In the early 1880s, the Michigan Central had sleepers between Chicago and New York/Boston, and coaches between Chicago and Buffalo. Boston cars operated via the Hoosac Tunnel Route (Fitchburg Railroad). By the late 1880s, Chicago–Grand Rapids service had begun with four daily trains. Although most Detroit trains operated via Battle Creek and Kalamazoo, some used the Air Line Division between Niles and Jackson, Mich.

At the dawn of the 20th century, the Michigan Central had 10 Chicago–Detroit trains, a Chicago–Kalamazoo round trip, and eight trains between Chicago and New Buffalo (Grand Rapids service). Boston sleepers now used the Boston & Albany (New York Central). The Michigan Central claimed to be the only railroad operating in full view of Niagara Falls. Since the 1850s, it had done a brisk business in excursion trains to the falls.

The *New York State Special* and the *Fast Mail* were all-Pullman, carrying New York/Boston sleepers. Sleepers also operated between Chicago and the Michigan cities of Bay City, Saginaw, Muskegon, and Grand Rapids. Chicago–Detroit service had reached 15 trains by 1904, and Chicago–Kalamazoo service had risen to 4 trains.

The *Detroit Night Express* became the *Wolverine* on May 14, 1905. Although it carried a Chicago–New York buffet library car, the *Wolverine* initially did not handle Chicago–New York sleepers. The *Michigan Central Special* became the westbound *Wolverine* in November. The *Wolverine* was the Michigan Central's premier Chicago–New York train, seeking to be a peer of the *Twentieth Century Limited*.

Chicago–Kalamazoo service peaked in the second decade of the 20th century at seven trains. Chicago–Detroit service had risen to 16 trains by 1907. The Boston to Chicago *New England Special* had become a section of the *Wolverine* (named *New England Wolverine*) by 1912. By January 1914, the Michigan Central operated 26 trains through Indiana including 18 between Chicago and Detroit and 6 between Chicago and Kalamazoo.

The all-Pullman *Motor City Special* (Chicago–Detroit) began October 16, 1916, increasing Chicago–Detroit service to 21 trains. During World War I, a mixed train operated between East Gary and Michigan City, but was gone by late 1919.

Chicago–Detroit service was still 21 trains in 1920, but Kalamazoo service had fallen to four trains. All-Pullman trains included the *Motor City Special*, *Wolverine*, and the eastbound *North Shore*. *Wolverine* passengers paid extra fare. Sleepers operated between Chicago and Grand Rapids, Boston, New York, Philadelphia, Montreal, Toronto, Saginaw, and Bay City. Through coaches operated between Chicago and Grand Rapids, Montreal, Buffalo, and New York. Parlor cars operated between Chicago and Grand Rapids and Buffalo. The *North Shore* had coaches by 1923, and in summer 1924 the Michigan Central began sleepers between Chicago and Mackinaw City, Petoskey, and Harbor Springs in Michigan's resort region via a connection with the Grand Rapids & Indiana (later Pennsylvania) at Kalamazoo.

By the mid-1920s, Chicago–Detroit service was 23 trains, 2 of them all-stops locals. Three trains operated between Chicago and Kalamazoo. A new all-first-class daylight Chicago–Detroit train began April 25, 1926. The *Twilight Limited* featured parlor cars and a diner, but no coaches. By the end of the 1920s, Chicago–Detroit service had peaked at 30 trains. The *North Shore Limited* was all-Pullman in both directions. The eastbound *Motor City Special* did not accept passengers at intermediate points.

Chicago–Detroit service had fallen to 22 trains by January 1932. Two years later it was 17 trains, and by 1936 it was 15. The Chicago–Kalamazoo locals were gone by 1933. Service had risen to 18 trains by 1937, including the *Michigan*, which featured coaches, parlor cars, and a diner.

Michigan Central passenger trains used Chicago Central Station, but by 1935 the *Wolverine* was using La Salle Street Station, the New York Central's Chicago home. The *Wolverine* was back at Central Station by 1938, and the *Twilight Limited* used La Salle Street Station. The *Twilight Limited* also had gained deluxe coaches.

Michigan Central sleepers ran through to New York, Boston, Philadelphia, Montreal, Toronto, Bay City, Saginaw, and Grand Rapids. Coaches served New York, Toronto, Montreal, and Buffalo. Parlor cars served Grand Rapids. The Toronto and Montreal cars operated on the Canadian Pacific east of Detroit.

Train of the Gods

The New York Central hired industrial designer Henry Dreyfuss to create a fast, streamlined train that could woo back travelers who had forsaken the train for other means of transportation. The Central could not afford to purchase new equipment, but Dreyfuss got the idea of rebuilding surplus commuter cars. The cars were rebuilt at the Big Four shops at Beech Grove near Indianapolis. The *Mercury* (the Roman messenger of the gods) featured reserved seat coaches, a diner, and parlor-observation. Christened June 25, 1936, in Indianapolis, the *Mercury* began service July 15, 1936, between Cleveland and Detroit.

The *Mercury* was so popular that another *Mercury* was created for Chicago–Detroit service, again using cars rebuilt at Beech Grove. The Chicago *Mercury* began November 12, 1939, on a brisk schedule of 4 hours, 45 minutes. The *Mercury* was a hit, and to keep up with demand the Central had to assign additional cars, including some heavyweights.

Chicago–Detroit service ranged between 17 and 18 trains during the early 1940s, increasing to 19 during World War II when the *Mercury* lost its parlor-observation cars. They returned after the war, but the *Mercury* was worn out. The *Mercury* received new lightweight streamlined cars from the postwar orders from Budd and Pullman-Standard.

Although Chicago–Detroit service fell to 17 trains in 1945, it was up to 20 by January 1947. Among the returnees was the westbound *New England Wolverine*, which had been terminating at Detroit. A newcomer was the eastbound *Advance Wolverine*.

This proved to be the apex of postwar Detroit service, which fell to 15 trains in 1948. The *Advance Wolverine* became the *Michigan*, a name that had disappeared in 1939. A year later, Chicago–Detroit service had fallen to 15 trains. The *New England Wolverine* once again began terminating at Detroit. The eastbound *Michigan* ended, but another train named the *Michigan* replaced the *New England Wolverine* from Detroit to Chicago. The *Wolverine* shifted to La Salle Street Station, and the *Twilight Limited* returned to Central Station.

The New York Central had 14 Chicago–Detroit trains in the early 1950s. The *Motor City Special* was all-Pullman through 1948, the last such train on the Detroit line. The *Twilight Limited* carried coaches and parlor cars. Observation-parlors ran on the *Twilight Limited*, *Mercury*, and the *Michigan*, all of which also had diners. The *Mercury* and the *Michigan* carried tavern-lounge coaches. Another pair of Chicago–Detroit trains had coaches.

Trains operating beyond Detroit included the *Wolverine*, which served New York, and the *North Shore Limited* with sleepers and coaches from New York and Toronto to Chicago, and a Boston to Chicago sleeper. All except the Toronto cars returned on the *New York Special*. The Toronto cars returned on the *Canadian–Niagara*, which also conveyed coaches and a sleeper-lounge from Chicago to Buffalo and a sleeper to Bay City.

Nos. 346/323 ended April 26, 1953, and the *Michigan* lost its tavern-lounge coach. The *Wolverine* began handling a New York to San Francisco sleeper in 1952, interchanged at Chicago with the Union Pacific's *City of San Francisco*. The car went back to the Chicago line in 1955 and briefly returned to the *Wolverine* in 1957.

The New York Central assigned the experimental *Aerotrain* to Chicago–Detroit service in May 1956. The *Great Lakes Aerotrain* averaged 224 passengers per trip and operated nonstop between Chicago and Detroit in 4 hours, 20 minutes. But it was removed in July.

Despite objections by the Illinois Central, the New York Central moved its Detroit trains to La Salle Street Station on January 18, 1957, which also ended passenger service at the former Michigan Central stations in Gary and Hammond.

The New York Central began scaling back on-board services in 1956. The *Chicago Mercury* lost its observation-parlor and, the next year, its parlor cars. The *Wolverine* lost its observation cars in 1957. The westbound *Chicago Mercury* was combined with the *Wolverine* on February 16, 1958, and the *New York Special* ended between Chicago and Detroit.

The eastbound *Chicago Mercury* regained its observation-parlor, but the train ended April 27, 1958. The *New York Special* resumed originating at Chicago, operating on the former *Mercury*'s schedule. The Chicago–Bay City sleepers also ended in 1958.

Limiteds in Twilight

There were five Chicago–Detroit round trips in 1960. The *Wolverine* had New York sleepers and coaches and a Chicago–Boston sleeper that interchanged at Buffalo with the *New England States*. The *New York Special/North Shore Limited* terminated at Buffalo and carried Chicago–New York sleepers and coaches. The *North Shore Limited* and the *Canadian–Niagara* carried Chicago–Toronto sleepers and coaches interchanged with the Canadian Pacific at Detroit. The *Michigan* and *Twilight Limited* had parlors and dining cars. The *Twilight Limited* also featured a tavern-lounge and observation-parlor. The *Motor City Special* had a lounge-sleeper that offered buffet breakfast service, but it was gone by 1961.

The *Canadian–Niagara* became simply the *Canadian* in April 1961. The *Canadian* and *North Shore Limited* lost their Toronto cars in October 1961. The *Wolverine* lost its Boston sleepers in January 1963. The *North Shore Limited* and the *Canadian* became the *World's Fair Special* in 1964, offering Chicago–New York sleepers and coaches, and a lounge-buffet between Chicago and Buffalo. A meal-a-mat car provided food service. The *World's Fair Special* was discontinued April 25, 1965, ending overnight service between Chicago and Buffalo via Detroit. The *New York Special* lost its New York coaches April 24, 1966.

The westbound *Motor City Special* ended October 30, 1966, in favor of a train originating at Buffalo. The eastbound *Motor City Special* lost its sleepers. The *Michigan* had lost its sleeper as parlor car and in fall 1966 its diner-lounge was downgraded to a buffet-lounge serving light meals. The *Twilight Limited* also lost its sleeper as parlor car. All trains lost their names on December 3, 1967.

Penn Central notified the Interstate Commerce Commission on May 17, 1968, of its intent to discontinue the westbound former *Twilight Limited* west of Ann Arbor, Mich. The railroad said patronage had fallen from an average of 102.6 per day in 1966 to 57.5 in 1968. Although the train made an operating profit of $128,536 in 1966, Penn Central said it lost $15,390 in 1967, due to the loss of a railway post office on August 4, 1967. Fifteen witnesses at public hearings opposed curtailing operation of the train, saying it was the most convenient evening train from Detroit to Chicago. But the ICC cited the financial losses and declining ridership in granting Penn Central's petition on October 15, 1968.

The former *Wolverine* lost its Chicago–New York sleepers in May 1968, but continued to handle Detroit–New York sleepers and a Chicago–Detroit diner-lounge. The eastbound former *Twilight Limited* and the former *Michigan* still had diner-lounge cars, but Penn Central ended dining service in favor of food-bar coaches in late 1969 on all but the former *Twilight Limited*, which lost its diner-lounge in 1970.

Another era ended October 26, 1968, when Chicago to Detroit No. 366 became the last former New York Central passenger train to depart La Salle Street Station. The next day all former New York Central trains began using Union Station, the Pennsylvania Railroad's longtime Chicago home.

The former *New York Special* ended November 30, 1969. Penn Central said it averaged fewer than 50 passengers a day and was losing $141,000 a year, largely due to the loss of mail and express revenue. Four of the six surviving Chicago–Detroit trains served Buffalo.

Penn Central sought to end all Detroit line trains in its March 10, 1970, petition to the Interstate Commerce Commission. Nos. 355/356 carried 45,974 revenue passengers in 1969, an average of 81.2 per trip westbound and 51.8 eastbound. Most patrons boarded or disembarked at Chicago. The former *Wolverine* carried 86,481 revenue passengers in 1969. Nos. 351/52 carried 44,289. On all four trains, just over half the passengers traveled between Chicago and Detroit. There was a significant through business with between 35.7 percent (No. 351) and 18.7 percent (No. 52) of the patrons boarding or disembarking beyond Buffalo. The former *Wolverine* lost $291,169 in 1969. Nos. 52/351 lost $255,720, and Nos. 355/356 lost $165,773. The ICC approved the discontinuance of Nos. 52/351 but required the four other trains be kept for six months.

Amtrak retained the former *Wolverine*, and No. 356 (former *Twilight Limited*) and No. 355 (formerly the *Michigan*). Nos. 351/52 began their last runs on April 30, 1971. The Detroit–Buffalo leg of the former *Wolverine* also was discontinued.

Chicago–Cairo, Ill.

The Chicago, Indiana & Southern opened January 21, 1906, between Indiana Harbor and Danville, Ill. Passenger service began with one Chicago–Danville round trip, but expanded to two round trips within a year and three round trips on June 28, 1908. One pair of trains had a through sleeper between Chicago and Cairo, Ill.

One pairing had begun operating by 1913 between Chicago and Kentland in Newton County, but these trains were gone within two years. Service then was two Chicago–Danville round trips, increasing to three on September 26, 1926, one of which was the *Egyptian* with Chicago–Cairo through coaches and sleepers.

One pairing began terminating at Sheff in Benton County on June 29, 1930, but within a year these trains were terminating at Kentland. The train began terminating at Schneider on September 27, 1931, and was discontinued December 13, 1931. A pairing that departed Chicago in late afternoon and Danville in early morning ended July 1, 1933. These trains did not connect with Big Four passenger trains operating south of Danville.

The *Egyptian* became a Chicago–Cairo train in 1934, operating on an overnight schedule. It began terminating at Harrisburg, Ill., on June 22, 1941, offering a sleeper, usually a 10-section, three double bedroom heavyweight, through the late 1950s. The *Egyptian* ended April 28, 1957.

Vincennes Branch

The Cairo & Vincennes began service February 2, 1873, with a Vincennes–Cairo round trip and a mixed train between Vincennes and Carmi, Ill. "The Great Short Line Route to and from the Southwest" operated one Vincennes–Cairo round trip during most of the 1870s.

The Paris & Danville began service between Danville and Vincennes on April 30, 1876, using the C&V between Vincennes and St. Francisville, Ill. After the Wabash gained control of the C&V in 1881, trains operated in shuttle fashion between Vincennes and St. Francisville, ranging from three to five round trips. After Wabash control ended May 27, 1885, four trains operated between Vincennes and Cairo.

Now known as the Cairo, Vincennes & Chicago, the road interchanged a Cairo–Indianapolis sleeper with the Indianapolis & Vincennes and Cairo–Chicago sleepers with the Chicago & Eastern Illinois. By 1887 one pairing was terminating at Mt. Carmel, Ill. One train operated Vincennes to Danville, and another ran from Danville to Vincennes to Cairo. The Indianapolis–Cairo sleepers ended in 1887, and service fell to one Vincennes–Mt. Carmel round trip.

After the Big Four began operating the CV&C in 1889, service became three Vincennes–St. Francisville round trips, one of which was extended in the early 1890s to Mt. Carmel and then to Cairo. Service had expanded by 1895 to two Vincennes–Cairo round trips and five Vincennes–St. Francisville round trips. By the late 1890s, service had fallen to nine trains. In 1899 the Big Four eliminated all but the Vincennes–St. Francisville trains. From four round trips in 1900, service increased to six round trips by 1907.

Service had fallen to two round trips by 1915, but briefly increased to three round trips during World War I and again in 1923. Two years later, one round trip became a mixed train. Service fell to two round trips on September 26, 1926, and to one round trip (a mixed train) on July 1, 1928. Passenger service ended October 1, 1928.

Evansville–Mt. Carmel, Ill.

Big Four subsidiary Evansville, Mt. Carmel & Northern opened this 35-mile branch on July 1, 1911, offering two round trips between Evansville and Mt. Carmel. By 1913, through coaches had begun operating between Chicago and Evansville. One round trip had been extended to Danville by 1915. In less than two years, all four trains served Danville. During World War I, service fell to an Evansville–Mt. Carmel round trip. The Chicago coaches ended.

The Chicago through coaches resumed in 1925. An Evansville–Indianapolis sleeper interchanged with St. Louis line trains at Paris, Ill. Service increased to two Evansville–Mt. Carmel round trips. Chicago–Evansville sleepers began September 26, 1926. Two of the four trains on the Evansville branch served Danville, but within a year all four trains operated Evansville–Mt. Carmel. Service had fallen to one round trip by 1929.

Service expanded February 22, 1931, when an Evansville–Danville train began. By April these trains were operating between Evansville and Paris as the *Crescent City Special* and carrying a diner-lounge. The Evansville–Mt. Carmel train became the *Egyptian*. The *Crescent City Special* lost its dining car in May 1932 and was discontinued March 18, 1939. The Chicago–Evansville sleepers ended in the late 1930s, and the Evansville–Indianapolis sleepers ended August 24, 1941. The Evansville–Chicago coaches survived until Evansville–Mt. Carmel passenger service ended in January 1942.

Evansville–Terre Haute

The Big Four acquired this line in 1920 from the Chicago & Eastern Illinois. The Big Four usually offered four passenger trains, Terre Haute–Evansville and Evansville–Washington (in Daviess County).

The Evansville–Washington trains ended in April 1922, but returned June 21, 1925. By then all four trains operated with motor cars. The Evansville–Washington trains ended for good on September 28, 1930. The Terre Haute–Evansville trains had been downgraded to mixed trains by 1933. Passenger service ended in December 1941.

Indianapolis–Peoria, Ill.

The Indianapolis, Bloomington & Western opened October 1, 1869, and operated three round trips between Indianapolis and Peoria. By late 1874 one pairing had begun terminating at Champaign, Ill. The IB&W hosted a Cincinnati–Kansas City through coach, a sleeper between Indianapolis and Galesburg, Ill., and an Omaha to Cincinnati coach.

Reorganized as the Indiana, Bloomington & Western on August 9, 1879, all six trains operated between Indianapolis and Peoria. The Kansas City and Omaha through coaches were gone, but a sleeper operated between Cincinnati and Rock Island, Ill. All through cars were gone by January 1879 when service reverted to two Indianapolis–Peoria round trips and an Indianapolis–Champaign round trip.

The IB&W leased the Indiana, Decatur & Springfield on January 1, 1882, and began operating three round trips between Indianapolis and Decatur, Ill., two of them mixed trains. All six IB&W trains now served Peoria. The IB&W also operated a commuter train between Indianapolis and Indianola, 2 miles west of downtown Indianapolis.

After an extension to Springfield, Ohio, opened in 1883, all Peoria passenger trains began operating between Peoria and Columbus, Ohio. Sleepers operated between Indianapolis and Creston, Iowa; Indianapolis and Chicago; Indianapolis and Burlington, Iowa; and Columbus and Peoria. Through coaches operated between Columbus and Kansas City, Indianapolis and Burlington, Columbus and Decatur, and Indianapolis and Sandusky, Ohio.

The IB&W entered receivership in 1886 and relinquished the ID&S (which later became part of the B&O) in 1887. Although all through sleepers had ended by January 1887, the IB&W operated through coaches between Indianapolis and Youngstown, Ohio; Sandusky, Ohio; Burlington, Iowa; and Lincoln, Neb.; between Peoria and Cincinnati; and between Columbus, Ohio, and Kansas City.

By the late 1880s, the six Peoria trains were operating between Peoria and Springfield, Ohio. The only through coaches operated between Springfield and Creston, Iowa. Sleepers operated between Indianapolis and Cleveland and Columbus. An Indianapolis–Champaign round trip had begun.

The road was reorganized on February 20, 1890, as the Peoria & Eastern and operated by the Big Four. Although leased by the New York Central in 1930, the P&E maintained a headquarters in Indianapolis and its own board of directors. The Big Four reduced passenger service to five Springfield–Peoria trains. All through cars had ended by January 1892. Springfield–Peoria service fell to one round trip with another pairing operating between Peoria and New Castle. Other trains operated Indianapolis–Champaign and Indianapolis–Peoria.

The Peoria–New Castle trains began terminating at Indianapolis by January 1895. Within two years service had fallen to one Indianapolis–Peoria round trip. Service had increased to eight trains by late 1901. Three trains operated between Peoria and Springfield. Other trains operated Springfield to Champaign, Indianapolis to Peoria, Champaign to Indianapolis, Peoria to Lynn, Ind., in Randolph County, and Lynn to Indianapolis. Within two years Peoria–Springfield service had reverted to two round trips, one of which operated on an overnight schedule. Another round trip operated between Indianapolis and Champaign.

Passenger service had peaked by January 1906 at 10 trains. Peoria–Springfield, Ohio, service had fallen to three trains. Other trains operated Indianapolis–Springfield, Indianapolis–Lynn, Indianapolis–Peoria, and Indianapolis–Champaign. The Indianapolis–Peoria trains had vestibule coaches and buffet-parlor cars.

By January 1908, service had fallen to eight trains with the cancellation of the Indianapolis–Lynn trains. Trains no longer operated between Peoria and Springfield by 1911. The P&E had six trains between Indianapolis and Peoria and two trains between Indianapolis and Champaign. Sleepers operated from Indianapolis to Peoria and Peoria to Cincinnati.

In 1914, the P&E briefly carried a sleeper from French Lick, Ind., to New York that operated on Wednesday and Saturday and interchanged with the Monon at Crawfordsville. The P&E named this train the *Knickerbocker Special* and also advertised sleepers between Peoria and Cincinnati. The P&E had named five of its six Indianapolis–Peoria trains by 1917: *Knickerbocker Special, Day Express/Indiana–Ohio Local,* and *Night Express.*

The Indianapolis–Champaign trains disappeared during World War I but had returned by January 1920. The *Day Express,* which now carried that name in both directions, offered

Few New York Central locals survived into the 1950s, but those that did were pulled by GP7 diesel locomotives. This local was near Clarks Hill between Indianapolis and Lafayette circa 1954. Photo by John Stuckey; John Fuller collection.

broiler-buffet parlor cars. Within a year, the *Knickerbocker Special* name had been applied to its previously unnamed westbound counterpart. The Indianapolis–Champaign trains ended November 20, 1921.

By the end of the 1920s, the *Knickerbocker Special* had become the *Peoria Special/Indianapolis Special* and begun conveying sleepers between Peoria and New York and coaches and a broiler-buffet parlor between Peoria and Indianapolis. The Peoria–New York sleepers ended in April 1930.

The *Indianapolis Special* and westbound *Day Express* ended west of Champaign on July 10, 1931, and between Indianapolis and Champaign on July 3, 1932. A New York to Peoria sleeper conveyed by the *Southwestern Limited* to Indianapolis operated on the *Peoria Special*. The New York to Peoria sleeper ended in April 1933. At the same time the *Peoria Special/Day Express* lost their parlor cars and became all-coach trains. Sleepers still operated between Peoria and Indianapolis on the *Night Express*. Sleepers as parlor cars had been reinstated on the daylight trains by January 1935.

By the mid-1940s, all four Peoria–Indianapolis trains had lost their names and become coaches only. The overnight trains ended June 19, 1949. The daylight trains were rescheduled to depart each terminal at 7 A.M. The trains became the *Peorian* in April 1950 and began operating with GP7 passenger diesels on December 21, 1950. The *Peorian* carried 47,301 passengers in 1951, an average of 64 passengers each way per day. The train's primary business was mail and express, typically operating with three head-end cars and an air-conditioned coach.

To avoid the expense of using the Peoria & Pekin Union to reach Peoria Union Station, the *Peorian* began originating at Pekin on June 26, 1955, and was rescheduled to leave Indianapolis at 7 A.M. and return in early evening. The *Peorian* became the *Corn Belt Special* on October 30, 1955. Citing annual losses of $175,000, the New York Central ended the *Corn Belt Special* on October 14, 1957. It was the New York Central's last Indiana branch line passenger train.

For many years the P&E operated shuttle service between downtown Indianapolis and the Indianapolis Motor Speedway. On Indianapolis 500 race day, the P&E assembled four trains of 10 cars with a locomotive at each end. Service began at 2:15 A.M. and operated every 30 minutes (every 15 minutes during peak times).

Indianapolis–Springfield, Ohio

The Indiana, Bloomington & Western opened the route in 1883 and operated passenger trains between Springfield and Peoria, Ill. Acquired by the Big Four on February 22, 1890, trains operated between Springfield and Peoria for another two decades before being curtailed to Indianapolis–Springfield. One of the two pairings had ended by 1915, but service expanded to two round trips on April 9, 1916, when the *Chicago–Columbus Special/Columbus–Chicago Special* debuted between its namesake cities. The *Specials* ended in 1918.

Four mixed trains began operation in 1919, two between Springfield and Lynn in Randolph County, and two between Lynn and Belt Road in Indianapolis. The Belt Road trains stopped carrying passengers in September 1925. The Springfield–Lynn trains ceased passenger service on April 25, 1926.

The Indianapolis–Springfield trains had been assigned motor cars by the early 1930s. The train left Indianapolis at 8:15 A.M. daily except Sunday, reaching Springfield by early afternoon after serving 27 intermediate stations. It departed for Indianapolis nearly 3 hours later, arriving at 8 P.M. Aside from the westbound train operating an hour earlier beginning in the mid-1930s, the service changed little through the late 1940s.

Passenger service ended in Ohio on October 20, 1949. The trains operated between Indianapolis and Crete in Randolph County until passenger service ended in January 1950.

"Three I" Line

The Indiana, Illinois & Iowa first published schedules showing passenger service between Streator, Ill., and North Judson in LaPorte County in the July 1883 *Traveler's Official Railway Guide.* Initially offering two round trips, service had been halved by 1884. The Three I opened to Knox in Starke County on November 21, 1886.

The Three I began passenger service between Wheatfield in Porter County and New Buffalo, Mich., on December 15, 1889, using a future C&EI branch to La Crosse in LaPorte County and a future Pere Marquette branch between there and New Buffalo. This service, which briefly increased to two round trips in 1892–93, ended in December 1894.

A Streator–South Bend round trip began December 16, 1894. Within two years, service had expanded to include a round trip between South Bend and Kankakee, Ill. A train that began operating in 1897 from South Bend to Knox had no scheduled return. This train was extended to Kankakee in 1898. South Bend–Streator service became two round trips in 1899. A round trip also operated between South Bend and Kankakee, and another train ran from South Bend to North Judson.

The Three I leased the St. Joseph, South Bend & Southern between 1900 and 1905 and operated two round trips between South Bend and St. Joseph, Mich. Effective July 15, 1900, the South Bend to North Judson train began operating in both directions, and a mixed train began operating round trip between Streator and North Judson. That December one South Bend–St. Joseph pairing began operating between St. Joseph and Streator. South Bend–Streator service fell to one round trip.

Although the map in the January 1902 *Official Guide of the Railways* showed the Three I reaching East Clinton, Ill., passenger trains never operated west of Zearing, Ill. The Three I operated a train from Zearing to St. Joseph, but the return train terminated at Streator. Other service included trains operating South Bend–Streator, South Bend–St. Joseph, South Bend–Kankakee, South Bend to St. Joseph, South Bend to Zearing, and St. Joseph to North Judson.

Passenger service shrank from 11 to 10 trains in 1902, although South Bend–St. Joseph service increased to two round trips. Other trains operated Kankakee–South Bend, Zearing to St. Joseph, St. Joseph to Streator, South Bend to Zearing, and Streator to South Bend.

Service had fallen to six trains by January 1904, operating South Bend–St. Joseph, St. Joseph–Streator, St. Joseph to Streator, and Zearing to South Bend. After the Michigan Central took over the St. Joseph line in 1905, the South Bend–St. Joseph trains began operating between South Bend and Kankakee. The train to Streator that had originated at St. Joseph now originated at South Bend.

By 1911, the South Bend–Kankakee trains had begun terminating at Walkerton in southwest St. Joseph County. These trains were gone within two years. This dropped service to four trains: South Bend–Streator, South Bend to Streator, and Zearing to South Bend.

A Vanderbilt satellite since the 1890s, the Three I was folded into the Chicago, Indiana & Southern in 1906 and merged with the New York Central in 1915. The South Bend–Walkerton trains returned in 1916 for the purpose of conveying the Lake Erie & Western (later Nickel Plate) South Bend–Indianapolis trains. This service increased to two round trips in 1920, but ended in 1921.

The Zearing to South Bend train began originating at Streator on January 18, 1926. All four trains on the former Three I in Indiana now operated between South Bend and Streator. Motor cars had been assigned to all trains by 1928.

South Bend–Streator Nos. 2 and 3 ended June 29, 1930, and Nos. 1 and 4 began operating between South Bend and Kankakee. Downgraded to mixed trains in the late 1930s, passenger service ended March 18, 1940.

South Bend–St. Joseph, Mich.

The 37-mile Indiana & Lake Michigan opened between South Bend and St. Joseph, Mich., on August 4, 1890. Operated for eight years by Pennsylvania Railroad partner Terre Haute & Indianapolis, the line was sold at foreclosure on December 8, 1898, and acquired the next month by the St. Joseph, South Bend & Southern. The road offered three round trips between South Bend and St. Joseph until leased on February 23, 1900, by the Indiana, Illinois & Iowa, which cut service to two round trips on July 15, 1900.

After the road's lease was transferred to the Michigan Central on February 15, 1905, service reverted to three South Bend–St. Joseph round trips. Service had fallen to two round trips by 1909 and one round trip in 1918, which terminated at Benton Harbor, Mich. The trains ended between South Bend and Galien, Mich., on April 27, 1924.

Lake Station–Joliet, Ill.

The Joliet & Northern Indiana opened a 45-mile Chicago bypass in 1854 between a junction with the Michigan Central at Lake Station in Lake County and Joliet, Ill. The Michigan Central leased the line in September 1854. Scheduled passenger service was not shown in the *Traveler's Official Railway Guide* until January 1872. Initially two round trips, service had fallen to one round trip within a year, but increased to three round trips by 1874, which remained through the late 1880s when one pairing ended.

Service remained two round trips until one round trip ended in 1915. Trains had begun terminating at East Gary five years earlier. Passenger service ended in May 1925. The last schedule allotted more than 4 hours to make the 44.4-mile journey between East Gary and Joliet.

Northwest Indiana Branches

Commuter trains operated for about a year on two branches in Northwest Indiana. Beginning May 30, 1909, 26 trains operated on a 2.4-mile branch between Hammond and Gibson. Eighteen trains used a 9.5-mile branch between Gibson and Gary. This service last appeared in *The Official Guide of the Railways* in May 1910.

South Bend–Niles, Mich.

The Michigan Central began service July 23, 1871, on this 11.6-mile branch between South Bend and Niles, Mich. Initially three round trips, service had increased to four round trips by 1874, but fallen to two round trips by 1877. One pairing ended in 1918. The Michigan Central faced fierce competition from the parallel Southern Michigan, an interurban railway with 10 South Bend–St. Joseph trains and 9 Niles–South Bend trains.

The Michigan Central in 1921 began a round trip between downtown South Bend and the University of Notre Dame. This service ended in February 1922. The South Bend–Niles round trip ended April 27, 1924.

Goshen–Sturgis, Mich.

The Canada & St. Louis opened a 29-mile branch between Goshen in Elkhart County and Sturgis, Mich., on December 29, 1888. The line was subsequently extended 7 miles to Findley, Mich., to connect with a Michigan Central branch to Battle Creek, Mich. The Lake Shore & Michigan Southern leased the line on February 1, 1890.

Passenger service was two round trips between Goshen and Findley through 1899 when all four trains began operating to Battle Creek. Within two years the trains had resumed terminating at Findley, but by 1905 all trains again served Battle Creek. One pairing became mixed trains in 1921, and all four trains began operating triweekly the next year. The mixed train became a regular passenger train in 1923, but the frequency of service remained unchanged. One round trip ended September 26, 1926, and the surviving pair became mixed trains. Passenger service in Indiana ended May 11, 1931.

Elkhart–Grand Rapids, Mich.

The Lake Shore & Michigan Southern began passenger service between Elkhart and Grand Rapids, Mich., in 1897. Trains used the Old Road between Elkhart and White Pigeon and reached Grand Rapids via Kalamazoo. Service was two round trips through 1911 when it increased to three round trips. The third pairing ended in 1917, and service fell to one round trip on November 16, 1930. A motor car was assigned to the route in 1932. Passenger service ended December 27, 1937.

Fort Wayne–Jackson, Mich.

The Fort Wayne, Jackson & Saginaw began service in 1870 between Fort Wayne and Jackson, Mich., with three round trips, one of which was a mixed train. Service had fallen to two round trips by 1872. Three years later, trains were operating Jackson to Fort Wayne and Angola (in Steuben County) to Jackson. These trains subsequently become an Angola–Jackson round trip, but within two years these trains were operating between Fort Wayne and Jackson.

Service peaked in the early 1880s at seven trains; five trains operated between Fort Wayne and Jackson and trains operated Jackson to Waterloo in DeKalb County and Waterloo to Fort Wayne. By 1885 service had fallen to two Fort Wayne–Jackson round trips. Service increased to three round trips in 1903, fell back to two round trips in 1917, increased to three in 1920, fell back to two in 1922, and increased to three again on May 28, 1923. One pairing was assigned a motor car in 1928.

One round trip was curtailed to Fort Wayne–Hillside, Mich., on April 27, 1930, and discontinued November 16, 1930. Another pairing ended September 25, 1932. The trains began terminating at Hillside, Mich., on September 25, 1938, and made their final runs in July 1943.

Martinsville–Fairland

The Martinsville & Franklin opened May 17, 1853. Operations ended in 1858, but were revived following the Civil War by Gen. Ambrose Burnside. An extension later opened to

Fairland in Shelby County. Service was two round trips that briefly terminated at Gosport in Owen County in the late 1860s (via the Indianapolis & Vincennes).

Service had fallen to one round trip by 1876 and did not increase to two round trips until 1901. Another pairing had begun between Fairland and Franklin by 1913. The Fairland–Franklin leg ended in 1917, and a year later this train began operating from Franklin to Martinsville. But in 1919 operations reverted to Franklin–Fairland. The train regained its return leg in 1920, lost it a year later, and regained it in 1924.

The Fairland–Franklin train ended September 1, 1924. Its counterpart ended November 30, 1924, only to resume in December 1925. All of the trains on the branch became mixed trains in 1928. One Martinsville–Fairland round trip ended September 30, 1928. Also discontinued was the Franklin–Fairland train. Fairland–Martinsville passenger service ended in December 1941.

Greensburg–Columbus

The 26-mile branch opened April 10, 1884. The Big Four began passenger service May 4, 1884, with two round trips between Columbus and Greensburg in Decatur County. An additional train had begun operating from Columbus to Greensburg by 1911. A return leg was added within two years, giving the branch six passenger trains. Service fell to five trains in 1917, three trains from Columbus to Greensburg and two returning.

Four of the five trains had become mixed trains by the late 1920s. Service fell to one round trip on February 27, 1928. Passenger service ended in December 1941.

Louisville, Ky.–Benton Harbor, Mich.

The longest New York Central passenger route in Indiana (303 miles) began as the Warsaw, Goshen & White Pigeon, which opened August 17, 1870, between Goshen in Elkhart County and Warsaw in Kosciusko County. Following an 1871 reorganization, the road became the Cincinnati, Wabash & Michigan. It published its first schedules in the *Traveler's Official Railway Guide* in March 1873, two round trips between Elkhart and Wabash, one a mixed train. After opening to Anderson on May 21, 1876, the CW&M offered two round trips between Anderson and Elkhart.

The Vernon, Greensburg & Rushville opened in July 1881 between Greensburg and North Vernon. Passenger service was two round trips.

The CW&M opened an extension to Niles, Mich., on September 3, 1882. Service was four trains: Niles–Anderson and Anderson–Elkhart. The CW&M opened to Benton Harbor on November 12, 1882. The six passenger trains all served Anderson and terminated at Benton Harbor, Niles, or Wabash. Eighteen days later, the Anderson–Niles round trip ended.

The CW&M had increased Anderson–Benton Harbor service to two round trips and added a Benton Harbor–Elkhart mixed train by early 1885. Another pairing operated Anderson–Wabash. On the south end, service was one round trip between North Vernon and Rushville.

By the late 1880s the CW&M had begun through cars between Indianapolis and Benton Harbor (interchanged with the Big Four at Anderson). The CW&M adopted the slogan "The Elkhart Line" and featured a deer head logo. However, service had fallen to six trains, four between Anderson and Benton Harbor and two between Anderson and Elkhart. The south end had four trains: Greensburg–Rushville and North Vernon–Rushville. By 1890 service had increased to six trains, a North Vernon–Rushville round trip and two pairings between Greensburg and North Vernon.

The CW&M operated all six of its trains between Anderson and Benton Harbor. All carried Indianapolis–Benton Harbor coaches. Four trains carried parlor cars between the two cities. Sleepers and parlor cars also operated between Indianapolis and Grand Rapids. Within a year, though, one pairing had been curtailed to Elkhart–Anderson.

After the CW&M opened between Anderson and Rushville on May 3, 1891, the Elkhart–Anderson trains began operating between Benton Harbor and North Vernon. The Big Four had taken stock control of the CW&M in 1890 and leased the company, along with the Vernon, Greensburg & Rushville, on July 1, 1891.

The Big Four made the route a busy passenger artery, although many trains operated over relatively short distances and most trains terminated at Anderson. Within two years the Big Four operated 15 passenger trains including round trips operating North Vernon–Anderson, North Vernon–Benton Harbor, Anderson–Warsaw, Anderson–Benton Harbor, Benton Harbor–Warsaw, and Elkhart–Benton Harbor. Other trains operated North Vernon to Wabash, Anderson to North Vernon, and Wabash to Anderson. Through coaches operated between Indianapolis and Benton Harbor and Indianapolis and Warsaw.

Passenger service to Louisville began August 18, 1895, with three round trips between there and Greensburg. Trains used the Ohio & Mississippi (later B&O) between North Vernon and Louisville. The Big Four began operating through coaches and sleepers between Chicago and Louisville on October 20, 1895, and coaches between Louisville and Indianapolis. One Louisville–Greensburg round trip began serving Anderson.

Louisville service had fallen to two round trips by the late 1890s, and the Chicago–Louisville coaches had ended. The Louisville–North Vernon trains were extended to Benton Harbor in 1897. Overall the line hosted 12 trains a day, none of which served any one station. Through coaches had begun operating between Cincinnati and Anderson by 1901. The Indianapolis–Wabash coaches were extended to Elkhart.

Service had fallen to 10 trains by 1903, and the Cincinnati coaches were gone. Service was back to 12 trains by 1907 by which time the Elkhart–Benton Harbor trains were mixed trains. Four trains operated between Elkhart and Anderson, and two trains between Anderson and Greensburg. Louisville service was unchanged, but the Indianapolis–Louisville through coaches were gone.

The Big Four had cut service to 10 trains by 1915. Trains operated Louisville–Benton Harbor, Louisville–Greensburg, North Vernon–Anderson, Anderson–Elkhart, and Elkhart–Benton Harbor. Through coaches operated between Benton Harbor and Indianapolis and Louisville. Sleepers and parlor cars operated between Chicago and Louisville.

The New York Central line between Louisville and Benton Harbor, Mich., was the road's longest in Indiana and at one time one of its busiest branch line passenger routes. The fireman of No. 4802, an Alco 4-6-2, checks on passengers boarding at Jonesboro, Ind. Jay Williams collection.

By World War I, eight of the trains had names: *Lake Special, Northern Express/Southern Express, Michigan Express/Indianapolis Express,* and *Chicago Night Special/Louisville Night Special.* Service fell to eight trains in 1918: Louisville–Elkhart, North Vernon–Greensburg, Greensburg–Anderson, and Anderson–Benton Harbor. The Louisville trains resumed serving Benton Harbor in 1919. The Elkhart–Benton Harbor mixed trains ended in 1920 in favor of an Elkhart–Anderson pairing that carried Indianapolis through coaches. All eight of the route's trains served Anderson.

The North Vernon–Anderson trains began terminating at Rushville and became mixed trains on December 5, 1926. The Louisville–Benton Harbor trains began terminating at Elkhart, although the southbound train resumed originating in Benton Harbor in 1927. A motor car operating between North Vernon and Anderson replaced the mixed trains, but this service ended June 3, 1928. The Louisville–Anderson trains ended January 2, 1928, and service fell to four trains: Anderson–Benton Harbor and Louisville–Elkhart. The latter carried Chicago–Louisville parlor cars.

The Big Four extended the Benton Harbor to Anderson train to Louisville in 1930 and resumed operating through coaches between Indianapolis and Benton Harbor. The Louisville to Elkhart train began running through to South Bend. Another train originated at South Bend and terminated at Anderson.

By 1933, four trains operated between South Bend and Anderson and one pair between Anderson and Louisville. Passenger service to Benton Harbor had ended. One South Bend–Anderson round trip, the *Winona,* operated with a motor car. The *Michigan Express/Indianapolis Express* offered through coaches between Indianapolis and South Bend.

South Bend service had ended by 1938. Service to Louisville ended April 27, 1941, when the *Louisville Express/Chicago Express* began terminating at Greensburg. Service ended between Anderson and Greensburg on August 24, 1941. The *Indianapolis Express/Michigan Express* names were gone by the mid-1940s along with the Indianapolis through coaches. The Anderson–Elkhart trains made their final trips on April 6, 1950.

Whitewater Valley Branch

The Whitewater Valley Railroad opened July 21, 1868, between Hagerstown in Wayne County and Harrison, Ohio. The line was later extended to Valley Junction (near Cleves, Ohio) on the Indianapolis, Cincinnati & Lafayette, which leased the Whitewater Valley through 1871. Four trains operated between Hagerstown and Cincinnati, and two trains ran between Cincinnati and Brookville in Franklin County. Through cars operated to Chicago and Indianapolis.

After regaining its independence, the Whitewater Valley operated two Cincinnati–Hagerstown round trips. By the early 1880s service had fallen to one pairing between Hagerstown and Harrison. The line also hosted through cars between Fort Wayne and Cincinnati, interchanged at Connersville with the Lake Erie & Western.

Service expanded after the Big Four began operating the line in 1890. Six trains operated between Hagerstown and Valley Junction, four of which served Cincinnati. By 1892 four of these trains had begun terminating at Cambridge City in Wayne County. Trains operated Hagerstown–Cincinnati, Cambridge City–Valley Junction, and Cambridge City–Cincinnati. The latter had begun operating to Hagerstown by 1894, and within two years the Cambridge City–Valley Junction trains were gone.

All four Whitewater Valley passenger trains had begun terminating at Valley Junction by 1899. When Fort Wayne–Cincinnati service began, service increased to six trains, two of which terminated at Connersville. Two trains served Cincinnati. Four trains operated to Cincinnati by 1905 with pairings operating Hagerstown–Cincinnati, Hagerstown–Valley Junction, and Cincinnati–Cambridge City. Service to Hagerstown had begun to diminish by 1909.

Although service had increased to 10 trains, only 2 served Hagerstown. Other service included round trips operating Connersville–Beesons (in Wayne County) and Cincinnati–Brookville, two trains from Cincinnati to Cambridge City, a train from Cambridge City to Cincinnati, and a train from Connersville to Cincinnati.

Within two years service had fallen to eight trains with the loss of the Connersville–Beesons trains. A schedule restructuring two years later resulted in three round trips between Hagerstown and Connersville, two round trips between Connersville and Cincinnati, and one round trip between Cincinnati and Brookville.

Connersville–Hagerstown service fell to one round trip during World War I. The Connersville–Cincinnati trains and the Brookville–Cincinnati trains operated on a commuter schedule. The Brookville trains began operating Cincinnati–Harrison, Ohio, in 1922. One of the two Connersville–Cincinnati pairings ended August 28, 1927. By the end of the decade, the other Connersville–Cincinnati pairing had begun terminating at Valley Junction.

All four Whitewater Valley trains became mixed trains in 1930 with the southbound leg of the Hagerstown pairing having been extended to Valley Junction. Service to Hagerstown ended in March 1931. The Cincinnati–Valley Junction mixed trains became regular passenger trains that were extended to Cincinnati and later used a motor car. These trains ended April 2, 1933.

Aurora–Lawrenceburg Junction

The Indianapolis, Cincinnati & Lafayette built a bypass around Lawrenceburg in 1875, shortening the Cincinnati–Indianapolis route by 6 miles and reducing the original line to a branch. The Big Four operated a Cincinnati–Lawrenceburg round trip in the early 1880s, but most passenger service shuttled between Lawrenceburg and Lawrenceburg Junction. From three round trips in the late 1870s, service on the 3-mile branch had increased to 13 trains by early 1887.

A subsidiary company, the Cincinnati & Southern Ohio River, was incorporated April 30, 1887, to extend the branch 3 miles to Aurora. Sixteen passenger trains operated between Aurora and Lawrenceburg. By the early 1890s, 25 trains used the branch, with one train originating at Cincinnati and terminating at Aurora. Other trains operated Aurora–Lawrenceburg, Aurora–Lawrenceburg Junction, and Lawrenceburg–Lawrenceburg Junction. Service had increased to 26 trains by the late 1890s, but no trains operated beyond Lawrenceburg Junction.

This changed in 1899 when six trains began operating between Cincinnati and Aurora. Although these trains were gone two years later, the branch hosted 22 passenger trains, all but one of which operated between Aurora and Lawrenceburg Junction. Service fell incrementally, and by 1908 the branch had 18 trains.

Within two years the Big Four had reinstated direct service to Cincinnati. Five trains operated from Cincinnati to Aurora and four trains from Aurora to Cincinnati. One train operated from Cincinnati to Lawrenceburg. Twelve other trains operated Lawrenceburg Junction–Aurora, Lawrenceburg Junction–Lawrenceburg, or Lawrenceburg–Aurora.

The Cincinnati service again proved to be short-lived. By January 1914 service had fallen to 17 trains between Lawrenceburg Junction and Aurora. Four years later service had fallen to 12 trains. Service fell to 10 trains on April 29, 1923, which remained until passenger service ended January 1, 1931.

Pennsylvania Railroad

To Grand
Rapids

To Chicago

Gary

80

South
Bend

Lagrange

Butler

LaCrosse

Plymouth

Fort
Wayne

To Pittsburgh

Effner

Logansport

65

Ridgeville

Frankfort

69

To Columbus

Muncie

74

Indianapolis

To Pittsburgh,
Dayton,
Columbus

Greencastle

Richmond

To Peoria

70

To Cincinnati

Terre
Haute

74

To St. Louis

Columbus

Worthington

65

Madison

Vincennes

64

Evansville

Louisville

PENNSYLVANIA
RAILROAD

A dying man summoned his sons to his bedside to divide his stocks and bonds, but kept some Pennsylvania Railroad shares under his pillow. Asked what he planned to do with them, the man replied, "Keep them, my boys. Pennsylvania shares are negotiable everywhere."

Such was the mystique of the "Standard Railroad of the World," which carried more passengers than any other railroad. "Do not think of the Pennsylvania Railroad as a business enterprise. Think of it as a nation," wrote *Fortune* magazine. Conservative and efficient, the Pennsy never suffered a bankruptcy and avoided the financial manipulations that plagued other railroads.

The Pennsylvania's 1,556 miles in Indiana (21 percent of the state's mileage) were second only to the New York Central. Four components made up the Pennsylvania in Indiana: the Panhandle (56 percent), the Vandalia (30 percent), Pittsburgh, Fort Wayne & Chicago (10 percent), and Grand Rapids & Indiana (4 percent). The Pennsylvania acquired these companies after the Civil War and absorbed most of them on March 1, 1920.

Chicago Line

The Ohio & Indiana began construction in 1852 between Fort Wayne and Crestline, Ohio. The first train arrived to a tumultuous welcome in Fort Wayne on November 15, 1854. The Fort Wayne & Chicago began service in January 1856 between Fort Wayne and Columbia City in Whitley County. Passengers paid 80 cents for the 90-minute ride in an open freight car jury-rigged with boards for seating.

With financial backing from the Pennsylvania, the O&I, Ohio & Pittsburgh and FtW&C merged on July 29, 1856, to form the Pittsburgh, Fort Wayne & Chicago, which had reached Plymouth by late 1856. The Cincinnati, Peru & Chicago (later Nickel Plate) linked Plymouth with LaPorte, and a connection with the Michigan Southern (later New York Central). This created a Chicago–Pittsburgh route, but different gauges and high fees created an unfavorable situation. Pennsylvania president J. Edgar Thomson became chief engineer of the PFtW&C to ensure its completion to Chicago. Service to Chicago began January 1, 1859.

Following the Civil War, the PFtW&C offered four Chicago–Pittsburgh round trips. Through sleeper service between Chicago and Jersey City, N.J., began in January 1868, via

Allentown, Pa. Locals operated Chicago–Valparaiso, Fort Wayne–Plymouth, Fort Wayne–Lima, Ohio, and Chicago–Crestline.

The *New York and Chicago Limited* began October 31, 1881, on a 26-hour schedule. Its well-heeled clientele demanded a better class of service, and the Pennsylvania assured them, "You pay for exclusive privileges and get them. You pay for strictly first-class accommodations and get them. You pay for first-class meals and get them."

For the remainder of the 1880s, the Chicago line hosted eight Chicago–Pittsburgh expresses. Through trains often carried different names east and west of Pittsburgh. The *New York and Chicago Limited* ran as the *Limited Express* west of Pittsburgh until the late 1880s when it became the *Pennsylvania Limited.* By the late 1890s, nine expresses operated between Chicago and Pittsburgh. Commuter service had begun between Chicago and East Chicago by early 1894 with one round trip, reaching four round trips by 1900 and six round trips by 1902. A year later, 12 trains operated between Chicago and Clarke Junction (Gary) and 8 between Chicago and Kennedy Avenue (East Chicago).

The *Pennsylvania Limited* received new equipment on January 15, 1898, painted Brewster green below the windows and a yellowish-cream above, which gave the train the nickname "Yellow Kid." The consist included a parlor-smoking-library car, a dining car, three drawing room sleepers, and an observation car.

The competition between the Pennsylvania and New York Central intensified when both introduced 20-hour Chicago–New York luxury trains on June 15, 1902. The *Pennsylvania Special* accepted passengers between Chicago and Pittsburgh only at Fort Wayne and Englewood, Ill. With its Tuscan red livery and swift schedule, it became known as the "Red Ripper."

Chicago–Pittsburgh service was 11 trains. Passengers paid extra fare on the *Pennsylvania Special*, *Pennsylvania Limited*, and the eastbound *Atlantic Express*. The *Pennsylvania Special* was suspended February 1, 1903, due to congestion in Pittsburgh. The Pennsylvania spent $100 million to reduce grades and straighten curves on its Chicago–New York mainline. That same year, the *Seashore Limited* became the *Manhattan Limited*, a name that lasted through 1971.

The *Pennsylvania Special* resumed June 11, 1905, on an 18-hour schedule. The first westbound run was 26 minutes late into Crestline due to a hotbox near Mansfield, Ohio. Engineer Jerry McCarthy ran the 131 miles to Fort Wayne in 115 minutes, hitting a record 127 mph near Elida, Ohio, and arriving in Fort Wayne two minutes early.

The Chicago–Valparaiso commuter trains ended in 1906, but returned in 1907 as Sunday-only service. Resuming daily operation in 1909, service was four trains by the early 1920s.

The November 27, 1910, opening of the North River tunnels and Pennsylvania Station enabled the Pennsylvania to serve New York City. Previously, trains had terminated at Jersey City. Chicago–Pittsburgh service had grown to 15 expresses. Fifteen commuter trains operated between Clarke Junction and Chicago. There were 22 trains between Chicago and East Chicago.

Regards to Broadway

To prevent confusion with the *Pennsylvania Limited*, the Pennsylvania renamed the *Pennsylvania Special* the *Broadway Limited* on November 24, 1912. By some accounts the Pennsy intended the name to be *Broad Way Limited* in honor of the multiple track mainline between New York and Pittsburgh. But newspaper stories spelled it *Broadway*, leading many to erroneously believe the train was named for New York's theater district.

For more than 60 years, the *Broadway Limited* and New York Central's *Twentieth Century Limited* vied to be America's foremost passenger train. Both were all-Pullman and extra-fare trains, personifying the epitome of luxury travel. Every change in equipment, schedules, or on-board services of one train was immediately matched by the other.

Nine expresses operated between Chicago and Pittsburgh by 1912. The Pennsylvania gained a third Chicago–New York all-Pullman pairing when it renamed the westbound *Chicago Limited* the *Manhattan Limited*. Its eastbound counterpart already was all-Pullman. The *Broadway Limited* was suspended between December 1, 1917, and May 25, 1919, due to World War I travel restrictions. The Chicago line had 11 eastbound and 7 westbound expresses, but northwest Indiana commuter service was declining. There were 15 trains, all of which ended July 20, 1919.

The Pennsylvania called its premium trains the Blue Ribbon Fleet. As the 1920s began, 8 of the 29 Chicago–Pittsburgh trains carried no coaches. The fourth all-Pullman Chicago–New York pairing was the *Metropolitan Express/New York Day Express*. Another extra-fare train, the eastbound *Gotham Limited*, began July 16, 1922. The *Chicagoan*, an extra-fare all-Pullman train, began operating westbound a year later. In response to the launch of the Baltimore & Ohio's *Capitol Limited*, the *Broadway Limited* gained a Washington cousin, the *Washington–Broadway*, on May 6, 1923, with equipment and service identical to the New York section, but operating as a separate train.

Local service sharply diminished in the 1920s beginning with the April 26, 1925, discontinuance of the Chicago–Plymouth trains and the downgrading of the Chicago–Crestline locals to mixed trains. Chicago–Pittsburgh service stood at 10 round trips in the mid-1920s. The *Chicagoan* had ended, and the *Washington–Broadway* became the *Liberty Limited* on September 27, 1925. The Pennsylvania restructured service September 25, 1927, by creating mixed trains operating Chicago to Crestline, Crestline to Fort Wayne, and Fort Wayne to Chicago. The net effect was a loss of two trains. The Chicago–Crestline and Crestline–Fort Wayne trains ended April 28, 1929, in favor of Chicago–Fort Wayne mixed trains, which ended November 25, 1934.

The *Broadway Limited* began losing ground to the *Twentieth Century Limited* in the 1920s. Arguably a peer of the *Century* in every aspect, the *Broadway* could not match the *Century*'s cachet as *the* train of the leaders of finance, fashion, and professional celebrity. Each train had a loyal clientele, but Pennsy management lamented that the patron who upgraded from the *Manhattan Limited* or *Pennsylvania Limited* to the *Broadway Limited* was soon lost to the *Century* in the belief that his or her personal prestige was enhanced by being on the *Century*.

The *Broadway Limited* averaged 13.5 passengers per trip eastbound and 16.3 westbound in July 1939 compared with 50.1 and 71.4, respectively, for the *Twentieth Century Limited*. On August 5, 1939, the *Broadway* departed New York with no passengers, picked up two at Philadelphia, and served but two the remainder of the way. An early 1930s schedule tightening to 16.5 hours and the assignment of new equipment in 1938 did little to bolster patronage. Some Pennsylvania executives suggested the *Broadway Limited* had outlived its usefulness.

However, H. E. Newcomer, vice president of the western region, argued persuasively that giving up the *Broadway Limited* would be conceding defeat to the New York Central and would have negative consequences for the rest of the fleet. "The Pennsylvania would be immediately recognized as being in the same class as the Erie and the B&O," Newcommer wrote in a 1941 memorandum.

Modernizing the Fleet

Inauguration of the eastbound *Rainbow* and westbound *Red Knight* on April 28, 1929, boosted Chicago–Pittsburgh service to 22 trains. Four additional trains operated between Chicago and Fort Wayne, including the Chicago–Florida *Southland* and a pair of mixed trains. The *Golden Arrow* began September 29, 1929, as an extra-fare all-Pullman train operating on a 20-hour, 50-minute schedule, similar to the *Broadway Limited* and *Pennsylvania Limited*. Chicago–Pittsburgh service had reached 24 trains by early 1930. Another new service was the Chicago–Pittsburgh *Valley Special* (via Youngstown and Niles, Ohio), which passed through Indiana on the eastbound *Gotham Limited* and westbound *Pennsylvania Limited*.

Pennsylvania passenger revenue fell from $134 million in 1929 to $60 million in 1934, a 55 percent decline. The New York Central surpassed the Pennsylvania in passenger traffic in 1929. The Pennsylvania responded by consolidating trains, ending extra fare on all but the *Broadway Limited*, assigning coaches to some all-Pullman trains, tightening schedules, and air-conditioning much of the long-distance fleet. To lessen the cost of their rivalry, the Pennsylvania and New York Central agreed to remove such costly features as club cars and observation cars from all but a few headliner trains.

But their boldest move was a joint announcement on March 9, 1937, of plans to redesign and streamline their respective flagship trains and to jointly negotiate with Pullman for new equipment. The Pennsylvania hired industrial designer Raymond Loewy, whose work over the next 18 years redefined the Pennsylvania's passenger image. The Pennsy labeled its new equipment the Fleet of Modernism.

The *Broadway Limited* became an all–private room train on June 15, 1938. Unlike the *Twentieth Century Limited*, the *Broadway Limited* had rebuilt heavyweights (diners and head-end cars). The Central assigned most of its new lightweight equipment to the *Century*, but the Pennsy spread its new equipment among the *Broadway Limited*, the *General*, *Liberty Limited*, and *Spirit of St. Louis*.

Loewy's use of bright colors (white, orange, and lemon) with touches of black accenting contrasted with the dark grays and browns favored by the Central's designer, Henry Dreyfuss. Loewy gave car exteriors a livery of two shades of Tuscan red with black roofs and gold pinstripes. A typical *Broadway Limited* consist included a baggage-mail car, midtrain lounge, four sleepers, diner, and observation car. The *General* and *Liberty Limited* had similar consists but without a barbershop and secretary.

The Pennsylvania debuted the all-coach Chicago–New York *Trail Blazer* on July 28, 1939, the same day the New York Central began its all-coach *Pacemaker*. The *Trail Blazer* featured an observation car, four coaches, and twin-unit diner (the Pennsylvania's first), offering dinner for 75 cents and breakfast for 25 cents. The *Trail Blazer* averaged 524 passengers per day in each direction during its first two months of operation and carried more than 300,000 annually during its first two years of operation. The *Pacemaker* carried just over 280,000 passengers annually.

The *General* began April 25, 1937, as a heavyweight sleeper and coach train second in prestige only to the *Broadway Limited*. Created with the idea of competing with the New York Central, the *General*, as Pennsy management had feared, also diverted traffic from the *Broadway Limited*. Nonetheless, Pennsylvania management was pleased enough with the *General* to create a second eastbound section, the *Advance General*, in June 1940. Renamed the *Admiral* in April 1941, it acquired a westbound counterpart in April 1942 when the westbound *General* became all-Pullman.

The Pennsylvania and Wabash launched Chicago–Detroit service April 2, 1933, with four trains a day. The *Detroit Arrow* and *Mid-City Express* used the Pennsylvania between Chicago and Fort Wayne. A third Detroit train, the *Red Bird*, began April 27, 1941. The morning train to Chicago became the *Chicago Arrow*.

World War II travel demands boosted traffic, but strained the fleet. Passenger revenue doubled from $89 million in 1941 to a record $260 million in 1944. The Pennsylvania owned 15 percent of the nation's passenger car fleet and experienced the highest volume of passenger traffic during the war. But the service quality was inconsistent, thousands had to stand, and trains often ran late.

Patronage skyrocketed to 13 billion in 1944, more than four times what the Pennsylvania carried in 1939 and 88 percent higher than the record set in 1920. Trains routinely operated in extra sections, many of which were not shown in published schedules. The *Liberty Limited* acquired an all-Pullman section in August 1943 that did not accept passengers between Englewood and Baltimore and that operated through early 1947. Extra fare on the

In 1942 the Pennsylvania introduced the T1, a sleek and stylish 4-4-4-4 steam locomotive designed by Raymond Loewy. Fifty of these locomotives were built between 1945 and 1946, but they proved to be unsatisfactory due to poor traction. Jay Williams collection.

Broadway Limited ended in February 1943. The Pennsylvania had 22 scheduled Chicago departures and 18 arrivals in November 1944, including 28 Chicago–Pittsburgh trains.

Postwar Optimism

The Pennsylvania hoped that new lightweight equipment and more powerful locomotives would enable it to operate longer trains with more spacious accommodations following the war. Pennsy employees received refresher courses in providing courteous service. The Pennsy began taking bids in December 1945 for 129 sleepers, 21 coaches, 11 twin-unit diners, 6 regular diners, 4 baggage-dorms, and 2 coach-lounges. The Pennsy shops rebuilt hundreds of cars with exteriors repainted one shade of Tuscan red.

The Pennsylvania was slow to embrace diesel locomotives because 40 percent of its revenue came from hauling coal and because steam locomotives were cheaper to operate. Although the Pennsylvania received its first passenger diesels in September 1945, it would be the late 1940s until the use of diesels for passenger service became widespread.

A newly equipped *Broadway Limited* debuted March 15, 1949, six months after the New York Central had reequipped the *Twentieth Century Limited*. The *General* had been all-Pullman westbound since 1942, but shortly after the war became all-Pullman eastbound on a 16-hour schedule. Departing an hour ahead of the *Broadway Limited*, the *General* handled its running mate's overflow traffic.

Assigned lightweight equipment in April 1949, the *Liberty Limited* still trailed the B&O's *Capitol Limited*. Once the faster train, the *Liberty Limited* held its own until 1929 when the *Capitol Limited* began bypassing Pittsburgh to avoid a backup move into the Pittsburgh station. Hindering the *Liberty Limited* were street running in York, Pa., and swapping the steam locomotive for a GG1 electric engine at Baltimore.

The *Liberty Limited* could not match the *Capitol Limited*'s air of courtly service similar to a fine hotel. *Liberty Limited* patrons feasted on broiled pork chops, but the *Capitol Limited* served crab imperial. Some travelers felt the *Liberty Limited*'s ambience was aloof in comparison with the southern hospitality of the *Capitol Limited*.

The Pennsylvania began transcontinental sleeper service on March 31, 1946. West of Chicago, the New York–Los Angeles sleepers used the Overland Route (Chicago & North Western/Union Pacific) and the Santa Fe. Sleepers between New York/Washington and San Francisco used the Overland route with Southern Pacific conveying the cars to Oakland.

A New York–San Francisco service conducted jointly with the New York Central began April 1, 1946. West of Chicago, it used the Burlington, the Denver & Rio Grande Western, and the Western Pacific. A New York–Los Angeles sleeper via the Golden State Route (Rock Island/Southern Pacific) began June 2, 1946, operating every other day.

The transcontinental sleepers attracted 200 passengers a day in each direction, but there were complaints about long layovers and transfers between terminals in Chicago. An elderly woman was marooned in her room for several hours in a rail yard without heat or food. The New York–Los Angeles and New York–San Francisco sleepers had an occupancy rate of 70 percent, but the Washington sleepers averaged 3.7 passengers per trip. The Washington–San Francisco sleepers lasted less than two years, and Washington–Los Angeles serviced ended in 1949.

With three New York–Los Angeles routes, the Pennsylvania had too many sleepers for the market. The Golden State Route sleepers ended July 10, 1951. The remaining transcontinental sleepers ended October 27, 1957.

By the early 1950s, the Pennsylvania's passenger service was losing $71 million a year under the Interstate Commerce Commission formula, the nation's largest passenger deficit. In January 1949, the Pennsylvania had 26 Chicago–Pittsburgh trains, 6 Chicago–Detroit trains, and 4 Valparaiso commuter trains. Detroit service shrank to 4 trains with the January 23, 1949, discontinuance of the *Chicago Arrow* and eastbound *Red Bird*. The westbound *Red Bird* became the *Detroit Arrow*. Detroit service ended September 25, 1949, reportedly because the Pennsylvania was reluctant to invest in new equipment for a short split-profit route.

Chicago to Pittsburgh No. 34 ended east of Crestline on April 24, ending eastbound passenger service via Youngstown, Ohio. Westbound service via Youngstown ended December 16. At year's end there were 22 Chicago–Pittsburgh trains. The *General* and *Trail Blazer* merged September 30, 1951, although they operated independently during peak travel periods with the *General* all-Pullman and the *Trail Blazer* all-coaches.

The Pennsylvania's passenger losses eased to $43 million in 1954, but beginning in 1952, passenger revenue dropped every year in the 1950s except for 1956. The Pennsylvania had 18 Chicago–Pittsburgh trains by 1955. The *Manhattan Limited* had consolidated with the *Golden Triangle*, but otherwise service was largely what it had been for the previous three years.

A major restructuring of April 29, 1956, shrank Chicago–Pittsburgh service to 14 trains. The *Pennsylvania Limited* became a local and consolidated with the *Gotham Limited*. The westbound *Admiral* became a local east of Pittsburgh. The *Liberty Limited* lost its sleeper-observation cars and ended October 27, 1957, its Chicago–Washington cars transferred to the *General*.

One bright spot was the *Broadway Limited* overtaking the *Twentieth Century Limited*. As both observed their golden anniversaries in 1952, the *Broadway Limited* was 30 minutes faster than the *Century*, which ran on a 16.5-hour schedule. The *Broadway* had begun besting the *Century* in patronage by 1954. Recognizing it had the better track, the Pennsylvania cut the *Broadway Limited*'s running time to 15.5 hours eastbound and 15.75 hours westbound, its fastest schedules ever.

But the defining moment that enabled the *Broadway Limited* to gain the upper hand occurred August 4, 1957, when the Central temporarily combined the *Century* and the *Commodore Vanderbilt*, giving the *Century* its first coaches. Celebrities deserted the *Century* in droves for the *Broadway Limited*, which gained an additional 13,000 patrons, a 14 percent increase. Seizing the moment, the Pennsylvania tidied up the *Broadway Limited*'s equipment, added new entrees to the dining car menu, and launched a marketing campaign.

A 1958 recession dropped the Pennsylvania's passenger revenue by $18 million, but the passenger deficit also fell by $20 million. Nonetheless, the Pennsylvania continued to whittle away service. The westbound *Admiral* ended east of Pittsburgh in February 1958 and west of there on October 26, 1958, reducing Chicago–Pittsburgh service to 11 trains.

Benign Neglect

The eastbound *Fort Pitt* was curtailed to Gary to Fort Wayne operation on February 14, 1960. The coach-only train, which departed Gary at 5 A.M., ended in July. Chicago–Pittsburgh service was 10 trains, a frequency of operation that changed little over the next 10 years. But the quality of the service changed greatly.

The Pennsylvania began deferring maintenance as a cost-cutting move in 1957, and by 1961 the fleet was showing the effects of neglect. Although not as aggressive as the New York Central or the Erie Lackawanna in ending passenger service during the 1960s, the Pennsylvania was unable to maintain its physical plant and simply wore itself out.

There were a few shining moments. Spurred by the success of its service to the 1964 New York World's Fair, the Pennsylvania mounted one last marketing campaign in 1965 on behalf of the *Broadway Limited*, which had not been advertised since 1962. An advertisement poked mild fun at the airlines, saying the train had better food and more legroom and was a more relaxing way to travel.

Through 1967, the *Broadway Limited* and the *General* had covered their direct costs by $145,000 (*Broadway Limited*) and $205,000 (*General*) while earning $3.1 million and $3.7 million, respectively. But the Pennsylvania convinced state regulators that it could save $1.4 million annually by consolidating them.

The "old" *Broadway Limited*, America's last all-Pullman passenger train, departed for the final time on December 12, 1967. The "new" *Broadway Limited* had the numbers, consist, and schedule of the *General*. The "old" *Broadway* had stopped between Chicago and Pittsburgh only at Englewood, Fort Wayne, and Crestline. The "new" *Broadway* made six additional stops including Gary and Plymouth in both directions and Warsaw westbound.

Sleeping car service west of Pittsburgh on the westbound *Pennsylvania Limited* and in both directions on the *Manhattan Limited* ended March 3, 1968. Also that day, the *Broadway Limited* lost its Chicago–Washington sleepers and coaches.

Penn Central told the Interstate Commerce Commission in March that it would discontinue the *Admiral* (No. 50) and *Fort Pitt* (No. 53) on April 21. The *Admiral* and *Fort Pitt* had been mail and express workhorses, but most of their mail had been diverted to mail and express trains. Mail had accounted for 61 percent of 1967 revenue of the *Admiral* and 70 percent of the *Fort Pitt*. The trains had been profitable until losing most of their mail and express business. Penn Central argued that without mail and express, Nos. 50/53 were unprofitable and patronage was steadily falling due to travelers' increasing preference to drive or fly. Some in Indiana used the *Admiral* as a commuter train because it left Chicago at 6:30 P.M. and stopped at Gary, Valparaiso, Plymouth, and Warsaw.

Critics accused Penn Central of diverting mail and express in order to weaken the performance of its passenger trains to justify service reductions. Penn Central said it acted in response to the desire of the Post Office Department to dispatch mail once a day from major mail-generating cities and to remove bulk mail from passenger trains. The ICC reached no conclusion as to whether Penn Central had acted on its own or at the prompting of the post office. But the commission acknowledged that diverting mail and express to freight trains had weakened the passenger trains and may have prevented them from covering their operating costs. In its August 15, 1968, order to keep the *Admiral* and *Fort Pitt* operating for nine months, the ICC found "a significant public demand for the service."

Only two trains in America were still all-Pullman in 1967. In December, the Pennsylvania's *Broadway Limited* would be the last of the two to gain coaches. The train with observation sleeper "Tower View" is at Englewood, Ill., on August 29. Photo by Dave McKay.

Penn Central was back before the ICC on June 30, 1969, in another effort to extinguish Nos. 50/53, again claiming declining patronage and financial losses. Although some of the 84 people who opposed the discontinuance accused Penn Central of deliberately downgrading service, the ICC disagreed. But the ICC's order of November 25, 1969, allowing Penn Central to discontinue both trains, was stayed four days later by a federal judge in Pittsburgh.

Penn Central told the ICC on March 10, 1970, it would end the remainder of passenger service on the former Pennsylvania between Chicago and Harrisburg, Pa., except the Valparaiso commuter trains. The *Broadway Limited* was still a formidable train with a baggage car, two coaches, two lounge cars (one a coach lounge), twin-unit diner, and four sleepers. The *Manhattan Limited* and *Pennsylvania Limited* had one or two coaches, a snack-bar coach, and various head-end cars. The *Pennsylvania Limited* had a Chicago to New York sleeper.

The ICC noted that collectively the six trains carried 548,469 revenue passengers and 106,580 non-revenue passengers in 1969, of which 37.1 percent boarded at Pittsburgh or points west and 43.2 percent detrained between Pittsburgh and Chicago (an average of 500 per day). The commission said if these trains ended, 283,000 of the 1969 passengers could not have completed their journey.

The ICC decided on September 22, 1970, that because the *Manhattan Limited* had the highest operating loss in 1969 and generally the lowest patronage, it could be discontinued, but the *Broadway Limited* and *Pennsylvania Limited* would continue for six months. A federal judge in Pittsburgh stayed the ICC order and the Rail Passenger Service Act of 1970, which created Amtrak, froze the nation's rail passenger network in place until May 1, 1971. Amtrak announced in March 1971 that the *Broadway Limited* would be its sole Chicago–New York train. The *Manhattan Limited*, *Pennsylvania Limited*, *Admiral*, and the former *Fort Pitt* began their final runs on April 30, 1971.

St. Louis Line

The Terre Haute & Richmond opened February 16, 1852, between Terre Haute and Indianapolis, and became the Terre Haute & Indianapolis on March 6, 1865. The Indiana Central opened between Indianapolis and New Paris, Ohio, in 1853. Ten years later, an extension opened from New Paris to Bradford, Ohio, creating an Indianapolis–Columbus, Ohio, route. The St. Louis, Vandalia & Terre Haute (Vandalia Road) formed in 1865. The TH&I agreed in 1868 to lease the Vandalia, which opened April 26, 1870, between St. Louis and Terre Haute.

Following the Civil War, the TH&I operated four Indianapolis–Terre Haute round trips. The Columbus, Chicago & Indianapolis had one Indianapolis–Richmond round trip and three Indianapolis–Columbus round trips, two of which operated via Piqua, Ohio. The third went through Dayton, Ohio. There were three round trips between Richmond and Xenia, Ohio, via Dayton. Through sleepers operated between St. Louis and New York, and between St. Louis and Cincinnati and Louisville.

Indianapolis–St. Louis service had grown to four round trips by the early 1880s with the Piqua route the preferred path for Indianapolis–Columbus expresses. By the late 1880s, the Richmond–Xenia trains had begun serving Indianapolis, which meant that 14 trains a day operated between Indianapolis and Richmond.

In the early 1890s, the Pennsylvania had four St. Louis–Columbus round trips, all via Piqua. Another train operated from St. Louis to Indianapolis. Locals operated between Indianapolis and Terre Haute, Indianapolis and Effingham, Ill., and Indianapolis and Richmond. The *Day Express* and the *Night Express/Fast Line* had St. Louis–Columbus sleepers.

The *Pennsylvania Special* originated at Indianapolis and ran through to Baltimore and Washington. Its westbound counterpart was the *Western Express*. The premier westbound train was the *St. Louis Special*, which had sleepers for St. Louis from New York and Columbus. The *St. Louis and Cincinnati Express* and the *Atlantic Express* were first-class-only trains.

Indianapolis–St. Louis service had increased to five round trips by the late 1890s. No. 20, the former *Atlantic Express*, was an all-vestibule train from St. Louis to New York. Three of the five St. Louis line round trips carried St. Louis–New York sleepers. Sleepers also operated between St. Louis and Washington, and Indianapolis and Evansville, via a connection with the Evansville & Terre Haute (later C&EI [Chicago & Eastern Illinois]) at Terre Haute. A local operated on a spur that came off the mainline at Seelyville east of Terre Haute and terminated at Harmony in Clay County.

Service increased in 1900 to six Indianapolis–St. Louis round trips and 17 trains between Indianapolis and Columbus, 9 of them going via Piqua. Six trains carried sleepers between St. Louis and New York. Two trains had St. Louis–Washington sleepers. Locals operated Indianapolis–Effingham and Indianapolis–Richmond. Another local briefly operated between Indianapolis and Bradford, Ohio.

The *St. Louis Limited/New York Limited* were all-Pullman and had a dining car, library-smoking car, and an observation car with compartments. St. Louis line service had risen to eight round trips by 1906, a schedule pattern that remained largely unchanged through 1908. Many of these trains carried St. Louis–New York cars. Another premium train debuted November 7, 1909. The *24-Hour New Yorker/24-Hour St. Louis* were extra-fare all-Pullman trains. The Pennsylvania spruced up the *New York Limited/St. Louis Limited*, adding electric lighting and such services as a ladies' maid, stenographer, and barber.

St. Louis line service had fallen to six Indianapolis–St. Louis round trips by 1913. The *24-Hour New Yorker* and *24-Hour St. Louis* names were shortened to *New Yorker/St. Louisan*. The eastbound *Pittsburgh Express* was an extra-fare train from St. Louis to New York. By 1915, the Pennsylvania had seven round trips between St. Louis and Columbus. A miners' train operated between Seelyville and Harmony and locals operated Indianapolis–Effingham and Indianapolis–Columbus. A year later, the Seelyville–Harmony trains were gone.

During World War I, 11 trains operated between St. Louis and Pittsburgh. St. Louis–Boston sleepers were apparently a casualty of wartime travel restrictions and were gone by January 1919. Shortly after the end of the war, St. Louis–Pittsburgh service increased to six round trips. However, local service diminished January 14, 1923, with the discontinuance of Terre Haute to St. Louis No. 807 and Columbus to Indianapolis No. 803.

A New Spirit

The Pennsylvania introduced a new 24-hour "train de luxe," the *American*, on April 26, 1925, between St. Louis and New York. The *American* featured new Pullmans with drawing rooms and compartments, and such services as stenographer, barber, valet, bath for men, and ladies' maid and manicurist. The club car was stocked with periodicals and a writing desk and offered the latest baseball scores and stock market quotations. Telephone service was available while the train was parked at major terminals. The Pennsylvania said the observation car had been designed expressly to accommodate women with its "commodious ladies' lounge and bath."

Midway through the 1920s, the Pennsylvania had six St. Louis–Pittsburgh round trips. But many stations barely saw these trains. Their service was a pair of St. Louis–Indianapolis mixed trains, which made 49 stops eastbound and 51 stops westbound. Locals also operated Indianapolis to Columbus (No. 302) and Terre Haute to Indianapolis (No. 88).

The *American* and the *New Yorker/St. Louisan* had similar equipment, including sleepers, club car, observation car, and diner. The *American* carried coaches, but the *New Yorker/St. Louisan* did not. The *New Yorker/St. Louisan* were renamed the *Spirit of St. Louis* on June 15, 1927, in honor of the airplane that Charles A. Lindbergh piloted on the first nonstop, transatlantic solo flight on May 20–21, 1927.

The St. Louis–New York travel time of the *Spirit of St. Louis* and the *American* was cut to 23 hours in 1930. Air-conditioned cars operated on major east-west trains by 1934 and extra fare was no longer charged on any St. Louis line train. As the 1930s began, the Pennsylvania operated 15 St. Louis–Pittsburgh trains, an Indianapolis–St. Louis round trip, and a local from Terre Haute to Pittsburgh. The *Spirit of St. Louis* carried a St. Louis to Boston sleeper that returned on the *Fast Mail*. An Indianapolis to Evansville sleeper interchanged at Terre Haute with the C&EI.

St. Louis–Pittsburgh service was 12 trains by January 1934. The St. Louis–Boston sleepers were gone, and the *Spirit of St. Louis* was no longer all-Pullman, having been assigned coaches in 1932. By 1936, the *Spirit of St. Louis* flew between St. Louis and New York in just under 21 hours, and by the end of the decade it was on a 20-hour schedule, which would be its fastest.

In the mid-1930s, the Pennsylvania had plans to purchase new lightweight cars for the *Spirit of St. Louis* and *American* and to rebuild the St. Louis route to enable faster operation. But cost considerations forced the Pennsylvania to scale back the track rehabilitation project. The modernized *Spirit of St. Louis* was christened on June 15, 1938. By the late 1930s, the Pennsylvania had 12 St. Louis–Pittsburgh trains, an Indianapolis to Pittsburgh local, and an Indianapolis–St. Louis local that served 38 stations. The locals ended April 28, 1940.

Encouraged by the success of its all-coach *Trail Blazer*, the Pennsylvania on April 27, 1941, created an all-coach St. Louis–New York train, the *Jeffersonian*, which featured rebuilt heavyweight equipment, typically four coaches, a diner, observation car, and a combined passenger-baggage car. One coach operated between St. Louis and Washington. The *Jeffersonian* ran between St. Louis and New York in just over 20 hours.

The *Spirit of St. Louis* reverted to all-Pullman status, operating just minutes apart from the *Jeffersonian*. The addition of the *Jeffersonian* resulted in a net increase of just one train between St. Louis and Pittsburgh because an eastbound train had ended. The *Spirit of St. Louis* began operating in two sections in April 1942. The St. Louis–New York section was all-Pullman with Washington sleepers interchanged at Indianapolis with an Indianapolis–St. Louis section of the *Spirit* that carried Indianapolis–Washington coaches.

The *American* was primarily a St. Louis–New York train with coaches and sleepers and one St. Louis–Washington sleeper. The *Jeffersonian* had coaches between St. Louis and New York/Washington, an Indianapolis–New York coach, a diner, and a buffet coach and broiler coach, all operating between St. Louis and New York. The *St. Louisan* had St. Louis–New

York sleepers, coaches, and diner, St. Louis–Washington sleepers, St. Louis–Pittsburgh sleepers, and a Louisville to Pittsburgh and a New York to Louisville sleeper.

The Indianapolis–Washington section of the *Spirit of St. Louis* ended March 2, 1947, but the *American* and *St. Louisan* continued to handle St. Louis–Washington sleepers. St. Louis to Pittsburgh No. 6 became the *Allegheny* in October 1948. It had sleepers, coaches, and a lounge originating in St. Louis, a diner originating in Indianapolis, and sleepers from St. Louis to Indianapolis and Columbus.

At the end of the 1940s, the Pennsylvania had 13 St. Louis–Pittsburgh trains, 2 of which operated via Piqua. Other trains operated Columbus to St. Louis (via Piqua) and Pittsburgh to Indianapolis. The *Spirit of St. Louis* was reequipped with new lightweight cars in August 1949. The first passenger diesel locomotive on the St. Louis line began service in August 1946.

Southwest Service

The *Sunshine Special*, the first train to operate through St. Louis, debuted July 7, 1946, using the Missouri Pacific to reach Dallas 37.5 hours after leaving New York. The train conveyed sleepers between New York and Houston/Galveston, Dallas, San Antonio, Mexico City, and El Paso, and coaches for Dallas and San Antonio. Other sleepers operated between Washington and Fort Worth. The dining and baggage cars also ran through.

The MoPac soon became disenchanted with the *Sunshine Special* and wanted to limit through operation to sleepers. Patronage had fallen to an average of 18 passengers per day traveling through St. Louis. The *Sunshine Special* began terminating at St. Louis on April 25, 1948. Many Missouri Pacific trains had Eagle in their name and the *Sunshine Special* became the *Texas Eagle* on August 15, 1948. But the Pennsylvania's pride wouldn't allow another railroad's name to grace one of *its* passenger trains, so the *Texas Eagle* became the *Penn Texas* on the Pennsylvania on December 12, 1948.

The Pennsylvania also began interchanging New York–San Antonio and New York–Oklahoma City sleepers with the Frisco/Katy on July 7, 1946. The San Antonio cars were conveyed by the *American* and (west of St. Louis) the *Texas Special*. The Oklahoma City cars used the Frisco's *Meteor*.

Soon after the service began, the Oklahoma City sleepers began terminating at Tulsa. Never well patronized, the Tulsa sleepers ended in late 1949. That same year, the *Texas Special* sleepers began using the *Penn Texas*. The New York–Mexico City sleeper also was short-lived.

The Pennsylvania had 16 St. Louis–Pittsburgh trains in 1950, but service had shrunk to 14 by December 1952. The eastbound *Mail and Express* began originating at Indianapolis on January 28, 1953. Another *Mail and Express* operated from Columbus to Richmond.

The Pennsylvania had appointed a vice president whose duties included reducing the road's passenger deficit. The first significant step in this endeavor reached the St. Louis line on April 25, 1953, when the *Jeffersonian* was discontinued and its coaches were assigned to the *Spirit of St. Louis*. At the same time, the Pennsylvania inaugurated the *Indianapolis Limited*, which featured coaches and sleepers for New York/Washington, and a diner, lounge, and observation car for New York. Other changes included the creation of a Monday-only Richmond–Terre Haute train. These trains ended later in the year in favor of a daily *Mail and Express* round trip between Richmond and Xenia, Ohio.

The *American* was no longer an elite train by the 1950s. Still impressive with its coaches, sleepers, lounge, and diner, the *American*'s schedule too closely approximated the *Penn Texas*, leaving St. Louis two hours ahead of the *Penn Texas*, but beating it to New York by just 15 minutes. The westbound *American* trailed the *Penn Texas* by three hours out of New York and arrived in St. Louis three hours and 40 minutes after the *Penn Texas*.

The *American* ended April 29, 1956, the same day that the eastbound *Mail and Express* began originating at Indianapolis, and Pittsburgh to St. Louis No. 27 began terminating

The through cars between Texas and New York have disappeared, but the *Penn Texas* still makes an impressive sight as it departs St. Louis Union Station on April 2, 1967. Photo by Dave McKay.

at Indianapolis and was renumbered No. 7. This left the *Spirit of St. Louis, Penn Texas, St. Louisan,* and the *Allegheny* between St. Louis and Pittsburgh.

The *Indianapolis Limited* was consolidated with the *Cincinnati Limited* (Cincinnati–New York) east of Columbus on June 24, 1956, and became all-Pullman between Indianapolis and Columbus with sleepers between Indianapolis and New York/Washington and an Indianapolis–New York lounge with six double bedrooms. The New York coaches and the observation car were gone. The *Indianapolis Limited* was running on borrowed time. In its final months, it had coaches from Columbus to Indianapolis, but none eastward. The Washington to Indianapolis sleeper had disappeared. The *Indianapolis Limited* ended October 27, 1957.

The *Spirit of St. Louis* began carrying Indianapolis–New York sleepers, but had lost its St. Louis–Washington sleepers on October 28, 1956. Also that day the Pennsylvania created a new pair of trains named *Mail and Express* that operated via Dayton. No. 14 originated at Indianapolis and ran to Pittsburgh. No. 13 originated at Pittsburgh and terminated at St. Louis. Indianapolis–Pittsburgh *Mail and Express* Nos. 11/12 only carried passengers between Pittsburgh and Richmond, ending passenger service via Piqua from west of Richmond.

Mail and Express Nos. 11/12 ceased handling passengers on June 30, 1957. Also ending that day was a Columbus to Indianapolis train that apparently had been a second section of the *Indianapolis Limited.*

King of a Diminishing Hill

The New York Central reduced its St. Louis–New York service to one round trip in 1958, all but ceding the market to the Pennsylvania. The April 26, 1959, discontinuance of the westbound *St. Louisan* left the Pennsy with only two trains from the Hudson to the Mississippi, the *Penn Texas* and *Spirit of St. Louis*. Eastbound service included the *Penn Texas*, *Spirit of St. Louis*, and *St. Louisan*. Also discontinued were Indianapolis to Pittsburgh No. 14, Pittsburgh to Indianapolis No. 7, and the St. Louis to Pittsburgh *Allegheny*.

The *Penn Texas* through services began lessening with the truncating of the New York–El Paso sleeper to Fort Worth on January 24, 1958. The New York–San Antonio sleepers interchanged with the *Texas Special* ended October 1, 1958. The last Washington through sleeper (serving Fort Worth) ended June 10, 1959. The *Penn Texas* lost the remainder of its through cars when sleepers operating between New York and Houston, San Antonio, and Fort Worth ended June 26, 1961.

The *St. Louisan* lost its St. Louis to Pittsburgh lounge car in April 1964, and in June 1965 the *Penn Texas* lost its Indianapolis–Washington sleepers and Indianapolis–New York lounge cars. The lounge-sleeper on the *Spirit of St. Louis* was curtailed to Indianapolis–New York. The *Spirit of St. Louis* diner stopped operating west of Indianapolis in September 1966 when the St. Louis to New York sleeper on the *St. Louisan* ended. The *St. Louisan* name and its St. Louis to New York coach disappeared in January 1967. The New York coach returned in November, but ended July 7, 1968.

The Pennsylvania twice unsuccessfully sought Interstate Commerce Commission permission to discontinue the *Spirit of St. Louis* in the mid-1960s. The first effort, announced September 25, 1964, to take effect a month later, was denied February 15, 1965. The Pennsylvania said the *Spirit* had covered its operating costs in 1962, 1963, and the first six months of 1964 by, respectively, $659,013, $126,225, and $67,943. However, the Pennsy described the *Spirit*'s financial performance as marginal and argued that the declining patronage was not enough to justify the train's continuance. Witnesses criticized the Pennsylvania for antiquated equipment, unsanitary conditions, and poorly maintained stations. In ordering the *Spirit* kept for another year, the ICC said the *Spirit of St. Louis* offered a useful, not wasteful, service.

A year later, the Pennsylvania tried again to terminate the *Spirit of St. Louis*, saying it had an operating profit of $285,469 in 1964, but lost $151,557 in 1965. However, after the ICC disallowed some terminal expenses, the *Spirit* showed an operating profit of $383,404 for 1965. The *Penn Texas* had operating profits of $954,079 in 1964 and $198,790 in 1965. Between July 1965 and February 1966, the *Spirit* carried an average of 378 per trip westbound and 248 eastbound, a slight decline from the previous discontinuance case. In a decision reached August 15, 1966, the ICC conceded the *Spirit*'s financial performance had been marginal, but ordered it to continue for another year, citing strong patronage and the Pennsylvania's overall good financial health.

Soon after the Penn Central merger, the railroad said it would end the westbound *Penn Texas* (No. 3) and eastbound *Spirit of St. Louis* (No. 30) on May 29, 1968. All four St. Louis–New York trains were losing patronage and had a collective $2.5 million operating loss in 1967. The westbound *Penn Texas* averaged 127.9 passengers per day; the eastbound *Spirit of St. Louis* averaged 187.1. Comparable figures for the eastbound *Penn Texas* and westbound *Spirit of St. Louis* were 211.7 and 237.0, respectively.

Loss of mail and express figured prominently in the declining performance, and several Penn Central employees accused their employer of shifting mail and express to freight trains to weaken the passenger trains financially. The ICC said the shift "may have destroyed the ability of the trains to earn revenues adequate to cover operating expenses." In a decision reached September 24, 1968, the ICC ordered Nos. 3/30 to continue for four months, saying there remained a need for the trains and suggested Penn Central could save money by ending St. Louis–Pittsburgh Nos. 13/32.

Penn Central sought to consolidate Nos. 3/30 and Nos. 4/31 on March 20, 1969. All four trains had 1968 operating losses. Nos. 3/30 lost $833,213 and $967,837, respectively. Nos. 4/31 lost $857,773 and $418,895. The average daily patronage of the westbound *Penn Texas* was 124.3 whereas the eastbound *Spirit of St. Louis* averaged 153.4. On an average day, only 34 people got off No. 30 west of Richmond and 33 got off No. 3.

The ICC agreed Penn Central would likely retain most of the revenue of Nos. 3/30 because displaced passengers would ride Nos. 4/31. The commission said Penn Central trains were consistently dilapidated, dirty, and late, and such comforts as air conditioning, heat, restrooms, water coolers, pillow rental, and reclining seats were often missing or inoperative. Many stations were unmanned or undermanned, and the reservation service was inadequate. Yet the ICC exonerated Penn Central of trying to discourage business. The prevalence of bad conditions was "caused by the railroad's inability to support the trains over the same route in [the] luxury known in the by-gone days of railroad passenger service." Citing Penn Central's precarious financial condition, the ICC drew a distinction between deliberately downgrading service in an effort to make a case for discontinuance and cutting the costs of supporting two round trip passenger trains "where it is highly questionable that the public would support one." The commission on July 11, 1969, approved the discontinuance of Nos. 3/30, but a court challenge kept the trains operating until June 1970. Penn Central subsequently renamed No. 4 *Spirit of St. Louis* and extended operations of the *Spirit's* diner to St. Louis.

In the meantime, Penn Central had removed the Indianapolis–New York sleepers in February 1969 only to restore them in November 1970, when the *Spirit's* dining car again was curtailed to Indianapolis–New York operation. A St. Louis–New York lounge car offered snacks and beverages west of Indianapolis. The *Spirit* also had a St. Louis–New York sleeper and one to three coaches. These equipment assignments remained largely unchanged through 1971.

St. Louis–Pittsburgh Nos. 13/32 typically operated with one coach and one to seven head-end cars. No. 32 operated overnight to Pittsburgh, where it had a convenient connection to the *Pennsylvania Limited*. St. Louis line passenger trains shifted to the faster former New York Central route between Indianapolis and Terre Haute on March 1, 1969.

The *Spirit of St. Louis* and Nos. 13/32 were among the trains Penn Central sought to remove with its March 10, 1970, petition to end virtually all passenger service west of Harrisburg. Penn Central claimed Nos. 13/32 had an operating loss of $1.1 million in 1969, and the *Spirit of St. Louis* lost $1.8 million, the largest operating losses of the 34 trains Penn Central wanted to discontinue.

The westbound *Spirit of St. Louis* was the best patronized of the four trains, carrying 72,862 revenue passengers in 1969. The eastbound *Spirit* handled 47,871 passengers. No. 32 carried 4,485 revenue passengers in 1969, while No. 13 carried 3,235 passengers. Patronage of the *Spirit of St. Louis* became progressively less as the train made its way westward. It typically left Newark with an average of 108 passengers, left Pittsburgh with 54, left Indianapolis with 34, and arrived in St. Louis with an average of 20 on board.

The eastbound *Spirit of St. Louis* left St. Louis with an average of 17 passengers. Patronage steadily increased as the train traveled eastward, arriving in New York with an average of 84 on board. Patronage of No. 32 was typically 10 passengers upon leaving St. Louis and 7 upon arrival at Pittsburgh. No. 13 typically left Pittsburgh on its daylight run with 3 passengers with patronage peaking at 6 leaving Indianapolis.

Although the ICC said the losses claimed by Penn Central were overstated, it concluded that the route needed just one pair of trains. It allowed Penn Central to discontinue Nos. 13/32, but ordered the *Spirit of St. Louis* continued for six months. A court challenge and the coming of Amtrak kept all four trains in operation through April 30, 1971. Amtrak retained the *Spirit of St. Louis*, combining it with a Missouri Pacific train to create a New York/Washington–Kansas City route.

Cincinnati Line

The Cincinnati, Logansport & Chicago opened in 1853 between Richmond and New Castle by which time construction had begun from Logansport to Kokomo. Service began between Logansport and Tabor's Creek, a distance of 2 miles, on July 4, 1855. Two years later, trains were operating between Logansport and Richmond.

Reorganized in 1860 as the Cincinnati & Chicago Airline, the company the next year opened an extension to Valparaiso to connect with the Pittsburgh, Fort Wayne & Chicago. The Valparaiso line was abandoned north of La Crosse in 1865 after a merger with the Chicago & Great Eastern, which had built from La Crosse to Chicago via Crown Point in Lake County.

The Richmond & Miami opened between Richmond and Cincinnati about the time the Richmond–Kokomo route opened. By the late 1860s it was known as the Cincinnati, Richmond & Chicago and was a part of the Cincinnati, Hamilton & Dayton (later B&O). The Pennsylvania leased the line in 1888.

Chicago–Cincinnati travelers needed 18 hours to complete their journey in the 1860s, changing trains at Logansport and Richmond. Known as the Columbus, Chicago & Indiana Central after February 12, 1868, the route had two Richmond–Logansport round trips. Chicago–Cincinnati sleeping cars had begun in 1867.

Through the late 1870s, three round trips operated between Chicago and Logansport, and two operated between Richmond and Logansport. Other trains operated Logansport–Kokomo and Chicago–Crown Point. One train operated through from Cincinnati to Chicago. Three round trips operated between Richmond and Cincinnati.

Direct Cincinnati–Chicago service increased in the early 1880s when two of the three Richmond–Logansport round trips began operating between Chicago and Cincinnati. Trains also operated Chicago–Crown Point, Logansport–Kokomo, and Richmond–Anderson. During much of the 1880s, Chicago–Logansport service was four round trips.

During the 1890s, the Pennsylvania operated two Chicago–Cincinnati round trips. Other trains operated Cincinnati–Logansport, Richmond–Logansport, Chicago–Crown Point, and Logansport–Winamac. Chicago–Logansport service varied between 8 and 10 trains. By the late 19th century, Logansport was a prosperous hub with routes radiating in seven directions. The Panhandle rebuilt the track between Chicago and Logansport for high-speed operation, double-tracking the route by 1906.

Seven routes radiating in all directions made Logansport an important Pennsylvania Railroad passenger hub in Indiana. The platform was a busy place at the turn of the 20th century. Indiana Historical Society, negative C8880.

At the dawn of the 20th century, there were five round trips between Chicago and Logansport, two of which were Chicago–Cincinnati trains. Overnight trains carried sleeping cars between Chicago and Cincinnati and Springfield, Ohio, the latter interchanging with St. Louis line trains at Richmond. Day trains carried buffet-parlor cars. Locals operated Logansport–Richmond and Cincinnati–Logansport.

The Pennsylvania participated in the *Chicago and Florida Special*, a seasonal all-Pullman luxury train operating on a one-night-out 32-hour schedule between Chicago and St. Augustine, Fla., that began January 6, 1902. The train operated six days a week, using three routes between Chicago and Cincinnati. The Pennsylvania hosted the train on Tuesday and Friday.

The *Chicago and Florida Special* lasted just a year, but in 1909 the Louisville & Nashville began a Cincinnati–Jacksonville, Fla., train that advertised connections with the Pennsylvania at Cincinnati. Perhaps prompted by the 1913 debut of the *Royal Palm* via the Big Four (later New York Central), the Pennsylvania began the Chicago–Jacksonville *Southland* on November 1, 1915. Billed as a year-round all-steel train, the *Southland* had through cars from Chicago, Indianapolis (via Louisville), and Grand Rapids, Mich. It featured drawing room sleepers, coaches, diner, and observation car.

South of Cincinnati, the *Southland* traversed the L&N (Cincinnati–Atlanta), Central of Georgia (Atlanta–Macon, Ga.), Georgia Southern & Florida (Macon–Tifton, Ga.), and Atlantic Coast Line (Tifton–Jacksonville). Over the years, the *Southland* used three routes between Chicago and Richmond. Between Logansport and Richmond, the *Southland* traveled either via Kokomo or via Marion and Ridgeville. The third route was via Fort Wayne and Ridgeville. The *Southland* replaced the *Chicago Express/Southern Express*. The Pennsylvania also had a Chicago–Richmond train that had ended by the time the *Southland* appeared.

During World War I, the Pennsylvania operated two Chicago–Cincinnati round trips. The *Cincinnati Daylight Express/Chicago Daylight Express* had parlor cars and a diner. The *Cincinnati Night Express/Chicago Night Express* had sleepers, including drawing room sleepers, and a diner. Other service included two Cincinnati–Logansport round trips and a Cincinnati–Richmond local. The *Southland* was suspended.

Through Service Expansion

The *Southland* returned November 1, 1920, with Chicago–Jacksonville sleepers and a new route south of Atlanta. The train used the Central of Georgia to Albany, Ga., and the Atlantic Coast Line to Jacksonville. The Pennsylvania had begun handling Chicago–Norfolk, Va., sleepers interchanged at Cincinnati with the Norfolk & Western. The *Southland* acquired sleepers between Jacksonville and Indianapolis and Grand Rapids on November 12, 1922, both via Cincinnati. The *Southland* was again a year-round train with sleepers and coaches between Chicago and Jacksonville.

In the mid-1920s the Pennsylvania operated three Chicago–Cincinnati round trips including sleepers operating between Chicago and Winston-Salem, N.C., and Norfolk. Locals operated Richmond–Logansport and Chicago–Winamac. The latter was gone by 1925.

The Winston–Salem sleepers were gone by 1926. Later that year, the *Southland* acquired sleepers between Chicago and Miami, Sarasota, and St. Petersburg. The Indianapolis and Grand Rapids sleepers had ended. By 1930, an observation-sleeper had been assigned between Chicago and St. Petersburg, and a second section of the *Southland* had begun operating between Chicago and Richmond to serve Indiana points bypassed by the Florida train, which now operated via Fort Wayne.

As the 1930s began, the Pennsylvania scheduled two Chicago–Cincinnati round trips via Kokomo. Locals operated Chicago–Richmond and Cincinnati–Richmond. Another train operated from Chicago to Richmond. The *Southland* operated via Fort Wayne for most of the 1930s and had sleepers only for the Florida West Coast cities of St. Petersburg and Sarasota.

Late in the decade, the *Southland* operated for a while as the *New Southland,* the re-naming coinciding with the addition of Chicago–Miami and Detroit–Miami sleepers. The *New Southland* continued to be oriented toward Florida's West Coast. Chicago–Fort Myers sleepers began in 1931 and were gone by 1936.

The Pennsylvania began a Chicago–Logansport local using gas-electric cars in 1931. This train ended in 1934. Another short-lived service was the Chicago–Richmond *Indiana Arrow,* which began September 27, 1936. The *Indiana Arrow* had three sections, terminating at Richmond, Louisville, and Dunkirk, Ind. All three operated as one train between Chicago and Logansport. The *Indiana Arrow* name disappeared April 25, 1937, although the train continued to operate between Logansport and Richmond until September 26, 1937.

The Pennsylvania on April 2, 1933, launched a Chicago–Cincinnati train named the *Union* that operated via Fort Wayne, shifting to the Kokomo route the same day the *Indiana Arrow* was shortened to Richmond–Logansport. This increased Chicago–Cincinnati service via Kokomo to three round trips.

Southland Returns

At the beginning of the 1940s, the Pennsylvania operated four Chicago–Cincinnati round trips. The northbound *Chicago Night Express* operated in two sections, one an Indiana local. A second Chicago–Jacksonville sleeper began in 1940, interchanging at Cincinnati with the *Flamingo,* which used the same route as the *Southland.* The southbound *Union* and the *Chicago Daylight Express* carried a seasonal Chicago–Jacksonville sleeper and sleeper-lounge.

Presidential candidate Wendell Willkie conducted a whistle stop campaign in his home state in 1940. Willkie's train is north of Anderson on the Cincinnati line. Photo by George Witt; John Fuller collection.

For the 1941–42 season, the *Southland* operated in two sections from Cincinnati to Chicago. The *Chicago Night Express* was operating as two sections north of Logansport by January 1942. The *Southland*'s Sarasota sleepers now operated to Fort Myers.

The Jacksonville cars via the *Flamingo* were a war era casualty, and the *Southland* and *Chicago Night Express* ceased operating in two sections. For the 1942–43 season, the *Southland* had sleepers between Chicago and St. Petersburg, Fort Myers, Jacksonville, and Cincinnati. The next year the *Southland* picked up a Chicago–Miami sleeper. At the height of World War II, the Pennsylvania had four Chicago–Cincinnati round trips. But the Norfolk sleepers were suspended during the war.

After the war, the *Southland* operated in two sections, one terminating at Miami and the other at St. Petersburg. Sleepers operated between Chicago and St. Petersburg, Tampa, Jacksonville, and Miami. The *Southland* became solely a Florida West Coast train in 1948, handling sleepers between Chicago and Jacksonville, St. Petersburg, and Sarasota. The *Southland* permanently returned to the Kokomo route on April 30, 1950, although it was a few months before it began serving stations between Logansport and Richmond.

Faced with a staggering passenger deficit in the early 1950s, the Pennsylvania didn't need two pairs of overnight trains between Chicago and Cincinnati. The *Chicago Night Express/Cincinnati Night Express* were curtailed to Richmond–Logansport on June 30, 1952, and discontinued November 2, 1952. The next month, the Pennsy renamed the *Chicago Daylight Express/Cincinnati Daylight Express* the *Red Bird*, a name previously used in Chicago–Detroit service. Cincinnati line service changed little through the mid-1950s. The *Southland*'s St. Petersburg and Sarasota sleepers shifted in late 1957 to the *South Wind* (which operated via Louisville), and the *Southland* became the *Buckeye* on December 13, 1957.

Barely Hanging On

At the close of 1958, the *Red Bird* was coaches only, departing Chicago at midmorning and Cincinnati in early afternoon. The *Union* carried coaches, a diner-lounge and the Norfolk sleeper, departing Cincinnati in early morning and Chicago at midafternoon. The overnight *Buckeye* carried coaches and sleepers. The Norfolk sleepers ended July 26, 1959.

The southbound *Union* and northbound *Red Bird* were curtailed to Richmond–Crown Point on October 25, 1959. The *Red Bird* and *Union* names were dropped from surviving Nos. 70/71, and a café coach replaced the diner-lounge cars. The Richmond–Crown Point trains ended in April 1960. The café coaches of Nos. 70/71 were replaced on April 24, 1960, by a tavern-lounge with limited food service. This car ended in February 1961 in favor of a vendor selling sandwiches and drinks between Logansport and Norwood, Ohio. The *Buckeye* lost its sleepers October 29, 1967.

Less than three months after Penn Central began operations, the *Buckeye* name was dropped and the railroad said it would discontinue the train on May 12, 1968. Penn Central claimed Nos. 70/71 were losing more than $500,000 annually. Nos. 70/71 had two locomotives, two coaches, and seven head-end cars and carried 59,066 revenue passengers in 1966 and 49,333 in 1967, an average of 90.85 (1966) and 70.97 (1967) per day for No. 70 and 73.16 (1966) and 62 (1967) per day for No. 71. Many passengers originated on other railroads beyond Cincinnati or Chicago.

The Interstate Commerce Commission found Nos. 70/71 had been profitable until losing much of their head-end busi-

Picking up and setting out head-end cars along the way was once common practice for passenger trains, but had all but vanished by 1970. A Penn Central crewman hangs a rear marker on a Railway Express Agency car that No. 70 has just picked up at the former Pennsylvania Railroad station in Kokomo. Photo by John Fuller.

ness in September 1967. No. 70 netted $74,291 in 1966, and No. 71 netted $78,673, but the trains lost $231,818 and $207,916, respectively, in 1967. The ICC on September 9, 1968, ordered Penn Central to keep Nos. 70/71 going another year, saying it was too soon after the removal of the head-end business to know what the trains' financial performance would be and that there remained a public need for the service.

Penn Central said it would discontinue the former *Buckeye* (Nos. 67/68) on January 5, 1969, claiming an annual loss of more than $381,000. During the first nine months of 1968, Nos. 67/68 carried fewer than 50 revenue passengers per day. The ICC delayed the discontinuance while it investigated whether Penn Central had given proper notice. The commission decided on February 20, 1969, that it had, and Nos. 67/68 soon ended.

Penn Central made a second attempt to discontinue Nos. 70/71 (now numbered 65/66) on February 1, 1970, saying the trains lost $496,924 in 1968 and $387,707 in 1969. Patronage was on a steady decline, dropping from 59,066 to 36,792 in 1969 when No. 65 carried an average of 53.7 passengers. No. 66 averaged 51.2 passengers per day.

Public hearings attracted 124 witnesses opposed to the removal. Their most common complaint was dirty coaches. Penn Central conductors testified that slow orders covered 20 percent of the 298-mile route, and the trains seldom ran on time. "The public use of these trains has no doubt been deterred by the erratic and declining service. The evidence indicates a failure on the part of carrier management rather than a failure on the part of the public to support the service," the ICC wrote in its decision of May 26, 1970, ordering Nos. 65/66 to continue for six months. Unwanted by Amtrak, Nos. 65/66 made their final runs on April 30, 1971.

Trains that once had 15 cars needed just one coach as passenger service declined sharply in the 1960s. Penn Central's Chicago to Cincinnati No. 66, formerly the *Red Bird*, passes Anoka Tower in Logansport in 1970. Photo by John Fuller.

Columbus Line

The Columbus, Chicago & Indiana Central (the Panhandle) opened between Union City on the Ohio border and Anoka Junction (Logansport) in 1868 and began three round trips between Chicago and Columbus, Ohio. During the 1870s, service was generally one

Chicago–Columbus round trip and a Logansport–Columbus round trip. By the late 1870s, another train had begun operating between Logansport and Bradford, Ohio.

Chicago–Columbus service was two round trips by late 1883. Two years later, all four Chicago–Columbus trains had names (*Western Express*, *Eastern Express*, *Fast Line*, and *Day Express*) and had begun operating between Chicago and New York by January 1886. In the early 1890s, the Panhandle had three Chicago–Columbus round trips, a Logansport–Columbus round trip, a Logansport–Marion round trip, and a pairing operating Columbus to Chicago and Logansport to Columbus. The latter had ended by January 1895. The Logansport–Marion trains were gone by the late 1890s.

At the dawn of the 20th century, all four Chicago–Columbus trains carried Chicago–New York sleepers. The *Atlantic Express/Chicago and St. Louis Express* also carried a Chicago–New York diner. The other Chicago–Columbus trains, the *New York and Chicago Limited*, operated on the Pennsylvania as the *Pennsylvania Limited*. Other trains operated Columbus–Logansport, Columbus to Chicago, and Logansport to Columbus.

By 1904, only the *Keystone Express/Chicago and St. Louis Express* carried Chicago–New York sleepers. The *Eastern Express* carried Chicago–Columbus sleepers. The *Pacific Express* originated in New York, but its sleepers operated only to Columbus. Nos. 20/21 had become the *Keystone Express* in both directions by January 1908. During the first decade of the 20th century, Chicago–Columbus service was two round trips. Other trains operated Logansport–Columbus and Logansport–Bradford. Chicago–Columbus service had expanded to three round trips by January 1911. The premier Chicago–New York train was now called *Seaboard Express/Chicago Express*.

In late 1912 the Panhandle began the *Pan Handle Limited*, an all-Pullman Chicago–New York train that operated via Richmond, where it combined with the *24-Hour New Yorker/24-Hour St. Louis*. The Panhandle had five Chicago–Columbus round trips, four of which operated via Union City. Locals operated Bradford to Logansport and Logansport to Columbus.

The *Chicago Express* became the *Panama–Pacific Express* in June 1913. The March 1914 discontinuance of the *Pan Handle Limited* reduced Chicago–Columbus service to four round trips. The *Panama–Pacific Express* became the *Pan-Handle Express* in 1915.

Through Service Ends

Throughout the early 1920s, service remained two Chicago–Columbus round trips, a Columbus to Chicago train, a Logansport–Columbus round trip, and Bradford–Logansport and Logansport–Columbus locals. By 1923, local service had declined to a Logansport–Bradford round trip, which by the mid-1920s had begun operating with a motor car that made 27 intermediate stops. These trains ended November 29, 1931.

The New York cars came off the *Pan-Handle Express/Seaboard Express* in August 1932 in favor of sleepers and a café car between Chicago and Pittsburgh. Within a year, the Pittsburgh cars had been replaced by Chicago–Columbus parlor cars. Columbus line trains received new names in April 1935. The *Pan-Handle Express/Seaboard Express* was renamed the *Fort Hayes*, and Nos. 108/109 became the *Ohioan*. The Chicago–Cincinnati *Union* had a Columbus section that operated via Fort Wayne and Richmond.

A local that began between Chicago and Bradford on September 27, 1936, was curtailed to Logansport–Dunkirk on November 29, 1936, and named the *Indiana Arrow*. The *Arrow* ended April 25, 1937, along with the Logansport–Ridgeville segment of a Chicago–Dayton–Springfield, Ohio, train. Although the latter trains returned December 9, 1937, they were gone by the following spring.

Except for a brief return in the late 1940s of the Chicago–Springfield train between Logansport and Ridgeville, Columbus line passenger service changed little during the 1940s and into the 1950s. The *Fort Hayes* was a daylight train, and the *Ohioan* traveled by night. By 1951 the Pennsylvania had assigned a 10-section bar lounge to the *Ohioan* and a parlor buffet lounge to the *Fort Hayes*. The *Union*, a Chicago–Cincinnati train that operated via Kokomo, had a Columbus section that carried coaches and a parlor.

The *Fort Hayes* ended October 28, 1956. The *Ohioan* lost its lounge-buffet-sleeper in April 1957 and its name and sleepers in April 1958 when the Chicago–Columbus sleepers were assigned to the *Buckeye* between Chicago and Richmond via Kokomo.

The remnant of the former *Ohioan* was discontinued December 31, 1958, which ended scheduled passenger service on the Chicago–Columbus line via Marion and Ridgeville. The Chicago–Columbus sleepers on the *Buckeye* continued until October 29, 1967. The *Buckeye*'s Chicago–Columbus coaches ended with the discontinuance of the train in spring 1969.

Grand Rapids & Indiana

The Grand Rapids & Indiana opened between Fort Wayne and Grand Rapids in October 1870, to Petoskey, Mich., on the south shore of Little Traverse Bay in November 1873 and to Mackinaw City, Mich., on July 3, 1882. The Cincinnati, Richmond & Fort Wayne had built an 86-mile route between Richmond and Adams (Fort Wayne). The GR&I leased the CR&FtW in 1871.

The lumber trade was the impetus for creating the GR&I, and when this business faltered in the 1890s, the company was sold to a representative of the Pennsylvania at a July 1896 foreclosure sale. The Pennsylvania absorbed the GR&I on January 1, 1921.

The GR&I called itself "The Fishing Line" because of its service to northern Michigan's resort region. The GR&I published guides to Michigan fishing holes and resorts. The Pennsylvania even had a bureau that provided fishing information. The GR&I and the Michigan Central funded construction of several hotels, including the renowned Grand Hotel on Mackinac Island.

In the early 1870s, the GR&I operated one round trip each between Fort Wayne and Kalamazoo and Paris, Mich. The CR&FtW offered two round trips between Richmond and Winchester in Randolph County. By late 1873 one round trip operated between Richmond and Fort Wayne, the other between Richmond and Portland in Jay County.

By July 1877, the GR&I and CR&FtW offered two round trips between Cincinnati and Petoskey, both featuring sleepers and cars with reclining seats. Trains also operated Richmond–Fort Wayne, Grand Rapids–Richmond, Grand Rapids–Fort Wayne, and Richmond–Ridgeville. During the 1880s, the GR&I generally operated single pairings between Richmond and Grand Rapids, Fort Wayne and Grand Rapids, and Fort Wayne and Richmond. Additional trains operated between Sturgis, Mich., and Fort Wayne or Richmond.

Quite a crowd has gathered at the Grand Rapids & Indiana depot at LaGrange, Ind., in this 19th century scene. The train was the primary means that most people used then for intercity travel. Indiana Historical Society, negative C8886.

The GR&I generally operated three round trips between Fort Wayne and Richmond during the 1890s, two of which served Grand Rapids. A third pairing operated between Fort Wayne and Grand Rapids. Sleepers and parlor cars operated between Cincinnati and Grand Rapids and in the summer between Cincinnati and Mackinaw City.

Building the Resort Business

In its early years, the GR&I operated excursion trains to the area of Michigan called "up north," including some that originated in Indianapolis. Sleepers began year-round operation between Mackinaw City and Cincinnati in 1903. Seasonal Mackinaw City sleepers originated at Pittsburgh, St. Louis, and Louisville. By 1910 the GR&I had sleepers between Grand Rapids and Indianapolis, and twice-weekly sleepers between Grand Rapids and Jacksonville, Fla. Parlor cars operated Cincinnati–Mackinaw City, Cincinnati–Grand Rapids, Fort Wayne–Grand Rapids, and Fort Wayne–Mackinaw City.

During the first decade of the 20th century, there were two Cincinnati–Grand Rapids round trips and various other combinations between Grand Rapids and Richmond that made for six to eight trains per day within Indiana. From January 1913 through 1920, three trains usually operated between Fort Wayne and Richmond, and four trains operated between Fort Wayne and Grand Rapids. Three trains operated through Fort Wayne northbound, and two operated through Fort Wayne southbound. A diner operated between Grand Rapids and Kendallville in Noble County.

Service increased by one round trip when the seasonal Cincinnati–Mackinaw City train began service with sleepers for Mackinaw City and Traverse City and sleepers operating between Louisville and Mackinaw City. Parlor cars operated between Cincinnati and Grand Rapids. The seasonal Cincinnati–Grand Rapids train became the all-Pullman *Northland Limited* in the 1921 *Official Guide of the Railways* with through sleepers between Mackinaw City and St. Louis, Indianapolis, Louisville, Cincinnati, and Columbus, Ohio. A dining car operated between Mackinaw City and Grand Rapids. That winter, the *Southland* carried a sleeper between Mackinaw City and St. Petersburg.

The *Northland Limited* was shortened to the *Northland* in 1922, but it gained Cincinnati–Traverse City sleepers. The following summer, the dining car on the *Northland* began operating between Mackinaw City and Cincinnati, but there were no Cincinnati–Traverse City sleepers.

By the mid-1920s, four pairs of trains operated between Richmond and Grand Rapids, two of which served Mackinaw City, even during the winter. However, the *Northland* name had disappeared from the *Official Guide*. Cincinnati–Traverse City sleepers returned in 1925.

Through sleeper service peaked in 1927 when sleepers operated between Mackinaw City and Cincinnati, Indianapolis, Louisville, St. Louis, and Columbus, Ohio. Sleepers also operated between St. Louis and Petoskey, Grand Rapids and Cincinnati, and Grand Rapids and Indianapolis. The Indianapolis and Louisville sleepers ran via Logansport and reached Fort Wayne via the Wabash. After the summer season ended, passenger service reverted to two pairs of trains between Richmond and Fort Wayne and three pairs between Fort Wayne and Richmond.

The Mackinaw City seasonal sleepers for St. Louis and Columbus did not return in 1929. Sleepers operated between Mackinaw City and Cincinnati, Louisville and Indianapolis, and Cincinnati and Traverse City. Another train conveyed sleepers between Grand Rapids and Cincinnati and Indianapolis. An Indianapolis–Detroit sleeper operated via Richmond, reaching Detroit on the Wabash north of Fort Wayne.

The *Southland* began operating between Chicago and Cincinnati via Fort Wayne in 1930, which increased Fort Wayne–Richmond service to six trains. Between 1931 and 1949, the *Southland* carried Detroit–Florida cars conveyed to Fort Wayne by the Wabash. The resumption of the seasonal Cincinnati–Mackinaw City train increased service between Fort Wayne and Richmond to eight trains. The Pennsylvania reinstated the *Northland* name in *The Official Guide of the Railways* in 1931. Also that year, a pair of Chicago–Cincinnati trains began operating between Richmond and Ridgeville.

The Indianapolis and Louisville sleepers on the *Northland* began operating to Harbor Springs in 1932. Sleepers also operated Cincinnati and Harbor Springs, Traverse City and Mackinaw City.

The Chicago–Cincinnati *Union* began operating between Fort Wayne and Richmond on April 2, 1933. With the resumption of the seasonal *Northland*, 10 trains operated between Fort Wayne and Richmond and 8 between Fort Wayne and Grand Rapids.

The *Northland* began conveying sleepers between Harbor Springs and St. Louis in 1933, but the sleepers between Harbor Springs and Indianapolis and Louisville were gone. The train also carried its first coaches. The *Northland* became the *Northern Arrow* in 1935. Its only Indiana stops were Richmond and Fort Wayne. It carried coaches, a lounge, and a diner between Cincinnati and Mackinaw City, and sleepers between Harbor Springs and St. Louis and Cincinnati, Traverse City and Cincinnati, and Mackinaw City and Cincinnati.

Parlor cars that had operated for four years between Fort Wayne and Cincinnati ended in April 1937. The sleepers between Grand Rapids and Indianapolis and Cincinnati ended in June 1937. Four pairs of trains operated Richmond–Fort Wayne and Fort Wayne–Grand Rapids.

The *Union* moved to the Kokomo route on April 25, 1937. A year later, service between Fort Wayne and Richmond dropped to six trains including the seasonal *Northern Arrow*, the *Southland*, and a Richmond–Fort Wayne local. Fort Wayne–Grand Rapids service was six trains including two unnamed locals, one of which served Mackinaw City. The *Southland* moved back to the Kokomo route in December 1939, which dropped service between Richmond and Fort Wayne to four trains, six in the summer. The *Southland* began operating between Ridgeville and Richmond at the end of the 1939–40 winter travel season.

The War Years

The *Northern Arrow* made conditional stops at Winchester, Portland, and Decatur, but no stops in Indiana north of Fort Wayne. After the *Northern Arrow* went into winter hibernation in 1940, service fell to four trains between Richmond and Fort Wayne, four trains between Fort Wayne and Grand Rapids, and the *Southland* between Ridgeville and Richmond. That winter the *Southland* gained a quad-weekly sleeper between Grand Rapids and Miami.

The *Southland* resumed operating via Fort Wayne in December 1940, which increased Richmond–Fort Wayne service to six trains, but only Nos. 501/502 stopped at intermediate stations. Four trains operated between Fort Wayne and Grand Rapids. By January 1942, the *Southland* had moved back to the Kokomo route. Travelers could no longer connect from the train from Mackinaw City to Grand Rapids and any train operating beyond Fort Wayne.

The *Northern Arrow* did not operate in 1943, and the only sleeper for the Michigan resort country operated between Cincinnati and Petoskey. A café-parlor car operated between Fort Wayne and Mackinaw City. During the 1942–43 winter season, the *Southland* operated from Ridgeville to Richmond, but returned to the Kokomo route after the end of the season.

During World War II, service was a Richmond–Fort Wayne round trip, a Richmond–Grand Rapids round trip that connected with the Grand Rapids–Mackinaw City trains, and a Fort Wayne–Grand Rapids round trip. All trains serving Richmond conveyed Cincinnati cars, which generally operated on Chicago–Cincinnati trains south of Richmond.

In the summers of 1944 and 1945, the Pennsylvania offered sleepers and coaches between Cincinnati and Mackinaw City. During the off-season, these sleepers operated between Cincinnati and Grand Rapids. The *Southland* had resumed operating via Fort Wayne in combination with the Richmond–Grand Rapids trains.

The *Northern Arrow* returned in 1946 with a consist closely resembling its prewar status. Sleepers, coaches, a diner, and a lounge operated between Cincinnati and Mackinaw City. Sleepers also operated between Harbor Springs and Cincinnati, St. Louis, and Chicago. The latter were interchanged at Fort Wayne, an operation that began in the early 1940s. Previously, Chicago sleepers had interchanged with the Michigan Central at Kalamazoo, Mich.

Whither the Northern Arrow

The Harbor Springs sleepers did not return in 1947. Instead, the Chicago and St. Louis sleepers operated to Mackinaw City. The *Northern Arrow* continued to carry sleepers, coaches, a diner, and a lounge between Cincinnati and Mackinaw City.

The November 1947 discontinuance of Nos. 501/502 (Richmond–Fort Wayne) left only the *Southland* between Richmond and Fort Wayne, and it made no intermediate stops. The *Southland* also conveyed the coaches and sleepers that operated between Cincinnati and Grand Rapids. Service increased to two pairings with the resumption of the *Northern Arrow*, which made flag stops at Winchester, Portland, and Decatur.

Fort Wayne–Grand Rapids Nos. 508/511 were discontinued between Fort Wayne and Sturgis, Mich., on January 11, 1948. The *Southland* was permanently rerouted via Kokomo on April 30, 1950, replaced by a Cincinnati–Grand Rapids train with coaches and sleepers. After the *Northern Arrow* went on winter hiatus in October 1950, year-round passenger service to Mackinaw City ended.

The Cincinnati–Grand Rapids sleepers ended in April 1953. In June, the Cincinnati–Grand Rapids coaches began originating at Richmond. When the train that conveyed these cars was curtailed to Grand Rapids–Sturgis operation on December 8, 1954, the only passenger service left on the GR&I in Indiana was the seasonal *Northern Arrow*.

The *Northern Arrow* did not operate daily when it resumed operation on July 1, 1955, making 20 round trips through September 11. Travel between Richmond and Fort Wayne was permitted, but at Winchester, Portland, and Decatur the train only accepted passengers bound for stations north of Grand Rapids. The train did not serve any Indiana stations north of Fort Wayne.

The *Northern Arrow* began its final northbound trip on September 1, 1961, and its final southbound trip on September 4. In the final seven years of operation, sleepers operated between Mackinaw City and Cincinnati, St. Louis, and Chicago. A diner and coaches operated between Cincinnati and Mackinaw City. The *Northern Arrow* made 13 round trips during its final season.

Louisville Line

The oldest Pennsylvania line west of Pittsburgh dated to the February 3, 1832, chartering of the Ohio & Indianapolis. Later reorganized as the Jeffersonville Railroad, the road was completed to Columbus in 1852. Trains reached Indianapolis via the Madison & Indianapolis north of Edinburgh in Johnson County. The two competitors merged May 1, 1866, to form the Jeffersonville, Madison & Indianapolis. The Pittsburgh, Cincinnati & St. Louis leased the JM&I in 1871.

The JM&I and the Louisville & Nashville reorganized the Louisville Bridge Company after the Civil War in a renewed attempt to replace the car ferries used to cross the Ohio River. Construction began in 1867, and the bridge opened February 24, 1870.

In the late 1860s, the JM&I operated four Jeffersonville–Indianapolis round trips and in 1867 began what may have been Indiana's first commuter train operation with eight round trips between Jeffersonville and New Albany. The JM&I also fielded a Jeffersonville–Columbus round trip and four Jeffersonville–Indianapolis round trips.

After the opening of the Ohio River bridge, the JM&I had three Indianapolis–Louisville round trips and Indianapolis–Seymour and Indianapolis–Jeffersonville accommodation trains. Several Jeffersonville–New Albany commuter trains served Louisville. Through sleepers operated between Louisville and New York, St. Louis, and Chicago.

Service between Louisville and Indianapolis varied between three and four round trips for the remainder of the 19th century. The day trains carried Chicago–Louisville parlor cars and coaches; the night trains had sleepers and coaches. The New Albany–Jeffersonville–Louisville commuter service operated almost hourly by 1873, hourly by the end of the 1870s, and every half-hour between 5 A.M. and midnight by 1890.

Two of the three Indianapolis–Louisville trains continued to Chicago by 1890, using the Lake Erie & Western (later Nickel Plate) via Kokomo. Indianapolis–Louisville service was four round trips by 1896. Most trains used Louisville Union Station and a depot at 14th and Main in Louisville.

The 1893 World's Columbian Exposition in Chicago prompted the creation of the Pennsylvania's first Florida through service through Indiana, a Chicago–Tampa sleeper that interchanged at Louisville with the L&N and operated via Montgomery, Ala.

At the turn of the 20th century, there were four Indianapolis–Louisville round trips, two of which served Chicago, and an Indianapolis–Columbus local. A sleeper operated between Louisville and New York. Louisville–Indianapolis service rose to five round trips in 1901, with four of these pairs originating at Louisville Union Station. The fifth originated at 14th and Main.

The first Florida through train, the *Florida Limited*, began seasonal service in January 1903. The train used the Southern to Oakdale, Tenn., the Queen & Crescent Route to Atlanta, the Southern to Jacksonville, and the Florida East Coast to St. Augustine, Fla. Operating on an overnight schedule through Indiana, the train featured Pullman drawing

The Pennsylvania shared Louisville Union Station with the Louisville & Nashville. Until 1969, the two interchanged here such Chicago–Florida trains as the *South Wind*, *Florida Arrow*, and the *Jacksonian*. Bob's Photo.

room sleepers. The *Florida Limited* did not return the next year, but in 1917 the Pennsylvania began a through sleeper between Indianapolis and Jacksonville, conveyed by the *Night Express* to Louisville and interchanged with the L&N.

A New Path to Chicago

The opening of a line between Frankfort and Indianapolis on June 16, 1918, enabled the Pennsylvania to stop using the Lake Erie & Western between Indianapolis and Logansport. Trains used the Terre Haute–South Bend branch between Frankfort and Logansport.

By 1916, the New Albany commuter trains no longer served Louisville and service had fallen to three New Albany–Jeffersonville round trips. The service ended in 1920.

During the early 1920s, the Pennsylvania restructured service so that four round trips operated between Chicago and Louisville, three round trips operated between Louisville and Indianapolis, and one round trip operated between Indianapolis and Chicago. Most day trains carried parlor cars or buffet-parlor cars.

The Pennsylvania assigned a gas-electric car to a Chicago–Frankfort local in 1929. Two Indianapolis–South Bend trains had begun serving Louisville by 1931.

For several years, the Pennsylvania had offered Indianapolis–Jacksonville sleepers on the *Southland.* For the 1929–30 winter season, these sleepers were switched to the *Flamingo.* Sleepers also began operating between Miami and Chicago and Indianapolis.

The Indianapolis–Florida sleepers did not return in 1931, but the following year sleepers operated between Indianapolis and Miami on a quad-weekly basis via the *Flamingo.* No Indianapolis–Florida sleepers operated in 1933 or 1934, but the *Flamingo* carried quad-weekly Chicago–Miami sleepers in 1933 and sleepers between Chicago and Fort Myers, Fla., in 1934. A lounge car also operated between Chicago and Jacksonville.

A Chicago–Florida seasonal train began January 2, 1935. The triweekly *Florida Arrow* carried sleepers between Chicago and Miami/St. Petersburg. Coaches, a lounge, and a diner operated between Chicago and Jacksonville. The Indianapolis–Miami sleepers returned to the *Flamingo,* which also carried Indianapolis–St. Petersburg sleepers. The *Florida Arrow* returned for the 1935–36 season on a daily schedule.

The Pennsylvania named the overnight Chicago–Louisville trains the *Kentuckian* in April 1936. Service was two Chicago–Louisville round trips, and two Indianapolis–Louisville round trips, one of which was extended to Chicago on September 27, 1936, and named the *Indiana Arrow.* It had coaches, drawing room parlors, and a diner. Although the train survived, the *Indiana Arrow* name disappeared after May 1937.

For the 1936–37 season, the *Florida Arrow* carried daily Chicago–Miami sleepers, triweekly Chicago–St. Petersburg sleepers, and quad-weekly sleepers between Indianapolis and Miami and between Chicago and Sarasota. A recreation-lounge car with buffet operated between Chicago and Miami. Coaches and a diner operated between Chicago and Jacksonville. The only through car on the *Flamingo* was a Chicago–Jacksonville lounge-observation. These equipment assignments remained largely unchanged over the next three winters.

A New Wind Blows

The Pennsylvania and eight other railroads announced in 1940 plans to operate a trio of every-third-day coach streamliners over three routes on one-night-out 29.5-hour schedules between Chicago and Miami. Tickets were interchangeable among the trains. The fare was $23.25 one-way ($41.85 round trip), and even the dining car prices were standardized.

The *South Wind* left Chicago Union Station on December 19, 1940, on its maiden run. The *South Wind,* which followed the *Florida Arrow* route, had the longest trek at 1,559 miles and had to average 52.8 mph to make its schedule, which included 16 intermediate stops.

The *South Wind* had a diner, observation lounge, and five coaches, all built by Budd and adorned in the Pennsylvania's Tuscan red livery.

The popularity of the trains prompted the railroads to operate them year-round and to plan a trio of all-Pullman trains and a trio of trains with Pullmans and coaches. The Pennsylvania's all-Pullman train, the *Jacksonian*, debuted December 18, 1941, with four Chicago–Miami sleepers, a Chicago–Tampa sleeper, a Chicago–Miami lounge, and a Chicago–Jacksonville diner. The *Florida Arrow* resumed service on January 1, 1942, with two Chicago–Miami sleepers, a Chicago–St. Petersburg sleeper and coach, Chicago–Sarasota sleeper, Chicago–Miami lounge, and Chicago–Indianapolis diner.

The *South Wind, Florida Arrow*, and *Jacksonian* operated on alternate days. The *Jacksonian* and *South Wind* departed Chicago at midmorning on one-night-out schedules. The *Florida Arrow* departed in the evening on a two-night-out schedule. Daily service included two unnamed Chicago–Louisville trains and the Indianapolis–Louisville *Pennsylvania Limited*. The *Kentuckian* had been suspended.

With the nation mobilizing for war, the grand plan for Midwest–Florida service changed. The *Florida Arrow* ended January 16, 1942, after just five trips, and the *Kentuckian* was revived. The *Jacksonian* made its last run on April 6, 1942, and carried coaches and Pullmans when it returned for the 1942–43 season. The *Jacksonian* was the last all-Pullman train between Chicago and Florida on any railroad.

The Louisville–South Bend through cars ended in 1942. Through April 1943, the Louisville line hosted five Chicago–Louisville round trips including the every-third-day *South Wind* and every-third-day *Jacksonian*, which did not return after it ended for the season in April 1943.

The *Florida Arrow* returned December 14, 1946, with Chicago–Miami and Chicago–Jacksonville sleepers. The coaches, diner, and lounge operated between Chicago and Miami, operating on an every-third-day, one-night-out schedule. Indianapolis was the only Indiana station served by the *South Wind* and *Florida Arrow*.

Chicago–Louisville service was three round trips. Sleepers operated Louisville to Pittsburgh and New York to Louisville. The daylight Chicago–Louisville trains were named the *Chicago Daylight Express/Louisville Daylight Express* in 1948. Indianapolis to Louisville No. 312, an all-coach train, ended April 25, 1948. Chicago–Louisville Nos. 319/320 became the *Union* in November 1948, giving names to all Louisville line trains.

The *Florida Arrow* began its last southbound run on April 20, 1949, and its final northbound run the next day. The *South Wind* received its first sleepers on April 24, operating Chicago–Miami and Chicago–Jacksonville. Also for the first time the *South Wind* had Chicago–Jacksonville coaches. The observation broiler buffet, lounge coach, and diner continued to operate between Chicago and Miami. By January 1950, the Louisville–Pittsburgh sleeper was operating to New York.

The *South Wind* received new lightweight sleepers and coaches in 1950. To compensate for the loss of the *Florida Arrow*, the *South Wind* operated for the 1950–51 and 1951–52 winter seasons on two of every three days. K-4 Pacifics regularly pulled the *South Wind* on the Pennsylvania through the late 1940s when diesels began to take over. Baldwin "shark noses" pulled the *South Wind* before giving way to E units. The Pennsylvania and Atlantic Coast Line established a *South Wind* power pool on a mileage-balancing basis, and purple and silver ACL diesels with gold trim became a common sight in Indiana.

The Pennsylvania dropped the *Union* name on June 30, 1952, and renamed the trains the *Blue Grass Special* on August 2, 1952, when the *Kentuckian* began conveying the Louisville–New York sleepers. The *Chicago Daylight Express/Louisville Daylight Express* name disappeared in late 1952 and the trains ended in 1953, dropping Chicago–Louisville service to two daily round trips and the every-third-day *South Wind*. Indianapolis–Louisville Nos. 326/327 ended April 26, 1953.

By the early 1950s, the *South Wind* was accepting passengers at Logansport, and by the mid-1950s it was making conditional stops at Frankfort, Columbus, Seymour, and Jeffersonville. On September 27, 1953, the Pennsylvania began a Chicago–Louisville train on days the *South Wind* did not operate. The train carried coaches and a café-parlor car.

The November 29, 1957, discontinuance of the *Dixieland* on the C&EI and the downgrading of the *Southland*, the Pennsylvania's other Chicago–Florida train, resulted in the *South Wind* taking on additional cars. The *South Wind* began handling the *Southland*'s Chicago–Sarasota sleeper on November 20, a Chicago–St. Petersburg sleeper on November 30, a Chicago–Jacksonville sleeper on November 27, and coaches between Chicago and St. Petersburg and Sarasota on November 30. The *South Wind* also began operating every other day, alternating with the Illinois Central's *City of Miami*.

On September 8, 1957, the Chicago–Louisville train that had alternated with the *South Wind* was discontinued southbound and shortened northbound to Louisville to Indianapolis. The *Blue Grass Special* name disappeared in April 1957. The New York–Louisville sleepers ended April 27, 1958, as did Louisville to Indianapolis No. 93. The former *Blue Grass Special* was curtailed to Indianapolis–Louisville on May 24, 1958, and was gone by early 1960. By now the *Kentuckian* had lost its lounge-bar car.

Carrying On

The *South Wind* continued to carry healthy loads with sleepers between Chicago and Miami, St. Petersburg, Sarasota, and Jacksonville, coaches between Chicago and Miami, St. Petersburg, and Sarasota, and a diner and lounge between Chicago and Miami. The *South Wind* acquired an unusual addition in October 1959 when leased Northern Pacific dome-sleepers in two-tone green began seasonal operation between Chicago and Miami. The domes did not return the next year, but made a repeat appearance for four winter seasons beginning in 1964.

The *Kentuckian*'s sleepers ended October 29, 1967. Shortly after the Pennsylvania and New York Central merger of February 1, 1968, Penn Central said it would discontinue the *Kentuckian*, saying it was losing $320,000 a year. In an order issued April 10, the ICC allowed the discontinuance effective April 21.

The *South Wind*'s Chicago–Sarasota coaches and sleepers ended after the 1967–68 winter season. For the 1968–69 season, the *South Wind* had a slimmer consist of two Chicago–Miami sleepers, a Chicago–St. Petersburg sleeper, coaches between Chicago and Miami/St. Petersburg, and a diner and lounge for Miami.

Penn Central pulled out of the *South Wind* pool on November 21, 1969, substituting a connecting train with two coaches and a coach-buffet car. The latter was removed in November 1970. Penn Central sought to kill the *South Wind* connecting train in its March 10, 1970, train-off petition to the Interstate Commerce Commission, claiming Nos. 90/93 had an operating loss of $728,325 in 1969. But the ICC ordered Nos. 90/93 kept in service for six months. The trains continued until May 1, 1971, when Amtrak re-created the *South Wind*, although it shifted the train north of Indianapolis to the former New York Central via Lafayette.

Brazil–Center Point

Built between Knightsville and Center Point in Clay County in 1870, the branch typically hosted four passenger trains and served coal miners. One round trip ended June 26, 1924, and the other became a mixed train. Passenger service ended June 15, 1925.

Columbus–Cambridge City

The Rushville & Shelbyville opened between its namesake cities in 1850 and reached Columbus in December 1853. The Lake Erie & Louisville opened from Rushville to Cambridge City in Wayne County on July 4, 1867. A through train between Jeffersonville and New York began in May 1869 on a 36-hour schedule but was short-lived.

The branch usually hosted four trains between Columbus and Cambridge City. These trains began terminating at Richmond in September 1909. Service fell to one round trip on January 14, 1923. Downgraded to a mixed train on September 20, 1928, passenger service ended September 13, 1930.

Indianapolis–South Bend

Indianapolis–South Bend service began in June 1919. One pairing operated jointly with a Louisville train between Indianapolis and Logansport. Another pairing, the *Capitol Express/Logansport and South Bend Express*, operated independently. All four trains carried broiler-buffet parlor cars. The train names disappeared in September 1921.

One round trip ended September 6, 1930. The surviving trains operated on daylight schedules with broiler-buffet parlor cars, which within a year had become parlor coaches.

Service reverted to two round trips in 1932. By now all South Bend cars were conveyed by Louisville trains between Indianapolis and Logansport. One pairing had a parlor coach; the other featured a buffet–drawing room parlor car.

The parlor coach ended in September 1935; the buffet–drawing room parlor came off in September 1936. Service fell to one round trip on April 25, 1937, which ended in November 1947. This also was the end of passenger service between Logansport and South Bend.

Indianapolis–Vincennes

Construction of the Indianapolis & Vincennes began in 1867. The first scheduled passenger operation was a round trip between Indianapolis and Gosport in Owen County. After opening to Vincennes in 1869, service expanded to four trains, two between Indianapolis and Vincennes and two between Indianapolis and Spencer in Owen County. Service between Indianapolis and Vincennes involved four trains by 1872.

The I&V built four coal branches in the 1880s near Bicknell in Knox County and Dugger in Sullivan County that hosted miners' trains but no scheduled service. A miners' train operated between Bushrod in Greene County and Dugger until December 27, 1923.

During the 19th century, the line hosted between six and eight trains, four of which usually operated between Indianapolis and Vincennes. Other trains originated at Indianapolis or Vincennes and terminated at various intermediate points in Greene and Knox Counties.

The line hosted eight trains in 1900, four between Indianapolis and Martinsville in Morgan County, and four between Indianapolis and Vincennes. Service peaked at 10 trains in 1901 when Indianapolis–Martinsville service expanded to three round trips and one of the Vincennes pairings began terminating at Spencer. A year later, service had fallen to eight trains with the discontinuance of one Indianapolis–Martinsville pairing.

There were six trains by May 1906, all operating between Indianapolis and Vincennes. Two short-lived trains began operating Worthington–Vincennes and Bicknell–Vincennes in June 1916. A year later, an Indianapolis–Vincennes train began terminating at Spencer, but this had ended by late 1918. Indianapolis–Vincennes service had reverted to three round trips by July 1918.

In the late 19th century, the Pennsylvania began conveying sleepers between New York and French Lick in Orange County. The cars interchanged with the Monon at Gosport. The two roads had begun an Indianapolis–French Lick parlor-diner by 1908.

Suspended during World War I, French Lick service returned in 1921 with coaches, parlors, and a diner originating at Indianapolis. New York service resumed in September 1925, but ended in December. A coach and parlor originating at Indianapolis continued until July 19, 1931.

Indianapolis–Vincennes service fell from three to two round trips on January 14, 1923. An Indianapolis–Martinsville pairing that began August 2, 1925, lasted less than a year. Indianapolis–Vincennes service fell to one round trip in August 1930 and ended in June 1941.

Logansport–Butler

Originally the Eel River Railroad, passenger service began in 1872. The Wabash leased the route between August 22, 1879, and September 12, 1901, when it was sold under court order to the newly organized Logansport & Toledo, which became part of the Vandalia on January 1, 1905.

The L&T initially operated three Logansport–Toledo round trips, using the Wabash east of Butler. The trains began terminating at Butler in 1902, and service diminished to two round trips.

Through service between Toledo and Chicago and St. Louis began in May 1913. The Chicago cars, which included coaches, sleepers, and a buffet-parlor, interchanged with Fort Wayne line trains at Columbia City in Whitley County. St. Louis coaches and sleepers interchanged at Logansport and operated via Terre Haute. Logansport–Butler service increased to three round trips, two of which carried through cars. A Columbia City–Butler round trip handled some of the Chicago cars.

The Chicago cars and Toledo–Columbia City trains ended in November 1913. The buffet-parlor continued to operate between Toledo and Columbia City through January 1914 when the Toledo–St. Louis sleepers ended and service fell to two Logansport–Butler round trips. The St. Louis–Toledo coaches ended in August 1918, although the cars briefly continued to operate between St. Louis and Butler. By December, service was one Logansport–Butler round trip.

Service had increased to two round trips by the end of 1919, but dropped to one round trip on November 28, 1920. A gas-electric car was assigned to the line in November 1926. The train began terminating at LaOtto in Noble County on July 7, 1929, and at Columbia City on August 12, 1929. For the final three months of operation, service was a mixed train. Passenger service ended March 29, 1930.

Logansport–Effner

The Logansport, Peoria & Burlington opened in December 1859 between Logansport and State Line (later Effner), where it connected with the Peoria & Oquawka (later Toledo, Peoria & Western). The first passenger operation was an excursion train from Logansport to Peoria, Ill., on December 27, 1859.

The route's two round trip passenger trains originated at Richmond in 1868, but this had ended by 1869 and trains terminated at Logansport thereafter. In connection with the TP&W, the route hosted a Peoria–Columbus, Ohio, sleeper in 1870. Two years later, sleepers operated between Columbus and Burlington, Iowa. This service ended in 1873.

Effner–Logansport service was three round trips by 1871, which remained the norm for the remainder of the 19th century except in the mid-1890s when it increased to four round trips. After 1902, service was generally two round trips with schedules coordinated to connect with the TP&W. Service fell to one round trip on February 10, 1924.

A gas-electric car was assigned to the route in November 1926. A mixed train operating on a different schedule replaced the motor car in December 1928, which broke the connection with the TP&W. Passenger service ended March 1, 1929.

Knightstown–Shelbyville–Edinburgh

The 16-mile Shelbyville Lateral Branch opened August 1, 1849, between Shelbyville and Edinburgh. Passenger service was one round trip. The Jeffersonville Railroad purchased the line on July 1, 1851, with the intention of using it to connect with a proposed railroad between Shelbyville and Indianapolis. But the Jeffersonville soon began using the Madison & Indianapolis to reach Indianapolis, and operations ended in 1855.

The 26-mile Knightstown & Shelbyville opened between its namesake cities on October 26, 1849. Its lone passenger train connected at Shelbyville with the Shelbyville Lateral Branch. The K&S faltered and ceased operations in 1854, becoming Indiana's first railroad to be abandoned.

Madison–Indianapolis

Construction of the Madison & Indianapolis, Indiana's first intercity railroad, began in 1837. The M&I's first passenger train operated on November 29, 1838, from North Madison to Graham's Ford (15 miles). Service began to Vernon in Jennings County on June 6, 1839, and to Indianapolis on October 1, 1847.

As other railroads opened, the M&I lost much of its business and it merged with the Jeffersonville in 1866. Passenger service usually was two Indianapolis–Madison round trips that operated in combination with Louisville trains between Indianapolis and Columbus.

Trains began terminating at North Madison on July 1, 1931, ending use of the fabled Madison 5.89 percent grade for passenger service. One pairing began operating as a mixed train in February 1934 and ended in June 1935. Passenger service ended in September 1937.

Muncie–Converse

The Chicago, Indiana & Eastern began building in 1895 between Matthews and Fairmount in Grant County. Two round trips had begun by late 1899 between Converse in Miami County (on the Chicago–Columbus line) and Matthews. Service between Converse and Muncie began January 20, 1901.

Service expanded June 2, 1901, to two Muncie–Converse round trips and a Matthews–Converse round trip. Service was four Muncie–Converse round trips by April 1902. A Chicago–Muncie sleeper interchanged with the Panhandle at Converse.

After the Pennsylvania purchased the CI&E on May 1, 1907, passenger service fell to two Muncie–Converse round trips. One round trip ended August 11, 1920. The surviving train became a mixed train on October 30, 1921, and ended April 25, 1925.

Terre Haute–South Bend

The Logansport, Crawfordsville & Southwestern built in 1871 between Rockville in Parke County and Logansport. The first passenger service was two round trips between Frankfort and Colfax in Clinton County. A year later, the LC&SW leased the Terre Haute–Rockville line of the Evansville & Crawfordsville, which had opened in 1860. Passenger service was three Terre Haute–Logansport round trips and trains operating Terre Haute–Crawfordsville and Rockville–Logansport.

Later reorganized as the Terre Haute & Logansport, the Terre Haute & Indianapolis acquired the route in 1879 with plans to extend it to South Bend. Construction began in early 1883 and reached Culver (then called Marmont) in Marshall County in September 1884, Plymouth in June 1884, and South Bend on November 24, 1884.

A subsidiary company, the Indiana & Lake Michigan, opened an extension to St. Joseph, Mich., on August 4, 1890. One of the two Terre Haute–South Bend pairings began serving St. Joseph. A Logansport–St. Joseph pairing had begun by early 1897.

The TH&L entered receivership in 1898, and the St. Joseph line was sold at a foreclosure sale. Passenger service became two Terre Haute–South Bend round trips and a Logansport–South Bend round trip, which began operating between Terre Haute and South Bend in 1903.

Over the next 15 years, most of the route's six to seven trains operated between Terre Haute and South Bend. Terre Haute–South Bend service fell to one round trip in June 1918 with another pairing operating between Logansport and Terre Haute. A year later, the northbound leg of the Terre Haute–South Bend train was discontinued north of Logansport and not reinstated until January 12, 1923.

The Terre Haute–Logansport trains ended in 1924. The Terre Haute–South Bend round trip was downgraded to mixed trains in September 1926, assigned gas-electric cars on September 29, 1929, and discontinued north of Frankfort in December 1931. The gas-electric car operated daily except on Sunday when a steam train handled the run. Downgraded to mixed trains on July 11, 1937, passenger service ended in February 1938.

Terre Haute–Peoria

Service between Terre Haute and Arcola, Ill., began in 1872, using the Terre Haute & Alton (later New York Central) between Terre Haute and Paris, Ill. After 1874, trains used the Vandalia between Terre Haute and a junction just over the Illinois border. The route generally hosted four trains, operating Terre Haute–Peoria, Ill., and Terre Haute–Decatur, Ill. Service briefly rose to six trains in the late 1870s and again between March 1907 and October 1914. All four trains operated between Terre Haute and Peoria between 1901 and late 1904. A Terre Haute–Arthur, Ill., mixed train that began in November 1914 lasted until April 30, 1922, when a Terre Haute–Decatur Sunday-only round trip began, lasting until January 14, 1923.

The daily Terre Haute–Decatur trains became mixed trains on September 27, 1925, were assigned gas-electric cars in 1928, and ended August 1, 1931. The Terre Haute–Peoria trains began terminating at Decatur on August 20, 1932, became mixed trains on January 30, 1938, and became regular passenger trains on May 30, 1948. The Pennsylvania's last Indiana branchline passenger trains were discontinued between Terre Haute and Paris on January 23, 1949.

CHAPTER 7

ERIE/ERIE LACKAWANNA

The Erie was the first railroad to link the Atlantic seaboard with the Great Lakes, the first to use a telegraph to coordinate train movements, and the first to install a systemwide radio network. But it was never the top passenger carrier between Chicago and New York. The Erie had a longer and slower route than its chief competitors, the New York Central and Pennsylvania Railroads. Whereas they went the distance in 16 hours in 1950, the Erie needed nearly 24 hours. If the Erie was "a first-class freight railroad, but a second-class passenger one," it was a pleasurable way to travel with its friendly, courteous crews, clean sleeping cars, excellent meals, and well-maintained equipment.

The Erie was chartered by New York on April 24, 1832, to serve the state's southern tier. The first passenger excursion occurred on June 30, 1841, at Piermont, N.Y. Scheduled service began September 23, 1841, between Piermont and Goshen, N.Y. Six months later, the Erie was bankrupt, the first of five receiverships it would incur during its lifetime. When completed between Piermont and Dunkirk, N.Y., on May 14, 1851, the Erie was the longest railroad in America.

Beginning in the late 1860s, the Erie made several unsuccessful attempts to reach Chicago. It tried to affiliate with the Michigan Southern, which instead aligned with the New York Central. After financier Jay Gould took over the Erie, he agreed in 1869 to lease the Columbus, Chicago & Indiana Central (the Panhandle). But the Pennsylvania persuaded the Panhandle to break its pact with Gould and sign a lease with the Pennsy. Gould then bought a majority share of the Pittsburgh, Fort Wayne & Chicago. But at the behest of the Pennsy, the Pennsylvania legislature made it impossible for Gould to take over the Fort Wayne road's board of directors. Gould subsequently sold his stock to the Pennsy.

The Erie leased the Atlantic & Great Western on June 24, 1874, but the A&GW never made good on a promise to obtain a controlling interest in the Cleveland, Columbus, Cincinnati & Indianapolis (later Big Four). The Erie finally reached Chicago in the early 1880s when a subsidiary, the Chicago & Atlantic, completed a line between Marion, Ohio, located on the Atlantic & Great Western, and Hammond, Ind.

Arguably, the Erie had the best-engineered right-of-way between Chicago and Ohio, rebuilt west of Marion in the early 20th century as a double-track split line with grades related to the heaviest flow of traffic. Typical of the hyperbole of the era, the Erie proclaimed in 1883: "No railroad was ever constructed with closer attention to scientific detail. . . . The route was located with such masterly skill that the road may be called an almost literal straight line, and there is no perceptible grade from one terminal to the other."

Erie Lackawanna

Passenger operations in Indiana began April 2, 1883, with a Chicago–Huntington round trip. Chicago–New York service began on June 17, 1883, when service expanded to two pairs of Chicago–Marion express trains, one of which carried the New York through cars. The other train conveyed Pullmans between Chicago and Hornellsville, N.Y. The Erie described the equipment that it purchased from the Pullman Palace Car Co. as "the most magnificent ever used by any railroad." Accommodation trains operated Chicago–Huntington and Marion–Huntington. Within a year, the Erie was offering Chicago–Boston sleepers.

The Erie charged no extra fare for its 28-hour Chicago–New York express service, which terminated in Jersey City, N.J., and was 2 hours slower than the New York Central and Pennsylvania Railroads. Unable to offer expeditious schedules, the Erie marketed scenery, calling itself the "Landscape Route of America."

Erie train names first appeared in the June 1885 *Traveler's Official Railway Guide*. Eastbound trains were named *New York Express*, *Mail Express*, and *Atlantic Express*. Westbound trains were named *Chicago Express* and *Pacific Express*. The *Atlantic* and *Pacific Express* names would last into the 1960s.

The Erie's premier train, the *Vestibule Limited*, first appeared in July 1889 as the *New York and Chicago Vestibule Limited*. The name was shortened in November 1892. The *Vestibule Limited* featured dining cars, sleepers, and first- and second-class coaches built by Pullman, all with vestibules.

For a brief time in 1890, the *Pacific Express* and *Atlantic Express* carried a Chicago–Ashland, Ky., through sleeper interchanged at Marion with the Hocking Valley (later Chesapeake & Ohio). For most of the 1890s, the Erie had two Chicago–New York trains, the *Vestibule Limited* and the *Atlantic Express/Pacific Express*. The Erie added a third pair of long-distance trains on June 5, 1904, the Chicago to New York *Excelsior Express* and the Buffalo to Chicago *Buffalo Chicago Express*. The *Chicago, Cincinnati and Buffalo Express* replaced the *Excelsior Express* on December 4, 1904. Its westbound counterpart, the *Buffalo, Chicago and Cincinnati Express*, operated between its namesake cities. Chicago–New York service reverted to two pairs of trains.

The Chicago to Buffalo train came off on October 20, 1907, but the Buffalo to Chicago train continued until May 2, 1909, when it was replaced by the Chicago–Hornell *Night Express*. The latter carried Chicago–Boston sleepers. A Youngstown, Ohio–Chicago train began at the same time. These trains operated for less than two years.

A New Flagship

The *Vestibule Limited*, *Atlantic Express*, and *Pacific Express* continued during World War I, but all Erie train names were dropped on January 1, 1919. Following the war, all trains carried sleepers, but there was no diner service on Nos. 7/8 through Indiana. The diner on Nos. 3/4 operated between Huntington and Marion eastbound and between Kent, Ohio, and Huntington westbound. In October 1921, Nos. 7/8 again became the *Atlantic Express* and the *Pacific Express*. No. 3 became the *Chicago Express*, and No. 4 the *New York Scenic Express*. The diner on Nos. 3/4 began operating the length of the route.

Service remained largely unchanged until the June 2, 1929, debut of the *Erie Limited*. Previously, Erie's flagship train had been the Buffalo–Jersey City *Southern Tier Express*. Erie president John J. Bernet ordered the train upgraded and extended to Chicago. Advertisements described the *Erie Limited* as the Erie's new standard-bearer, with new Pullmans, diners, coaches, and a luxurious club lounge for coach passengers. Cars had aisle carpet strips that extended across the vestibules. Operated on an overnight 25-hour schedule, the Erie charged an extra fare of $4.80 for travel between New York and Chicago. This was still less than the $5.20 surcharge for the New York Central's *Twentieth Century Limited* and the Pennsylvania's *Broadway Limited*.

Inauguration of the *Erie Limited* helped to boost employee morale and signaled a willingness to compete in the Chicago–New York market. Revamped schedules made Erie passenger service more attractive to long-distance travelers. Three pairs of trains, all with sleeping cars, operated between Chicago and Jersey City. The *New York Scenic Express* was renamed the *New York Express*.

The Erie's efforts to rejuvenate long-distance service came just before the Depression. Passenger revenue fell 50 percent between 1929 and 1933. In response, the Erie cut fares, promoted tours, and offered coach luncheons (meals served by attendants from baskets). Although the *Erie Limited*'s Pullman bookings held steady in the 1930s, coach travel declined.

The Erie discontinued the *Chicago Express/New York Express* on April 30, 1933. The *Atlantic Express* carried a lounge-restaurant car from Chicago to Hornell, N.Y., but the *Pacific Express* offered no food service through Indiana. After the Erie entered receivership on January 18, 1938, it discontinued most of its branch line passenger trains and focused on serving Chicago, Cleveland, and Buffalo. It began bus service between Jersey City and New York City.

Chicago–New York service increased on June 3, 1939, with the inauguration of the *Midlander*, which offered Chicago–New York sleepers and a Chicago–Hornell diner. However, sleeping car service ended through Indiana on the *Pacific Express*. The *Midlander* departed Chicago in midmorning and arrived in late afternoon. The *Erie Limited* departed Chicago in late afternoon and arrived in early morning. The *Atlantic Express* departed about 10 P.M. The *Pacific Express* arrived around midnight.

On June 19, 1942, the Erie declared a dividend of 50 cents a share on its common stock, the first such dividend in more than 60 years. For years Wall Street wags had quipped that the day that "weary Erie" declared a dividend, "icicles will freeze in hell."

World War II travel demands boosted the Erie's passenger traffic from 23 billion revenue passenger miles in 1940 to 95 billion in 1944; a figure never equaled again. Before the war, passenger revenue had been 6 percent of the Erie's gross operating revenue whereas at the New York Central and Pennsylvania it had been 15 percent. Erie passenger revenue was 10 percent of total operating revenue by 1945.

The public liked the Erie's passenger service, but more often than not the "weary Erie" was an also-ran in the Chicago–New York market. An Erie train is shown here leaving Chicago Dearborn Station. Bob's Photo.

Into the Lightweight Era, Slowly

Although Erie management believed that passenger prosperity would continue after the war, the railroad's purchase of new streamlined equipment was conservative, limited to 7 lightweight sleepers, 22 baggage/express cars, and 8 baggage/mail cars. The Erie focused on modernizing its passenger fleet at its Susquehanna, Pa., shops. In 1947, just 8.4 percent of Erie passenger equipment was more than 30 years old, compared with the industry average of 38.2 percent. Erie management did not believe the railroad could afford to simultaneously switch to diesel engines, upgrade its freight fleet, and buy new passenger equipment. The Erie had rebuilt 35 coaches and 8 diners by 1951. The refurbished cars had flush-rounded roofs, larger windows, and air conditioning. Coaches received larger seats, which reduced capacity from 84 to 52.

Assignment of diesel locomotives to the passenger fleet began in 1947 with the purchase of seven F3 units from the Electro-Motive Division (EMD) of General Motors. These locomotives were assigned to the *Erie Limited*, the *Midlander*, and, east of Marion, the *Atlantic Express/Pacific Express*. The Erie later ordered 12 Alco PA-1 diesels for delivery in 1949. By 1951, diesels pulled all passenger trains operating west of the New Jersey commuter district. The Erie took delivery of 2 more PA units and 14 E8A units from EMD in 1951. The latter introduced a new two-tone green passenger livery.

Erie's marketing focused on travel from intermediate points to Chicago or New York. The Erie served mostly small towns and medium-sized cities, the largest being Akron, Ohio. The *Midlander* was renamed the *Lake Cities* in November 1947, a name previously carried by the Cleveland and Buffalo sections of the *Midlander*. The *Erie Limited* also had a Buffalo section, but it ended on February 12, 1951.

Erie's postwar passenger revenues held steady until 1948, when ridership began to decline. Nonetheless, the early 1950s were a time of financial prosperity for the Erie, and management was not overly concerned about declining passenger revenue. The Erie heavily promoted passenger travel in newspaper and radio advertisements.

The Erie and the Delaware, Lackawanna & Western announced in 1956 that they were studying a merger. The Erie shifted its intercity passenger service on October 13, 1956, from Jersey City to the Lackawanna terminal in Hoboken, N.J. The two railroads had long competed in the New York–Buffalo market, and the Lackawanna was a rival in the Chicago–New York market through its alliance with the Nickel Plate Road. The Interstate Commerce Commission approved the merger, which became effective October 17, 1960. That year the two railroads collectively lost $7.2 million. For the five-year period through 1962, the two had a combined annual $13 million passenger deficit.

The first significant postmerger change was the January 1961 renaming of the *Erie Limited* to *Erie–Lackawanna Limited*. The *Erie–Lackawanna Limited* and the Lackawanna's Hoboken–Buffalo *Phoebe Snow* were consolidated between Elmira and Hoboken on April 30, 1961, and began operating over the former Lackawanna between Binghamton and Hoboken. The *Lake Cities*, renamed the *Chicago Lake Cities/Buffalo Lake Cities*, began carrying New York–Buffalo cars and operating over the former Lackawanna between Hoboken and Binghamton. The route of the *Atlantic Express* and *Pacific Express* remained unchanged. The *Erie–Lackawanna Limited/Phoebe Snow* began operating over the former Erie between Hoboken and Hornell on October 28, 1962, and the *Phoebe Snow* name disappeared.

The expected benefits of the merger did not materialize. Erie Lackawanna lost $26.4 million in 1961 and $16.6 million in 1962. To cut expenditures, it deferred maintenance on its physical plant and passenger equipment.

The *Chicago Lake Cities/Buffalo Lake Cities* names were shortened on April 29, 1962, to *Lake Cities*. Operation of the diner was shortened to Huntington–New York. The *Lake Cities* lost its sleepers on October 28, 1962. Sleeping car operations on the *Erie–Lackawanna Limited* were reduced to Chicago–Binghamton and a sleeper from Youngstown to Chicago that returned to Youngstown on the *Atlantic Express*.

Fleeting Wisp of Glory

William H. White, the retiring president of the Delaware & Hudson, became chairman and chief operating officer of the Erie Lackawanna on June 18, 1963. White had begun his career in 1913 on the Erie and served as president of the Lackawanna from 1941 to 1952. He would preside over a short-lived passenger revival, but further cuts came first.

Sleeping car operations on the *Erie–Lackawanna Limited* were curtailed on October 27, 1963, to Chicago–Hornell. A Chicago–Youngstown sleeper also operated in both directions following the removal of that sleeper from the *Atlantic Express*. Food service aboard the *Lake Cities* was downgraded to a buffet-lounge operating from Huntington to Jamestown, N.Y., and Meadville, Pa., to Huntington. The diner-lounge on the *Erie–Lackawanna Limited* no longer ran west of Youngstown.

White had fond memories of the Lackawanna's flagship train, the *Phoebe Snow*. Shortly after taking office, he ordered the *Phoebe*'s tavern-lounge cars removed from storage and placed in service between New York and Meadville on the *Erie–Lackawanna Limited*, which subsequently was renamed *Phoebe Snow*. Sleeping car operations on the *Phoebe Snow* were extended from Chicago to Elmira, N.Y., on December 3, 1963, and to Hoboken on December 31.

In an effort to tap the travel market to the 1964 New York World's Fair, Erie Lackawanna remodeled 25 coaches and 8 diners, and placed advertisements encouraging fairgoers to sleep aboard Pullmans en route to the fair rather than in New York hotels. The *Lake Cities* was renamed *The World's Fair* on April 26, 1964, and a diner-lounge began operating in June between Chicago and New York, replacing a coach sandwich service begun earlier in the year between Huntington and Marion. By August, the *Phoebe Snow*'s diner-lounge had been restored between Chicago and New York. The *Atlantic Express* received a Chicago–Youngstown sleeper.

But retrenchment had begun by summer's end. The Chicago–Youngstown sleepers came off the *Phoebe Snow* in September. On October 25, the sleeper came off the *Atlantic Express*, and the *World's Fair* reverted to the *Lake Cities* name. Passenger revenues fell from $24.3 million in 1963 to $21.4 million in 1965. The struggling Erie Lackawanna could ill afford these passenger deficits.

On February 1, 1965, the Erie Lackawanna sought Interstate Commerce Commission approval to end passenger service on the *Atlantic Express* and *Pacific Express*, which by now were primarily mail and express trains that carried one coach. Chairman White said that the need to handle passengers required the Erie Lackawanna to maintain a rigid schedule and stop where there was no mail and express business. Ending passenger service would afford the Erie more flexibility to serve the needs of mail and express shippers.

The *Pacific Express* had posted a 1964 profit of $494,721, but the *Atlantic Express*, which carried far less mail and express, lost $174,796. The ICC said discontinuance of dining and sleeping car service in 1963 had adversely affected patronage, which declined from an average of 75.3 passengers per day in 1962 to 46.6 in 1964 on the *Pacific Express* and from 94.4 in 1962 to 39.7 in 1974 on the *Atlantic Express*. Most patrons traveled 200 miles or less.

Few people opposed the discontinuance. The ICC figured that Erie Lackawanna would save 30 percent of the passenger revenue of Nos. 7/8 by diverting passengers to its other trains. The *Atlantic Express/Pacific Express* made their final runs as passenger trains in July 1965.

That same month, operation of the *Phoebe Snow*'s diner was curtailed to New York–Meadville, although on April 24, 1966, the diner again began operating between Chicago and New York. A year later, the Erie Lackawanna notified the ICC of its intent to discontinue the *Phoebe Snow*. The railroad's perilous financial footing again swayed the commission. The westbound *Phoebe* had been profitable through 1966, but the eastbound *Phoebe* had lost money, thus creating an adjusted $93,340 deficit for the *Phoebe Snow* in 1965.

Diversion of express traffic in early 1966 to piggyback and freight trains had further exacerbated the *Phoebe Snow*'s paltry financial performance. Although 130 people opposed

The Erie Lackawanna's *Lake Cities* ran in the shadow of the better-known *Phoebe Snow*, but would outlast the former Lackawanna train by more than 3 years. The *Lake Cities* is at Wadsworth, Ohio, in December 1966. Photo by Dave McKay.

removal of the *Phoebe Snow*, the ICC dismissed them as occasional patrons. Ridership had steadily declined since 1963. The *Phoebe Snow* began its final runs on November 27, 1966. The next day the *Lake Cities* was assigned sleepers and a diner between Chicago and Hoboken. Discontinuance of the *Phoebe Snow* also ended Erie Lackawanna passenger service in Indiana at Decatur in Adams County, North Judson in Starke County, and Crown Point in Lake County.

The *Lake Cities* had long played second fiddle to the *Erie Limited*. Renowned railroad photographer Phillip R. Hastings once described the *Lake Cities* as "old-school passenger railroading in the best sense of the phrase," operating in 1968 as though it were still 1948. By August 1967, the sleeping cars no longer operated west of Marion. Operation of the diner was curtailed to Huntington–Hoboken on April 27, 1969.

In June 1969, the Erie Lackawanna sought ICC approval to discontinue its last intercity passenger trains, citing declining revenue. The *Lake Cities* earned $2.3 million in 1968, but had cost $2.8 million to operate. Head-end income had dropped from $2.3 million in 1967 to $1.3 million in 1968, largely because of the 1967 removal of the railway post office. Of the 128 people who

The bleak future of Erie Lackawanna passenger service is reflected in the faces of conductor William Bellam (right) and trainman Kenneth Bartee at Huntington in December 1969. Photo by John Fuller.

Huntington was a major station for the Erie in Indiana. In the final years of service, the westbound *Lake Cities* dropped off its diner at Huntington, to be picked up 50 minutes later by its eastbound counterpart, shown departing in December 1969. Photo by John Fuller.

Waving through a cloud of steam, the conductor gives the second-to-last westbound *Lake Cities* a highball at Rochester on January 6, 1970. Photo by John Fuller.

Passengers board the last eastbound *Lake Cities* at Rochester on January 6, 1970. To the very end, the Erie Lackawanna still provided such amenities as fresh flowers, clean linens, and cloth napkins in the diner. Photo by John Fuller.

opposed the discontinuance at ICC hearings, 16 admitted to never having ridden the train. Many others were occasional patrons who wanted the service as a backup transportation option in poor weather. This prompted railroad attorney Wallace Steffen to comment, "The public liked the trains, but they didn't use them, and this cost us a bundle after we lost the mail business."

The ICC absolved the Erie Lackawanna of downgrading service in an effort to discourage business. Some witnesses said the railroad still provided such touches as fresh flowers, clean linens, and cloth napkins in the diner. Erie Lackawanna diners also featured a novelty item called Krusty Korn Kobs, a muffin baked in the shape of an ear of corn. Erie Lackawanna president Gregory Maxwell said the railroad's philosophy was "If you are going to be in the passenger business, you had better do it right."

By ICC calculations, the *Lake Cities* was losing $2,700 a day and cost $18 per passenger to operate. Yet the ICC granted permission to end the service with reluctance, saying that by law it was obligated to allow the discontinuance. But the commission commented, "We urge the railroad to muster its managerial acumen in an all-out effort to save this last brace of trains." The *Lake Cities* could have ended on December 30, 1969, but the train continued to operate through the New Year's holiday period.

Discontinuance opponents made an eleventh-hour effort to keep the *Lake Cities* running. The public service commissions of Illinois, Indiana, Ohio, Pennsylvania, and New York asked a federal district court in Columbus, Ohio, to issue a temporary restraining order blocking the train's discontinuance. The court refused, and U.S. Supreme Court Justice Potter Stewart denied an emergency appeal for a stay of the lower court's decision. The *Lake Cities* began its final runs on January 6, 1970.

Local Service

Most Erie locals in Indiana operated west of Huntington, terminating at North Judson, Rochester, and Huntington. These trains served Chicago, but during the 1890s Erie operated a Huntington–North Judson local. Locals operating east of Huntington usually terminated at Marion, although a local sometimes operated to Lima, Ohio.

In 1900, the Erie operated nine locals in Indiana: Chicago–Rochester (two pairs), Huntington–Lima, Chicago–Marion, and Marion–Chicago. Erie's local service in Indiana peaked in 1901 at 11 trains: Chicago–Rochester, Chicago–Huntington, Rochester–Huntington, Huntington–Lima, Chicago–Marion, and Marion–Chicago.

On September 21, 1902, service fell to eight trains, including two Chicago–Huntington round trips, a Huntington–Marion round trip, Huntington–Marion, and Marion–Chicago. The number of locals varied from 6 to 10 for the remainder of the decade. Although having commuterlike schedules, these were not true commuter trains due to the long distances involved and the lack of frequent stops. The Erie did offer Chicago–Hammond commuter service (one round trip) between January 8, 1905, and June 23, 1907.

The 1.7-mile line to Bass Lake in Starke County opened in June 1898. The line's daily passenger train often pulled private passenger cars. A Sunday-only Chicago–Bass Lake round trip begun on June 25, 1905, lasted through the fall. The Bass Lake branch was abandoned in August 1928.

By January 1918, local service operations had stabilized at three pairs of trains: Chicago–North Judson, Chicago–Huntington, and Huntington–Marion. This pattern remained until removal of the North Judson trains on June 19, 1921.

In 1908, the Erie became the first major railroad to experiment with a gasoline-powered car for passenger service. It took delivery of three Brill gas-electric cars in 1926 for branch line service and assigned one on April 25, 1926, to the Huntington–Marion trains. The car remained in service until December 1, 1928, when the trains were downgraded to mixed trains.

A year later, a motor car was assigned to the Chicago–Huntington trains, departing Chicago in early morning and returning in late afternoon. The Huntington–Marion mixed trains were truncated to Huntington–Lima, departing each terminal in the morning. The motor car was removed from the Chicago–Huntington run on September 28, 1930, and the Erie began operating three pairs of mixed trains: Hammond–Rochester, Rochester–Huntington, and Huntington–Lima. The Rochester mixed trains were consolidated into a Hammond–Huntington round trip on March 5, 1933. Erie discontinued the Hammond–Huntington and Huntington–Lima mixed trains on September 24, 1933.

CHAPTER 8

NICKEL PLATE ROAD

In the late 19th century, nickel was used interchangeably with silver to describe something of prestige or quality. The glittering prospects and substantial financial means of the Nickel Plate's founders prompted Ohio newspaper editor F. R. Loomis of the *Norwalk Chronicle* to label it "the great New York and St. Louis double track, nickel plated railroad" in an editorial published March 10, 1881. Built for $23 million in 1881–82 between Chicago and Buffalo, the Nickel Plate made its mark with fast freight service on a mostly single-track line. Unable to match the speed or frequency of service of the New York Central, its principal rival, the Nickel Plate excelled at on-board service and was known for friendly crews, excellent dining, and low fares.

The Nickel Plate's 1923 acquisition of the Lake Erie & Western and the Toledo, St. Louis & Western (Clover Leaf) made it Indiana's third-largest railroad with 773 miles or 10 percent of the state's peak rail mileage.

Chicago–Buffalo

George I. Seney created a syndicate that organized the New York, Chicago & St. Louis on February 3, 1881. William H. Vanderbilt's Lake Shore & Michigan Southern (later New York Central) held a virtual monopoly along the southern rim of the Great Lakes, but he seemed unconcerned about his new competitor.

The Nickel Plate was built in 500 days. Construction began in Indiana on April 15, 1881, at Knox in Starke County. The first Indiana passenger operation was a special that arrived in Fort Wayne from Fostoria, Ohio, on November 3, 1881. A ceremony at Sidney, Ind., in southeastern Kosciusko County on April 5, 1882, marked the completion of the Nickel Plate in Indiana. The first passenger train to run the length of the Nickel Plate left Chicago on August 30, 1882, and reached Buffalo the next day. The Nickel Plate had long tangents, gentle grades, and majestic bridges, but served an area already saturated with railroads.

Scheduled service began on October 23, 1882, with trains operating Buffalo–Bellevue, Ohio, and Chicago–Cleveland. The Nickel Plate's Pullman-built passenger car fleet included 24 first-class coaches and 10 second-class coaches pulled by 4-4-0 locomotives built by the Brooks Works of Dunkirk, N.Y.

Three days after opening, the Nickel Plate was sold to William H. Vanderbilt for $7 million, leading to speculation that it had been built to force Vanderbilt to buy it to elimi-

Nickel Plate Road

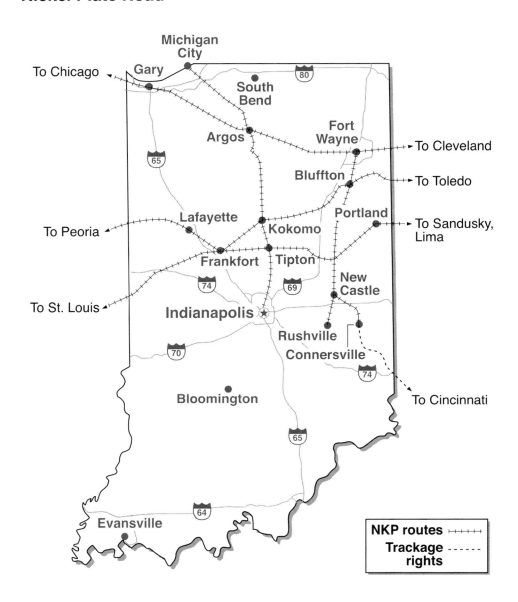

nate a competitor. Whatever the truth of those claims, the Nickel Plate did not prosper under New York Central control.

At first, the Nickel Plate offered only local service. Indiana service in early 1888 included a Chicago–Cleveland accommodation train and a local operating between Stony Island (Chicago) and Erie Junction near the Illinois border. By 1891, three pairs of trains served Indiana: Chicago–Cleveland, Fort Wayne–Stony Island, and Fort Wayne–Bellevue. The Nickel Plate was a decade old before it scheduled passenger trains to operate the length of its system. The *Chicago Express/Buffalo Express* debuted October 23, 1892, between Chicago and Buffalo on overnight schedules.

The World's Columbian Exposition in Chicago prompted the Nickel Plate's first through car arrangement. On May 28, 1893, the Nickel Plate began interchanging Chicago–New York sleepers with the West Shore (later New York Central) at Buffalo. Cleveland to Chicago No. 3 became a Buffalo to Chicago express and a new Chicago to Buffalo train, the *Western Express*, commenced. Operating on 16-hour Chicago–Buffalo schedules, these trains had Ohio Falls passenger cars and Wagner dining cars. No. 3 reverted to Cleveland–Chicago operation after the fair closed, but the Nickel Plate began interchanging New York cars at Buffalo with the Delaware, Lackawanna & Western. A Chicago–Boston sleeper began operating via the West Shore and the Fitchburg (later Boston & Maine) railroads.

The *Chicago Express/New York and Boston Express* were renamed the *Standard Express* on May 30, 1897, and Nos. 3/4 began serving Buffalo. No. 3 was named the *Erie, Cleveland, Fort Wayne and Chicago Express*. No. 4 became the *Nickel Plate Express*. The *Western Express* lost its name and the *Eastern Express* was renamed the *Fort Wayne, Cleveland, Erie, Buffalo and Eastern Express*. Nos. 2/3 ran on a 15-hour Chicago–Buffalo schedule. Nos. 3/4 carried New York cars interchanged at Buffalo with the Lackawanna. Cars interchanged with the West Shore were conveyed by Nos. 5/6. These schedules remained largely unchanged through 1916. The Nickel Plate labeled its express trains "the peerless trio." Advertisements showed a hand holding three trains and a banner proclaiming "excellent dining service."

At the beginning of the 20th century, the Nickel Plate's Chicago–Buffalo schedule included the *Standard Express*, the *Nickel Plate Express*, the *Erie, Cleveland, Fort Wayne, and Chicago Express*, and the *Fort Wayne, Cleveland, Erie, Buffalo, and Eastern Express*. The 28-hour Chicago–New York schedule of the *Nickel Plate Express* was 8 hours slower than the premier trains of the New York Central and Pennsylvania, but the Nickel Plate's first-class fare was $3 lower.

The Nickel Plate used several terminals in Chicago, including the Illinois Central depot, Van Buren Street Station, and Grand Central Station, before settling in at La Salle Street Station in 1903. Between 1892 and 1898, the Nickel Plate had its own Chicago depot a mile south of Van Buren Street Station.

The Van Sweringens Take on the Central

To avoid antitrust problems, the New York Central sold the Nickel Plate in 1916 to Cleveland bachelor brothers Oris P. and Mantis J. Van Sweringen. Some described the Nickel Plate as "a streak of rust" because it had done little to improve its physical plant. It owned just four all-steel passenger cars.

The Nickel Plate left the Erie's Buffalo terminal in March 1917 for the Lackawanna terminal and ended its last interchange arrangement with the West Shore, a Boston sleeper. A United States Railroad Administration order led to the January 12, 1918, discontinuance of Nos. 3/4, leaving Nos. 5/6 to convey the New York cars. The "peerless trio" returned on June 6, 1920, when Nos. 3/4 resumed service between Chicago and Cleveland. Upgraded on April 30, 1922, to Chicago–Buffalo express trains, Nos. 3/4 were assigned New York coaches and sleepers.

The Transportation Act of 1920 encouraged railroad consolidation. The Van Sweringens purchased the Lake Erie & Western on January 11, 1922, and the Clover Leaf on February 7, 1922. The three roads initially did not integrate passenger schedules. Neither the LE&W nor the Clover Leaf possessed a fleet of modern passenger cars. The Nickel Plate lacked a general passenger agent. The Nickel Plate's nonchalant attitude toward passenger service began to change following the 1926 appointment of Walter L. Ross as president. Ross had been general passenger agent of the Clover Leaf. If the Nickel Plate hoped to compete with the New York Central's leading passenger trains, it would need faster schedules, new passenger cars, and powerful locomotives.

In mid-1926, the Nickel Plate began designing a new passenger locomotive, a 4-6-4. The first four of these arrived from Alco's Brooks Works in March 1927 and began service between Chicago and Conneaut, Ohio. Although innovative, the Nickel Plate's L-1 Hudsons were overshadowed by the Hudsons built at the same time for the New York Central. The Nickel Plate received two new dining cars from Pullman in 1927, its first all-steel diners. Between 1927 and 1930, the Nickel Plate also purchased new coaches and café-coaches.

Chicago–Buffalo schedules were tightened in 1928. Nickel Plate No. 5 and the Central's all-Pullman *Forest City* both departed Cleveland at 11:30 P.M. Although the *Forest City* stopped only at Toledo, Elkhart, and Englewood, Ill., No. 5 arrived at La Salle Street Station just 15 minutes later.

Railroads operating in the Chicago–New York market charged extra fare on trains making the run in less than 28 hours. For each hour below that, the fare went up by $1.20. If a train failed to meet its schedule, passengers were entitled to a proportional refund. The Nickel Plate and Lackawanna had marketed their service for its lower fares, operating in 1927 on the same 28-hour schedules of 1897. Although the Nickel Plate's Chicago–New York running time was chiseled to just under 24 hours, an improvement of 4 hours, this still did not match the New York Central's best schedules.

The Delaware, Lackawanna & Western conveyed the Nickel Plate's New York cars between Buffalo and Hoboken, N.J. The Lackawanna route was shorter than the Central's route but slower because of multitudinous curves and steep grades in the Pocono Mountains. Nickel Plate through cars also had long dwell times in Buffalo.

Ross had faced a similar situation at the Clover Leaf in competing with the Wabash between Toledo and St. Louis. His philosophy was to try harder to please passengers. Cars were cleaner and more comfortable, food was prepared better and served faster, and employees were more congenial and helpful. Nickel Plate diners had more spacious pantries and kitchen areas to expedite food service. The Nickel Plate also scheduled trains at convenient times at intermediate cities.

The competition intensified in April 1929. The Nickel Plate named Nos. 4/5 the *Nickel Plate Limited* and went after the high-end business by charging extra fare. The Nickel Plate had not had a named passenger train since 1906. The Chicago–Hoboken running time was trimmed to 23 hours. The *Nickel Plate Limited* received two Pullman club cars and four 12-section, one–drawing room Pullmans. A Cleveland–Fort Wayne sleeper was established. The next day the New York Central beefed up its Chicago–Cleveland service with additional Pullmans and faster schedules. The Central also announced plans to assign new equipment to the *Forest City*.

The Nickel Plate ordered four Hudsons from Lima in June 1929 and placed an order with Pullman for 21 all-steel cars including eight 80-seat coaches, three diners, two café-parlor cars, and eight baggage and mail cars. Pullman agreed to furnish 12 sleepers of the latest design. Two new sleepers assigned to the *Nickel Plate Limited* on December 21, 1929, featured six single bedrooms and a sun parlor–observation room and lounge. The lounge section had plush carpeting, table lamps, deep-seated armchairs, and settees upholstered in green, buff, black, and gold. Five refurbished 10-section, one-compartment, two–drawing room sleepers replaced the 12-1 sleepers.

The Nickel Plate's passenger network peaked with the release of the April 28, 1929, time-table, which listed 28 daily trains and 11 daily-except-Sunday mixed trains. The Nickel Plate had just 25 passenger locomotives, so 86 freight engines had been pressed into passenger duty.

Waving the White Flag

The spirited competition with the New York Central lasted just over a year. No. 4 ended on September 28, 1930. No. 8 became the eastbound *Nickel Plate Limited*, operating on a daylight schedule between Chicago and Cleveland with the luxury lounge-buffet-sleepers from No. 4, a 26-seat parlor car, a new diner, and Buffalo coaches.

The Fort Wayne–Cleveland sleepers ended on July 19, 1936. The Nickel Plate began converting diners to diner-lounges in 1937. Two café-coaches became café-lounges. Nos. 5/6 received New York coaches and sleepers in May 1938. The best-patronized and most profitable Pullmans were Chicago–Cleveland sleepers.

For the 1934 Century of Progress Fair in Chicago, the Nickel Plate revived No. 4, which along with No. 3 became extra-fare trains between Chicago and New York. But as the fair wound down, the Nickel Plate on September 8, 1934, permanently pulled the plug on the "peerless trio" by slicing Chicago–Buffalo service to two round trips.

In the early 1930s, the Nickel Plate had lost $4.4 million. Government loans helped stave off bankruptcy. Patronage, average trip length, and passenger-train miles remained constant between 1932 and 1942. The Nickel Plate completed air-conditioning its passenger fleet in 1934 and cut fares by a third in 1936. These moves helped offset the general passenger service decline that had bedeviled eastern railroads since the mid-1920s.

The Nickel Plate experienced sharply increased passenger travel during World War II when passenger revenue peaked at $5.35 million. A shortage of passenger locomotives forced the assignment of 22 freight engines to troop trains and some scheduled service.

The lightweight car era began on the Nickel Plate on August 5, 1940, when two Pullman demonstrators, each with 18 roomettes, replaced a pair of 12-1 sleepers between Chicago and Cleveland. The Nickel Plate purchased the cars in 1945 and named them *Moses Cleaveland* (the founder of Cleveland) and *Robert de La Salle* (an early French explorer). The Stony Island shops in Chicago rebuilt 10 coaches and converted seven diners to diner-lounge cars. The Nickel Plate ordered 25 stainless-steel lightweight cars from Pullman-Standard in 1947,

The Nickel Plate's first passenger diesel locomotives were Alco PA1s, which quickly became known as "bluebirds" because of their blue and gray livery. A pair of "bluebirds" hustles the *Westerner* across northern Indiana. Jay Williams collection.

including 10 52-seat coaches, two bedroom-lounge-diners, and 13 10-roomette, six double bedroom sleepers.

The Nickel Plate dieselized mainline passenger trains with 11 Alco PA1 locomotives, the first 7 of which arrived in December 1947. The Hudsons were relegated to backup duty, and K-1 Pacifics replaced R-class 4-6-0 locomotives on branch line trains. Nicknamed "Bluebirds" after their blue and gray livery, the PA1s cost $204,099 apiece and ran in pairs on Chicago–Buffalo trains and as a single unit on Cleveland–St. Louis trains.

The Cleveland–Fort Wayne sleepers were revived on September 15, 1946, using the last heavyweight sleepers to operate on the Nickel Plate. Lightweight 10-6 sleepers were assigned in 1954. At 186 miles, the Cleveland–Fort Wayne sleeper line was one of the shortest in the country. The Fort Wayne sleepers ended on August 2, 1956.

The heavyweight sleepers continued in Chicago–Hoboken service until replaced on July 21, 1949, by new Lackawanna lightweight 10-6 sleepers, sporting Lackawanna maroon and gray. The Nickel Plate's lightweight equipment was adorned in blue, silver, and gray. In the early 1880s, Nickel Plate passenger cars were Tuscan red with gilt stripes, which later gave way to Pullman green with gold lettering.

The Nickel Plate and Lackawanna posted their best Chicago–New York schedules in the late 1940s. The eastbound *Nickel Plate Limited*/westbound *New Yorker* went the distance in 20 hours, 35 minutes. However, the crack expresses of the New York Central and Pennsylvania were 4 hours faster. The *Nickel Plate Limited* was renamed *City of Chicago* (westbound) and *City of Cleveland* (eastbound) in September 1954. No. 8 became the *New Yorker* on October 28, 1956, to match its Lackawanna counterpart. No. 7 had been the *Westerner* for several years.

New equipment and schedule enhancements helped to reverse a trend of steadily declining passenger revenue. The Nickel Plate earned a record $3.15 per passenger train mile in 1952. Passenger revenues increased 50 percent over 1949 levels.

By the end of 1953, the Pacifics had been retired and the Hudsons relegated to back-up and excursion train duty. The 1955–56 arrival of GP9 diesels from the Electro-Motive Division of General Motors prompted retirement of the Hudsons. The new diesels were painted black with yellow striping to match the Nickel Plate's freight locomotives.

The *City of Chicago/City of Cleveland* carried bedroom-buffet-lounge sleepers (Chicago–Cleveland) and 10-6 sleepers (Chicago–Hoboken). The *New Yorker* and the *Westerner*

Despite having just six passenger trains during most of the 1950s, the Nickel Plate did quite well. No. 8 (later named the *New Yorker*) is at Bellevue, Ohio, on May 15, 1956. Jay Williams collection.

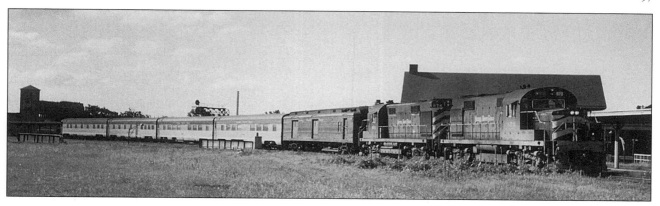

carried diner-lounges and Chicago–Hoboken coaches and sleepers. The *City of Cleveland* lost its New York sleepers in late spring 1958. That same year, the heavyweight diner-lounges on the *New Yorker* and the *Westerner* stopped operating east of Cleveland. Despite service reductions and scant marketing, the Nickel Plate in 1959 earned a post–World War II record $3.4 million in passenger revenue.

The last "Bluebirds" came off the Nickel Plate roster in May 1962, replaced by Alco RS36 Nos. 874 and 875. Built in July 1962, the Alcos were the last passenger locomotives purchased by the Nickel Plate.

The *City of Chicago* poses at Englewood, Ill., on Chicago's South Side on August 28, 1965. Though operated by Norfolk & Western, the *City* still retained its Nickel Plate identity. Thirteen days later, the *City of Chicago* and *City of Cleveland* were gone. Photo by Dave McKay.

End of Service

The 1960 merger of the Erie and the Lackawanna led to the assignment of Erie passenger cars to the Chicago–Hoboken equipment pool. The Chicago–New York sleepers were curtailed to Cleveland–New York on August 6, 1962, leaving the Hoboken–Chicago coach on the *City of Chicago* as the Nickel Plate's only through car through Indiana.

The Nickel Plate said in December 1962 that it would end the *New Yorker/Western* (Nos. 7/8) on January 7, 1963. An Interstate Commerce Commission investigation found that Nos. 7/8 carried more passengers than the *City* trains but had a greater out-of-pocket loss. The Nickel Plate said those using Nos. 5/6 generally traveled longer distances than those patronizing Nos. 7/8. Patronage on Nos. 7/8 had fallen from 92,918 in 1960 to 77,119 in 1961. The corresponding figures for Nos. 5/6 were 70,937 and 58,830. No. 7 carried an average of 102.6 passenger per trip in 1961; No. 8 averaged 108.7. The Nickel Plate said Nos. 7/8 had net losses of $376,787 in 1960, $422,999 in 1961, and $198,140 in the first 6 months of 1962.

Those opposed to the discontinuance spoke highly of Nickel Plate service, and the ICC concluded there was no evidence the railroad had sought to discourage service. However, the opponents did not consider the schedule of Nos. 5/6 to be an acceptable alternative to Nos. 7/8. In a decision reached May 15, 1963, the ICC approved the discontinuance, citing the losses and alternative transportation choices. The *New Yorker* and the *Westerner* departed for the final time on June 2, 1963, ending diner-lounge service on the Nickel Plate. Shortly thereafter, the Hoboken to Chicago coach ended.

The cover of the final Nickel Plate timetable, issued August 23, 1964, still featured a "Bluebird," even though they had been retired from the Nickel Plate roster for more than 2 years. In the final years of service, a low-nose RS36 freight locomotive followed by a passenger Geep or RS36 pulled Nos. 5/6. The usual consist was a railway post office, two coaches, a 10-6 sleeper, and a buffet-lounge-sleeper. The sleepers did not operate east of Cleveland.

Following the October 16, 1964, merger of the Nickel Plate and the Norfolk & Western, Nos. 5/6 continued to operate with Nickel Plate equipment, although at least one coach and some locomotives were painted in N&W Tuscan red. Otherwise, passenger cars remained in Nickel Plate blue and gray with Norfolk & Western in gold script on the letter board.

Six months after the merger, the N&W notified the Interstate Commerce Commission of its intent to discontinue Nos. 5/6. *City of Chicago* patronage had declined 39.9 percent from 27,238 in 1962 to 16,395 in 1964. *City of Cleveland* patronage was down 24.1 percent from 22,832 to 17,370. The trains lost $771,675 in 1964 due to a sharp reduction in head-end business including the removal of the Chicago–Cleveland RPO on January 15, 1965.

The ICC received several letters opposing removal of the trains, including one from the state of Indiana, but only one person opposed the discontinuance at a hearing in Cleveland and only four protested at a Fort Wayne hearing. "The demonstrated need for continued operation of these trains is light," the ICC said. The commission brushed aside allegations that the N&W had failed to adequately promote the service. Commissioner Kenneth H. Tuggle remarked, "We have consistently held that prospective patrons who must be coaxed to use the service evidently have no urgent need for it." The *City of Cleveland* and *City of Chicago* ended September 10, 1965.

Indiana Local Service

In the late 1890s, local service in Indiana included trains operating Knox–Stony Island, Fort Wayne–Knox, and Fort Wayne–Leipsic Junction, Ohio. These schedules remained through 1914 when the Knox–Stony Island trains began operating between Knox and Rock Island Junction (Chicago). These trains were gone by 1918. The Fort Wayne–Knox and Chicago–Knox locals ended in 1920.

Nine years later, on April 28, 1929, the Nickel Plate instituted a Chicago–Fort Wayne local so that it could speed up the *Nickel Plate Limited* by skipping all stops except Englewood (Chicago), Hammond, and Knox. The local and the *Nickel Plate Limited* interchanged a through coach at Fort Wayne. The Fort Wayne locals ended September 28, 1930.

For a while, beginning in 1883, the Nickel Plate offered summer excursion service between Indiana and Niagara Falls, N.Y. A train originated at Valparaiso and ran nonstop east of Fort Wayne. A second train originated at Fort Wayne. The service featured sleepers, discounted fares, and guided tours.

Lake Erie & Western

The Lake Erie & Western began August 4, 1879, with the merger of three railroads operating between Fremont, Ohio, and Bloomington, Ill. Envisioned as the middle segment of a Boston–Kansas City route, the LE&W ultimately operated between Sandusky, Ohio, and Peoria, Ill.

The LE&W featured the oldest line in the Nickel Plate system, the Peru & Indianapolis, chartered January 19, 1846, and opened on March 12, 1851, between Indianapolis and Noblesville in Hamilton County. The P&I's mixed trains began operating to Peru in 1854.

Development north of Peru began with the June 23, 1853, formation of the Cincinnati, Peru & Chicago, which opened between LaPorte and Plymouth in 1855. Financial problems stalled further expansion until 1867. By now the Chicago, Cincinnati & Louisville, it reached LaPorte in July 1869. Peru–LaPorte service began September 4, 1869.

The push to Michigan City began with the June 4, 1870, organization of the Michigan City & Indianapolis, which reached Michigan City in December. Passenger service began April 9, 1871. A month later, the Michigan City & Indianapolis and the Chicago, Cincinnati & Louisville were taken over by the Indianapolis, Peru & Chicago to complete the Indianapolis–Michigan City route. Briefly operated by the Wabash in the 1880s, the Michigan City route was absorbed by the Lake Erie & Western on March 15, 1887.

The Sandusky–Peoria route began with the 1853 organization of the Fremont & Indiana. Two decades and three receiverships later, the company, now known as the Indianapolis & Sandusky, began building toward Muncie, reaching Portland, the Jay County seat, by late 1879. Passenger service began in late May 1880.

Construction of the La Fayette, Bloomington & Mississippi began at Lafayette in March 1870. A separate company chartered in Illinois began in October 1869 to build from Bloomington, Ill., to the Indiana border. Construction crews drove the last spike on March 22, 1872, at the border. Passenger service began on May 1, 1872.

Construction westward from Muncie began in June 1875. The line reached Tipton by October and Frankfort a month later. By the end of the year, the line had reached Altamont, a junction near Lafayette, where it connected with the Indianapolis, Cincinnati & La Fayette (later New York Central).

A stockholders' special on February 1, 1876, was the first passenger operation between Muncie and Lafayette. A Muncie–Tipton accommodation train that began 10 days later was extended to Frankfort on February 24. Service began between Muncie and Lafayette on July 19, 1876, but there was no coordination of schedules at Lafayette with western division trains until November when service began between Muncie and Bloomington, Ill. The LM&B also operated a daily Frankfort–Bloomington accommodation train.

The third of the Lake Erie & Western's Indiana lines began October 10, 1863, as the Connersville & New Castle Junction. Completed between Connersville and Cambridge City in western Wayne County in April 1865, the line was extended to New Castle in early 1867. Renamed the Cincinnati, Connersville & Muncie on January 2, 1868, the line opened to Muncie in February 1869.

A subsidiary, the Fort Wayne, Muncie & Cincinnati, was organized on October 3, 1868, to finish the route to Fort Wayne. The line reached Bluffton in Wells County on November 10, 1869, and Fort Wayne in 1870. Service between Fort Wayne and Connersville began September 12, 1870. The Fort Wayne, Muncie & Cincinnati used the Wabash to reach Fort Wayne until opening its own route by 1873.

The FWM&C in 1880 created a subsidiary, the New Castle & Rushville, to build between those two points. The branch opened in 1881. The FWM&C reorganized on December 6, 1881, becoming the Fort Wayne, Cincinnati & Louisville. Through 1890, the FWC&L operated passenger trains to Cincinnati on the White Water Valley Railroad (later New York Central) south of Connersville. The Lake Erie & Western purchased the FWM&C on May 28, 1890.

The LE&W completed an extension to Sandusky, Ohio, on February 20, 1881. For a while, the LE&W operated a pair of Sandusky–Kansas City express trains that interchanged with the Chicago & Alton (later Gulf, Mobile & Ohio) at Bloomington, Ill. The LE&W completed an extension to Peoria, Ill., in April 1888. Sandusky–Peoria passenger service began May 27, 1888. After a natural gas boom of the late 1880s saved it from financial ruin, the LE&W began using the slogan, "The Natural Gas Route." During New York Central control of the LE&W between 1900 and 1922, the railroad rebuilt its physical plant but otherwise stagnated.

The Elwood & Alexandria interurban railway, which opened in 1899, paralleled the LE&W for 9 miles. Four years later, interurban railways paralleled 150 miles of the LE&W and half of it by 1913. Competition with the interurbans was brutal, and the LE&W's passenger and express business suffered enormously.

Interurban railways offered more frequent service, lower fares, and better access to the commercial districts of many cities. Among the first passengers to forsake the LE&W were traveling salesmen, who for years had derisively called the LE&W "Leave Early and Walk." With little prospect of offsetting its losses with long-haul passenger business, the LE&W fought back by reducing the running time of some trains and purchasing new equipment, including 84-seat coaches with vestibules and smoother riding six-wheel trucks. The LE&W also purchased 20 rebuilt 4-4-0 locomotives from the Big Four.

The unrelenting competition from interurban railways forced the LE&W to reduce service. Most of the LE&W's excursion business to Lake Erie was lost to interurban railways. In 1904 LE&W management discussed electrifying some central Indiana lines, but shelved the idea.

Nickel Plate No. 152, a
Baldwin R Class 4-6-0 built
in 1907, has a local in tow
on the former Lake Erie &
Western at Celina, Ohio, in
December 1934. The Nickel
Plate acquired the LE&W
in 1923. Jay Williams
collection.

Increasing automobile ownership and an expanding highway network robbed the interurban railways and steam railroads alike of passengers in the 1920s. Nickel Plate passenger traffic fell 30 percent between 1923 and 1927.

The Nickel Plate considered purchasing gasoline-powered motor cars in 1925 to replace worn-out steam locomotives on former LE&W passenger trains. Motor cars operated at half the cost of a steam train, but the Nickel Plate still needed steam trains to provide adequate capacity to meet peak passenger demand. With the future of passenger service on the former LE&W lines in doubt, the Nickel Plate discarded the idea of buying motor cars. Cleveland–St. Louis Nos. 9/10, which used the LE&W between Frankfort and Arcadia, Ohio, were the only diesel-powered passenger trains ever to use former LE&W rails in scheduled service.

Passenger service ended over 174 miles of the former L&EW in August 1929, mostly on routes paralleled by interurban railways. The last competing interurban railway went out of business in 1938, but by then passenger service on the former LE&W was six pairs of trains on the Sandusky–Peoria line.

Fort Wayne–Connersville

In its early years, service on this line was oriented toward Cincinnati. Through cars operated between Connersville and the Queen City through 1881 using the Cincinnati, Hamilton & Indianapolis (later Baltimore & Ohio) and after that on the White Water Valley. The line hosted two round trips between Fort Wayne and Connersville in 1900 and a Fort Wayne–Muncie round trip. Cincinnati service ended in 1890 but was restored in 1905 via the White Water Valley route. The *Cincinnati Fast Mail* connected at Fort Wayne with a Lake Shore & Michigan Southern train from Jackson, Mich., and made the 166-mile trek to Cincinnati in just over 6 hours. The train featured buffet-parlor cars serving a la carte meals. Another train operated between Muncie and Cincinnati.

Fort Wayne–Indianapolis through service began at the same time, interchanging at Muncie with the Big Four. These trains featured vestibule parlor cars. The Muncie–Cincinnati and Fort Wayne–Indianapolis through cars ended in 1908. Three Fort Wayne–Connersville round trips and one Muncie–Connersville round trip remained. Indianapolis and Cincinnati through cars were restored in 1909, the same year the Muncie–Connersville train ended. The Indianapolis and Cincinnati cars ended in 1913, and service fell to two Fort Wayne–Connersville round trips. This was one round trip by 1918.

A Fort Wayne–Muncie round trip and Fort Wayne–Indianapolis parlor cars and coaches were inaugurated in December 1920. This ended January 22, 1922, when service reverted to one Fort Wayne–Connersville round trip, which made its final runs on August 3, 1929.

New Castle–Rushville

Passenger service on the Rushville branch was always minimal: one daily round trip in 1900. The branch had competition from a parallel interurban railway, and service never increased. By 1917, the Rushville–New Castle train no longer connected with Fort Wayne–Connersville trains. Nos. 95/96 became mixed trains and made their final runs on August 3, 1929.

Indianapolis–Michigan City

A bustling passenger route in the early 1920s, bolstered by excursion business to Michigan City and Indianapolis–South Bend through cars, service peaked in that era at eight trains. During Wabash control in the early 1880s, the line hosted two Indianapolis–Michigan City round trips, three Indianapolis–Peru round trips, and a Michigan City–Peru round trip. Sleepers also operated between Indianapolis and Detroit. By late 1883, service had fallen to one Indianapolis–Michigan City round trip and two Indianapolis–Peru round trips.

At the dawn of the 20th century, seven trains used the Michigan City line, some connecting at Tipton with Sandusky–Peoria line trains. The schedule included Indianapolis–Michigan City and Indianapolis–Plymouth round trips and trains operating Indianapolis to Michigan City, Michigan City to Peru, and Peru to Argos in Marshall County on the Nickel Plate's Chicago–Buffalo mainline. Over the next 15 years, service held steady at three pairs of trains: two Indianapolis–Michigan City round trips and one round trip between Indianapolis and Peru, LaPorte, Plymouth, or Walkerton (southwestern St. Joseph County).

Indianapolis–South Bend service began about 1915 and featured café-parlor cars displaced from Fort Wayne–Cincinnati service. Trains operated between Walkerton and South Bend on the New York Central. Service expanded to four round trips on March 23, 1919, two operating Indianapolis–Michigan City and two Indianapolis–Walkerton. This schedule remained until November 21, 1920, when one Michigan City train ended. Five of the remaining six trains carried South Bend cars.

South Bend service ended in 1921, and service was trimmed to two round trips: Indianapolis–Michigan City and Indianapolis–Plymouth. Service expanded to three Indianapolis–Michigan City round trips on June 18, 1922, but by the end of the year it had fallen to two round trips, one of which ended in 1922. With the inauguration of Indianapolis–Toledo service on February 19, 1928, Nos. 23/24 were combined with the Toledo trains between Indianapolis and Kokomo, where the Michigan City line crossed the former Clover Leaf.

Unlike many LE&W trains, the Indianapolis–Michigan City trains never became mixed trains. Nos. 23/24 made their final runs on April 16, 1932, ending 80 years of passenger service on the Nickel Plate's oldest route.

Sandusky–Lafayette–Peoria

The LE&W operated a Sandusky–Kansas City through train in the early 1880s. The travel time of the westbound *Kansas City Express* to Bloomington, Ill., where it interchanged with the Chicago & Alton, was 16 hours. The eastbound *Denver Express* ran from Bloomington to Sandusky in 17 hours.

The LE&W upgraded passenger service in 1902 by assigning café-parlor cars to Nos. 1/2 between Sandusky and Peoria, and cutting the running time by 3 hours. Six additional trains were added, terminating at Lima, Ohio, Rankin, Ill., Lafayette, or Muncie. With competition from interurban railways heating up, the LE&W tightened schedules in 1906, reducing the Sandusky–Peoria running time to 13 hours, 45 minutes. By year's end, the schedule had been tweaked to provide four one-way trains: Sandusky to Lafayette, Muncie to Sandusky, Peoria to Muncie, and Lafayette to Peoria.

Service peaked at 10 trains in 1907: Nos. 1/2 (Sandusky–Peoria), Nos. 3/4 (Sandusky–Muncie), Nos. 9/10 (Lafayette–Peoria), and Nos. 5/6 7/8 (Muncie–Lafayette). A year later, service had fallen to eight trains with an emphasis on shorter-distance pairings. The Peoria–Sandusky trains remained unchanged, but Nos. 3/5 had been shortened to Sandusky–Tipton, Nos. 5/6 to Tipton–Bloomington, and Nos. 7/8 to Lafayette–Rankin.

Between 1909 and 1912, the line hosted six trains. By early 1913, this had risen to eight and included Nos. 1/2 (Sandusky–Peoria), Nos. 5/6 (Muncie–Peoria), and trains operating Lima to Lafayette, Rankin to Lima, Lafayette to Peoria, and Peoria to Rankin. Within a year, Nos. 1/2, the last passenger trains to operate the length of the LE&W, had been curtailed to Lima–Bloomington. Service had fallen to six trains by 1918, which continued through the early 1920s: Nos. 1/2 (Lima and Bloomington), Nos. 3/4 (Sandusky and Lafayette), and Nos. 5/6 (Lafayette and Peoria).

The day after the Nickel Plate took over the LE&W on July 2, 1922, passenger service fell to two pairs of trains, operating Sandusky–Bloomington and Lafayette–Peoria. Within a year, the latter had begun operating between Frankfort and Peoria. Service between Fostoria, Ohio, and Sandusky ended August 31, 1929, when Nos. 21/22 were curtailed to Fostoria–Bloomington. Nos. 25/26 (Frankfort–Peoria) no longer connected with other

By the time this photo of No. 22 leaving Peoria, Ill., was taken on May 12, 1951, the train had already been gone in Indiana for more than a month. Locomotive No. 167 was a K-1b Pacific built by the Brooks Works in 1923. Jay Williams collection.

Nickel Plate trains at Frankfort. The usual consist for Nos. 25/26 was a Ten-Wheeler steam locomotive, a railway post office, and a day coach.

No. 26 became a mixed train between Peoria and Frankfort on March 15, 1932. No. 25 became a mixed train between Frankfort and Rankin two months later and a mixed train all the way to Peoria on June 26. The same day, Nos. 21/22 ended between Frankfort and Tipton and began operating as mixed trains between Tipton and Fostoria. The Frankfort–Tipton segment was reinstated on June 25, 1933. Service remained largely unchanged for the remainder of the 1930s.

The Nickel Plate discontinued Nos. 25/26 on June 13, 1943, extended Nos. 21/22 from Bloomington to Peoria, but discontinued the train between Fostoria and Lima. The trains departed both terminals in early morning and arrived at their terminus by early evening. The schedule listed 55 stops, including 26 in Indiana.

Nos. 21/22 soldiered on during World War II. The usual consist was an RPO-express car and a coach pulled by a steam locomotive. Passengers could purchase a box lunch at Frankfort, where both trains arrived at midday. The Nickel Plate asked state regulatory authorities in late 1949 for permission to discontinue Nos. 21/22, claiming an out-of-pocket loss of $34,127 in 1948 and $30,349 for the first nine months of 1949. Ohio acted first, and the trains ended between Lima and Portland, Ind., on March 12, 1950. The trains were discontinued east of Frankfort on June 4 and between Frankfort and Cheneyville, Ill., on March 20, 1951. The rest of the run in Illinois ended July 1, 1951.

Agent C. W. Morris hoops up train orders to the flagman of No. 22 at Boswell, Ind., on May 24, 1949. No. 22 was the last passenger train on the former Lake Erie & Western and operated between Peoria, Ill., and Lima, Ohio. NKP photo by John Burger; John B. Corns collection.

Clover Leaf

Frequently in financial straits, the Clover Leaf was saved by the natural gas boom of the late 1880s. To commemorate its good fortune, the company in 1886 adopted a three-leaf clover as its corporate symbol, each leaf representing a state that the road served. The "Little Giant Line" was the longest narrow-gauge railroad east of the Mississippi River.

The Clover Leaf began May 23, 1879, as the Toledo, Delphos & Burlington. Joseph W. Hunt, a Delphos, Ohio, pharmacist, envisioned a narrow-gauge railroad stretching from Lake Erie to the Mexico border. The TD&B planned to build across Indiana and connect with the Havana, Rantoul & Eastern (later Illinois Central). The TD&B purchased the standard-gauge Frankfort & Kokomo and converted it to narrow gauge.

Formed December 27, 1870, the F&K began building in 1873. Its first passenger operation occurred on March 28, 1874, between Frankfort and Michigantown in northeastern Clinton County. The line reached Kokomo in August 1874, and weekend mixed train service began August 10. After July 1876, a daily Kokomo–Frankfort train connected at Frankfort with the La Fayette, Muncie & Bloomington (later Lake Erie & Western).

Construction between Delphos and Kokomo began July 17, 1878, at Delphos and July 8, 1878, at Bluffton. The first passenger operation was an October 11, 1878, excursion from Bluffton to Warren in southern Huntington County. Most of the line in Indiana was completed in 1879. Service between Warren and Delphos began December 16, 1879. Scheduled mail and express trains began January 5, 1880.

The route was completed to Toledo in 1880, and the gap between Warren and Kokomo closed in late December. Service between Marion and Delphos began December 2, 1880, the same day that service began to Toledo. Service began to Kokomo on July 24, 1881.

After the Wabash took control of the Havana route in 1880, the TD&B decided to build to St. Louis. Construction began in Illinois in 1880. Service between Toledo and Frankfort began October 3, 1881, and was extended to Veedersburg in Fountain County on May 28, 1882. Completion of a Wabash River bridge enabled mixed train service to begin August 25, 1882, between Frankfort and Charleston, Ill.

The line reached the outskirts of East St. Louis, Ill., in December 1882, but a financial crisis delayed completion until the next year. Service between St. Louis and Toledo began May 14, 1883. The westbound *St. Louis Express* had Pullman palace coaches and made the run in less than 24 hours. The road also operated accommodation trains between Toledo and Frankfort and between Delphos and Frankfort.

Financial problems plunged the Clover Leaf into receivership, and a judge ordered passenger service slashed to a mixed train in each direction effective January 6, 1885. The road added service between Frankfort and Bluffton on August 9, 1885. Later that year, a Frankfort–Bluffton accommodation train began, and a Frankfort–Charleston train soon followed. Clover Leaf passenger trains during the 1880s typically terminated at Frankfort and ran to Delphos, Toledo, Bluffton, Decatur, Ind., or Charleston.

The last narrow-gauge passenger train east of Frankfort operated between Delphos and Frankfort on June 25, 1887. The track east of Frankfort was converted to standard gauge in 11 hours on Sunday, June 26, by a workforce of 2,000. Passenger service resumed the next day operating Delphos–Frankfort and Delphos–Toledo. Travelers bound for St. Louis endured a 16-hour wait in Frankfort and another 12-hour wait in Charleston to make connections.

Conversion to standard gauge reached Cayuga in Vermillion County in late June 1887 and Charleston by late August. But it would be May 31, 1889, before the Clover Leaf operated its last narrow-gauge passenger train and finished the conversion to standard gauge the next day.

Express Trains Return

The Clover Leaf had used Toledo's Union Depot since May 13, 1889, and St. Louis Union Station (via Eads Bridge) since July 4, 1889. Much of the track west of Frankfort lacked adequate ballast for high-speed operation. The Clover Leaf operated four pairs of passenger trains in Indiana in January 1888, three of which terminated at Frankfort and ran to Toledo, Delphos, and Decatur, the Adams County seat. The fourth pair operated between Toledo and Charleston.

Clover Leaf president Samuel R. Callaway hoped to operate Detroit–Kansas City through sleepers, and in the summer of 1890 he launched a rebuilding project. A high-speed test run on August 14, 1890, from Delphos to East St. Louis was made without incident. The Clover Leaf extended Toledo–Frankfort Nos. 3/4 to St. Louis on August 31. An overnight train, Nos. 5/6, began operating between Toledo and St. Louis on May 3, 1891, with Wagner combination buffet-sleeping cars.

But the Clover Leaf's luck had run out. Unable to pay its Illinois taxes in 1892, the road entered receivership on May 19, 1893. The case languished in the courts for 7 years. The Clover Leaf emerged on July 31, 1900, as the Toledo, St. Louis & Western, which had the dubious distinction of having higher fixed charges than had its predecessor.

At the beginning of the 20th century, the Clover Leaf operated six pairs of passenger trains in Indiana, two of them Toledo–St. Louis express trains. Nos. 3/4 offered parlor service and sleepers on a daylight schedule between Toledo and Frankfort. Overnight Nos. 5/6 had sleepers and coaches. Nos. 1/2 between Toledo and Frankfort offered coaches. The remaining service was mixed trains operating Frankfort–Charleston, Frankfort–Bluffton and Bluffton–Delphos.

The Clover Leaf fancied itself a major player in the passenger business. An advertisement in the February 1909 *Official Guide of the Railways* proclaimed the Clover Leaf to be America's most popular railroad, offering "perfect passenger service." With the Pan-

American Exposition scheduled to open in Buffalo on May 1, 1901, the Clover Leaf seized an opportunity in January by naming Nos. 5/6 the *Commercial Traveler*, operating on a 12.5-hour schedule eastbound and a 13-hour schedule westbound. The Clover Leaf purchased four new Baldwin Class E Ten-Wheelers equipped with electric headlights, the first on the railroad. Each train featured a combination baggage-mail car, 72-seat reclining-chair car, 46-seat buffet car (all built by the American Car & Foundry), an older coach, and a 12-section observation–drawing room sleeper from Pullman. The sleepers were named *Advance* and *Progress*. The new equipment featured vestibules and state-of-the-art Pintsch gas lamps. The train's name, chosen in a public contest, was emblazoned on the side of each car.

The *Commercial Traveler* offered convenient connections at St. Louis with western railroads and at Toledo with New York Central trains. Nos. 3/4 were upgraded with new 4-6-0 locomotives purchased from Richmond Locomotive Works in February 1901 and operated on 14-hour and 15-hour schedules between St. Louis and Toledo.

The opening of the Louisiana Purchase Exposition in St. Louis in 1904 prompted another equipment makeover for the *Commercial Traveler*. The Clover Leaf purchased two smoking cars, two 86-seat day coaches, and a buffet-chair car from Barney & Smith. The road bought a pair of 4-4-2 Atlantics from Brooks, which were used east of Frankfort. Baldwins continued to pull the train west of Frankfort. The *Commercial Traveler* was slightly faster than the Wabash's St. Louis–Toledo trains. But the Wabash had a station at the fair, and the Clover Leaf did not try to compete with the Wabash's day trains to St. Louis.

The *Commercial Traveler* was renowned throughout the Midwest. Its popularity with newlyweds bound for Niagara Falls earned it the nickname "Honeymoon Special." Couples had time in Toledo to shop before taking the Lake Shore Electric to Cleveland for dinner and then embarking by boat for Buffalo, where they transferred to another interurban to complete the journey to Niagara Falls.

The *Commercial Traveler* survived an encounter with a tornado near Hanfield in northern Grant County on the night of March 12, 1916. The twister lifted the train off the track and dropped it about 20 feet away. The coaches were turned on their sides, but the Pullman remained upright. Miraculously, no one was killed, and only five passengers were seriously injured.

The Clover Leaf named its express trains in 1906. Nos. 1/2 became the *Toledo and Frankfort Express/Frankfort and Toledo Express*. No. 3 became the *Eastern Express*, No. 4 the *Western Express*. When Nos. 1/2 became Toledo–Charleston trains a year later, they were renamed *Toledo and Charleston Express/Charleston and Toledo Express*.

The Clover Leaf lacked feeder lines, so it negotiated joint tariffs with Indiana and Ohio interurban railways, which proved to be a lucrative source of traffic. In Frankfort, the Clover Leaf station was situated across from the Indianapolis & North Western Terminal, and the two companies coordinated schedules. A Dayton–St. Louis arrangement involved taking the *Interstate Limited* of the Dayton & Western Traction Company to Indianapolis and changing to an interurban for Frankfort. The Pennsylvania Railroad had direct and faster service, but by riding the *Interstate Limited*, travelers saved $1.40 on the first-class fare.

The interline ticketing arrangements with the interurban railways appealed to budget-minded travelers, but these journeys began taking longer. The St. Louis–Toledo day trains became progressively slower until they were long-distance locals that did not operate west of Delphos when patronage was low. Discontinued west of Charleston in April 1918, Nos. 3/4 were shortened to Toledo–Frankfort on June 18, 1922, and replaced by a Toledo–Indianapolis train in February 1928. Nos. 1/2 changed from Toledo–Charleston to Toledo–Frankfort operation in 1908 and were renamed the *Toledo and Frankfort Express*. They disappeared in 1912.

Aside from Van Buren in northeast Grant County replacing Bluffton as the terminus of a Frankfort–Bluffton mixed train, local service remained unchanged through 1911 when the Van Buren–Frankfort mixed trains began operating between Marion and Frankfort, and the Delphos–Van Buren trains began operating between Delphos and Warren. Another pair of mixed trains briefly operated between Warren and Ohio City, Ohio.

The Delphos–Warren trains had reverted to Delphos–Bluffton operation by 1914, the Frankfort–Charleston trains now operated between Cayuga and Charleston, and another mixed train pair operated between Frankfort and Cayuga. This continued until 1930. The Delphos–Bluffton mixed trains ended in 1930. The four Cayuga mixed trains were combined on November 1, 1930, into a Frankfort–Charleston mixed train, which operated until July 11, 1932.

Requiem for a King

The heady times of the early 1900s prompted the Clover Leaf to adopt the slogan "The Lucky Way" and to modify its logo from a three-leaf to a four-leaf clover. Flush with success and motivated by grandiose expansion dreams, the Clover Leaf acquired control of the Chicago & Alton in 1907. Unable to pay the Alton's bond interest payments, the Clover Leaf lapsed into its third receivership. During its eight-year stay in receivership, the Clover Leaf's physical plant deteriorated. It finally began making money once it was rid of the Chicago & Alton. The Van Sweringen brothers of Cleveland believed the Clover Leaf would fit with the Lake Erie & Western because the two crossed at Frankfort, Kokomo, and Bluffton.

In its halcyon years, the *Commercial Traveler* was called the "King of the Rails." But the train suffered a pauper's death. Since 1918, the *Commercial Traveler* had been the only Clover Leaf passenger train to operate between St. Louis and Toledo.

Until 1928, Nos. 5/6 met in the dead of night between Frankfort and the Wabash River. The Nickel Plate launched Cleveland–St. Louis Nos. 9/10 in 1928 and scheduled them to meet in Frankfort shortly after midnight. Nos. 9/10 began conveying the *Commercial Traveler* between St. Louis and Frankfort.

The Nickel Plate discontinued the Toledo–St. Louis sleepers on May 3, 1931, and cut operation of the coaches to Toledo–Frankfort. The *Commercial Traveler*'s storied name vanished from *The Official Guide of the Railways*. The eastern terminus shifted on July 5, 1932, from Toledo's Union Station to a freight house. The former *Commercial Traveler* was downgraded to mixed train operation east of Delphos on October 1, 1932.

The Nickel Plate on August 29, 1939, asked Indiana regulatory officials for permission to discontinue the remains of the *Commercial Traveler*, which had carried 2,251 passengers in the first six months of 1939. The Indiana Public Service Commission denied the petition on December 27, 1940, saying the Nickel Plate had not shown that Nos. 15/16 had lost money.

The former *Commercial Traveler* made its final trips in Ohio on March 8, 1941. It operated as a mixed train between Frankfort and Pleasant Mills in Adams County near the Ohio border. The train actually operated to Delphos, but passengers were not permitted to ride beyond Pleasant Mills. Further discouraging patronage, the Nickel Plate put the train on a 7-hour schedule that made no connections at Frankfort. On April 4, 1943, the onetime "King of the Rails" made its final trip. It was the last scheduled passenger operation on the former Clover Leaf east of Frankfort.

Toledo–Indianapolis

As part of a campaign to boost long-haul travel, the Nickel Plate created a Toledo–Indianapolis train on February 19, 1928. Nos. 13/14 used the Clover Leaf between Toledo and Kokomo and the Michigan City line of the Lake Erie & Western between Kokomo and Indianapolis.

The new trains replaced Toledo–Frankfort Nos. 3/4 and combined with Michigan City line Nos. 23/24 between Indianapolis and Kokomo. Connections were offered at Tipton with the Bloomington, Ill., to Sandusky, Ohio, local and at Continental, Ohio, with Chicago to Buffalo No. 2. No. 13 left Toledo at 8:15 A.M. and arrived in Indianapolis at 3:15 P.M. No. 14 departed Indianapolis at 10 A.M. and arrived in Toledo at 6:45 P.M. The trains made their final runs on May 2, 1931.

Cleveland–St. Louis

Probably the least heralded Nickel Plate long-distance train was Cleveland–St. Louis Nos. 9/10. Inaugurated February 19, 1928, the trains went unnamed until October 28, 1956, when they became the *Blue Arrow* (westbound) and the *Blue Dart* (eastbound).

The only Nickel Plate passenger trains to operate over all three predecessor railroads, Nos. 9/10 ran on the New York, Chicago & St. Louis (Cleveland–Arcadia, Ohio), the Lake Erie & Western (Arcadia–Frankfort), and the Clover Leaf (Frankfort–St. Louis). Consequently, Nos. 9/10 were the last scheduled Nickel Plate passenger trains to operate on the Clover Leaf and the Lake Erie & Western.

In its early years, No. 9 dropped a parlor-café car at Lima, which was picked up by No. 10, which had dropped its diner at Charleston, to be picked up by No. 9. The trains usually operated with a Pacific east of Frankfort and a Baldwin west of Frankfort.

In 1930, the Nickel Plate began operating a Buffalo to St. Louis coach and parlor-café car that originated on No. 7 and interchanged to No. 9 at Cleveland. On September 28, 1930, No. 7 was renumbered No. 9 and became a Buffalo to St. Louis train that at 721 miles was the Nickel Plate's longest passenger run. No. 10 was never extended to Buffalo, and No. 9 reverted to Cleveland–St. Louis operation on May 9, 1942. For a few years, No. 10 arrived in Cleveland in time for an across-the-platform connection with the eastbound *Nickel Plate Limited.* The connection ended on April 24, 1949, when the trains were rescheduled to miss each other by less than 30 minutes.

Initially, Nos. 9/10 carried a 12-1 sleeper, but within a year this had changed to a 10-section lounge-observation car. The trains were assigned buffet-lounge-observation sleepers in 1939, which remained in service until replaced in 1949 by a pair of Pullman 10-section, one-compartment, one–drawing room heavyweight sleepers and modernized diner-lounges.

On March 21, 1948, Alco PA diesels replaced aging K-1 Pacific locomotives that had been pulling Nos. 9/10 since 1930. The Nickel Plate assigned new 10-6 lightweight sleepers to the trains in the early 1950s. A typical consist of Nos. 9/10 was a "Bluebird" diesel, a railway post office–express car, a coach, a sleeper, and a diner-lounge.

The *Blue Arrow/Blue Dart* were not heavily patronized, but their financial losses were not excessive, either. They just faded away. Operation of the diner-lounge was reduced to Cleveland–Lima in June 1957, and food service ended altogether on April 27, 1958.

Nickel Plate officials in late spring 1958 weighed public reaction to discontinuance. Railroad union leaders accused the Nickel Plate of discouraging patronage by ending food service and replacing lightweight coaches with heavyweight coaches. Nonetheless, the Nickel Plate petitioned regulatory authorities in Illinois, Indiana, and Ohio for permission to end the trains, saying the service had lost $400,000.

The Illinois Commerce Commission acted first. The last *Blue Arrow* arrived in St. Louis on March 14, 1959. The *Blue Dart* departed that night with a GP9 diesel, four deadhead baggage cars, an RPO-express car, 10-6 sleeper *City of Painesville*, and a coach. For another week, the trains operated between Cleveland and Cayuga, although the sleepers had been removed when the trains were discontinued in Illinois. The Indiana Public Service Commission on March 13 approved discontinuance of the trains in Indiana. Nos. 9/10 were cut back on March 21 to Cleveland–Coldwater, Ohio.

Opposition to the discontinuance had been strongest in the Buckeye State, and the Ohio Public Utilities Commission ordered the trains to continue. The Nickel Plate appealed, and Ohio authorities eventually relented. Nos. 9/10 made their final runs between Cleveland and Coldwater on October 17, 1959.

Wabash

CHAPTER 9

WABASH

The *Wabash Cannon Ball* never jingled, rumbled, or roared from the great Atlantic Ocean to the wide Pacific Shore, but the fabled folk song correctly described a fast train. Wabash management often looked the other way when an engineer exceeded the speed limit in order to make up time. Wabash passenger trains were not only fast but also clean and comfortable. Named for Indiana's most celebrated river, the Wabash once leased or owned 677 miles of track in the state.

Ohio and Indiana businessmen met in Toledo in 1852 to plan a railroad between Toledo and the Mississippi River. The Indiana segment was the Lake Erie, Wabash & St. Louis, the first use of the Wabash name. Built parallel to the Wabash and Erie Canal, the Wabash was the first Indiana railroad to compete with a canal.

Construction began in 1854, and by early 1855 it had reached New Haven in Allen County. The railroad followed the Wabash River for 100 miles between Huntington and Attica in northern Fountain County, reaching Danville, Ill., in 1856. The Wabash then entered receivership, the first of nine it would endure during its lifetime. By the end of 1857, the route between Toledo and Quincy, Ill., on the Mississippi River, was complete.

Seeking to create a transcontinental railroad, financier and stock manipulator Jay Gould gained control of the Wabash in 1879. Recognizing that Detroit rather than Toledo would emerge as a more prosperous industrial and transportation center, Gould set out to create a St. Louis–Detroit route. He leased the Eel River Railroad (Logansport and Butler) in 1879 and acquired the Detroit, Butler & St. Louis. Organized in 1880 with financial backing from the Detroit Board of Trade, the DB&StL was completed between Detroit and Butler on August 15, 1881. However, it would be 1885 before Wabash passenger trains routinely operated between St. Louis and Detroit without change.

Gould expanded the Wabash prodigiously, but borrowed too much money and engaged in too many rate-cutting wars. The Wabash defaulted on its interest payments in May 1884. The Wabash leased and lost six Indiana railroad lines. These included the Eel River Railroad (later Pennsylvania), the Peru & Detroit Railway, the Indianapolis, Peru & Chicago (later Nickel Plate), the Lafayette, Bloomington & Mississippi (later Nickel Plate), the Havana, Rantoul & Eastern (later Illinois Central), and the Cairo, Vincennes & Chicago (later New York Central).

An interchange with the Grand Trunk for Chicago–Detroit business was so successful that the Wabash built its own Chicago–Detroit route, which opened May 4, 1893, between Gary and Montpelier, Ohio, on the St. Louis–Detroit line. The Wabash constructed a

15-mile line in 1881 in Fountain County between Attica and Covington and a 5-mile line in 1900 between Helmer, located on the Chicago line in southwestern Steuben County, and Stroh in southeastern LaGrange County.

St. Louis Line

During its first two decades, the Wabash operated a mail train and an express train between Toledo and the Mississippi River ports of Quincy, Ill., and Keokuk, Iowa. After completing a line between Decatur, Ill., and Illinoistown (later East St. Louis, Ill.) in 1870, trains began operating between Toledo and St. Louis with Quincy cars interchanged at Decatur.

By early 1871, the Wabash had instituted a Lafayette–St. Louis train, the *Cincinnati Express*. The train had been curtailed to Lafayette–Decatur by fall 1871 and was gone by November. St. Louis–Toledo trains had acquired names by 1874. The westbound *Pacific Express* originated in Cleveland on the Lake Shore & Michigan Southern and conveyed cars for St. Joseph, Mo., and Atchison, Kans. Its eastbound counterpart, the *Atlantic Express*, carried Kansas City to Toledo coaches. The *Through Express* and *Lightning Express* carried sleeping cars between Toledo and St. Louis and Quincy.

By late 1878, the *Atlantic Express/Pacific Express* no longer served Cleveland but continued to carry Kansas City–Toledo sleepers and coaches. The *Through Express* name was given to the westbound leg of a Toledo–Springfield, Ill., train that had been in operation since 1877. The St. Louis train that had operated as the *Through Express* was renamed the *Fast Express*. The Toledo–Springfield trains were gone by early 1880. St. Louis–Toledo service remained two round trips, both of which carried Quincy cars. The *Fast Line* operated from Toledo to St. Louis but had no eastbound counterpart.

At the pinnacle of the Gould years in 1884, the Wabash offered coaches between Toledo and the Iowa cities of Burlington and Keokuk. This service soon ended along with the use of names for Toledo–St. Louis/Quincy trains.

Wabash sleeping cars had begun operating between St. Louis and New York by 1882 via the Lake Shore & Michigan Southern (Toledo–Buffalo, N.Y.) and the West Shore (Buffalo–New York), both later New York Central. St. Louis–Boston sleepers followed the same route but reached Boston on the Fitchburg Railway (later Boston & Maine). St. Louis–Toledo trains carried dining cars and a Lafayette–Buffalo sleeper. The New York cars began taking a different path on May 12, 1889, going on the Michigan Central from Toledo to Detroit and thence on the New York Central & Hudson River Railroad.

After leasing the Peru & Detroit Railway on December 1, 1890, the Wabash shifted most passenger trains away from the Eel River Railroad between Chili in Miami County and Logansport. Instead, trains used the Peru & Detroit between Peru and Chili. Wabash trains continued to use the Eel River Railroad between Chili and Butler.

The Wabash in March 1898 began using the Grand Trunk in southern Ontario between Windsor (opposite Detroit) and Fort Erie (opposite Buffalo). Wabash crews and locomotives handled the trains while in Canada.

The Wabash launched the *Continental Limited* between St. Louis and New York/Boston in June 1898. It featured the finest and newest sleeping cars, vestibule coaches, and diners. East of Buffalo the *Continental Limited* used the West Shore to Weehawken, N.J. (opposite New York). The St. Louis–Boston sleepers did not operate continuously in the early 20th century. Removed in 1901, they resumed in 1902, ceased again in early 1909, were reinstated in 1911, and were gone less than a year later. Revived in 1913, the Boston sleepers ended for good in 1914.

The *Continental Limited* no longer conveyed St. Louis cars east of Detroit by January 1913, those cars having been switched to another train. New York to St. Louis sleepers continued to run on the *Continental Limited*. Later that year sleepers from St. Louis to New

York and Boston were back on the *Continental Limited*. The Wabash removed the *Continental Limited* name from the St. Louis–Detroit route in December 1916, making it exclusively a Chicago–New York train.

Meet Me in St. Louis

St. Louis through car service expanded in 1904 for the Louisiana Purchase Exposition. The only railroad with a station on the fairgrounds, the Wabash had through service between St. Louis and Cincinnati, Pittsburgh, Toronto, and Montreal. During the fair, the Wabash operated two St. Louis–Toledo round trips, four St. Louis–Detroit round trips, and one pairing that operated St. Louis to Toledo but returned as a Detroit–St. Louis train. Ten of these 14 trains stopped at the fairgrounds station.

Cincinnati trains (two round trips) used the Cincinnati, Hamilton & Dayton (later Baltimore & Ohio) between Cincinnati and Decatur via Indianapolis. The service included sleepers and a café-parlor car. Montreal and Toronto sleepers were conveyed east of Detroit by the Canadian Pacific. Pittsburgh cars operated east of Toledo on the Wheeling & Lake Erie and the Wabash Pittsburgh Terminal Railway. The Cincinnati cars operated through November. The Montreal and Toronto cars operated a month longer.

Wabash passenger service between St. Louis and Detroit had increased to three round trips by January 1900 and grown to four round trips by January 1904. One round trip was discontinued in early 1905, and three round trips remained the norm until 1924 when service again increased to four round trips.

With its right to use the Eel River Railroad set to expire on January 1, 1902, the Wabash built a 25.6-mile line between New Haven and Butler. For about a month, the Wabash routed Detroit trains to Toledo and used the Michigan Central to reach Detroit. The New Haven–Butler cutoff opened on February 1, 1902.

In the early 20th century, the Wabash operated sleepers between St. Louis and Buffalo and beginning in 1902 offered St. Louis–Buffalo coaches. The St. Louis–New York coaches and St. Louis–Buffalo sleepers ended in 1907, but the Buffalo sleepers returned in 1909.

The Wabash began operating all-steel coaches in 1913 from Detroit to St. Louis on the *Continental Limited*, but, curiously, the timetable initially did not show these cars returning to Detroit. The St. Louis–Buffalo sleepers ended in 1914, and the St. Louis–Buffalo coaches ended in early 1918. The last through cars between St. Louis and points east of Detroit, St. Louis–New York sleepers, ended in May 1918.

St. Louis–Detroit No. 50 was curtailed to Decatur–Detroit, on May 27, 1931. No. 50 and Detroit–St. Louis No. 51 became locals operating between Fort Wayne and the yard at Tilton, Ill., near Danville on September 27, 1931. A third St. Louis–Detroit round trip was reinstated later in 1931, but discontinued on April 2, 1933. St. Louis–Detroit service remained at two round trips until the overnight trains were discontinued in June 1968.

The 1933 shift of the Wabash's Chicago–Detroit passenger trains to the Pennsylvania Railroad between Chicago and Fort Wayne increased service on the Detroit line to four round trips between Detroit and Fort Wayne. The Wabash named its St. Louis–Detroit trains in spring 1938. The overnight trains became the *St. Louis Limited/Detroit Limited*. The daylight trains became the *St. Louis Special/Detroit Special*. The Wabash generally assigned coaches and diners to both trains. Sleepers ran on the overnight trains. Parlor and observation cars were assigned to the day trains.

In 1929 the Wabash built a stone station on Delmar Boulevard in St. Louis's West End near Washington University and Forest Park. Nearly 40 percent of the Wabash's St. Louis passengers boarded there. It later became the transfer point for the guaranteed connection between the *Wabash Cannon Ball* and the *City of St. Louis*, which began operating June 2, 1946, in conjunction with the Union Pacific and Southern Pacific, between St. Louis and Los Angeles and Oakland, Calif.

The Wabash hosted a handful of interline services in Indiana beginning with a short-lived Detroit–Indianapolis sleeper in 1885 that operated between Indianapolis and Peru on the Indianapolis, Peru & Chicago (later Nickel Plate). A South Bend–Detroit sleeper that began in 1920 originated in South Bend on the New Jersey, Indiana & Illinois, which the Wabash purchased in 1926. The sleepers interchanged at Pine on the Chicago line in southern St. Joseph County. The sleeper was discontinued on April 2, 1933.

A Detroit–Evansville sleeper began in spring 1926. The cars interchanged at Danville, Ill., with the Chicago & Eastern Illinois. Discontinued in August 1933, the Evansville sleepers returned on July 14, 1935, but ended again in August 1936.

The longest operating interline service involved the Detroit–Florida *Southland.* The Wabash conveyed the cars on regular passenger trains between Detroit and Fort Wayne. The Pennsylvania Railroad carried the cars between Fort Wayne and Cincinnati. Service began on September 13, 1931, with Detroit–St Petersburg sleepers.

The *Southland* sleepers changed to Detroit–Miami operation beginning with the 1936–37 winter travel season. Two years later, the *Southland* sleepers began operating between Detroit and Miami and St. Petersburg. The two railroads also instituted Detroit–Cincinnati coaches. The Detroit–Miami sleepers ended in May 1941. The Detroit–St. Petersburg sleepers and coaches began terminating at Tampa in 1944. Two years later, the *Southland* sleepers reverted to Detroit–St. Petersburg operation. The Detroit–St. Petersburg sleepers shifted to the B&O between Detroit and Cincinnati via Dayton, Ohio, on September 25, 1949.

The Cannon Ball *Legend*

The premier train on the St. Louis–Detroit line was the *Wabash Cannon Ball,* although its fame was due principally to a song of the same name. Country singer Roy Acuff recorded *Wabash Cannon Ball* in the 1940s and sold millions of copies. More tribute to the life of hoboes than paean to the Wabash Railroad, *Wabash Cannon Ball* became one of America's best-known train songs.

The Wabash twice operated a train named *Cannon Ball.* The first *Cannon Ball* debuted in early 1887 and briefly operated between Chicago and Kansas City on the Wabash, the Toledo, Peoria & Western, and the Missouri Pacific.

Perhaps seeking to cash in on the popularity of the Roy Acuff song, on February 26, 1950, the Wabash renamed the *St. Louis Special/Detroit Special* the *Wabash Cannon Ball.* Assigned Nos. 1/4, once the numbers of the *Continental Limited,* the *Wabash Cannon Ball*

Norfolk & Western had a pair of E units that occasionally saw service on former Wabash passenger trains. The locomotives headed the Detroit to St. Louis *Wabash Cannon Ball* at Peru on April 1, 1967. Photo by Dave McKay.

The *Wabash Cannon Ball* was the best-known passenger train on the St. Louis–Detroit route. Open platform observation cars were becoming scarce in 1954 when the "Queen Anne" reposed at Lafayette. Photo by Ron Stuckey; John Fuller collection.

The Wabash followed Indiana's best-known river for 100 miles between Huntington and Attica, but was not known as an Indiana railroad in the same manner as the Monon. The *Wabash Cannon Ball* has a mix of lightweight and heavyweight equipment as it rumbles into Lafayette in 1954. Photo by Ron Stuckey; John Fuller collection.

The Wabash received four Alco PA1 diesel locomotives in 1949. Although usually assigned to the *St. Louis Limited* and *Detroit Limited*, on this day in 1954 two of them were seeing duty on the *Wabash Cannon Ball*. Photo by Ron Stuckey; John Fuller collection.

of the 1950s carried chair cars, a diner-lounge, and an observation parlor. Much of this equipment had been rebuilt to make it modern and luxurious. The Wabash also speeded up the *Cannon Ball*'s schedule.

New streamlined sleepers were assigned to the *St. Louis Limited/Detroit Limited*. The Wabash took delivery of four Alco PA1 diesels in 1949 and assigned them to the overnight St. Louis–Detroit trains. The *St. Louis Special/Detroit Special* received diesels built by the Electro-Motive Division of General Motors and delivered in fall 1949. Most Wabash trains were diesel-powered by 1953.

The on-board service of the *Wabash Cannon Ball* and the overnight trains changed little in the 1950s. The diner-lounge of the *St. Louis Limited/Detroit Limited* was curtailed to St. Louis–Decatur operation in late October 1958 and removed by early 1960. However, breakfast into Detroit was offered in a lounge-buffet sleeper.

Mergers in the 1960s involving the Nickel Plate and Norfolk & Western and New York Central and Pennsylvania Railroads resulted in the folding of the Wabash flag. The Pennsy, which owned 99.5 percent of the Wabash, suggested it be included in the N&W/Nickel Plate merger, a proposal that won unanimous approval of the Interstate Commerce Commission on June 24, 1964, and became effective October 16, 1964.

The N&W was rule and safety conscious, and the Wabash practice of exceeding the speed limit to make up time quickly ended. The N&W also discovered how many people revered the *Wabash Cannon Ball* when it dropped the "Wabash" from the name. Following a public outcry, the N&W restored the original name. N&W management viewed passenger service as an incurable money-losing operation, but it would not be as successful in eliminating passenger service on the former Wabash as it was in doing so on the former Nickel Plate.

In its final years, the Wabash still offered good service and did not actively seek to discourage patronage, although it did reduce on-board service. In April 1960, the *Wabash Cannon Ball* carried parlor cars, a diner-lounge, and chair cars. The *Detroit Limited/St. Louis Limited* carried chair cars, a buffet-lounge-bar, two sleepers, a 10 roomette, six double bedroom car, and a six double bedroom car with buffet-lounge. A diner-lounge operated between St. Louis and Decatur.

The Wabash removed the *Wabash Cannon Ball* parlor cars in September 1960. The overnight trains by late 1963 had begun operating with one sleeper, a 12 roomette, four double bedroom car. At the same time, operation of the lounge-buffet-bar car was curtailed to St. Louis–Decatur. Shortly before the N&W merger, the Wabash ended food service on the *St. Louis Limited/Detroit Limited*.

By 1968 the trains had lost most of their head-end business, their consists now a locomotive, two baggage cars, a coach, and a sleeper. The railway post office car came off on October 6, 1967, and the storage mail cars were discontinued on November 7, 1967. A mail interchange with the Erie Lackawanna at Huntington ended on February 18, 1968. Collectively these cuts cost the N&W $564,458 annually in mail revenue. Railway Express Agency pulled its business off the trains on February 2, 1968, a revenue loss of $58,891. The *St. Louis Limited* had carried a significant number of military travelers, but this business ended in January 1967, a revenue loss of $43,968. The January 30, 1968, termination of the N&W's *City of Kansas City* between St. Louis and Kansas City deprived the *St. Louis Limited* of $2,930 in feeder traffic revenue.

The N&W announced plans to discontinue the trains on February 10, 1968, saying the losses incurred by the *Detroit Limited* had grown from $180,158 in 1965 to $236,237 in 1966 to $205,460 in the first eight months of 1967. The *St. Louis Limited* had profits of $33,628 in 1965 and $31,701 in 1966, but lost $5,370 in the first eight months of 1967. An ICC analysis concluded that collectively the trains lost $146,530 in 1965, $204,536 in 1966, and $389,013 in 1967. The ICC projected the 1968 losses at $462,000 and concluded there was no hope of reversing the downward financial slide. Discontinuing sleeping-car service would reduce the losses slightly to $353,276.

Largely because of the military business, ridership had been higher on the *St. Louis Limited*. The average number of revenue passengers per month in 1965 aboard the *St. Louis Limited* was 62, a figure that grew to 70 in 1966, but fell to 58 in 1967. Excluding military passengers, however, the monthly figures were 60 (1965), 59 (1966), and 50 (1967), which was comparable to the average monthly patronage of the *Detroit Limited* of 59 (1965 and 1966) and 55 (1967).

The ICC found that 65 percent of the *Detroit Limited*'s passengers boarded at St. Louis with nearly half of them bound for Detroit. The *St. Louis Limited* boarded 60 percent of its passengers in Detroit, and 65 percent of its passengers disembarked in St. Louis. The busiest Indiana stations were Fort Wayne and Lafayette, with an average on/off count per month of four and six, respectively.

Thirty-nine witnesses testified, including 14 at Lafayette and 9 at Fort Wayne. Most opposed removal of the trains because they preferred traveling by rail rather than by bus or because they feared flying. ICC Commissioner George Stafford noted, "Generally, the passenger witnesses testified that the equipment was reasonably satisfactory and no real problems had been encountered in the use of the trains." That combined with the prospect of increased losses and the existence of other transportation options, including the *Wabash Cannon Ball*, was enough to persuade the ICC on May 29, 1968, to allow removal of Nos. 302/303. The trains were discontinued on June 10, 1968.

Cannon Ball *Reprieve*

Getting rid of the *Wabash Cannon Ball* was a tougher challenge for the N&W, which on May 10, 1967, sought to discontinue the *Cannon Ball* and the Chicago–St. Louis *Banner Blue*. The *Wabash Cannon Ball* combined with the *Banner Blue* from Decatur to St. Louis. From St. Louis to Decatur the *Cannon Ball* combined with the St. Louis to Chicago *Blue Bird*, which was unaffected by the discontinuance proceeding.

The *Wabash Cannon Ball* had not lost significant mail and express revenue, but the Post Office Department had said on June 19, 1967, that it probably would switch mail from the *Cannon Ball*'s railway post office to closed pouches. Storage mail carried by the *Cannon Ball* would be diverted to the *St. Louis Limited/Detroit Limited*. Neither the post office nor the Railway Express Agency opposed discontinuance of the *Wabash Cannon Ball*.

The *Cannon Ball* in 1966 carried an average of 96 passengers eastbound and 91 westbound. However, patronage was dropping, falling from 89,800 in 1962 to 68,100 in 1966, a 24 percent decline. Fort Wayne and Lafayette were the only Indiana stations to board and detrain more than five passengers per train. The N&W said the *Wabash Cannon Ball* had an out-of-pocket loss of $119,008 in 1965 and $218,580 in 1966.

At ICC hearings, witnesses criticized the N&W's handling of the *Wabash Cannon Ball*, with some accusing the railroad of allowing service to deteriorate in an effort to discourage patronage. N&W employees testified that the trains were dirty, the air conditioning and water coolers were prone to malfunctioning, car wheels had flat spots, doors were difficult to open, and the trains frequently were late due to locomotive problems or freight train interference. An N&W conductor said he received complaints almost every day.

Briefs submitted by labor and government officials claimed that "N&W has not made a genuine effort on these trains to provide efficient service, increase traffic, or reduce its alleged operating losses." Yet an inspector for the Indiana Public Service Commission who rode the *Wabash Cannon Ball* in both directions between Danville, Ill., and Fort Wayne on June 1, 1967, found the coaches presentable and clean, the equipment in good working order.

ICC Commissioner Kenneth Tuggle expressed doubt that an advertising campaign could have reversed the decline in patronage. Nor did Tuggle believe the evidence proved that the N&W had downgraded service to discourage patronage. However, Tuggle said the N&W had placed the *Cannon Ball* "in an operating status subordinate to its profit producing operations." The N&W had not done all it could to reduce operating expenses.

Tuggle suggested operating the train with one locomotive instead of two and replacing the dining-lounge cars with a "satisfactory refreshment service." The commission estimated this would save $272,000 annually and result in the *Wabash Cannon Ball* posting a profit of $54,000. In ordering the N&W to keep the *Cannon Ball* running for another year, Tuggle acknowledged the "substantial reliance upon the trains" by its patrons.

The N&W removed the diner-lounge in early 1968 in favor of a buffet coach. But a year later the N&W was back before the ICC, seeking to discontinue the *Wabash Cannon Ball* on March 3, 1969.

The 1969 hearings were largely a repeat of the 1967 hearings. The N&W said the train's losses had increased by $116,223 between 1967 and 1968. The *Cannon Ball* earned $696,139 in 1968, but had cost $1.2 million to operate, resulting in an out-of-pocket loss of $576,466. The N&W presented a gloomy picture of declining patronage. Whereas the *Cannon Ball* in 1966 had averaged 90.7 passengers per trip westbound and 96.0 per trip eastbound, by 1968 those numbers had fallen to 83.4 westbound and 76.6 percent eastbound. In 1968 the *Cannon Ball* boarded 4,847 passengers at Fort Wayne and 4,369 at Lafayette. The N&W conceded that its 1968 efforts to market passenger service had been minimal. The railroad spent $48,000, most of which was for publication of timetables in *The Official Guide of the Railways*. A marketing consultant retained by the N&W testified that an advertising campaign would have had little or no effect on the demand for rail passenger service.

Opponents of the discontinuance made many of the same arguments that they had made in 1967. The ICC again found those arguments persuasive and on June 26, 1969, ordered the N&W to keep the *Wabash Cannon Ball* going for yet another year. Commissioner Willard Benson said the *Wabash Cannon Ball* was needed because it was the last passenger train between St. Louis and Detroit. Bus service to many stations was limited or circuitous. As it had in 1967, the ICC said that the losses incurred by the *Cannon Ball* did not threaten the solvency of the N&W, which in 1968 had a net income of $74 million.

Commissioner Kenneth Tuggle, who had made virtually the same argument two years earlier in supporting continuance of the *Cannon Ball*, disagreed. In a sharply worded dissent, Tuggle said the need for the *Wabash Cannon Ball* was less every year and the public demand did not support continued operation. Pointing out that the losses had to be made up from the N&W's profits, Tuggle said the 58,500 passengers who rode the *Cannon Ball* in 1968 each received a $10 subsidy from the railroad. "The point has been reached when the remaining number of riders do not justify the overwhelming loss which the carrier is forced to bear," Tuggle wrote. If bus service to some cities served by the *Wabash Cannon Ball* was limited, Tuggle said, it was because of lack of demand for public transportation at those points.

After the ICC refused to reconsider its decision, the N&W asked a federal court in Missouri to overturn the ICC action. The suit was the first filed by a railroad against the ICC stemming from a case in which the ICC had denied permission to discontinue a passenger train. Supporting the ICC were the state public service commissions of every state served by the *Wabash Cannon Ball* and the city of Fort Wayne.

In a decision reached July 2, 1970, the court upheld the ICC decision to keep the *Cannon Ball* running. The court rejected the N&W's contention that the commission had failed to give adequate weight to a marketing study commissioned by the railroad that found little demand for the *Cannon Ball*. Nor did the court accept the N&W's argument that the ICC decision had been inordinately "'based on the intensity of the public opposition' rather than on the evidence of record." The court said many who testified in favor of keeping the *Cannon Ball* were among the train's regular patrons. The ICC could have concluded that they were sincere and concerned with the public good, the court said.

The court turned aside the N&W's plea that the ICC had failed to make sufficient and adequate findings with respect to the National Transportation Policy that bus service had an inherent cost advantage over rail passenger service. The court said the ICC had taken this into account but found it to be outweighed by mitigating circumstances that supported the view that keeping the *Cannon Ball* was in the public interest. Besides, the Missouri

Norfolk & Western was one of six railroads still operating passenger trains in Indiana when Amtrak began operations on May 1, 1971. However, only trains of the Penn Central were included in the Amtrak basic system. On April 30, 1971, the *Wabash Cannon Ball* took passengers for the final time at Wabash, Ind. Photo by John Fuller.

court said, other courts had ruled the ICC was not required by law to make specific reference to the National Transportation Policy.

The *Wabash Cannon Ball* continued to glide along the woodlands, through the hills, and by the shore, as the lyrics of the song had it. Three months after the Missouri court ruled for the ICC, Congress created Amtrak. The N&W's St. Louis–Detroit route was not included in Amtrak's basic route structure, and the *Wabash Cannon Ball* made its final runs on April 30, 1971.

Chicago Line

The Wabash began passenger service between Chicago and the East in August 1883 in conjunction with the Baltimore & Ohio and Great Western Railroads. The B&O conveyed the trains between Chicago and Auburn, Ind., and the Great Western, a division of the Grand Trunk, hosted the trains between Windsor and Buffalo through southern Ontario. The Wabash operated the trains between Auburn and Detroit. East of Buffalo, trains followed the same route as the St. Louis–New York/Boston trains.

The initial schedule showed three Chicago–Detroit round trips, two of which offered through cars for Boston, New York, and Philadelphia. Another train operated from Niagara Falls to Chicago. These trains were named the *Night Express*, the *Day Express*, the *Pacific Express*, and the *Limited*. The Wabash claimed to have the shortest Chicago–New York route by 30 miles.

By the late 1880s, Chicago service had begun operating between Chicago and Laketon Junction in northwest Wabash County on the Erie. Wabash passenger trains reached Chicago's Dearborn Station on the Baltimore & Ohio Chicago Transfer (Gary–Hammond) and the Chicago & Western Indiana (Hammond–Chicago), of which the Wabash was a part owner. During this era, the Wabash operated two round trips between Chicago and Buffalo. The Wabash opened its own line between Gary (Clarke Junction) and Montpelier, Ohio, on May 4, 1893. That line was extended to Toledo in 1901.

In April 1896, the Wabash began offering sleepers between Chicago and Montreal and Toronto via the Grand Trunk. Later that year, the Wabash added a third Chicago–Detroit round trip. Chicago–Buffalo trains also carried Niagara Falls cars and sleepers between Chicago and New York and Boston.

Within a year all three Chicago–Detroit round trips were operating to Buffalo and through coaches had begun between Chicago and New York. Another pair of trains that operated Chicago to Detroit and Buffalo to Chicago brought service on the Chicago line in Indiana to eight trains a day.

At the beginning of the 20th century, the Wabash offered three Chicago–Buffalo round trips and trains operating Chicago to Montpelier and Detroit to Chicago. Sleepers operated between Chicago and Toronto, Montreal, Detroit, New York, and Boston. Coaches operated between Chicago and Buffalo and New York. By 1902 the Wabash had begun interchanging the Montreal and Toronto sleepers with the Canadian Pacific at Detroit. About the same time, a Detroit to Chicago train began originating at Suspension Bridge in Niagara Falls.

The Suspension Bridge to Chicago train acquired a Buffalo section in 1906, increasing Buffalo to Chicago service to four trains. Service from Suspension Bridge to Chicago was discontinued on January 30, 1909. The Buffalo section also ended, although this train continued to operate from Detroit to Chicago. The other Chicago–Buffalo trains were unaffected. Chicago line service increased on July 20, 1909, with the establishment of a local operating between Montpelier and North Liberty in southwest St. Joseph County.

In 1911 the Wabash operated sleepers between Chicago and New York, Boston, Toronto, and Montreal, and coaches between Chicago and Buffalo, New York, Pittsburgh, Toronto, and Montreal. A Chicago–Buffalo train had been named the *Continental Limited* by 1913. The Montreal sleepers came off in July 1914, the Toronto sleepers in February 1915. By now the Boston sleepers operated triweekly. The North Liberty–Montpelier locals were discontinued on June 17, 1914. In 1915 a Detroit–Chicago train began originating at Buffalo. Four trains now operated from Buffalo to Chicago and three from Chicago to Buffalo. A year later, three Buffalo trains were discontinued. This brought service to three Chicago–Detroit round trips, two of which were Buffalo trains. Service to Buffalo fell to one round trip on June 2, 1918, and all cars operating to New York and Boston were removed, leaving the Chicago line with two round trips between Chicago and Detroit.

The Chicago–New York sleepers and coaches returned on July 11, 1920, operating east of Buffalo on the Lackawanna. Previously, the West Shore and the New York, Ontario & Western Railroads had conveyed these cars. At the same time, Chicago–Detroit service increased to three round trips, one of which was a Buffalo train.

The North Liberty–Montpelier locals resumed in 1924 as mixed trains. The Wabash had three Chicago–Detroit round trips, one of which operated to Buffalo with New York coaches and sleepers. The eastbound leg of another Chicago–Detroit train operated to Buffalo with a sleeper. By the late 1920s, Chicago–Detroit service had fallen to two round trips, one a Buffalo train. The Wabash named the trains the *Detroit Special/Chicago Special* and the *Detroit Midnight Special/Chicago Midnight Special*. Service increased to three round trips in 1931. The trains also received new names: *Mid-City Express*, *Detroit Arrow*, and *Detroit Express/Chicago Express*.

A New Path to Detroit

The Pennsylvania Railroad acquired control of the Wabash in 1928. Although the Wabash was operated and managed independently of the Pennsy, one change was the April 2, 1933, transformation of Chicago–Detroit passenger service into a joint Pennsylvania–Wabash operation. The discontinuance of Wabash passenger service between Chicago and Buffalo on April 2, 1933, ended the Wabash's New York through cars.

Chicago–Detroit trains operated on the Pennsylvania between Chicago Union Station and Fort Wayne and on the Wabash between Fort Wayne and Detroit Fort Street Station. The advantage of the 295-mile joint operation was speed. With the Pennsylvania allowing

90 mph operation, the trains covered the 141 miles between Chicago Englewood Station and Fort Wayne in 115 minutes. The Chicago–Detroit travel time (5 hours) made it one of the nation's fastest passenger routes.

Both railroads consolidated some Detroit trains with other trains. On the Wabash, the *Detroit Arrow* usually combined with the *St. Louis Special/Detroit Special* between Detroit and Fort Wayne. The other Chicago–Detroit trains operated independently between Fort Wayne and Detroit. On the Pennsylvania, the *Arrow* typically operated independently and the other Chicago–Detroit trains combined with Pittsburgh trains between Chicago and Fort Wayne. This began changing in the late 1930s when the *Mid-City Express* began operating independently to Fort Wayne.

The *Detroit Arrow* featured one of the last Atlantic-type steam locomotives used in mainline service in America. The daylight trains carried coaches, parlor-lounges, diners, and parlor observation cars. The overnight trains carried coaches and sleepers.

Several changes occurred on April 27, 1941. The *Detroit Arrow* was renamed the *Chicago Arrow/Detroit Arrow*. The *Chicago Express/Detroit Express* became the *Red Bird*. All six Chicago–Detroit trains began independent operation between Chicago and Fort Wayne. Operations on the Wabash were unchanged.

In the late 1940s, the *Arrows* carried coaches, a diner, and a Pullman observation–drawing room–parlor. The *Red Bird* carried a Pullman parlor lounge, Pullman drawing room–parlor, diner, coaches, and observation buffet (for coach passengers). The overnight *Mid-City Express* carried sleepers and coaches. Trains stopped at both the Pennsylvania and Wabash stations in Fort Wayne. Chicago–Detroit service shrank on January 23, 1949, with the discontinuance of the westbound *Chicago Arrow* and the eastbound *Red Bird*, both morning trains. The westbound *Red Bird* was renamed the *Detroit Arrow*.

The Wabash–Pennsylvania operation always had vigorous competition from the New York Central, which dominated the Chicago–Detroit market. The Pennsy was reportedly unwilling to purchase new streamlined equipment for a short split-profit route. The *Detroit Arrow* and *Mid-City Express* were discontinued on September 25, 1949.

The Last "Plug"

The Wabash extended its North Liberty–Montpelier mixed trains to Gary in 1931. The last passenger service on the Chicago line, the "Gary Limited," as the trains were jokingly called, was scheduled to take 7 hours to complete its 145-mile run. But when the crew had many freight cars to switch, the trip could take up to 16 hours. Nos. 51/52 were freight trains with a coach attached. Few passengers rode in the 18-seat coach, which still had oil lamps.

Indiana's last mixed trains lasted as long as they did because many Amish farmers relied on them to send and receive shipments. Among the items carried by the trains were drugs, shotgun shells, rugs, furnace castings, and shoes. By the time the trains were discontinued in April 1960, they had become a triweekly operation scheduled to depart Gary at 6 A.M. on Tuesday, Thursday, and Saturday, and return at 1:30 P.M. on Monday, Wednesday, and Friday.

Indiana Mainline Local Service

The Wabash operated various Indiana locals that originated and terminated in Fort Wayne, Lafayette, Logansport, and Peru. One of the earliest was an accommodation train in the early 1880s that ran from Lafayette to Fort Wayne and Toledo to Lafayette. By 1883, the latter train had begun operating to Danville, Ill., and the Lafayette to Fort Wayne train had ended. The Toledo to Danville train had begun terminating at Lafayette by 1885.

By late 1889, Wabash locals operated Lafayette–Fort Wayne and Logansport–Detroit. The latter later began originating at Peru. By early 1899, the Wabash's Indiana locals operated Peru–Montpelier, Ohio, Decatur–Lafayette, and Peru–Logansport.

Peru was a hub for Wabash passenger service because Detroit and Toledo trains diverged there. Some Detroit and St. Louis trains terminated at Peru in the late 19th century. During the 1890s, locals also operated between Fort Wayne and Lafayette and between Lafayette and Decatur. At the dawn of the 20th century, two pairings operated Peru–St. Louis, Peru–Montpelier, and Peru–Logansport (Eel River Railroad).

After the 1902 opening of the New Haven–Butler line, Fort Wayne supplanted Peru as the Wabash's major Indiana passenger hub. The Peru–St. Louis trains ended in 1900, and the Peru–Logansport trains ended on January 1, 1902. Also in 1902, the Wabash revived the Lafayette–Decatur locals. The four Peru–Montpelier trains, which also had used the Eel River Railroad, began operating between Toledo and Fort Wayne.

The Wabash instituted locals in 1907 between Lafayette and Litchfield, Ill., near St. Louis. These trains supplemented Nos. 50/51, the Lafayette–Decatur locals. Within a year the Litchfield trains were gone and No. 50 had begun originating at Tilton, Ill. This arrangement soon changed to locals operating Lafayette–Tilton and Lafayette–Decatur.

This continued through 1920 with the only significant changes the addition of a Fort Wayne–Detroit local in early 1918 and a St. Louis–Fort Wayne train in 1919. Within a year the Fort Wayne–Detroit train was gone. The Wabash revamped service in Indiana in 1920. Two trains now operated from Tilton to Lafayette, but only one made the return trip. Two trains operated from Fort Wayne to Detroit and one Detroit to Fort Wayne. The St. Louis–Fort Wayne trains were discontinued.

In 1921, all three Fort Wayne–Detroit trains ended and a Fort Wayne–Decatur local began. But this train was gone within a year. The Lafayette–Tilton locals were restructured into a Lafayette–Decatur round trip. These trains were curtailed to Lafayette–Tilton on October 11, 1925, and downgraded to mixed trains.

Indiana local service then remained largely unchanged through May 27, 1931, when a pair of mixed trains began operating between Fort Wayne and Peru. St. Louis to Detroit No. 50 began operating as a Decatur to Detroit train. Effective April 2, 1933, the Indiana mixed trains began operating Tilton–Peru and Peru–Montpelier. No. 50 began operating from Tilton to Detroit. Its counterpart, No. 51, began operating as a mixed train from Fort Wayne to Tilton. No. 50 became a mixed train on January 14, 1934.

Within a year Nos. 50/51 were operating Tilton–Peru. Peru–Tilton mixed trains 74/75 now operated triweekly. By 1939 the four Indiana locals, all of them mixed trains, were operating Peru–Tilton and Peru–Fort Wayne. These trains were designated local freights on October 4, 1942, which continued into the 1950s. The Wabash in 1958 finally received regulatory approval to end its obligation to carry passengers on these trains, which were last shown in the October 1958 *Official Guide of the Railways*.

Toledo Service

Concurrent with the launching of direct St. Louis–Detroit passenger service in 1885, the Wabash increased Toledo–St. Louis service to three round trips. The Wabash also had Toledo–St. Louis and Toledo–Lafayette trains, neither of which had an eastbound counterpart. St. Louis–Toledo service peaked in the late 1890s at four round trips. By March 1899, this had fallen to three round trips, and by early 1901 it was two round trips. All through car service between St. Louis and the East now operated via Detroit.

Following the 1901 extension of the Chicago line from Montpelier to Toledo, the Wabash established two passenger routes between Fort Wayne and Toledo. The original Wabash route via Defiance, Ohio, usually hosted the Toledo–St. Louis trains. But the Wabash also routed Toledo–Fort Wayne passenger trains via Butler and Montpelier. In the early 20th century, each route hosted six trains between Fort Wayne and Toledo. Fort Wayne–Toledo service reached its high-water mark in late 1904 when eight trains operated via Montpelier and six via Defiance. But by July 1905 each route had six trains. Toledo–St. Louis service fell to one round trip on November 19, 1905, and a Fort Wayne–Toledo train via Montpelier was discontinued.

The Wabash temporarily ended Fort Wayne–Toledo passenger service via Montpelier in 1907, leaving three round trips between the two cities via Defiance. The eastbound Toledo–St. Louis train was the *Fast Mail*. The Wabash dropped this name in January 1909, but renamed it *Mail and Express* in March, a name that stuck until 1911. The St. Louis to Toledo train went unnamed in this era.

Toledo service remained unchanged until November 21, 1915, when the Wabash added another round trip between Fort Wayne and Toledo, bringing the number of passenger trains on the line via Defiance to eight including the Toledo–St. Louis expresses. This schedule remained until November 24, 1918, when Toledo–Fort Wayne service fell to three round trips.

In 1920 the St. Louis–Toledo trains were named *St. Louis–Toledo Mail and Express/ Toledo–St. Louis Mail and Express*. The next year the Toledo to St. Louis train was discontinued west of Fort Wayne and the St. Louis to Toledo train began terminating at Fort Wayne. However, service between Fort Wayne and Toledo remained six trains. St. Louis–Toledo sleepers were interchanged at Fort Wayne, but the St. Louis–Toledo coaches ended.

Three years later, Fort Wayne–Toledo trains were shifted from the Defiance route to the Montpelier route. Toledo service remained relatively unchanged until March 31, 1928, when Nos. 53/58 were discontinued and service fell to two round trips. One pair of trains became mixed trains in late 1931, originating and terminating at Toledo Yard. Two years later, food service ended on the Fort Wayne–Toledo trains.

Service expanded to three round trips, including a mixed train pairing, in late 1935. However, the new pair of trains was discontinued April 3, 1938, dropping Fort Wayne–Toledo service to two round trips, one of which conveyed the St. Louis–Toledo sleepers. The trains were later shifted back to the Defiance route. This service remained in place into the early 1950s. The St. Louis–Toledo sleepers ended in August 1954. The Fort Wayne–Toledo Yard mixed trains ended in October 1958. In the final months of operation, the coaches on the Toledo–Fort Wayne trains operated to St. Louis, conveyed by the *St. Louis Limited/Detroit Limited* west of Fort Wayne. Wabash passenger service between Fort Wayne and Toledo ended on August 23, 1959.

Kansas City Service

The Wabash began offering through coaches between Toledo and Kansas City in the 1870s via St. Louis. After negotiating an agreement in 1894 with the Missouri–Kansas–Texas to use its line between Hannibal and Moberly, Mo., where the MKT connected with the Wabash's St. Louis–Kansas City line, the Wabash initiated a Detroit–Kansas City route that bypassed St. Louis. This made the Wabash the only major railroad to cross the imaginary line between Chicago and St. Louis that separated eastern and western railroads.

In May 1889, the Wabash launched the *Wabash Flyer*, operating between Toledo and Kansas City on a 23-hour schedule. But by the late 1890s, through Toledo–Kansas City passenger service had ended in favor of Detroit–Kansas City coaches and sleepers. Some of these cars operated between Kansas City and Buffalo. Wabash passenger service between Kansas City and Detroit was minimal, usually sleepers and coaches interchanged at Decatur or St. Louis.

In 1902–1903, the Wabash operated a diner between Kansas City and Detroit, through coaches between Hannibal, Mo., and Detroit, and a Buffalo–Detroit sleeper. The Hannibal cars were soon dropped, and Kansas City service settled into a Buffalo coach and Detroit sleeper. The Kansas City–Buffalo coach operated until late 1915.

The Wabash upgraded Kansas City–Detroit service in June 1929 with the debut of the *Central States Limited*, which carried coaches, sleepers, and a dining car between the two cities. The *Central States Limited* ran combined with the overnight Detroit–St. Louis trains between Detroit and Decatur. The *Central States Limited* had the misfortune of being launched on the eve of the Depression. Discontinued on September 27, 1931, it returned in May 1932 as a Kansas City–Detroit sleeping car service. Its discontinuance in April 1933 ended Wabash through car service between Kansas City and Detroit.

Pittsburgh Service

In the late 19th century the Wabash, then headed by Jay Gould's son George, proposed linking Andrew Carnegie's Union Railroad at Pittsburgh with the Wheeling & Lake Erie (Toledo–Wheeling, W.Va.). The 59.9-mile Wabash Pittsburgh Terminal Railway was an engineering marvel because of its moderate grades and lack of highway and railroad crossings. The Wabash wanted to open the line on April 30, 1904, the same day that the Louisiana Purchase Exposition began in St. Louis. Severe weather, labor unrest, and a smallpox epidemic dashed these hopes, and the line was not completed until June.

Wabash passenger service between Pittsburgh and St. Louis and Chicago began on July 3 with sleepers and coaches for St. Louis and sleepers for Chicago. Sleepers also operated between St. Louis and Wheeling.

Between Pittsburgh and St. Louis, the Wabash/W&LE competed with the Pennsylvania Railroad, whose route via Indianapolis was 89 miles shorter than the 710-mile Wabash/W&LE route. Wabash No. 16 made the trek in 18 hours, departing St. Louis at 12:30 P.M. and arriving in Pittsburgh 35 minutes after the 5:55 A.M. arrival of the Pennsylvania's *New York Limited.* Westbound, Wabash No. 19 departed Pittsburgh at 7:30 P.M. and arrived in St. Louis at 1:44 P.M. the next day. The St. Louis–Wheeling sleepers were short-lived. St. Louis–Pittsburgh through cars operated through June 1905 before ending. In the latter days of the service, the St. Louis–Pittsburgh travel time had expanded to 25.5 hours.

The Wabash/W&LE faced even stiffer competition between Pittsburgh and Chicago, competing against the Pennsylvania and B&O. Wabash No. 6 departed Chicago Dearborn Station at 3 P.M. and arrived in Pittsburgh 15.5 hours later. The Pennsy also had a 3 P.M. departure from Chicago Union Station but arrived in Pittsburgh 40 minutes earlier. The Pennsy route was 26 miles shorter than the Wabash/W&LE. Although the time saved by taking the Pennsylvania was of little consequence to many Pullman passengers, the Wabash could not match the opulence and swiftness of the *Pennsylvania Limited* or the B&O's *Chicago Limited.*

A 1907 financial panic triggered the collapse of George Gould's railroad empire, and the Wabash Pittsburgh Terminal Railway went into receivership on May 22, 1908, emerging in January 1917 as the Pittsburgh & West Virginia. The Wabash retreat from Pittsburgh ended the Chicago–Pittsburgh through cars on January 3, 1909, in favor of connecting service at Toledo. Two years later, Chicago–Pittsburgh service resumed with through coaches, but this ended on June 1, 1913.

Attica–Covington

Built on a former canal towpath, this 14.8-mile line was built by Wabash subsidiary Attica, Covington & Southern and opened on September 1, 1881, with two scheduled round trips daily except Sunday. By early 1888 the line hosted three round trips, a schedule that continued until February 18, 1899, when service reverted to two round trips. This remained the pattern until November 21, 1915, when service again increased to three round trips. This lasted less than a year, and service again fell back to two round trips.

Operations on the branch were leisurely, with crews sometimes stopping at Sugar or Shawnee Creeks to set out trotlines. If passengers were not in a hurry, the crew went hunting. Passenger service was reduced to one round trip on November 26, 1922, and discontinued on November 11, 1923.

Helmer–Stroh

The 4.6-mile line between Helmer on the Chicago line and Stroh in LaGrange County was built in 1900 to serve a cement plant at Stroh. However, a thriving passenger business also developed, with scheduled service beginning on December 8, 1907. The Wabash operated three round trips a day except on Sundays when service was two round trips.

The Sunday trains were discontinued in late 1913, and weekday service was curtailed to two round trips on January 4, 1914. However, on May 30, 1915, service again expanded to three weekday round trips, which remained until November 4, 1917, when service reverted to two round trips. Operations remained unchanged until June 1927 when service was reduced to one round trip. Nos. 31/32 operated at midday, taking 20 minutes to travel in each direction. Scheduled passenger service ended in January 1930.

Eel River Railroad

One of the more disputatious developments of the Jay Gould era involved the 93-mile Eel River Railroad in northern Indiana. Organized in 1852, the railroad endured two receiverships and several name changes before opening in 1872. Later extended to Logansport, it was completed to Butler in DeKalb County on October 18, 1873.

Passenger service began in early 1872 with two round trips between Auburn in De Kalb County and Roann in western Wabash County. Later that year, the southern terminus shifted to Denver in Miami County. Trains began operating between Logansport and Auburn on April 6, 1873. After opening to Butler, two passenger trains operated the length of the line, which also served South Whitley and Columbia City, on 7-hour schedules.

After Gould leased the Eel River Railroad on August 26, 1879, traffic dramatically increased, and the line hosted 14 passenger trains a day. In the late 1880s, Peru interests financed construction of the Peru & Detroit Railway, a 9.6-mile line between Peru and Chili in Miami County on the Eel River Railroad. Completed in 1889, the line was leased by the Wabash on December 1, 1890.

Consequently, the Wabash routed most Detroit traffic over the Peru & Detroit, moved its shops from Logansport to Peru, and curtailed passenger service to two round trips between Logansport and Chili. In part the Wabash favored the Peru & Detroit because the Eel River Railroad entered Logansport by looping around the city to the north before turning eastward into town. Trains thus faced the wrong way. Locomotives had to reverse direction, and the train ran backwards for the remainder of its journey.

By 1896, passenger service from Logansport on the former Eel River Railroad had diminished to one round trip and Peru had replaced Chili as the eastern terminus. Within two years, a Logansport–Chili round trip had been reinstated. All trains terminated at Peru by 1899. One of the Logansport–Peru pairings began operating Logansport–Chili in 1900. This train was discontinued on June 16, 1901, and service changed to trains operating Logansport to Peru and Chili to Logansport. The latter began terminating at Peru in late October.

The Wabash's downgrading of the Eel River Railroad prompted a lawsuit seeking to force it into receivership. The litigation bounced through courtrooms in Cass, Fulton, and Howard Counties for five years. Newspapers editorialized endlessly about the dispute. Much of the acrimony was between Peru and Logansport, the latter still smarting from having lost the Wabash shops to its neighbor.

Ultimately a court nullified the Wabash lease and ordered the Eel River Railroad into receivership. The Wabash appealed to the Indiana Supreme Court, which three years later denied the appeal. On September 12, 1901, the Wabash relinquished the Eel River Railroad, which was reorganized as the Logansport & Toledo Railway. The Peru & Detroit Railway was sold on August 8, 1906, to the Winona Interurban Railway, which electrified the line and began interurban service in May 1907.

Grand Trunk Western

CHAPTER 10

GRAND TRUNK WESTERN

A subsidiary of Canadian government–owned Canadian National Railways, the Grand Trunk Western faced challenges foreign to other U.S. railroads. CN managers were most concerned with their Canadian operations, viewing the U.S. subsidiaries—the Grand Trunk, Central Vermont, and Duluth, Winnipeg & Western—as comparatively insignificant. Yet Grand Trunk passenger service benefited from the CN affiliation when CN led the way among North American railroads in the 1960s in employing imaginative tactics designed to boost passenger traffic. Primarily located in Michigan, 81 miles of the Grand Trunk's Chicago–Port Huron, Mich., mainline passed through northwest Indiana via South Bend and Valparaiso.

The Peninsular Railway was incorporated in 1865 to build between Battle Creek and Lansing, Mich. A subsidiary, the Peninsular Railway Extension Company, was formed in January 1868 to build from Battle Creek to Chicago. The Peninsular began passenger service between South Bend and Lansing on September 11, 1871, with a mail train and a mixed train. By October, the trains were operated by the Chicago & Lake Huron Railroad, created April 5, 1873, to consolidate the Peninsular with the Port Huron & Lake Michigan.

In the 1960s, Grand Trunk Western No. 6323 pulled various passenger excursions. The 4-8-4 is shown on August 6, 1961, at South Bend Union Station, which the Grand Trunk shared with the New York Central. Bob's Photo.

Service began to Valparaiso on October 13, 1873, and between Valparaiso and Port Huron, Mich., on January 15, 1877. The schedule included a Valparaiso–Port Huron express and mixed trains operating from Lansing to South Bend, Battle Creek to Valparaiso, and Valparaiso to Lansing.

The Chicago & Lake Huron might have remained an undistinguished short line had it not become a pawn in a high-stakes struggle between William H. Vanderbilt, lord of the New York Central empire, and Sir Henry Tyler, president of the Grand Trunk Railway of Canada. The English bankers who financed the Grand Trunk realized that Canadian local trade was insufficient to ensure an adequate return on their investment. They hoped to boost revenue by hauling traffic between the American West and the Atlantic seaboard.

The Grand Trunk's desire to develop Chicago traffic could come only at Vanderbilt's expense. He tried to thwart the Grand Trunk's Chicago expansion plans by purchasing the Chicago & Northeastern Railroad (Lansing and Flint, Mich.), one of four railroads in the Chicago–Port Huron chain that fed traffic to the Grand Trunk at Sarnia, Ontario.

Lacking the financial resources to build to Chicago, Tyler purchased the 68-mile Port Huron & Lake Michigan (Port Huron and Flint) and the Chicago & Lake Huron. The Grand Trunk planned to build between Valparaiso and Thornton, Ill., to connect with the Chicago trackage that Tyler had acquired. Completing the Chicago–Port Huron route would be a new line between Lansing and Flint via Owosso, Mich. Realizing that he was trapped, Vanderbilt cut his losses by selling the Chicago & Northeastern to the Grand Trunk for $540,000 in November 1879.

Chicago Service Begins

On the eve of expansion to Chicago, Grand Trunk passenger service was two Valparaiso–Port Huron round trips, a mixed train from Port Huron to Valparaiso, and an express from Valparaiso to Battle Creek. Known as the North-Western Grand Trunk, this name remained through late 1880 when the road became the Chicago & Grand Trunk.

Chicago–Port Huron service began February 8, 1880, by extending one Valparaiso–Port Huron pairing to Chicago. A Chicago–Valparaiso train operating on a commuter schedule also began. Chicago–Port Huron service expanded to three round trips on May 16, 1880.

Trains reached downtown Chicago on the Chicago & Western Indiana, of which the Grand Trunk was a part owner. Initially, Grand Trunk trains used Chicago's 26th Street depot. One Port Huron round trip terminated at Corwith on Chicago's southwest side. By early 1882, the Grand Trunk had moved to a station at 12th and State Streets. By early 1885, the Grand Trunk was using a station at Polk and Fourth Avenue. The Grand Trunk then moved to Dearborn Station, built in 1885, where it remained until 1971.

In January 1882, the Grand Trunk established its first through service, sleeping cars operating between Chicago and Montreal, and Hornellsville, N.Y. Within a year, sleepers operated between Chicago and New York, Montreal, and Boston. Coaches operated to Hornellsville. The Hornellsville cars ended in 1883. That same year, the Grand Trunk instituted sleepers between Chicago and Bay City, Mich., a service that continued off and on into the 20th century. A Chicago–Detroit train that began in 1883 was short-lived. The Grand Trunk instead interchanged Chicago–Detroit cars at Durand, Mich., the crossing of Grand Trunk's Detroit–Grand Haven, Mich., line.

The Grand Trunk had the most circuitous Chicago–New York route, passing through Ontario and Niagara Falls. Initially, the Grand Trunk interchanged New York cars at Niagara Falls with the Erie, which conveyed them to Buffalo where they either continued on the Erie or interchanged with the West Shore Railroad. By January 1890, the Grand Trunk had begun interchanging Philadelphia sleepers with the Lehigh Valley at Niagara Falls. The Philadelphia sleepers had begun operating to New York by early 1894. A year later, the Lehigh Valley was conveying all Grand Trunk New York sleepers in a solid all-vestibule train.

Some Chicago–Boston sleepers stayed on Grand Trunk–owned rails, passing through Toronto and Montreal before being handed off at the Quebec border to Grand Trunk subsidiary Central Vermont. By the late 1880s, the Boston sleepers were following two paths. In addition to the Montreal route, some sleepers moved through Niagara Falls, reaching Boston via the West Shore, and the Fitchburg Railroad.

By early 1884, through coaches operated between Chicago and Buffalo. The Grand Trunk also offered coaches to New York and Boston and sleepers between Chicago and Detroit, Bay City, Saginaw, and Mount Clemens, Mich. A short-lived service began in 1896 between Chicago and Portland, Maine, via Toronto and Montreal. Known as the *Sea-Side and White Mountains Special,* the train featured a bathtub and an observation lounge.

The Grand Trunk placed its first dining cars into service in 1883. Ten years later, diners operated on four of the eight Chicago–Port Huron trains. Train names appeared in March 1887. No. 3 was the *Limited Express,* No. 4 the *Chicago Express,* No. 5 the *Atlantic Express,* and No. 6 the *Pacific Express.* By January 1890, Nos. 1/2 had become the *Day Express.* Seven of the eight Chicago–Port Huron trains had names by January 1892, the latest addition the *Mail and Express.* By 1894, No. 1 was the *Chicago Express,* No. 3 the *New York and Philadelphia Limited,* No. 4 the *Limited Express,* No. 6 the *Atlantic Express,* Nos. 7/8 the *Erie Limited,* No. 9 the *Pacific Express,* and No. 10 the *Mail and Express.* When the New York cars switched from the Erie to the Lehigh Valley, the *Erie Limited* became the *Lehigh Express.*

In the mid-1880s, the Grand Trunk offered three Chicago–Port Huron round trips and the Valparaiso commuter trains. A pair of Valparaiso–Battle Creek mixed trains began in March 1888. The Valparaiso commuter trains ended on June 23, 1889, when Chicago–Port Huron service expanded to four round trips. The Valparaiso trains were reinstated on June 26, 1892.

A New Grand Trunk

The Panic of 1893 triggered cutthroat competition that led to vicious rate cutting. Between 1894 and 1896, the Grand Trunk's revenue failed to cover the debt interest of its bonds. With the first of these bonds coming due in 1900, the Grand Trunk saw an opportunity to restructure its debt through a friendly foreclosure sale. The newly formed Grand Trunk Western emerged on November 20, 1900. Rebuilt and assigned new equipment in the first decade of the 20th century, the Grand Trunk Western was prospering by 1905.

A new luxury train, the *International Limited* from Montreal to Chicago, began on May 25, 1900. This train briefly carried a Montreal to St. Louis sleeper in 1904. The Grand Trunk changed some train names, retaining traditional names *Atlantic Express, Lehigh Express,* and *Limited Express,* but creating such new names as the *Detroit and New York Express* and the *Buffalo and Chicago Express.* All train names disappeared in 1907.

Chicago–Port Huron service increased to five round trips on June 30, 1907, and service fluctuated between five and four round trips over the next few years. A South Bend–Battle Creek round trip began operating to Port Huron on June 23, 1904. Although the Philadelphia cars ended in 1908, New York cars still passed through Philly on the Lehigh Valley. The Grand Trunk expanded through sleeper service in 1911 to include Portland, Maine, and Hamilton, Ontario. The Portland sleepers were short-lived, but service to Hamilton, which included coaches beginning in June 1911, lasted into the 1920s.

A Chicago–Durand, Mich., round trip began May 7, 1911, and South Bend service increased with the creation of a South Bend–Battle Creek local. The Durand trains were extended to Port Huron in 1912, and the South Bend–Battle Creek locals were curtailed to Battle Creek–Pavilion, Mich., on January 11, 1914. The Boston sleepers ended in December 1917, the New York cars in 1918. Chicago–Port Huron service fell to three round trips on January 20, 1918. Through service was limited to sleepers operating between Chicago and Detroit, Toronto, Montreal, and Hamilton and coaches between Chicago and Montreal. A diner operated between Chicago and Montreal.

The *International Limited* name was applied to Grand Trunk Western Nos. 1/14 in March 1919, the first use of a train name on the GTW in more than a decade. Chicago–Port Huron service increased to four round trips on June 27, 1920, and a Chicago–Flint sleeper began.

By the early 1920s, the Grand Trunk Western's parent company was in critical condition, its economic viability sapped by an extension into western Canada and rate cutting prompted by fierce competition for Midwest–Ontario traffic. The Canadian government created Canadian National Railways on June 6, 1919, a Crown corporation with quasi-independent status. Canadian National held its first board meeting on October 10, 1922, and placed the Grand Trunk of Canada under the CN banner.

Grand Trunk Western passenger service underwent a significant transformation in the mid-1920s. Chicago–New York service resumed on April 27, 1925, with No. 7, the *Chicagoan*, and No. 8, the *New Yorker*, featuring all-steel coaches, sleepers, and diners. Departing Chicago at 12:45 P.M., the train dropped its diner at Port Huron, traversed the Canadian National to Buffalo, picked up another diner, and followed the Lehigh Valley through Ithaca, N.Y., Wilkes–Barre, Pa., and Philadelphia, before arriving at New York Penn Station at 2:50 P.M. the next day. The train had Buffalo and Toronto sleepers.

The new service briefly increased Chicago–Port Huron service to six round trips, but this fell to five round trips on December 7. The discontinuance of the South Bend–Battle Creek locals in 1922 marked the end of Grand Trunk passenger trains originating at South Bend. The Valparaiso commuter trains ended on April 26, 1925. However, the Grand Trunk still had a Chicago–Port Huron local that made all stops.

Two years after launching the *Chicagoan/New Yorker*, Grand Trunk and Canadian National rolled out the *Maple Leaf* between Chicago and Montreal on May 15, 1927. Leaving Chicago at 9:05 a.m., the *Maple Leaf* arrived in Montreal at 7:30 a.m. the next morning. Departing Montreal at 12:05 p.m., the *Maple Leaf* arrived in Chicago at 10:15 a.m. the next day. It was one of three deluxe passenger trains launched by CN in 1927 that matched or exceeded the service of its chief rival, Canadian Pacific.

The *International Limited* remained the fleet leader, with Grand Trunk describing it as "the acme of travel" and "an extra fine train without any extra fare." It received new equipment in 1929, including 4-8-4 Alco steam locomotives. The *International Limited* carried coaches, sleepers, a diner, and a solarium-observation car. Inauguration of the *Maple Leaf* increased Chicago–Port Huron service to six round trips, the high-water mark of service between the two cities. Grand Trunk passenger service in Indiana had crested in 1914 when eight pairs of trains operated within the state, although no station saw all 16 of those trains.

The Grand Trunk dropped the *Chicagoan* name in May 1928 in favor of the *New Yorker* name in both directions. The next month, No. 6 became the *Atlantic Express*, a name dropped in May 1930 in favor of *Inter-City Limited*, a Canadian National name once applied to trains operating Ottawa–Toronto and Toronto–Montreal. Nos. 11/12 were named the *Chicago Express* and *Detroit Express*, respectively. Ten of the 12 Chicago–Port Huron trains were now named.

The Grand Trunk operated sleepers between Chicago and New York, Toronto, Montreal, Detroit, Flint, Lansing, and Pontiac, Mich. First-class coaches operated between Chicago and Montreal. One Montreal sleeper was an observation-library equipped with radio. Passengers listened through headphones. For a short time in the mid-1920s, the Grand Trunk operated a pair of Chicago–Detroit trains. Nos. 7/8 began in 1922, but were shortened to Chicago–Durand in 1924 with Detroit cars interchanged at Durand.

The Ax Falls

The onset of the Depression had no immediate effect on Grand Trunk passenger service in Indiana. But when the ax fell, it cut swiftly and deeply. The *Chicago Express/*

Detroit Express were discontinued May 1, 1932. Just over a month later, on June 26, the Grand Trunk discontinued the *New Yorker* and Nos. 9/10, eliminating Grand Trunk passenger service at all Indiana stations except South Bend and Valparaiso. The 1932 reductions temporarily eliminated sleepers between Chicago and Detroit and Lansing. The New York sleepers shifted to the *Maple Leaf*, and a New York coach operated for several months in 1935.

The Grand Trunk instituted a South Bend–Detroit sleeper in April 1935. The car opened at 9 P.M. at South Bend's Union Station and departed at 1:26 A.M. on the *Inter-City Limited*, interchanging with a Detroit train at Durand. The sleeper returned to South Bend on the *International Limited*, arriving in South Bend at 5:32 A.M. Passengers could remain aboard the 12 section, one drawing room car until 7:30 A.M. The service ended in November 1936.

Chicago–Port Huron service expanded on September 27, 1936, with the establishment of unnamed Nos. 7/20. In May 1937, No. 5 (the *Maple Leaf*) was renamed the *La Salle*. No. 8 retained its *Maple Leaf* name. In September 1938, No. 20 became the *Toronto Maple Leaf* and No. 8 the *New York Maple Leaf*. The Grand Trunk cut Chicago–Port Huron service to three round trips on September 25, 1938, dropping the *Toronto Maple Leaf* and No. 7. The *New York Maple Leaf* name was shortened to the *Maple Leaf* in 1939. The *Maple Leaf* name again graced trains in both directions with the April 28, 1940, reinstatement of Nos. 20/7, the latter assuming the *Maple Leaf* name.

Five months later, Chicago–Port Huron service fell back to three round trips, which remained the norm until Grand Trunk passenger service ended on May 1, 1971. Effective September 29, 1940, the Chicago–Port Huron schedule included the *International Limited* (Nos. 14/15), the *Inter-City Limited* (Nos. 6/17), the *La Salle* (No. 5), and the *Maple Leaf* (No. 20). The New York sleepers ended in September 1929. Henceforth the only through cars on the Grand Trunk Western through Indiana were Montreal and Toronto sleepers and coaches.

Grand Trunk passenger service remained relatively stable into the 1950s. The *La Salle* featured coaches to Chicago from Toronto and Detroit and sleepers from Detroit and Port Huron. The *Inter-City Limited* handled Toronto and Detroit coaches, Lansing, Port Huron, and Detroit sleepers, and a buffet parlor car between Chicago and Battle Creek. The *Maple Leaf* had a Chicago to Montreal coach and a diner that operated from Chicago to Lansing and returned on the *International Limited*. A typical consist of the *International Limited* during the 1940s was three sleepers, a buffet lounge, a diner, and at least three coaches. The *La Salle*, which did not offer food service, and the eastbound *Inter-City Limited* were overnight trains and carried most of the head-end traffic. The *Maple Leaf* and the westbound *Inter-City Limited* were day trains with Chicago–Toronto parlor cars.

The *Maple Leaf*, shown here on August 7, 1960, at Sedley, Ind., behind three GP9 diesel locomotives, was the Grand Trunk Western's daylight Chicago–Toronto train. Bob's Photo.

The *International Limited* and the *La Salle* arrived in Chicago in early morning an hour apart. The *Maple Leaf* departed Chicago at midmorning. The *Inter-City Limited* departed Toronto in the morning and arrived in Chicago that night. The *International Limited* left Chicago at 8 P.M. for an early morning arrival in Toronto. The *Inter-City Limited* departed at 11 P.M. for a midafternoon arrival in Toronto.

The Grand Trunk began replacing steam engines in the early 1950s with general-purpose diesel locomotives. The Grand Trunk was the last railroad to operate steam-powered intercity passenger trains to Chicago, ending the practice in 1957. After that, GP9 or GP18 diesels usually handled Chicago Division passenger trains. Canadian National F units sometimes pulled passenger duty on the Grand Trunk.

Canadian National president Donald Gordon had concluded in the early 1950s that passenger travel had no future. But in the face of strong public sentiment favoring rail passenger service, Gordon authorized an all-out effort to save the passenger train. Borrowing tactics used to solicit freight traffic, Canadian National launched a campaign to stimulate passenger traffic, created a tours department, and began offering group fares. But some Grand Trunk services disappeared. The Montreal sleepers on the *Maple Leaf* and westbound *Inter-City Limited* ended in February 1958. A Montreal–Chicago coach ended in 1961. Chicago–Lansing sleepers ended in 1958, and Chicago–Port Huron sleepers ended in 1963.

By the early 1960s, all Chicago–Port Huron passenger trains carried Toronto coaches. Sleepers operated between Chicago and Toronto and Detroit. The *Maple Leaf* and westbound *Inter-City Limited* carried a diner and parlor cars between Chicago and Toronto. The *International Limited* had a buffet lounge that offered food service between Chicago and Port Huron for sleeping car passengers. The train's diner operated between Port Huron and Toronto.

The Grand Trunk Western lost staggering amounts of money in the early 1960s, the red ink ballooning from $1.4 million in 1960 to $12.5 million in 1961. Nonetheless, the Grand Trunk tried hard to boost passenger traffic. One of Canadian National's most successful programs was the red, white, and blue plan, which grouped fares into bargain, economy, and standard classes with the lowest fares offered during slack travel periods. Extended to the Grand Trunk in 1963, the red, white, and blue plan was touted as the first fare experiment of its kind in the United States. The Grand Trunk also adopted such CN practices as eliminating the first-class step-up charge and complimentary meals for first-class patrons. Grand Trunk passenger equipment and stations were repainted red, white, and blue to match CN colors, and its logo was redesigned to match the CN "wet noodle" emblem.

The Grand Trunk Western was a subsidiary of Canadian National, whose influence is visible in the livery of the trailing passenger Geeps leading the *Maple Leaf* out of Chicago on August 13, 1967. The Grand Trunk logo was based on CN's "wet noodle" emblem. Photo by Dave McKay.

The Grand Trunk's passenger business received a boost from the April 1967 opening of Expo '67 in Montreal. Sleepers sold out, sometimes three months in advance, and additional cars were added. The Grand Trunk enjoyed its highest patronage in a single year since the end of World War II. The Grand Trunk began offering youth fares on June 1, 1968, the second U.S. railroad to do so. A stop instituted at East Lansing, Mich., attracted more than 500 Michigan State University students a week.

Nonetheless, the Grand Trunk continued to pare passenger service. The eastbound *Inter-City Limited* ceased operating to Toronto in May 1964, lost its name, and became a Chicago to Port Huron overnight train with a Detroit sleeper. The *Maple Leaf* name was temporarily dropped in June 1965. The Chicago–Toronto day trains were renamed *Maple Leaf* in May 1966, spelling the end of the *Inter-City Limited* name. The overnight Toronto to Chicago *La Salle* was renamed the *Mohawk*. The *International Limited* was shortened to the *International*.

Much of the head-end business previously handled by the former *La Salle* and eastbound *Inter-City Limited* had evaporated by October 1967. The railway post office cars were shifted to the *International*.

Enter the *Mohawk*

The Grand Trunk for several decades had offered Chicago–Detroit sleepers and coaches. But the cars were interchanged at Durand with a connecting train, which meant a time-consuming switching move. By the mid-1960s the sleepers sometimes ran empty. For years the Grand Trunk unsuccessfully sought to discontinue the Detroit connecting trains.

A service restructuring implemented October 29, 1967, substantially upgraded Chicago–Detroit service. Discontinued were the Toronto to Chicago *Mohawk*, the unnamed Chicago to Port Huron overnight train, and the Detroit–Durand trains. Inspired by the success of Canadian National's Toronto–Montreal *Rapido*, the Grand Trunk launched a streamlined Chicago–Detroit train named the *Mohawk*.

Designed to appeal to business travelers, the *Mohawk* departed at 4:30 P.M. and made the 320-mile Chicago–Detroit run in 5 hours, 40 minutes, besting the previous time of 8 hours. The faster running time was made possible by eliminating switching at Durand and bypassing some stations, including Valparaiso. The *Mohawk* received refurbished equipment including first-class accommodations in a rebuilt club-diner with 11 club seats in a 1-2 configuration. The club-diner, staffed by a porter and waiter, was open to all passengers even though one coach was a café-coach.

The Grand Trunk began a far-reaching marketing campaign that included radio and newspaper advertisements. It opened a city ticket office in downtown Chicago at Monroe and Clark Streets, an unusual thing for a railroad to do in the late 1960s. The *Mohawk* did well on weekends, often selling out. But weekday patronage was sparse. On weekends the *Mohawk* might have four coaches, a café-coach, and the club diner; on weekdays it carried a coach, café-coach, and club-diner.

Despite a positive attitude toward passenger service, the Grand Trunk was swimming against the tide. The *Mohawk* was faster and more elegant than the New York Central's Chicago–Detroit service, but that no longer guaranteed success. The *Mohawk*'s running time began lengthening, and first-class service ended with the removal of the club-diner in September 1969. The *Mohawk* began flag-stop service at Valparaiso in February 1970.

By the late 1960s Grand Trunk management could no longer ignore the railroad's passenger deficit, $2 million in 1968. In 1970, management studied ending passenger service. Club-diners removed from the *Mohawk* replaced parlor and dining cars on the *Maple Leaf*, now the Grand Trunk's premier train. Canadian National FP9 locomotives sometimes pulled the *Maple Leaf*, which usually consisted of five cars, typically four coaches and the club-diner, with 11 cars on weekends and busy travel periods.

At a time when most railroads did little to nothing to market passenger service, the Grand Trunk Western went all out to market its Chicago–Detroit *Mohawk*. The Grand Trunk opened a ticket office in Chicago, placed advertisements, and printed a full-color brochure. Author's collection.

fast new train
Mohawk
Detroit-Chicago
Chicago-Detroit

GT GRAND TRUNK WESTERN

The *International* did not fare as well. By 1968, the *International* usually had a railway post office, three coaches, a coach-lounge, two sleepers, and a sleeper buffet lounge. Food service was sandwiches in the coach-lounge, snacks and beverages in the buffet lounge out of Chicago in the evening, and continental breakfast into Chicago in the morning. One sleeper was removed in late 1968, and some head-end business was shifted to trucks. The coach lounge came off in late 1969.

On March 5, 1970, Canadian National notified the Grand Trunk of its intention to discontinue the *International* between Toronto and Sarnia. The Grand Trunk in turn notified the Interstate Commerce Commission of its intent to discontinue the train between Chicago and Port Huron on June 1. The CN segment of the *International* operated for the final time on June 12. Subsequently, the Grand Trunk removed the sleepers and food service cars, making the *International* a coach-only Chicago–Port Huron train.

Discontinuance of the *International* east of Port Huron had a precipitous effect on ridership. The *International* had averaged 100 passengers per day in each direction, most of them through passengers. But after discontinuance of the *International* in Canada, patronage fell to fewer than 40 passengers per day. The ICC lauded the Grand Trunk's efforts to promote passenger service, which had included spending $223,000 between 1966 and 1969 on advertising and the June 1969 purchase for $63,000 of 18 used lightweight coaches from the Union Pacific Railroad.

Mail had accounted for 25 percent of the *International*'s 1969 revenue. The May 28, 1970, removal of the RPO was expected to cost the Grand Trunk $187,000 in revenue. The ICC found that the *International* lost $224,263 in 1968, $200,469 in 1969, and was projected to lose $806,211 in 1970. The Grand Trunk lost $1.9 million on passenger service in 1969.

The 39 witnesses, most of whom opposed ending the train, who testified at ICC hearings in Chicago, Valparaiso, South Bend, Lansing, Flint, and Port Huron described Grand Trunk equipment as well maintained and its crews as efficient and courteous. Witnesses complained about a lack of convenient connections in Chicago, limited ticket agent hours, rough track, and antiquated station facilities. But no one accused the Grand Trunk of deliberately downgrading service to discourage patronage.

In giving the Grand Trunk approval to remove the *International*, Commissioner Donald L. Jackson cited the railroad's ever-widening losses, $28.5 million in 1969. The prospects were dim that the *International* could attract enough patronage and that the Grand Trunk could cut costs further to improve the train's financial performance. The *International* had lasted as long as it did largely due to Canadian National's financial support, Jackson wrote.

The freeze on intercity passenger train discontinuances imposed by the Rail Passenger Service Act of 1970 helped to keep the *International* operating until the coming of Amtrak. Passengers could connect with CN passenger trains at Sarnia, but had to make their own arrangements for crossing the border. The onetime Grand Trunk fleet leader carried two coaches and two baggage cars. The Grand Trunk removed the *International* name in spring 1971.

Amtrak did not want the Grand Trunk's six passenger trains, which began their final runs on April 30, 1971. The former *International* was held for an hour and a half at Chicago so that equipment from the inbound *Maple Leaf* and *Mohawk* could be added to its consist, which swelled to three locomotives and 12 cars. The former *International* was the last passenger train to depart from 81-year-old Dearborn Station, which closed 2 days later.

CHAPTER 11

CHICAGO & EASTERN ILLINOIS

If you were traveling from Chicago to Florida in the 1940s, you probably began your journey on the Chicago & Eastern Illinois, which carried the most Florida-bound passengers out of Chicago. Yet depending on your perspective, the C&EI was either the most typical or the most mediocre American railroad.

It was the first railroad to operate a full-length lounge car on an overnight train (1906), first to use automatic train control (1914), and first to operate a Mars Safety Signal on the rear of a passenger train (1946). A leader in sloganeering, its many mottoes included "The Danville Route," "The Evansville Route," "The Modern Route," "The Noiseless Route," "The Route of the Dixie Flyer," "The Chicago Route," and "The Boulevard of Steel." Seldom able to control its destiny, the C&EI was fortunate to have entered an alliance with the Louisville & Nashville to offer passenger service between Chicago and the South.

Through 1949, the C&EI's passenger train miles exceeded its freight miles. During the first decade of the 20th century, the C&EI operated 11 passenger trains on its 287-mile Chicago–Evansville line and 22 trains on its Indiana branches. By the early 1920s, the C&EI's Indiana route structure had shrunk due to the divestiture of most branch lines.

Chicago & Eastern Illinois passenger operations in Indiana peaked in the early 20th century at 33 trains. Locomotive No. 153, built in 1900, has a train ready to leave Chicago in 1905. Author's collection.

Chicago and Eastern Illinois

The C&EI began as the Evansville & Illinois Railroad. Chartered in 1849, its first passenger operation was a 2.6-mile excursion on July 4, 1851, between Evansville and Pigeon Creek Grove. By November, the E&I had begun passenger service between Evansville and the end of track near Princeton. Service to Princeton began in January 1852, to Vincennes on February 1, 1854, and to Terre Haute on November 24, 1854. It took 5.5 hours to travel the 109 miles between Evansville and Terre Haute. Renamed the Evansville & Crawfordsville, the railroad expanded to Rockville in 1860.

Another C&EI predecessor, the Evansville, Terre Haute & Chicago, began service on June 7, 1871, between Terre Haute and Perrysville in Vermillion County. Service was extended to Danville, Ill., on October 26, 1871. The Chicago, Danville & Vincennes began service between Chicago and Danville on November 16, 1871. By the following January the CD&V, ETH&C, and the E&C railroads had begun coordinating passenger schedules between Chicago and Evansville. The Chicago & Eastern Illinois was created by the September 1, 1877, merger of the CD&V and ETH&C. The E&C was renamed the Evansville & Terre Haute in 1877 and merged with the C&EI on July 20, 1911.

The 1869 organization of the Indiana North & South Railroad began development of the C&EI's Indiana Division. Passenger service had begun by July 1872 in Fountain County between Attica and Coalfield (later renamed Veedersburg). The IN&S entered receivership and was acquired by the Chicago & Block Coal Railroad in 1879.

The C&CB expanded from Veedersburg to Yeddo, also in Fountain County, in 1882, and merged in 1883 with the Chicago & Great Southern, which later that year completed a 57-mile extension from Attica to Fair Oaks in western Jasper County, a junction with the Monon. Service began between Fair Oaks and Pine Village in northern Warren County in April 1883. Service between Pine Village and Yeddo had begun by early 1884. The Mudlavia Sanitarium near Attica helped boost the C&GS's passenger business. The sanitarium claimed that its black, gooey mud could cure rheumatic ailments.

Henry M. Porter of Chicago purchased the C&GS at an 1886 foreclosure sale. A year earlier, his Lake Michigan & Ohio River Railroad had built a 42-mile line between Yeddo and Brazil in Clay County. In October 1885, Porter renamed his railroad the Chicago & Indiana Coal Railway and subsequently merged it with the C&GS, which had briefly operated as the Indiana Railway.

The C&IC began service between Chicago and Brazil on May 23, 1886, using the Monon north of Fair Oaks. The C&IC built a branch from Fair Oaks to La Crosse in southwest LaPorte County, and service began in August 1887 between La Crosse and Brazil. After acquiring a controlling interest in the C&EI, Porter built in 1888 between Momence, Ill., and Percy Junction, located just north of Goodland in southern Newton County. The C&EI purchased the stock of the C&IC in March 1889 and leased it in 1892. The former C&IC continued to be known as the Coal Road, a reflection of its major freight commodity.

The acquisition of the C&EI on October 1, 1902, by the St. Louis–San Francisco Railway (Frisco) brought the C&EI into the realm of Benjamin F. Yoakum, who also controlled the Chicago, Rock Island & Pacific. Consequently, on July 31, 1904, C&EI passenger trains switched from Chicago Dearborn Station to La Salle Street Station, which was used by the Rock Island.

Financially overextended, the Frisco forced the C&EI to declare high dividends to raise cash to pay the debt the Frisco incurred when it acquired the C&EI. The Frisco and C&EI entered receivership on May 27, 1913, effectively ending Frisco control of the C&EI. The C&EI was sold at a foreclosure sale on April 5, 1921, but dispossessed of the Coal Road lines and a Terre Haute–Evansville branch via Washington. The C&EI returned to Dearborn Station on August 1, 1913.

The Dixie Route

The C&EI–L&N Evansville interchange began on July 12, 1885, with Chicago–Nashville through car service. For nearly 83 years, the two railroads offered service between Chicago and Florida and the Gulf Coast. Through sleepers between Chicago and Jacksonville, Fla., via Evansville began in 1893 in time for the opening of the World's Columbian Exposition in Chicago. The first permanent Chicago–Florida through service on the C&EI began December 20, 1896. The *New Orleans and Florida Special* carried Jacksonville and Tampa cars.

The first Florida through train, the *Chicago and Florida Limited*, began seasonal service on January 4, 1901, to St. Augustine, replacing the *New Orleans and Florida Special*. Operating on a 31-hour one-night-out schedule, the train had sleepers (including some to New Orleans), a diner, and an observation car, all with vestibules, steam heat, and gas lighting. A St. Louis–St. Augustine observation-sleeper was conveyed to Evansville by the L&N. The C&EI, L&N, Nashville, Chattanooga & St. Louis, Western & Alabama, Central of Georgia, Georgia Southern & Florida, Atlantic Coast Line, and Florida East Coast handled the train over its 1,126-mile route.

The Chicago–Jacksonville *Dixie Flyer*, which debuted January 12, 1908, replaced the *Chicago and Florida Limited*. Offering Pullman drawing room cars, coaches, and a diner, the *Dixie Flyer* was the first year-round Chicago–Florida train on the Dixie Route. The *Dixie Flyer* departed in late evening and spent two nights out. The seasonal *Dixie Limited* debuted January 5, 1913, to Jacksonville with first-class coaches, a diner, a compartment-observation sleeper, and three drawing room sleepers.

The *Dixie Limited* did not return in 1919 due to World War I travel restrictions. Reinstated on December 2, 1923, as an all-Pullman train to Jacksonville, it began operating to Miami in late December. It also carried a Tampa sleeper. Since January 16, 1922, the *Dixie Flyer* had handled seasonal St. Petersburg sleepers and, later, Miami sleepers.

The Florida trains began taking a different route south of Atlanta on November 1, 1920, now using Central of Georgia between Atlanta and Macon, Ga., and the Atlantic Coast Line between Macon and Jacksonville via Albany, Ga. ACL also conveyed cars south of Jacksonville to Florida's West Coast. Six K3 Pacific 4-6-2 locomotives delivered in 1923 replaced Baldwin K1 and Alco K2 locomotives that the C&EI normally assigned to passenger duty. The superior accelerating ability of the K3s enabled C&EI to shave 20 to 30 minutes off the schedule.

The *Dixie Limited* carried coaches and sleepers during the 1924–25 season while the *Dixie Flyer* operated in two sections, one all-Pullman with Florida sleepers and the other with coaches for Jacksonville and sleepers for Atlanta and Augusta, Ga. A third train, the seasonal *Dixie Express*, debuted September 27, 1925, between Chicago and Jacksonville as a replacement for the second section of the *Dixie Flyer*. However, the *Dixie Express* and *Dixie Flyer* ran as one to Atlanta. The *Dixie Flyer* ran as an all-Pullman train between 1925 and 1928.

The *Dixie Limited* became the second year-round Florida train in April 1926 when the *Dixie Express* ended for the season. Stock market reports were available aboard all Florida trains, a perk that ended in 1927. The *Dixie Limited* continued to carry sleepers and coaches, but it reversed roles with the *Dixie Flyer* for the next 2 years beginning in 1928 with the *Dixie Limited* being the all-Pullman train.

The effects of the Depression became evident on September 28, 1930, when the *Dixie Limited* received New Orleans coaches and Nashville sleepers from the discontinued *New Orleans Special*. These assignments were temporary, for on January 1, 1931, the *Dixie Limited* reverted to all-Pullman operation when the *New Orleans Special* returned. The *Dixie Express* did not return for the 1930–31 season.

The *Dixie Express* made a comeback on January 2, 1932, between Chicago and Atlanta, consolidated with the *Dixie Limited* south of Nashville. The latter's Florida cars were assigned to the *Dixie Express* on April 24, 1932. The *Dixie Limited* returned on January 4, 1933, as a triweekly all-Pullman train. The *Dixie Express* began operating in the off-season when the *Dixie Limited* was on summer hiatus.

The C&EI implemented an odd schedule change on April 30, 1933, for the northbound *Dixie Flyer*. Sleepers were removed at Terre Haute and placed on another train. Pullman passengers thus arrived in Chicago 1 hour and 40 minutes later than coach passengers did. The *Dixie Flyer*, in the meantime, had begun handling Sarasota sleepers.

L&N Flirts with a New Partner

In September 1934, the L&N announced that on October 1 it would end the Evansville interchange with the C&EI in favor of an interchange with the New York Central. The C&EI took the L&N to court.

The stakes were enormous. In 1933 the C&EI had handled 70,212 through passengers. The Dixie fleet generated 56 percent ($1.1 million) of C&EI's passenger, mail, and express revenue and 17.4 percent of its total operating revenue. The C&EI's trustee told the court that a New York Central takeover of the Dixie fleet would diminish the earnings and sale value of the C&EI.

The Central's Chicago–Evansville route was mostly single track and lacked block signals south of St. John in Lake County, Ind. The Central had fewer curves and grades, but the C&EI had heavier rail and deeper ballast, a faster maximum speed (70 mph), automatic block signals the entire distance, and automatic train control and double track between Dolton, Ill., and Clinton, Ind.

Although the C&EI was able to keep the Dixie fleet, its passenger service was diminishing. Revenue fell by more than a half million dollars in 1927, much of that from declining patronage of locals, miners' trains, and Chicago commuter service. Revenue declined a half million dollars in 1928, $195,000 in 1929, and $792,000 in 1930.

The *Dixie Express* was renamed *Dixie Limited* on January 2, 1935, operating daily to Atlanta on a year-round schedule. Sleepers operated triweekly between Chicago and Jacksonville, Miami, and St. Petersburg. Florida-bound coach passengers changed trains in Atlanta. For the 1935–36 season, the *Dixie Flyer* began sprinting from Jacksonville to Chicago in 29.5 hours, 3 hours and 15 minutes faster. Miami sleepers operated daily, while Tampa and St. Petersburg sleepers operated every other day.

An even swifter train debuted January 2, 1936. The *Dixieland* made the southbound trek in 24 hours, the northbound trip in 25 hours, 3 hours faster than the Florida trains of the Illinois Central, Pennsylvania, and New York Central. The Chicago–Evansville running time was chopped to 5.5 hours. The *Dixieland* followed a different path between Atlanta and Jacksonville, using the Atlanta, Birmingham & Coast to Waycross, Ga., and the Atlantic Coast line to Jacksonville.

The *Dixieland* normally carried 8 to 10 cars including an observation-Pullman, coaches, a diner, two Miami sleepers, and a St. Petersburg sleeper. The *Dixieland* ran the wheels off the *Dixie Flyer* by 5 hours, 40 minutes and the *Dixie Limited* by 6 hours, 10 minutes southbound. It was 4.5 hours faster northbound. Meanwhile, the *Dixie Limited* now terminated at Atlanta and no longer was among the Dixie fleet elite.

The *Dixie Limited* resumed Chicago–Jacksonville operation on April 17, 1936, when the *Dixieland* ended for the season. That December, the *Dixieland* returned as an all-Pullman train. The Jacksonville to Chicago running time of the *Dixie Flyer* was trimmed by 2 hours. The *Dixieland*'s fastest Chicago to Jacksonville time was 23 hours, 40 minutes in 1939–40. On the C&EI, the *Dixieland* raced from Chicago to Evansville in 5 hours, 20 minutes. The northbound running time was 24.5 hours with the C&EI leg taking 5.5 hours.

The *Dixie Flyer*'s Miami coaches ended in April 1940, in favor of a connection at Jacksonville with the Florida East Coast's *Henry M. Flagler*. The *Dixie Flyer* continued to handle Miami sleepers, but coach passengers arrived in Miami 2 hours earlier even though they had to change trains at Jacksonville.

A Streamliner Trio

The streamliner era dawned on the C&EI the morning of December 17, 1940, at Chicago Dearborn Station when the theme girl of the Orange Bowl Festival broke a bottle of Florida orange juice across the nose of K3 Pacific No. 1008 to christen the maiden run of the all-coach Chicago–Miami *Dixie Flagler*. No. 1008 had been shrouded for a streamlined appearance, including a livery of black and aluminum with red pinstripes.

The train had seven lightweight stainless steel cars built by Budd, including five coaches (one a baggage-dormitory), a diner, and an observation-tavern-lounge. All seats were reserved at no extra fare. Breakfast was 50 cents, lunch and dinner 60 cents. The *Dixie Flagler* was part of a venture involving nine railroads and three all-coach trains operating on every-third-day schedules. The trio also included the *City of Miami* (Illinois Central) and *South Wind* (Pennsylvania Railroad). Each train operated on a 29.5-hour schedule, departing Chicago and Miami at the same time. Tickets were interchangeable.

The *Dixie Flagler* had the shortest route (1493 miles), using the traditional Dixie Route to Atlanta, and the Atlanta, Birmingham & Coast (via Waycross) south of Atlanta. Steam-powered to Jacksonville, a Florida East Coast Electro-Motive Division E6 diesel pulled the *Dixie Flagler* to Miami. The trio was envisioned as a seasonal operation, but business was good enough to warrant year-round service.

The 1941–42 winter season was the high-water mark of Dixie Route Florida service. Beginning December 17, 1941, five pairs of trains traversed the route including the *Dixie-land* (all-Pullman), *Dixie Limited*, *Dixie Flyer*, *Dixie Flagler*, and the *Dixiana*, a new train with coaches and sleepers on a 34-hour schedule to Miami and a 35-hour schedule to Chicago. The *Dixie Flagler*, *Dixiana*, and *Dixieland* operated every third day

The nation was mobilizing for war and the federal Office of Defense Transportation ordered the *Dixiana* discontinued. The *Dixiana* made its last run (Miami to Chicago) on January 14, 1942, having made just four round trips. The *Dixieland* returned on December 17, 1942, as a coach and Pullman train, but on April 18, 1943, it was suspended for the duration of the war. All Florida schedules were lengthened due to wartime conditions.

Tragedy struck on September 14, 1944, when the southbound *Dixie Flyer* and a northbound mail train collided north of Terre Haute, killing 29 and injuring 42. The accident occurred in early morning fog and was attributed to the *Flyer* running past the signal where it was to meet the mail train.

The *Dixieland* resumed service on December 12, 1946, on an every-third-day schedule with Miami sleepers displaced from the *Dixie Limited* and *Dixie Flyer*. The C&EI time-

The C&EI carried more passengers from Chicago bound for Florida than any other railroad. The *Dixie Limited*, shown in an undated photograph, was one of several "Dixie fleet" trains that the C&EI operated in conjunction with the Louisville & Nashville. Author's collection.

table contained a whimsical typographical error, showing the northbound *Dixie Flagler* as operating "every third year." The *Dixieland* made its final run on April 28, 1949. The *Dixie Limited* made its last runs on September 30, 1951, as a through train. Remnants of the train remained in service between Chicago and Evansville. The *Dixie Flagler* received its first sleepers, two for Miami and one for Jacksonville, on April 22, 1949.

C&EI patronage began declining after the end of World War II. Passenger train miles dropped from 2.4 million to 1.4 million between 1947 and 1950. By 1956, patronage was half of 1947's 1 million. Unprofitable trains were discontinued, and mail was diverted to trucks in order to speed up the remaining passenger trains. The strategy worked for a while, and C&EI passenger service operated close to a break-even basis. But by 1960, C&EI's passenger ratio was 120 percent, meaning that it was spending $1.20 for each $1 in revenue earned. By 1966, the ratio was 147 percent.

The *South Wind* and *City of Miami* received new lightweight coaches and sleepers in 1950, but it was December 16, 1954, before the *Dixie Flagler* received similar equipment. On the same day, the *Flagler* was renamed the *Dixieland*, although in late 1956 the C&EI called it the *New Dixieland*. The *Dixie Flagler* had been named for Henry M. Flagler, founder of the Florida East Coast Railway, who had died in 1913 and was no longer well known. The C&EI wanted to operate dome cars on the Dixie Route, but the idea was foiled by height restrictions at Jacksonville's Union Terminal.

The *Dixie Flyer*'s Chicago–Jacksonville sleepers ended on February 20, 1957. The *Dixieland* left Chicago for the final time on November 29, 1957. The last northbound *Dixieland* had traversed the C&EI the previous day. The C&EI no longer hosted Chicago–Florida sleepers. The *Dixie Flyer* carried Jacksonville coaches until August 3, 1965, when it was discontinued between Chicago and Danville, Ill. For the first time in nearly 70 years, a traveler could not board a C&EI train and step off in the Sunshine State.

Other Chicago–Evansville Trains

In 1868, the Evansville & Crawfordsville operated two Evansville–Terre Haute passenger trains, one of which was a mixed train. Accommodation trains operated Evansville–Vincennes and Terre Haute–Rockville. This schedule pattern remained through the 1870s. The Logansport, Crawfordsville & Southeastern (later Pennsylvania) acquired the E&C between Terre Haute and Rockville in 1875.

In the early 1890s, the Evansville & Terre Haute had four round trips between its namesake cities, three of which were Chicago trains. C&EI predecessor railroads also offered a train between Terre Haute and Watseka, Ill. By the mid-1890s, the locals operated through Terre Haute. These included the *Danville Express* (Danville to Evansville), an Evansville to Terre Haute train, and the *Chicago Mail* (Terre Haute to Chicago).

During this era, the C&EI and E&TH operated three Chicago–Evansville round trips, the *Chicago and Nashville Limited*, Nos. 1/2, and the *Southern Fast Mail/Northern Fast Mail*. The latter by the mid-1890s had been renamed the *Night Express* and began conveying Indianapolis–Evansville sleepers interchanged at Terre Haute with the Vandalia (later Pennsylvania). Chicago–Evansville service increased to four round trips with the July 11, 1897, inauguration of the *New Orleans and Florida Special*. Seeking to attract travelers bound for the Tennessee Centennial International Exposition, the C&EI offered two vestibule trains between Chicago and Nashville.

By the early 20th century, most Chicago–Evansville passenger trains were part of the Dixie fleet. However, through the mid-1960s the C&EI fielded locals that generally operated Chicago–Evansville, Chicago–Terre Haute, Terre Haute–Evansville, Danville–Terre Haute, or Danville–Evansville.

The Evansville station of E&TH was at Eighth and Main Streets. The L&N owned the Union depot at Fulton and Ohio Streets. When through service between Chicago and

7191. E. & T. H. Depot, Evansville Ind.

C&EI predecessor Evansville & Terre Haute built a depot at Eighth and Main in Evansville. For several years in the early 20th century, C&EI through trains used the E&TH and the Louisville & Nashville stations. This practice ended in 1933. Postcard in author's collection.

Nashville began in 1885, cars transferred between stations on a jointly owned 1.44-mile connection track in the middle of Division Street.

Trains that ran through Evansville stopped at both depots. This continued until 1915 when the southbound *Dixie Flyer* began stopping only at the L&N station. By the early 1920s, three through trains used only the L&N station, and two through trains stopped at both. Trains terminating in Evansville usually did not use the L&N depot. The *Dixie Express* was the last through train to use both stations, a practice that ended in 1933. When the E&TH station closed on July 14, 1935, only four trains still used it.

The growing Dixie Fleet increased Chicago–Evansville service to six round trips on February 18, 1919. The addition of a Chicago–Evansville local in 1918 increased service to seven round trips, but these trains were discontinued north of Terre Haute on March 27, 1921. Service to Evansville dropped to five round trips on December 16, 1922, when a Chicago–Evansville train and a Terre Haute–Evansville local ended. The Terre Haute–Evansville local was reinstated on April 29, 1923. The C&EI removed Nos. 13/14 in 1927 between Danville and Terre Haute.

Chicago–Evansville service reached seven round trips during the winter of 1924–25, which continued for the next 2 years. Five of the trains operated between Chicago and the South, primarily to Florida. In spring 1926, the C&EI and the Wabash established a Detroit–Evansville sleeper that was interchanged at Danville. Discontinued in August 1933, the Detroit sleepers returned on July 14, 1935, but ended in August 1936.

Terre Haute–Evansville Nos. 5/6 ended on June 28, 1931. However, the institution of the *Dixie Mail* from Chicago to Evansville picked up the slack. The *Dixie Mail* carried through coaches from Chicago to Montgomery, Ala., and raced from Chicago to Evansville in 7 hours, 5 minutes, the fastest schedule at the time. Its counterpart, No. 16, carried coaches from Atlanta to Chicago. This train had begun on September 26, 1926, but was not shown in public timetables until the *Dixie Mail* began.

During the 1930s, Chicago–Evansville service remained five round trips, three of them Dixie fleet trains. The addition of seasonal Chicago–Florida service would increase service to six round trips. Locals operated between Chicago and Evansville. A Danville–Evansville local operated through the late 1940s.

Whippoorwill *Takes Flight*

In 1944 the C&EI ordered 11 lightweight cars and two locomotives from EMD for two new streamliners. The locomotives arrived in May 1946, the passenger equipment that fall. The first streamliner, the *Meadowlark*, debuted October 6, 1946, between Chicago and Cypress, Ill. Following a christening ceremony in Evansville, the Chicago–Evansville *Whippoorwill* began November 10, 1946. With a running time of 5 hours, 10 minutes southbound and 5 hours, 9 minutes northbound, the *Whippoorwill* was the fastest train between Chicago and Evansville. The *Whippoorwill* and *Meadowlark* introduced a new blue, gold, orange, and silver livery.

The *Whippoorwill* and *Meadowlark* had identical consists of one diesel locomotive and seven cars. Five of the *Whippoorwill's* cars had Hoosier names: baggage-coach *Turkey Run*, coaches *Vigo Trail*, *Vincennes Trail*, and *Vanderburgh Trail*, and diner *Shakamak Inn*. Patronage of the *Whippoorwill* was disappointing, partly because it had to fight with its running mates for a declining share of passenger traffic. A month after its inauguration, a coach was transferred from the *Whippoorwill* to the *Meadowlark*.

With too many trains for the level of patronage, the C&EI and L&N discussed reducing the Dixie fleet. This led to the September 28, 1947, discontinuance of the *Dixie Express*. The *Dixie Mail* was removed on June 18, 1949. Chicago to Evansville No. 1 was curtailed to Danville on June 1, 1948. Evansville to Chicago No. 10 was discontinued and its counterpart, No. 9, was discontinued north of Danville. No. 9 vanished on December 12, 1948, and No. 1 again began operating from Chicago to Evansville.

The *Whippoorwill* got caught in the shuffle. When the Chicago–Atlanta *Georgian* began June 1, 1948, it assumed the *Whippoorwill's* schedule. The *Whippoorwill* began departing Chicago in early morning and Evansville in late afternoon. The *Whippoorwill* returned to its original schedule on May 8, 1949. Chicago to Evansville No. 1 was rescheduled to depart Chicago in early morning, but loafed along on a leisurely 10-hour schedule. The *Whippoorwill* ended between Evansville and Danville on November 6, 1949, just 4 days shy of its third anniversary.

This left Nos. 1/2 as the only Chicago–Evansville locals along with the *Dixie Limited*, *Dixie Flyer*, *Georgian*, and the every-third-day *Dixie Flagler*. No. 2 was named the *Shawnee* on August 12, 1950. The August 26, 1951, addition of a Chicago section of L&N's Cincinnati–New Orleans *Humming Bird* boosted Chicago–Evansville service to five daily round trips plus the every-third-day *Dixie Flagler*. This level of service remained through the mid-1950s.

When the running time of No. 1 was reduced to six hours on April 24, 1955, there was no longer time for a meal stop in Danville, so the C&EI assigned the train a diner-lounge. This car had been operating on the *Shawnee* since April 27, 1952. The *Shawnee* name disappeared on December 4, 1955, and Nos. 1/2 began operating on the schedule of the *Dixieland* on the days the *Dixieland* did not operate.

This lasted until April 29, 1956, when No. 1 began operating independently and lost its diner-lounge. No. 2 consolidated with the former northbound *Dixie Limited*. The former southbound *Dixie Limited* and *Dixie Flyer* were consolidated from Chicago to Evansville. The net effect was that Chicago–Evansville service fell to four daily round trips plus the every-third-day *Dixieland*. The diner-lounge was reinstated on No. 1 on December 16, 1956, but removed for good on February 20, 1957, the same day that the car was also removed from No. 2-92. The November 1957 discontinuance of the *Dixieland* combined with the January 26, 1958, consolidation of the *Georgian* and *Humming Bird* pared Chicago–Evansville service to three round trips.

For years the C&EI had operated a Chicago–Evansville setout sleeper. But this ended April 29, 1962, when the last Evansville sleeper was removed from the *Dixie Flyer*. The only sleeper now remaining on the *Dixie Flyer* on the C&EI operated to Nashville.

Discontinuance Games

The C&EI used the tactic of discontinuance by amputation to rid itself of four trains. The Illinois Commerce Commission allowed the C&EI to discontinue the *Dixie Flyer* between Chicago and Danville provided it reschedule Nos. 1/2-92 between Chicago and Danville. The schedule change of August 3, 1965, created four Evansville–Danville trains. The former *Dixie Flyer*, now Danville–Evansville Nos. 94/95, did not connect with other C&EI trains, but continued to connect with L&N's *Dixie Flyer*, now an Evansville–Jacksonville coach train.

The C&EI diverted the last head-end business from these trains to trucks or freight trains. Nos. 94/95 operated on a schedule that was hardly appealing to anyone, leaving Evansville at 9:32 P.M. and arriving in Danville at 1:40 A.M. The train left Danville for Evansville 19 minutes later. No. 1 departed Danville at 11:28 A.M. and arrived in Evansville at 4:40 P.M. No. 92 departed Evansville at 2 P.M. and arrived in Danville at 5:44 P.M.

The C&EI notified the Interstate Commerce Commission of its plan to discontinue all four trains on September 22, 1965. The C&EI claimed out-of-pocket losses of $64,000 in August and September 1965. Patronage averaged three to five riders a day. Trains sometimes ran empty. Revenue ranged from $85 in September for No. 95 to $537 for No. 92. The aggregate revenue for all four trains was less than $1,000.

Eight witnesses opposed removal of the trains, saying the service was needed for school travel and economic development. Terre Haute and Evansville officials criticized the C&EI for neglecting its passenger service. An inspector for the Indiana Public Service Commission described poor station facilities. The ICC dismissed the economic development argument as speculative and said the *Georgian/Humming Bird* provided alternative rail service. The C&EI should not be forced to lose money on what the ICC termed unnecessary and uneconomic service. The Danville–Evansville trains were discontinued on January 22, 1966.

The C&EI sought to discontinue the *Georgian/Humming Bird* between Chicago and Evansville on October 1, 1967. The C&EI said the trains had lost $247,057 in 1966 and $268,360 in the first six months of 1967. The ICC found that C&EI passenger operations had lost more than $1 million between 1962 and 1966. Some 20 percent of its freight net income had gone to make up the passenger deficits. This was not a case, though, of virtually empty trains. There was a high level of patronage between Chicago and the South, but the ICC said business on the C&EI was minimal. Excluding Chicago, the daily average of passengers boarding or disembarking on the C&EI was 176 southbound and 153 northbound.

The ICC dismissed the protesters as infrequent patrons who "desire the trains continued in what would be a standby service for use as convenience in bad weather, at holiday periods, and for shopping trips." The commission described the C&EI as a marginally profitable railroad that could ill afford the $400,000 deficit of the *Georgian/Humming Bird* when there was no prospect that the losses would diminish. The ICC served its order on January 31, 1968, and the *Georgian/Humming Bird* was promptly discontinued, triggering a court battle that lasted several years and is further recounted in chapter 12.

Mount Vernon Branch

The 38-mile Mount Vernon branch, which connected with the Chicago–Evansville mainline at Fort Branch in Gibson County, opened in 1882. Through the early 20th century, passenger service was two round trips between Prince-

The Chicago to Atlanta *Georgian* is ready to depart Dearborn Station on May 1, 1960, behind FP71 No. 1603. The train also carried the Chicago to New Orleans cars of the *Humming Bird*. Bob's Photo.

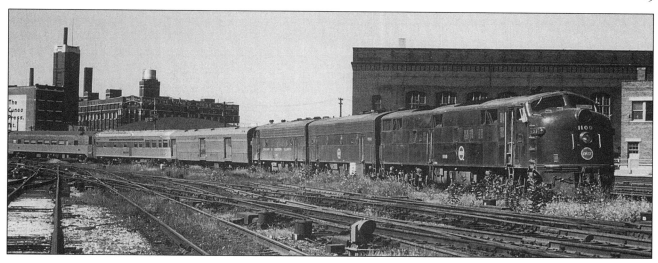

ton and Mount Vernon. One pair of trains had begun operating between Fort Branch and Mount Vernon by 1902. Service remained unchanged through December 8, 1918, when the trains began operating between Fort Branch and Mount Vernon. The midafternoon train was discontinued on July 29, 1923. The remaining trains departed Mount Vernon in the morning and returned in early afternoon.

Service was downgraded in the late 1920s to mixed trains. The trains began operation to Evansville on May 8, 1949, and became regular passenger trains in January 1950. The outbound train departed Evansville at 6:30 A.M. and arrived in Mount Vernon at 9 A.M. The return train left Mount Vernon at 10 A.M. and arrived in Evansville at noon. Nos. 302/303 made their final trips in May 1950.

The logo on E7 No. 1100 reflects the fact that the Missouri Pacific now owned the Chicago & Eastern Illinois. The *Georgian/ Humming Bird* nears Dearborn Station on August 13, 1967. No. 1100 was the C&EI's first E unit. Photo by Dave McKay.

Judyville Branch

The 15-mile branch between Judyville in western Warren County, and Rossville Junction, Ill., on the Chicago–Evansville mainline was built in 1903. The first scheduled passenger operation was a round trip between Rossville and Finney, Ind. Service to Judyville began on May 31, 1903. The service, one round trip, remained largely unchanged through the late 1920s when the trains became mixed trains that were discontinued in November 1935.

Freeland Park Branch

The 11-mile branch between Freeland Park in western Benton County and Milford, Ill., on the Chicago–Evansville mainline was built in 1901. Passenger service began November 10, 1901. Service expanded on January 6, 1902, to two round trips, one operating to Milford and the other to Watseka, Ill. In late 1905, all trains began operating to Watseka. The trains again terminated at Milford between November 4, 1910, and January 15, 1911. One round trip was discontinued on August 19, 1917.

Service remained unchanged until the late 1920s when mixed train operation began. The western terminus was changed from Watseka to Milford on December 1, 1924. Passenger service ended in November 1935.

Brazil–Saline City

Opened in 1887 by the Terre Haute & Indianapolis, this 12-mile branch was leased on June 3, 1887, by the Evansville & Indianapolis Railroad, later controlled by C&EI predecessor Evansville & Terre Haute. Passenger service was a round trip between Brazil and

Saline City in Clay County. Service was extended on July 9, 1900, to Worthington in Greene County and had increased by 1902 to two round trips that terminated at Clay City in Clay County. One round trip was briefly extended to Worthington in 1905 and discontinued in 1906.

The E&I entered receivership on February 20, 1916, and separated from the C&EI. The branch fell into the hands of the Vandalia (later Pennsylvania), which abandoned 7 miles of it in 1916. The last passenger operation was a Brazil–Saline City mixed train that made its final journey on May 30, 1916.

On November 11, 1887, at Stave Track, 2 miles south of Brazil, a southbound passenger train hit a mule, which apparently struck a switch stand, causing the switch to open and the train's coach to derail and turn over. All aboard escaped without serious injury just before the wooden coach burst into flames. The mule was last seen grazing in a nearby field.

The Coal Road

Goodland in southeastern Newton County was the center of passenger operations on C&EI's Indiana Division, the former Coal Road. In January 1900, trains originated at Goodland for Chicago, Brazil, and La Crosse. A Chicago–Terre Haute train also stopped there. Indiana Division passenger operations usually were fewer than 10 trains a day. Service ended when the line shut down on December 31, 1921. The Chicago, Attica & Southern took over most of the Coal Road a year later, but never offered scheduled passenger service.

La Crosse Branch

La Crosse was a busy railroad junction, but C&EI passenger operations were minimal. Service began August 28, 1887, with a round trip to Brazil. This train began terminating at Goodland on October 14, 1888. The trains again began operating to Brazil on January 8, 1917. That fall, operation reverted to Goodland. Nos. 200/201 made their final runs on December 31, 1921.

Chicago Trains

Chicago–Brazil service via Momence, Ill., began March 31, 1891. Previously, these trains had operated to Fair Oaks and reached Chicago on the Monon. This lasted until October 14, 1888, when the trains began operating between Brazil and Momence Junction, Ill. The trains began operating between Chicago and Terre Haute via Brazil on December 3, 1897. For a short time in the mid-1890s, the C&EI operated two round trips between Chicago and Brazil.

In May 1902, the C&EI named Nos. 209/210 the *Brazil and Mudlavia Express/Mudlavia and Brazil Express*. These names stuck until May 1907 when southbound No. 209 was renamed *Mudlavia and Brazil Accommodation*. The name for No. 210 was dropped. Four months later, No. 209 lost its name. Nos. 209/210 were shortened to Chicago–Brazil on April 15, 1906, and discontinued on December 31, 1921.

A handful of other trains operated between Chicago and other points on the Indiana Division. On the same day that service began between Chicago and Brazil, the Chicago & Indiana Coal railroad launched a Chicago–Attica train that ran for about eight months before being ending on November 22, 1891.

Service between Chicago and Goodland began January 14, 1901. Discontinued in 1902, the train was revived in spring 1907. Trimmed to Goodland–Momence operation on July 4, 1909, it became a mixed train later that year and operated to Momence Junction. Mixed train operation ended July 23, 1916, and the train again operated between Chicago and Goodland.

The C&EI extended Goodland–Momence Nos. 261/262 to Chicago on January 8, 1917, creating two Chicago–Goodland round trips. This continued until August 19, 1917, when one round trip was discontinued and the other began originating at Momence. The route was shortened to Tallmadge, Ill., on October 30, 1921. A Chicago–Veedersburg train began May 25, 1902. Named *Mudlavia and Veedersburg Express/Veedersburg, Mudlavia and Chicago Express* in February 1906, these trains ended on April 15, 1906.

The C&EI operated trains between Momence and Brazil, and Veedersburg and Attica in the 1890s. The Momence–Brazil service lasted the longest, through 1899, before changing to Momence–Goodland and Goodland–Brazil pairings. The former pairing was gone by 1901. The northbound train briefly operated beyond Goodland in 1903, terminating at Momence Junction. The Brazil–Goodland trains ran through late 1917.

Terre Haute–Evansville

Numerous companies developed the line between Terre Haute and Evansville via Washington in Daviess County. Development of the route, which was 29 miles longer than the C&EI mainline via Vincennes, began in 1853. It was not the intent of the predecessor companies to create a Terre Haute–Evansville route. The line resulted from the January 1, 1886, merger of three companies to form the Evansville & Indianapolis Railroad.

Passenger service in the early 1890s was three round trips operating Terre Haute–Evansville, Evansville–Washington, and Terre Haute–Worthington. By the middle of the decade, a Worthington–Washington round trip had joined the schedule. In April 1902, service changed to two round trips, Terre Haute–Washington and Terre Haute–Evansville. The Worthington–Washington train was reinstated later that year. The Terre Haute–Washington train was extended to Petersburg in 1906 and the Worthington–Washington train was replaced by a Washington–Evansville train.

This would be the zenith of the line's passenger service under C&EI control. By 1913, service had shrunk to two round trips, Terre Haute–Evansville and Worthington–Evansville. After the C&EI entered receivership, the line was spun off and eventually acquired by the Big Four (later New York Central).

Other Routes

C&EI predecessor Chicago, Danville & Vincennes built a line from Bismarck, Ill., to Coal Creek in western Fountain County that opened in July 1873. Passenger service was minimal. The C&EI ended operations between Covington, Ind., and Bismarck in favor of operating over the Indiana, Bloomington & Western (later Peoria & Eastern) between Danville, Ill., and Covington. Passenger service was two round trips between Coal Creek and Danville Junction. This service lasted through late 1887.

In the early 1900s, a branch was built from Standard, located 1.6 miles north of Shelburne in Sullivan County, through Hymera to New Pittsburg. Passenger service was offered between Standard and Hymera, but was gone by 1915.

The C&EI had two routes between Terre Haute and Brazil, both of which came off the Chicago line at Otter Creek Junction northeast of Terre Haute. The line via Bernett hosted passenger trains, including Chicago–Terre Haute service on the Indiana Division. The C&EI began an Otter Creek–Brazil local in 1882 that lasted through 1902. Passenger service between Otter Creek and Brazil ended in April 1906 when the Chicago–Terre Haute train began originating at Brazil.

Louisville and Nashville

CHAPTER 12

LOUISVILLE & NASHVILLE

Although the Louisville & Nashville Railroad cut across Indiana's southwest corner for just 39 miles, its importance far outweighed its diminutive presence. For nearly 83 years, trains arriving in Evansville on the Chicago & Eastern Illinois combined with L&N trains from St. Louis and crossed the Ohio River bound for Nashville, Tenn., Louisville, Ky., New Orleans, Atlanta, and Florida. L&N was a southern railroad, and many of its trains had *Dixie* in their names. L&N dining cars were renowned for fresh Gulf seafood gumbo and hickory-smoked ham. L&N offered comfortable, reliable service, but passenger traffic made up less than 10 percent of its overall revenue.

In the 1840s, the ability to attract railroads was essential to a city's future prosperity. With several railroads having built or planning to build to New Albany or Jeffersonville, Louisville interests created the L&N to link their city with the lower South. Chartered on March 5, 1850, L&N's first passenger train operated about 12 miles on August 28, 1855, from downtown Louisville to the end of track. Service between Louisville and Nashville began on October 31, 1859.

L&N's post–Civil War growth caused Evansville merchants to feel increasingly isolated from southern markets, and they decided in 1866 to build a railroad from Henderson, Ky., to a connection with L&N's Memphis branch at Guthrie, Ky. The Evansville, Henderson & Nashville was completed in January 1871 and opened to Nashville that April.

The St. Louis & Southeastern was established in 1869 to build from East St. Louis, Ill., to Evansville. Completed in late 1871, the StL&SE acquired the EH&N in 1872. The StL&SE's propensity toward egregious rate-cutting practices made it a thorn in the L&N's side. When the StL&SE declared bankruptcy in 1874, L&N saw an opportunity to eliminate a nefarious rival and break out of the South. L&N acquired the Tennessee and Kentucky Divisions of the StL&SE in 1879 and the Illinois and Indiana Divisions on May 1, 1880.

The Louisville, St. Louis & Texas never reached Evansville let alone St. Louis or Texas. Chartered in 1882, "the Texas" was completed between Henderson and West Point, Ky., in 1889 and extended to Strawberry, 6 miles south of Louisville, on April 1, 1905. It emerged from receivership in 1896 as the more realistically named Louisville, Henderson & St. Louis Railway.

Louisville–Evansville passenger operations began in 1897 using the L&N between Henderson and Evansville. Initially, the LH&StL used the Newport News & Mississippi Valley (later Illinois Central) to reach Louisville. L&N began taking stock control of the "Henderson Route" in 1905, although it operated as an independent entity until 1929.

St. Louis–Nashville

The St. Louis & Southeastern began passenger service in December 1871 with an Evansville–East St. Louis round trip. Service expanded to two round trips later that month, then three round trips in June 1873. Two of these trains had begun crossing the Ohio River on a steam ferry and serving Nashville by August 1873. The StL&SE advertised through Pullmans between St. Louis and Nashville.

Nashville service fell to one round trip in late November 1873. Another round trip operated between East St. Louis and Evansville. Mixed trains operated between Evansville and McLeansboro, Ill. After the StL&SE entered receivership, Evansville service was cut to two pairs of trains, both of which crossed the Ohio River, one serving Nashville, the other serving Nortonville, Ky. In its waning years the StL&SE operated two St. Louis–Nashville round trips, but one round trip was gone within a year after the L&N had purchased the StL&SE.

The 12-mile trip between Evansville and Henderson took 2 hours and couldn't operate in the winter when ice clogged the river. Differences in gauges meant that passenger car trucks had to be changed. Sleeping cars usually operated between St. Louis and Evansville, the standard-gauge portion of the route.

With the opening of a $2 million bridge at Henderson, the L&N's longest, on July 13, 1885, the St. Louis–Nashville travel time fell from 22 to 12 hours. The Chicago–Nashville travel time was cut to 16 hours. After the opening of the Henderson Bridge, service between St. Louis and Nashville doubled, and Chicago–Nashville through trains began. Initially named *Nashville Fast Line/Chicago Fast Line*, the trains were renamed *Chicago and Nashville Limited* on February 8, 1891.

Milton Hannibal Smith, who began his 32-year reign as L&N president in 1889, didn't care for passenger service. He took office at a time when travelers were demanding more opulent and comfortable accommodations. Smith reluctantly furnished them, but considered it a waste of money. During his presidency, the quality and quantity of L&N passenger equipment improved at a miserly rate, and passenger traffic grew slowly.

L&N instituted through sleepers between St. Louis and Jacksonville, Fla., in 1885, its first Florida service through Evansville. L&N also offered St. Louis–Nashville parlor cars and St. Louis–Atlanta sleepers. For the 1896–97 winter season, the sleepers operated between St. Louis and Tampa, Fla., on a 43-hour schedule. The Tampa cars did not return the following winter. Instead, the sleepers ran to Charleston, S.C.

L&N interchanged sleepers at Nashville with the Nashville, Chattanooga & St. Louis, which in December 1896 began advertising the St. Louis–Jacksonville sleepers as the *Quickstep*. The NC&StL later billed the Jacksonville–St. Louis sleepers (and those between Chicago and Jacksonville) as the *Dixie Flyer* and began calling itself the Dixie Route. Composed of the C&EI, Evansville & Terre Haute (later C&EI), L&N, and NC&StL, the 735-mile Dixie Route was the shortest way between Chicago and Atlanta.

Fewer travelers from the North, however, used St. Louis as a gateway to Florida than used Chicago or Cincinnati. L&N service between St. Louis and the South was of secondary importance compared with the vast Dixie Route fleet that originated in Chicago on the C&EI.

Prosperous Times

At the dawn of the 20th century, L&N offered through sleepers between St. Louis and Jacksonville, St. Petersburg, Fla., and Atlanta. Two round trips operated between St. Louis and Nashville. The 1901 debut of the *Chicago and Florida Limited* between Chicago and St. Augustine increased Evansville–Nashville service to three round trips. Service between Evansville and Nashville expanded and contracted with changes in seasonal service to the South. L&N usually operated more trains south of Evansville than west of Evansville,

L. & N. R. R. Passenger Station, Evansville, Ind.

"DIXIE FLYER."

Evansville Union Station opened in 1904 with the Louisville & Nashville as its primary tenant. All Dixie fleet trains from Chicago and St. Louis passed through this station. Author's collection.

where service remained at three pairs of trains until November 29, 1920, when the frequency increased to four pairings.

L&N had assigned chair cars to its overnight St. Louis–Nashville trains by 1902. That same year L&N purchased four café-coaches that were put into service in 1904 to serve travelers headed for the St. Louis World's Fair. Evansville Union Station also opened in 1904.

In 1916 the *Dixie Flyer*'s St. Louis–Jacksonville sleeper was named the *St. Louis Jacksonville Express*. The car began operating via Evansville on January 20, 1918, having been conveyed for several years by the Illinois Central between St. Louis and Martin, Tenn. Another Florida train, the *Dixie Limited*, began January 5, 1913, with St. Louis and Chicago sections operating independently between Evansville and Nashville.

L&N offered several sleepers between St. Louis and the South, many of them conveyed by the *Dixie Flyer*. For the 1923 winter season, L&N named Nos. 53/54 the *St. Louis–Jacksonville Express*. The train carried sleepers, a diner, and coaches between St. Louis and Jacksonville. Sleepers also operated St. Louis–Atlanta and St. Louis–Pensacola, Fla. The *Dixie Flyer* handled a weekly sleeper between Jacksonville and Peoria, Ill.

For the 1924 winter season, the *Dixie Limited* carried St. Louis–Miami sleepers. The Cincinnati–New Orleans *New Orleans Limited*, L&N's oldest named passenger train, carried the Pensacola sleepers south of Nashville. The Miami sleepers switched to the *Dixie Flyer* in 1925, but other through car service remained unchanged. Perhaps L&N's most extraordinary sleeper service operated in summer 1925 between Jacksonville and West Yellowstone, Wyo., passing through Indiana on the *Dixie Flyer* via St. Louis.

The Pensacola sleepers did not return for the 1926 winter season. Instead, the *New Orleans Limited* carried St. Louis–Birmingham, Ala., sleepers that returned the following year, but operated to Montgomery, Ala., for the 1928 season. There were no St. Louis–Alabama sleeping cars in the 1929 winter season. The 1920s were a decade of decline at L&N as ridership fell from 17 million in 1920 to 2.1 million in 1932. Passenger revenue fell from $27.7 million in 1921 to $5 million in 1932.

Leaner Times

The Depression had taken hold as the 1930 winter season began. St. Louis–Atlanta sleepers ended, but St. Louis–Montgomery sleepers resumed. Later that winter, L&N discontinued the *St. Louis–Jacksonville Express*, although sleepers continued to operate between St. Louis and Jacksonville on other trains. The *St. Louis–Jacksonville Express* returned for the 1931 season.

The following year, the Montgomery sleepers were dropped in favor of a resumption of service to Pensacola. The Miami sleepers were now carried by the *Dixie Limited,* and a St. Louis–Evansville setout sleeper had been established. The Miami sleepers did not return for the 1932 season. The St. Louis–Evansville sleeper ended in 1934, and St. Louis through sleeper service had shrunk to Pensacola, Nashville, and Jacksonville by January 1935.

By summer 1935, L&N had upgraded the *Dixie Limited* and *Dixie Flyer* by air-conditioning the Pullmans, coaches, and dining cars. Most mainline L&N passenger trains were air-conditioned by 1937. L&N also pioneered on-board radio entertainment. Passengers listened through headphones, but there never seemed to be enough to go around.

During the Depression, the L&N was the first major railroad to cut passenger fares in an effort to stimulate travel, which had plunged from 9.4 million passengers in 1927 to 2.1 million in 1932. On April 1, 1933, L&N cut Pullman fares from 3.6 cents to 3 cents per mile, reduced coach fares to 2 cents per mile, and ended the Pullman surcharge on parlor and sleeping car space. That December, L&N cut coach fares to 1.5 cents per mile and some Pullman fares to 2 cents per mile. Although patronage rose from 2.5 million in 1933 to 3.8 million in 1934, passenger revenue rose only slightly from $5.1 million to $5.3 million.

The *St. Louis–Jacksonville Express* disappeared for good in 1935, replaced by a St. Louis section of the *Dixie Limited.* The Pensacola sleepers were dropped, but sleepers were added to Atlanta and Birmingham. St. Louis–Nashville service was four round trips. St. Louis–Miami sleepers returned for the 1937 winter season, conveyed south of Evansville by the *Dixieland,* which had debuted January 2, 1936. St. Louis–Evansville service increased to five round trips in 1937 when a St. Louis–Louisville train began operating independently west of Evansville.

Service changed little through the early 1940s. L&N had five St. Louis–Evansville round trips, four of which were Nashville trains. The most notable change was the discontinuance of the St. Louis–Jacksonville sleepers in 1937. Another St. Louis–Nashville round trip

L&N gave K7 No. 295 streamlined shrouding in 1940 and assigned it to the Chicago–Miami *South Wind.* A 20,000-gallon tender enabled No. 295 to set a steam locomotive record for nonstop operation without servicing, 205 miles between Nashville, Tenn., and Birmingham, Ala. The engineer awaits a highball at Louisville Union Station. Bob's Photo.

ended on January 2, 1942, along with the St. Louis–Miami sleepers. The Birmingham sleepers began operating to Montgomery. St. Louis–Nashville service rose to four round trips a year later, but by January 1944, the St. Louis–Atlanta sleepers had ended. The only L&N sleepers from St. Louis went to Nashville and Montgomery.

The *Dixie Limited* operated in two sections south of Evansville, one for Florida, one for New Orleans. By November, the Montgomery sleepers had ended in favor of St. Louis–Atlanta sleepers carried by the *Dixie Limited* and the *Dixie Flyer*, which did not have a St. Louis section.

L&N took delivery of 16 E6 diesel locomotives from the Electro-Motive Division of General Motors in 1942, its first passenger diesels. Some of these locomotives pulled the *Dixie Limited*.

World War II stimulated explosive passenger growth. L&N carried 3.5 million passengers in 1941, 6.4 million in 1942, and 11.9 million in 1943. Patronage peaked in 1944 at 12.4 million. To handle the demand, L&N sold seats in lounges and observation cars. Its 29 dining cars dished up 2.3 million meals in 1943; half of them were served to military personnel. For the first time in its 42-year history, the dining department showed a profit.

L&N purchased only top-grade food and served generous portions. Trains leaving Gulf Coast cities were heavily stocked with fresh seafood, L&N's most popular dinner entrée. The hands-down morning favorite was the Kentucky country ham breakfast, featuring meat cured at the Old Hickory Farm near Peewee Valley, Ky.

The December 1940 inauguration of the all-coach, every-third-day Chicago–Miami *Dixie Flagler* increased Evansville–Nashville service, but the *Flagler* never had a St. Louis section.

Georgian *on Their Minds*

L&N's postwar passenger traffic strategy was to keep as much of the war era ridership as possible while enhancing existing service. The St. Louis–Atlanta and Cincinnati–New Orleans routes received rapid, diesel-powered daylight streamliners equipped with new lightweight equipment. In 1944, L&N placed a $2.5 million order with American Car and Foundry for 20 coaches, eight diners, and eight tavern-lounges, its first new equipment order since 1930. The cars were delivered in 1946. A year earlier the Electro-Motive Division had delivered eight E7 diesel locomotives, costing $1 million apiece.

A March 1946 contest to name the new trains attracted 300,000 entries. The winning names were *Humming Bird* (Cincinnati train) and *Georgian* (St. Louis train). L&N had operated a *Georgian* between Atlanta and Jacksonville in the late 1920s with a seasonal Cincinnati section in the early 1930s.

Both trains debuted November 17, 1946, the *Georgian* covering its 610-mile route in 13 hours. The trains also introduced a new passenger livery of dark blue and silver with imitation gold script lettering. Underbody equipment was painted light gray, and the trucks were black. The interiors featured shades of red and brown upholstery, maroon rugs, and ivory walls and ceilings. Previously, L&N passenger cars were painted dark olive green with gold Roman lettering.

The launch of the *Georgian* increased St. Louis–Evansville service to five round trips. With the *Dixie Limited* having Florida and New Orleans sections, Evansville–Nashville service had increased to five round trips.

Despite extensive promotion, patronage of the *Georgian* was below market forecasts. An internal study concluded that a Chicago–Atlanta routing would offer a stronger market. The switch was made on June 1, 1948, but did not affect St. Louis–Nashville service because the *Georgian* had a St. Louis section. The *Georgian* also was rescheduled for overnight operation, assigned heavyweight sleepers, and put on a schedule 4 hours faster than the *Dixie Limited* between Chicago and Atlanta. The move returned immediate dividends, as the *Georgian* became one of L&N's most popular trains.

Other postwar moves undertaken by the L&N to bolster passenger traffic included reducing running times and modernizing heavyweight cars. L&N dropped the blue and silver livery in favor of solid blue. Heavyweight sleepers received "shadowlining" to simulate the aluminum fluting of L&N's lightweight sleepers.

L&N received from Pullman-Standard eight lightweight sleepers in 1949 and 22 lightweight sleepers between 1953 and 1954. The latter were six roomette, four double bedroom, six section sleepers that were assigned to the *Georgian* and *Humming Bird*. L&N ordered 13 60-seat coaches in 1955 for the *Georgian* and *Humming Bird* from American Car and Foundry, which had a Jeffersonville assembly plant. These were the last new passenger cars that L&N would order.

Despite these efforts, ridership was declining steadily. Patronage was 2.6 million by 1950, which was 20 percent of the 1944 level of 12.4 million, and L&N's passenger deficit was $15 million by 1953. Removing 74 passenger trains and 34 mixed trains in the 1950s saved L&N $5.7 million as it refocused its passenger service by assigning new or modernized equipment to its better-performing trains.

The northbound *Georgian* and *Humming Bird* crossed paths in Nashville and interchanged cars operating between the Gulf Coast and Chicago and St. Louis. This shaved 5 hours off the travel time from the previous connection between the *Azalean* and *Dixie Limited*.

The *Humming Bird* acquired a Chicago–Nashville section on August 8, 1951. Chicago–Gulf Coast cars previously handled on the *Georgian* were shifted to the *Humming Bird*, which operated about 15 minutes apart from the *Georgian*. The *Humming Bird* operated between Evansville and St. Louis in combination with the *Georgian*.

Driving Old Dixie Down

As passenger traffic continued to decline and L&N management favored the *Georgian* and *Humming Bird* for new equipment assignments, the Dixie fleet began losing its grandeur. On the first morning that the *Georgian* highballed out of St. Louis Union Station for Atlanta, the *Dixie Limited* and *Dixie Flyer* were still leading trains. The *Dixie Limited* had Atlanta and Miami sleepers, a St. Louis–Evansville diner, and ran south of Evansville in separate Florida and New Orleans sections. The *Dixie Flyer* conveyed St. Louis–Atlanta sleepers. A year later, the Atlanta sleeper on the *Dixie Flyer* had begun terminating at Nashville.

The St. Louis–Miami sleeper did not return for the 1949 winter season, and L&N would never again operate St. Louis–Florida through service. St. Louis–Nashville service remained five round trips, but the only cars operating beyond Nashville were Atlanta coaches and sleepers on the *Georgian* and a Montgomery sleeper on the *Dixie Limited*.

St. Louis–Nashville service fell to four round trips in 1949 and three round trips in 1952: the *Georgian/Humming Bird*, St. Louis–Nashville Nos. 51/52, the *Dixie Flyer* to Nashville, and the former *Dixie Limited* (it lost its name on October 1, 1951) to St. Louis. Only the *Georgian/Humming Bird* still offered dining service between St. Louis and Evansville. The *Georgian/Humming Bird* had Atlanta coaches and sleepers and a Montgomery sleeper. A Nashville sleeper went south on the *Dixie Flyer* and returned on the *Georgian/Humming Bird*. On January 17, 1955, the Illinois Commerce Commission allowed Nos. 51/52 to end between St. Louis and Evansville. The trains continued to operate between Evansville and Nashville until March 3, 1955.

The *Dixie Flyer*'s Nashville sleeper lasted until 1958. Departing St. Louis at 10:40 P.M., the *Dixie Flyer* had a 3-hour layover in Evansville, where it consolidated with its Chicago counterpart. Passengers connected at Nashville with the former *Azalean* to New Orleans. No. 92 had a Nashville connection from the former *Azalean* and operated 3 hours later than it had as the *Dixie Limited*. For years it had been a coaches-only train. With the discontinuance of the *Dixie Flyer* and No. 92 on February 22, 1959, St. Louis–Evansville service was down to the *Georgian/Humming Bird*.

Not every L&N passenger train between Evansville and Nashville was part of the Dixie Fleet. Nos. 51 and 52 were all-stops, all-day locals between St. Louis and Nashville. The train slows for the stop at Hanson, Ky., on August 1, 1953. Bob's Photo.

The Chicago Dixie Fleet declined precipitously in the 1950s. The seasonal Chicago–Florida *Dixieland* made its final run on April 28, 1949. The *Dixie Limited* made its last run on September 30, 1951. The every-third-day *Dixie Flagler*, renamed *New Dixieland* on December 16, 1954, and shortened to *Dixieland* in 1956, ended in late November 1957. This left the *Dixie Flyer* as the last Dixie Fleet train between Chicago and Florida. Unlike most of its running mates, the *Dixie Flyer* died a slow and agonizing death, dismembered one section at a time. The oldest name in the Dixie fleet, the *Dixie Flyer* lost more patrons with each dismemberment.

The *Dixie Flyer* was principally a mail and express train by the 1960s. But this business began evaporating when the Post Office Department shifted much of the train's bulk mail to freight trains on July 1, 1964, saving itself $4,200 a month in handling expenses at the Atlanta passenger station. Nonetheless, there remained enough head-end business to make the *Dixie Flyer* a moneymaker, earning profits of $654,730 (1963), $419,577 (1964), and $84,636 in the first four months of 1965.

The *Dixie Flyer*'s fate effectively was sealed on July 15, 1965, when the Illinois Commerce Commission allowed the C&EI to discontinue the train between Chicago and Danville, Ill., in return for rescheduling Nos. 1/92 between Chicago and Danville. The new schedule, effective August 3, 1965, precluded travel on the *Dixie Flyer* between Chicago and the South. Shorn of its lucrative head-end business and without connections to Chicago, the *Dixie Flyer* became a coach-only Evansville–Jacksonville train. Concurrent with the end of service to Chicago was the removal of the *Flyer*'s last sleepers (Chicago–Nashville).

L&N told the ICC the *Dixie Flyer* would be discontinued on September 21, 1965, between Evansville and Atlanta, saying that once the *Dixie Flyer* stopped serving Chicago it began losing money, sustaining an out-of-pocket loss of $249,421 between August 4 and September 30, 1965. The ICC adjusted the loss to $181,066, but cited the losses, declining ridership, and other transportation alternatives in allowing L&N to discontinue the *Dixie Flyer* on January 21, 1966.

Humming Bird, *Don't Fly Away*

The *Humming Bird* had lost some of its glitter by 1967, but was still an impressive train with three locomotives and 10 cars—11 on weekends—including sleepers, coaches, a diner, and a lounge, most of them operating to Atlanta on the *Georgian*. Since the late 1950s, the *Humming Bird* had been gradually scaled back.

The Chicago–New Orleans cars began terminating at Mobile, Ala., in January 1958 and at Montgomery, Ala., on April 20, 1967. *Humming Bird* passengers bound for New Orleans had to transfer to the Cincinnati section, which combined with the Chicago section in Nashville. The campaign to ground the *Humming Bird* began on August 31, 1967, when the C&EI told the Interstate Commerce Commission it wanted to discontinue the train on October 1 between Chicago and Evansville. The C&EI expected to lose $400,000 on the train, which it described as "minimally used by consumers."

None of the subsequent ICC or court opinions discussed whether the C&EI and L&N might have conspired to discontinue the *Humming Bird*. Given how the *Dixie Flyer* had suffered once it no longer served Chicago, the L&N could have foreseen the advantage of having the *Humming Bird* cut off from Chicago. Indiana Senator Vance Hartke would later denounce the ICC for allowing the railroads to engage in piecemeal tactics to end passenger service.

In 1966, 82,213 passengers rode the *Humming Bird* from Chicago to Evansville, an average of 225 a day, 71 of them CE&I local passengers. That same year, 75,271 were on the northbound *Humming Bird* when it departed Evansville, an average of 205 a day, 40 of them local passengers. More than half of the ridership passed through Evansville, many of them traveling to and from Chicago.

Opponents of the discontinuance argued that what happened to the *Humming Bird* in Illinois and Indiana would affect the train's viability in other states. The ICC ignored this issue, asking only whether patronage between Chicago and Evansville justified forcing the C&EI to continue a money-losing operation. The ICC concluded that it did not. Patronage was minimal, the financial losses incurred by the C&EI were substantial, and there was little prospect that the situation would improve. The ICC rejected an argument that the CE&I's financial data were misleading because it ignored that the Missouri Pacific controlled the C&EI.

The ICC on January 31, 1968, served the order allowing discontinuance of the *Humming Bird* between Chicago and Evansville, and the train promptly ended. The cities of Chicago, Terre Haute, and Vincennes joined with four Illinois cities in asking the ICC to reconsider. Describing the *Humming Bird* as one of the best-patronized long-distance passenger trains in the country, the cities said the ICC had erred in not finding the CE&I portion to be part of a Chicago–Atlanta route. Noting that L&N was negotiating to purchase the C&EI between Woodland Junction, Ill., and Evansville, the cities said an L&N takeover would benefit C&EI passenger service.

The battle of the *Humming Bird* shifted south in April when L&N announced plans to discontinue the train between Cincinnati and New Orleans. Citing declining patronage and lost mail revenue, L&N said it expected patronage to decline further due to the truncating of the Chicago section of the *Humming Bird*. The ICC on May 15 declined to reconsider its C&EI *Humming Bird* decision, and on May 27 the Illinois and Indiana cities, joined by Nashville, Tenn., sued the ICC and the C&EI. The ICC on September 6, 1968, approved discontinuance of the Cincinnati section of the *Humming Bird*, but the Tennessee Public Service Commission obtained a federal court order restraining discontinuance while the courts considered Tennessee's challenge of the ICC order.

The Tennessee case was consolidated with the C&EI case, and a hearing was conducted on November 4, 1968. The U.S. District Court for the Northern District of Illinois dismissed both cases on January 8, 1969, ruling that Section 13a(1) of the Interstate Commerce Act (which gave the ICC legal authority to investigate a proposed discontinuance of an interstate passenger train) did not allow judicial review of an ICC decision to allow a discontinuance. The courts could review an ICC order that a train must continue operating, but the court said that by terminating an investigation, the ICC had not issued an order requiring action.

The next day L&N halted the southbound *Humming Bird* at Birmingham and put the passengers on a Greyhound bus. Although widely criticized for this, L&N said it feared labor unions and others might obtain an injunction to keep the *Humming Bird* operating. L&N said it wanted to discontinue the train as soon as possible because its overall passenger deficit was threatening the company's financial health.

The U.S. Supreme Court on December 9, 1969, overturned the Illinois court's decision, ruling that when the ICC investigates a proposed discontinuance and elects not to block it, it is reaching a decision on the merits of the case, an action reviewable by the courts. The case went back to the Illinois court, which on February 5, 1970, vacated the ICC orders in both *Humming Bird* discontinuance cases and ordered the ICC to reopen its investigation. The Supreme Court had cited a December 3, 1969, decision in which the ICC favored the L&N over the Illinois Central for acquisition of CE&I's Evansville line. Among other things, the ICC anticipated that L&N would maintain and improve passenger service between Chicago and the South.

This ICC statement was peculiar because nearly 2 years earlier it had allowed the discontinuance of the last through passenger train between Chicago and Atlanta. The ICC also had before it a petition that if approved would have meant discontinuance of the last L&N passenger trains between St. Louis and Atlanta. The Illinois court said neither the railroads nor the ICC had given cities south of Evansville adequate notice of the proposed discontinuance of the *Humming Bird* on the C&EI. The court observed that what happened in Indiana and Illinois affected Kentucky, Tennessee, and Georgia.

The *Humming Bird* discontinuance case again reached the Supreme Court, which disagreed with the district court's finding that residents downstream from the proposed discontinuance did not receive adequate notification. The Court ruled that federal law required notice only in states where the train was to be discontinued. Nonetheless, the Court acknowledged that what happened in one area could adversely affect a train's vitality elsewhere.

No Peace the Georgian Finds

In seeking to discontinue the *Georgian*, the L&N met its match with a small but persistent group of passengers who tirelessly fought to save passenger train service between St. Louis and Evansville. The skirmish began when L&N informed the ICC of its intent to discontinue the *Georgian* between St. Louis and Nashville on July 31, 1967.

Despite several attempts by the L&N to kill the train, the former *Georgian* lasted between Evansville and St. Louis until the coming of Amtrak in 1971. The train is at McLeansboro, Ill., in 1970. Photo by John Fuller.

The *Georgian* by now was hardly the illustrious streamliner upon which L&N had staked its passenger train future in 1947. The 1967 *Georgian* was a coach train that interchanged cars at Nashville with the Chicago section of the *Georgian*. L&N claimed the *Georgian* lost $386,800 out of pocket in 1965 and $529,984 in 1966. Clouding the train's future was the removal of the railway post office car on February 4, 1966, a shift by Railway Express Agency of some St. Louis–Evansville express business to trucks, and diversion to trucks of storage mail that had been carried from Evansville to St. Louis.

In the previous 7 months (beginning in October 1966), 7,569 passengers had ridden the southbound *Georgian*, 4,856 of them boarding at St. Louis. At Evansville, 566 had boarded and 1,414 detrained, while 2,327 had connected in Nashville with other L&N trains. Northbound, 4,016 passengers boarded at Nashville, of which all but 988 had connected from other L&N trains. The northbound *Georgian* carried 7,213 passengers, of whom 868 boarded at Evansville and 289 detrained there. At St. Louis, 3,517 passengers detrained.

Witnesses criticized L&N for poor on-time performance, freight train interference, unkempt coaches, and lack of food service. The Evansville station had dirty restrooms and inadequate heating and air conditioning. Passengers had a long walk from the station to the train. An Indiana Public Service Commission inspector testified that trains often stopped beyond the train shed to take on water. An L&N conductor said a lack of hostlers—employees who move engines at a terminal—was why the train stopped so far from the station. The conductor acknowledged receiving numerous complaints about dirty coaches and lack of food service, leading him to conclude that passengers were usually dissatisfied with L&N service.

L&N had removed the St. Louis–Montgomery, Ala., sleepers in September 1965. The St. Louis–Atlanta sleepers and St. Louis–Evansville diner had ended on April 24, 1966. Several witnesses said business would improve if the service and station facilities were better. But L&N executives disagreed. The railroad said it removed the diners and sleepers because of poor patronage. L&N officials did not believe it was possible to make passenger service attractive enough to significantly increase business. L&N had lowered fares for groups and spent $500,000 to advertise the service in 1961, but ridership had still declined.

The *Georgian* was the last passenger train between St. Louis and the Southeast, and the ICC seemed reluctant to let it go. The ICC acknowledged that the *Georgian* was losing money, but said L&N had "thrown in the sponge" on passenger service.

The *Georgian/Humming Bird* between Chicago and Nashville would continue to provide rail passenger service south of Evansville, but ending St. Louis–Evansville service would eliminate rail passenger service for 90 percent of the *Georgian*'s eastbound and westbound passengers. The ICC ordered L&N to keep the *Georgian* operating between St. Louis and Evansville for another year. L&N could discontinue the St. Louis section of the *Georgian* between Evansville and Nashville.

Some witnesses had suggested L&N had a covenant to provide passenger service. One mayor said he understood that the *Georgian* was a money loser, but the railroad was a public utility that owed a duty to the public other than taking the easy way out by discontinuing passenger service. Another witness said L&N owed the public a reasonable passenger service as the cost of doing business in the public domain.

L&N executives must have grimaced. They would later point out that L&N had spent $10.4 million on new equipment between 1946 and 1949 and $30 million to repair and rehabilitate passenger equipment between 1962 and 1968. The South Louisville shops had rebuilt 64 cars, installing new seats, disc brakes, and other appointments and improving heating and air-conditioning systems. L&N president William H. Kendall said the public overlooked the efforts that railroads had made to woo travelers before ending service. "It is apparent that the public did not respond to our investment and promotion," Kendall said.

L&N took its half loaf from the ICC and on December 15, 1967, discontinued the St. Louis section of the *Georgian* between Evansville and Nashville. The Chicago section of the *Georgian* continued to offer connections in Evansville with now-unnamed St. Louis–Evansville Nos. 5/10. When the C&EI received permission a month later to discontinue the *Humming Bird/Georgian* between Chicago and Evansville, L&N responded on February 3, 1968, by discontinuing the *Humming Bird*'s sleepers and the *Georgian*'s sleepers and dining car. The *Humming Bird* and *Georgian* names were dropped. The remains of the *Humming Bird/Georgian* were consolidated with Nos. 5/10 to create a St. Louis–Atlanta train, although for legal reasons L&N timetables presented the schedules as though the operation involved separate trains operating Atlanta–Evansville and Evansville–St. Louis.

L&N also asked the ICC to reopen the 1967 *Georgian* proceedings, but a hearing on that request was canceled at the railroad's request. Instead, L&N filed notice with the ICC of its intent to discontinue the St. Louis–Evansville–Atlanta trains on August 13, 1969. The L&N cited financial hardship, saying the service had lost $811,388 in 1967, $672,359 in 1968, and $519,055 in the first seven months of 1969. With the Post Office Department planning to remove the last storage mail cars on November 29, 1969, L&N projected the losses would balloon to $942,364 for 1969. The last express business had been removed between St. Louis and Evansville on April 1, 1968.

The former *Georgian* normally operated with one locomotive, a coach, and two head-end cars. During the 70-minute southbound layover at Evansville, passengers could patronize a restaurant located across the street from the station, and they had 10 minutes at Chattanooga to get breakfast. On the northbound trip, the only meal stop was 15 minutes at Chattanooga.

Fifty-one people testified against discontinuance, most hoping to save service between St. Louis and Evansville. Some accused L&N of trying to discourage patronage by removing food service and sleeping cars and cutting the maximum top speed from 70 mph to 50 mph due to rough track. Critics ripped the railroad for failures of the air conditioning and heat, poor lighting, lack of clean restrooms, and poor on-time performance.

Witnesses also said discontinuance of the *Humming Bird* had hurt patronage of the former *Georgian* because 30 to 36 percent of the passengers on the St. Louis–Atlanta trains had connected with the *Humming Bird* in Nashville in 1968. In response, L&N argued that the former *Georgian* was a hopeless money loser that would have to attract 300 daily riders, an 828 percent increase, just to break even. The trains cost $8 for each $1 of revenue earned.

As it had earlier, the ICC acknowledged that the trains were losing money, but in its decision of December 3, 1969, the Commission concluded that most of the service complaints were justified. "The . . . decrease in patronage was undoubtedly due in no small measure to a marked deterioration in the service provided by these trains, a matter wholly within the province and control of the railroad," wrote Commissioner Dale W. Hardin. Had the L&N been more diligent about taking care of its passenger service and promoting it, the ICC said, the railroad might have enjoyed higher revenues and smaller losses.

The ICC described the trains as having a hard core of regular passengers, and there was a significant likelihood that ridership would increase if the service was more attractive. The ICC ordered the former *Georgian* to continue for six months. L&N protested the ICC's decision, but to no avail. In asking the ICC to reconsider its decision, L&N said the former *Georgian* was "virtually running empty" and "nothing in the record justifies [its] continuance."

L&N's skeletal passenger network in 1969 earned $1.7 million in revenue compared with the $8.4 million it earned in 1960. About the only improvement that L&N made was a modification of three former C&EI coaches to provide a snack bar serving sandwiches, hot soups and stews, snacks, and beverages aboard the former *Georgian*.

The prolonged struggle to revive the *Humming Bird* and keep the former *Georgian* running may not have been as instrumental as the 1970 Penn Central bankruptcy in prompting the creation of Amtrak, but both cases contributed to a sense of urgency to find a solution to America's passenger train problem. Ironically, the law designed to save passenger service dealt Evansville's last rail passenger service a killing blow.

Initially, the Rail Passenger Service Act of 1970 prolonged the former *Georgian*. L&N went back to the ICC in June 1970 with plans to discontinue Nos. 5/10 (St. Louis–Evansville) and Nos. 3/4 (Evansville–Atlanta) on July 7. L&N again cited low ridership and high financial losses to justify ending service. Before the ICC investigation had ended, though,

Congress created Amtrak. The ICC ruled that the L&N trains were no longer subject to discontinuance proceedings under section 13a(1) of the Interstate Commerce Act and had to continue until Amtrak decided to keep them or allow them to expire.

The U.S. Supreme Court's second ruling in the *Humming Bird* case came after passage of the Rail Passenger Service Act. With the ICC now saying it could no longer review intercity passenger train discontinuances, the effort to get the ICC to reconsider its 1968 order allowing removal of the *Humming Bird* became moot.

Amtrak's basic route structure did not include the Chicago–Atlanta or St. Louis–Atlanta routes through Evansville. The *Humming Bird* was never revived, and the former *Georgian* trundled along until arriving in St. Louis and Atlanta for the last time on May 1, 1971.

Evansville–Louisville

After emerging from receivership in 1896, the Louisville, Henderson & St. Louis and L&N coordinated schedules at Henderson. At the time, the LH&StL operated two daily Louisville–Henderson round trips. In 1897, the L&N granted the LH&StL the right to use the Henderson Bridge, and the LH&StL entered Evansville on June 20, 1897, operating three daily Evansville–Louisville round trips, two of which carried St. Louis cars.

LH&StL trains used the L&N between Louisville Union Station and Strawberry. Located at 10th and Broadway, Union Station opened on September 7, 1891, and also served the Monon and Pennsylvania Railroads. The LH&StL periodically operated a local between Evansville and Cloverport, Ky., between 1900 and December 20, 1908, when it was curtailed to Henderson–Cloverport. Louisville–Evansville service briefly increased in 1907 when the LH&StL added a Saturday-only train from Louisville to Evansville. The train returned to Louisville on Sunday. This service lasted about a year.

The LH&StL had connections with the Illinois Central in Kentucky, but was dependent on the L&N at both ends of its system. The LH&StL had an excellent safety record, having never suffered a passenger fatality in its 40 years of independent existence.

The level of service on the LH&StL remained largely unchanged through the late 1940s. The LH&StL (and later the L&N) operated three Evansville–Louisville round trips, two of which had St. Louis cars, carried for the most part by L&N St. Louis–Nashville trains. The LH&StL offered Pullman drawing room sleepers and all-steel reclining chair cars on its night trains and observation parlor cars on its day trains. Some sections of the LH&StL followed the Ohio River.

The LH&StL added an Evansville–Louisville sleeper to the overnight trains in 1923, and two Louisville–Evansville round trips featured observation-parlor cars. A year later, the observation-parlors had been removed, but parlor car service remained on four of the six trains. The St. Louis–Louisville trains received names in September 1927: *Daylight Limited* and *St. Louis Limited/Louisville Limited*. The *Daylight Limited* had an observation-parlor by 1929, and the Evansville sleepers now operated between St. Louis and Evansville.

The LH&StL appeared as an independent entity for the final time in the May 1929 *Official Guide of the Railways*. In June, the schedules were included with L&N passenger schedules, and the train names were gone. Nos. 151/152 were day trains with buffet parlor cars. Nos. 155/156 were overnight trains carrying St. Louis–Louisville sleepers. Nos. 153/154 operated between Evansville and Louisville and had no food service, but made a meal stop at Irvington, Ky.

The Evansville sleeper reverted to Evansville–Louisville operation in 1930. L&N assigned a diner to one pair of St. Louis–Louisville trains, but the following year the St. Louis–Louisville observation-parlors were replaced by observation cars. The St. Louis–Louisville diner was removed in 1933, although dining cars still operated on L&N trains that conveyed the Louisville cars between Evansville and St. Louis.

The Evansville–Louisville sleepers were removed in March 1935. In the summer of 1935, L&N upgraded St. Louis–Louisville service by assigning air-conditioned Pullmans. Parlor cars came off the Evansville–Louisville trains in 1936 and off St. Louis–Louisville trains in May 1937. The latter had featured a broiler buffet and drawing rooms.

None of the Louisville trains offered dining or lounge cars during the 1940s. Following World War II, the L&N briefly operated coaches between St. Louis and Lexington, Ky. No. 152 (Louisville to St. Louis) and No. 153 (Evansville to Louisville) ended on December 14, 1949, leaving two trains from St. Louis to Louisville and one train each from Louisville to Evansville and St. Louis. This schedule continued through August 1953, when No. 151 (St. Louis–Louisville) was discontinued, leaving Nos. 153/154 (Evansville–Louisville) and Nos. 55-155/156-56 (St. Louis–Louisville). The Evansville–Louisville trains made their last trips on October 14, 1954.

The St. Louis–Louisville trains continued to offer sleepers and coaches through the late 1950s. From Evansville to St. Louis, the Louisville cars were attached to the *Georgian/Humming Bird*, which carried a diner that served breakfast into St. Louis. From St. Louis to Evansville, the Louisville cars were attached to the *Dixie Flyer*, which had no meal service. The St. Louis–Louisville sleepers ended in August 1958. The last assigned sleepers to this service were heavyweights with eight sections and five double bedrooms. The discontinuance of Nos. 55-155/156-56 on November 15, 1958, ended passenger service between Evansville and Louisville.

Evansville was the focal point of locals that provided service to Kentucky and Illinois on the St. Louis–Nashville mainline. Through the end of the 19th century, Illinois locals terminated at McLeansboro, Carmi, or Mount Vernon. The Illinois locals to Evansville were gone by 1890, although service had resumed by 1895 with an Evansville–McLeansboro round trip.

Kentucky locals to Evansville began after the opening of the Henderson Bridge in July 1885 when the L&N instituted an Evansville–Earlington round trip. These trains were combined with the Evansville–McLeansboro locals in 1899, an operation that continued until the trains separated into Evansville–Earlington and Evansville–McLeansboro trains in 1900. L&N began another short-lived Evansville run-through local (McLeansboro to Earlington) on January 14, 1901. The return train terminated at Evansville and another train operated from Evansville to McLeansboro. The Evansville–McLeansboro local was extended again to Earlington in 1903, an arrangement that lasted about a year.

L&N increased Evansville–Earlington service to two round trips in 1907, but the *Dixie Flyer* replaced one round trip. The Evansville–Earlington trains came off in 1909, but a year later L&N began an Evansville–Hopkinsville, Ky., local and extended the McLeansboro–Evansville local to Madisonville, Ky. The Hopkinsville local was gone by 1912, and L&N later added an Evansville–McLeansboro train to supplement McLeansboro–Madisonville service. L&N returned the McLeansboro local to Evansville–McLeansboro operation in 1915, but made the Kentucky local an Evansville–Nashville run. During World War I, these locals were consolidated into a McLeansboro–Nashville run.

The typical L&N local in 1920 featured one or two head-end cars and one or two coaches pulled by a smaller American or Ten-Wheeler steam locomotive. As the decade wore on, smaller Pacifics were relegated to local service duty as mainline passenger trains received heavier Mountain (4-8-2) or Pacific (4-6-2) locomotives. L&N passenger traffic took a hit during the 1920s, particularly in local service. The average trip length was growing, an indication that fewer passengers took the train from one neighboring town to the next. The average trip on the L&N grew from 48.7 miles in 1921 to 78 miles by 1929, 122 miles by 1940, and 273 miles by 1958.

The L&N operated three pairs of local service trains from Evansville in late 1921. Two operated between Evansville and McLeansboro and another between Evansville and Hopkinsville. The Hopkinsville trains were extended in 1922 to Guthrie, Ky., but discontinued on November 9, 1930. The McLeansboro locals ended in May 1931.

Illinois Central

CHAPTER 13

ILLINOIS CENTRAL

Long after others had decided that passenger trains had no future, the Illinois Central still described itself as a passenger-minded railroad. Yet IC Indiana passenger trains were principally slow-speed no-frills locals. And the Illinois Central was the first major railroad to discontinue passenger service within Indiana. All five of the Illinois Central's Indiana lines were built by other railroads and acquired by the IC in the late 19th or early 20th century.

Chartered on February 10, 1851, the Illinois Central was the first railroad created under the 1850 Land Grant Act. When finished on September 27, 1856, the 700-mile IC was one of the world's longest railroads, extending from Cairo to Dunleith near Galena with a branch to Chicago. The IC came to Indiana in October 1886 when it leased the Havana, Rantoul & Eastern Railroad. The terminus of two Illinois Central branches, Evansville was a hub of IC passenger operations, seeing 14 trains a day in the early 20th century, all of them using the Louisville & Nashville station on Fulton Avenue.

Illinois Central's passenger revenue declined from $32.8 million in 1920 to $24 million in 1929, and passenger train miles declined 20 percent. But the IC was prosperous and made no significant service cuts, instead purchasing new passenger cars and offering special fares and excursions. The Depression put the IC on the brink of bankruptcy, and the IC failed to pay a dividend for the first time in more than 60 years. The railroad escaped receivership in 1937 with the help of a $10 million loan from the Reconstruction Finance Corporation.

By 1933 passenger train miles had plummeted to 8.8 million, a 43 percent drop from 1929. The IC tried to stimulate travel by cutting fares from 2.6 cents per mile in 1929 to 1.65 cents in 1935 and to 1.59 cents in 1939. It also undertook a massive pruning of branch line passenger service. Consequently, just two IC passenger trains were still operating in Indiana by 1941.

West Lebanon Line

Benjamin Gifford was an eccentric Rantoul, Ill., lawyer who, after losing an argument with the Illinois Central over freight rates, reportedly decided to build his own railroad to give his adversary some competition. He disliked the IC so much that he once demanded that it pay him in gold coin.

Gifford organized the Havana, Rantoul & Eastern on January 1, 1873. Another company, the Mississippi & Atlantic Railroad, was chartered to build within Indiana. Construction of the 3-foot-gauge railroad began in summer 1875, opening in east central Illinois between Fisher and Alvin on December 1, 1876. A year later, the line opened to West Lebanon in Warren County, where it connected with the Wabash.

Indiana passenger service began December 16, 1877, with a pair of mixed trains between West Lebanon and Rantoul, a connecting point with the IC's Chicago–New Orleans mainline. Service was extended to Le Roy, Ill., after the road reached there on February 1, 1879. The HR&E owned two locomotives, two passenger cars, and 88 freight cars.

Poorly built and plagued by financial troubles, by 1880 the HR&E was being offered for sale by Gifford. The Illinois Central spurned his sale offer, but Gifford found a taker in Jay Gould, whose Wabash, St. Louis & Pacific leased the HR&E on May 1, 1881. Gould envisioned the HR&E as a link in a transcontinental railroad system that never developed. During Wabash control, HR&E passenger service was two West Lebanon–Le Roy round trips. The HR&E entered receivership in 1885, and the Illinois Central leased the line on October 27, 1886. The HR&E was in such poor condition that the IC issued $1 million in gold bonds for a rebuilding project that began in 1887 and included converting the HR&E to standard gauge.

The West Lebanon line was never a heavy carrier of passengers or freight. Passenger operations normally were four trains a day, pulled by 2-6-0 locomotives. In the first decade of the 20th century, trains operated between West Lebanon and Le Roy. One pair began operating between West Lebanon and Rantoul on May 5, 1912. Service remained unchanged until March 16, 1931, when the Le Roy trains ended. The IC downgraded the Rantoul trains to mixed trains on April 26, 1931. Passenger service to West Lebanon ended on January 15, 1934.

Perhaps the most noteworthy occurrence in the line's history was a head-on collision 4 miles west of West Lebanon between an empty passenger train and a freight train. Reportedly, the passenger train crew was eating lunch at West Lebanon when the engineer unexplainably bolted from the restaurant, ran to the train, and headed west. He died in the accident.

Indianapolis Line

The Indianapolis–Effingham, Ill., line began in 1868 as the narrow-gauge Springfield, Effingham & Southeastern. When it opened on October 3, 1880, between Linton in Greene County and the Effingham–Jasper county line in Illinois, it had been renamed the Cincinnati, Effingham & Quincy. Service between Effingham and Switz City in Greene County began December 5, 1880, with a daily round trip. A separate entity, the Bloomfield Railroad, was created on December 28, 1881, to operate the line within Indiana.

The two companies merged on April 9, 1883, to form the Indiana & Illinois Southern Railway, a ragtag operation whose tracks and equipment were in shoddy condition. Some passenger cars were coal cars with boards placed across the top for seats. Some stations were old boxcars. Two locomotives, the *Rackaramus* and the *Mother Holmes*, were notorious for derailing and breaking down.

Ice destroyed the approaches to the Wabash River Bridge in 1883, putting it out of service for 3 years. During this time, trains operated between Switz City and Merom Station in Sullivan County. The bridge was restored in 1886, and the line was converted the next year to standard gauge. The Illinois Central leased the line in 1900.

With financial backing from the Illinois Central, a group of Indianapolis businessmen organized the Indianapolis Southern in October 1899, expecting to prosper by hauling coal and limestone. The "Mineral Route" began passenger service between Indianapolis and Bloomington on July 16, 1906, with two pairs of trains. The line was completed between Bloomington and Switz City in December. The Indianapolis Southern operated independently until the IC absorbed it in 1909.

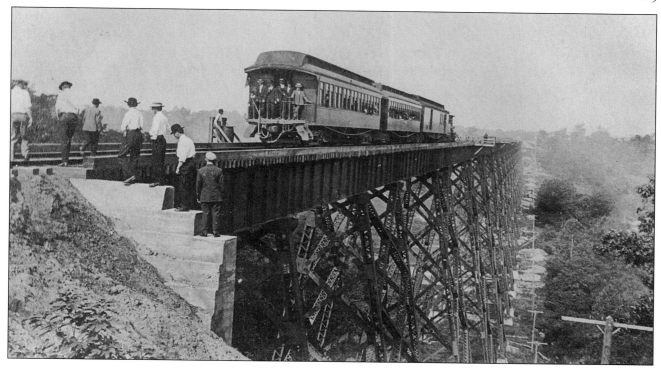

Tulip Trestle, 8 miles northeast of Bloomfield, spans Richland Creek and is Indiana's longest (2295 feet) and highest (157 feet) railroad viaduct. Excursionists on the then Indianapolis Southern Railroad admire the view shortly after the bridge opened in 1906. Indiana Historical Society, negative C8884.

Passenger service between Indianapolis and Effingham began on December 17, 1906. Trains operated Indianapolis–Effingham, Indianapolis–Linton, and Linton–Effingham. Previously, passenger operations had been two round trips between Switz City and Effingham, a connecting point with the IC's Chicago–New Orleans service. This schedule pattern remained until May 5, 1912, when service fell to two Indianapolis–Effingham round trips. This remained until January 3, 1932, when one pair was discontinued between Effingham and Palestine, Ill. Two weeks later, on January 17, the trains were discontinued between Indianapolis and Palestine.

Some Hoosiers called Nos. 333/334 the "Abe Martin Special," after the homespun philosopher created by Brown County author Kin Hubbard. The Illinois Central was the only rail-

Both the Illinois Central depot, shown here, and the Monon station in Bloomington were built of limestone. Both were demolished, although the freight house of the IC station (at left) survives. Author's collection.

road in Brown County. No. 334 departed Effingham at 5:30 A.M., arrived in Indianapolis at noon, and returned after a three-hour layover. Sunday operation ended on August 21, 1932.

A federal government order to discontinue lightly patronized trains to free equipment for use elsewhere during World War II prompted the discontinuance of Nos. 333/334 on March 1, 1945. The IC said the occupancy rate for November 1944 had been 17 percent. Bloomington civic leaders unsuccessfully sought restoration of service to Indianapolis. The Indiana Public Service Commission on November 8, 1945, ordered the Illinois Central to show cause why Nos. 333/334 should not be reinstated, saying the lifting of the federal curtailment order meant that passenger service should revert to the status that existed before the order's issuance. The IC countered that service abolished by a federal directive could not be ordered reinstated by a state government agency.

Following a November 20 hearing, Indiana officials ordered the trains reinstated. The IC appealed the order and lost the first round when a Bloomfield judge on September 4, 1946, ordered the trains reinstated in Indiana. But the IC ultimately prevailed, and Nos. 333/334 were never restored. The Indianapolis–Effingham trains were the last branch line passenger trains to operate on the Illinois Central north of the Ohio River.

Evansville Line

Dating to the 1839 formation of the Peoria & Warsaw Railroad, the Evansville line did not reach Indiana until 1881. Most of its 29 predecessor companies struggled. "Probably no segment of the Illinois Central Railroad has experienced more vicissitudes or suffered a closer acquaintance with the bankruptcy courts than has this line," wrote Carlton J. Corliss in *Main Line of Mid-America: The Story of the Illinois Central.*

In the early 1880s, the companies operating between Peoria and Parkersburg, Ill., merged to form the Peoria, Decatur & Evansville. Service between Peoria and Evansville began June 1, 1881. The PD&E had 21 locomotives, 12 passenger cars, five baggage cars, and 1130 freight cars.

It caused a stir when it placed an electric headlight on engine No. 2, a novelty at the time. Evansville businessman Daniel J. Mackey owned the Evansville & Terre Haute Railroad (later Chicago & Eastern Illinois) and took control of the PD&E in 1885, moving its headquarters from Mattoon, Ill., to Evansville. A depression in the early 1890s sank

A typical Illinois Central branch line passenger train in the 1930s had a coach and a baggage mail car. Locomotive No. 1026 was an Atlantic-type 4-4-2 built by Rogers in 1904. Date and location of this photo are unknown. Indiana Historical Society, Bass photo collection, negative 259055.

the PD&E into receivership in January 1894. Placed on the auction block on February 6, 1900, the Illinois Central submitted the winning bid and assumed control on August 1, 1900.

Initially, PD&E passenger operations had been a daily Evansville–Peoria round trip and an Evansville–Mattoon mixed train. Evansville–Peoria service increased to two round trips on November 19, 1882, a schedule pattern that remained until late spring 1890 when the mixed trains ended. In the late 1890s Evansville–Peoria service increased to three round trips, but one of those pairs was discontinued on May 20, 1900.

The PD&E's Nos. 3/4 offered the most luxurious service with parlor cars, sleepers, and dining service. However, the train had a 6-hour layover at Mattoon northbound and a 4.5-hour layover southbound. The Illinois Central began operating sleepers and coaches between Chicago and Evansville on October 21, 1900. A café car operated between Mattoon and Evansville. The IC later increased Evansville service to three pairs of trains, but only one pair operated to Peoria.

The Illinois Central's 1905 lease of the Tennessee Central between Hopkinsville, Ky., and Nashville enabled it to create a Chicago–Nashville route. On December 10, 1905, the IC launched the only named passenger trains that it ever operated in Indiana. The *Chicago Limited*/*Nashville Limited* offered coaches and sleepers and had an Evansville setout sleeper.

The names of the Chicago–Nashville trains disappeared from *The Official Guide of the Railways* in June 1907. Later that year, the train to Nashville began originating at Mattoon, although it still carried Chicago–Nashville cars. Chicago–Nashville service ended on July 1, 1908. At the time, the IC had three pairs of trains between Evansville and Mattoon, one of which served Peoria. Another pair of trains operated between Evansville and Olney, Ill.

The Chicago–Evansville coaches ended in spring 1909, but the Chicago–Evansville sleeper continued for 3 more years. Faced with fierce competition in the Chicago–Evansville market from the C&EI and the New York Central, the IC opted for a connection at Mattoon. The Evansville–Olney trains changed to Evansville–Newton, Ill., operation on May 9, 1909. Their discontinuance on June 12, 1910, left two Evansville–Mattoon round trips, one of which served Peoria, a schedule pattern that remained for more than a decade.

Peoria–Evansville Nos. 205/222 began terminating in Mattoon on April 3, 1921. Although discontinued on December 21, 1921, the trains were reinstated to Peoria on January 14, 1923. The Peoria trains came off for good on January 3, 1932, leaving one Mattoon–Evansville round trip. This train left Mattoon at 7:40 A.M., arrived in Evansville just before noon, and departed 5 hours later. A Pacific 4-6-2 locomotive usually pulled the train, which ceased operating on Sunday on August 21, 1932. On June 29, 1938, the IC announced plans to replace the Mattoon–Evansville passenger trains on July 3 with mixed train service. The Illinois Commerce Commission ruled in late January 1939 that the IC could discontinue the trains but at the last minute imposed a 30-day delay. Illinois regulatory officials eventually relented, and the trains made their final trips on March 15, 1939. About 42 passengers rode the final northbound run, most getting on at one station and off at the next. The mixed trains that replaced Nos. 235/236 stopped carrying passengers on August 13, 1939.

New Harmony Branch

New Harmony voters agreed in 1881 to pay $16,000 to the Peoria, Decatur & Evansville to construct a 6-mile line to Stewartsville, where it connected with the Evansville–Peoria line. Passenger service on this Posey County branch began in early 1882 with one round trip, which increased to two round trips in November 1882. Service increased to three round trips in the late 1890s, briefly rose to four round trips in 1907, dropped back to three, but increased to six round trips on May 9, 1909. This continued until June 1910, when service was cut to three round trips.

Service became two round trips in January 1924. The third round trip was reinstated on May 16, 1926, but service was cut again to two round trips on May 24, 1931. Downgraded to mixed trains on June 10, 1932, service ended in May 1933. A pair of mixed trains was reinstated 6 years later on March 26, 1939, apparently for a 1-year trial period that probably failed to generate enough ridership to justify continuance. The service ended in March 1940.

Hopkinsville Line

The Evansville–Hopkinsville, Ky., line did not reach Indiana proper. Trains crossed the Ohio River between Evansville and Henderson, Ky., on a ferry until 1904 when the IC began using the L&N Bridge at Henderson.

The Hopkinsville line dates to the March 15, 1871, creation of the South Kentucky Railroad by coal magnate and railroad organizer Dr. P. G. Kelsey. The line opened in November 1887 between Henderson and Princeton, Ky. Collis P. Huntington's Chesapeake, Ohio & Southwestern purchased the line in 1891 and extended it to Hopkinsville the next year. Huntington tried to sell the CO&SW to the L&N, but a court ruled the sale violated antitrust laws. The Illinois Central purchased a controlling interest in the CO&SW in December 1893, but complications delayed the acquisition until August 1, 1896.

Passenger service between Evansville and Princeton began November 15, 1903, with two round trips. Service expanded in late 1905 when the IC began offering three trains from Evansville to Nashville and one train to Hopkinsville. There were two trains to Evansville from Nashville and two trains from Princeton. The Kentucky terminals of these trains often changed.

The end of IC passenger service to Nashville in 1908 reduced Evansville–Kentucky service to three pairs of trains. A few months later, the IC briefly reinstated the fourth pair to increase service to two pairs of trains between Evansville and Hopkinsville, one pair to Morganfield, and a train that terminated at Hopkinsville but originated at Princeton. Service between Evansville and Kentucky had fallen by late 1909 to two pairs of trains.

During World War I, Kentucky service varied between two and three pairs of trains. Most trains terminated at Hopkinsville or Morganfield. A Sunday-only train operated between Evansville and Blackford for a few years and eventually became a daily train. There was an Evansville–Sturgis round trip until late 1916. During this period, the IC coordinated the schedules of some Evansville–Mattoon and Evansville–Hopkinsville trains to offer Chicago–Hopkinsville connecting service. The IC also advertised connections at Princeton with its Louisville–New Orleans service.

The IC had stopped showing the Chicago–Hopkinsville connections by November 1920 but had increased Evansville–Kentucky service. Effective November 20, 1920, the IC began operating two Hopkinsville round trips, a Blackford round trip, and a Morganfield round trip. The next year Evansville–Kentucky service shrank to three round trips with one pair each operating to Hopkinsville, Princeton, and Blackford. In December 1921, all three northbound trains began originating in Hopkinsville. Two southbound trains terminated there while the third train terminated at Princeton.

Evansville–Kentucky service remained at three round trips until the July 23, 1928, discontinuance of Evansville–Princeton Nos. 335/336. One pair of Evansville–Hopkinsville trains ended on March 29, 1931. Sunday-only Nos. 232/235 (Evansville–Princeton) ended on October 16, 1932. Illinois Central passenger service to Evansville ended in December 1940 when Evansville–Hopkinsville Nos. 231/235 began terminating at Henderson.

CHAPTER 14

MILWAUKEE ROAD

The Milwaukee Road's Indiana passenger trains were orphaned from the rest of the road's immense passenger network, which stretched from Chicago to the Pacific Northwest. Neither the Milwaukee Road nor any of its predecessors ever had passenger service between Indiana and Chicago. Although the Milwaukee Road *Hiawathas* were the nation's fastest steam-powered passenger trains, the Indiana trains were nondescript all-stops locals that ran at a turtle's pace and never did a substantial business. No Milwaukee Road passenger train in Indiana ever wore the esteemed *Hiawatha* name.

The Milwaukee Road's Indiana line extended 300 miles from Chicago Heights, Ill., to Westport in southwest Decatur County, making it the only western railroad to own trackage east of Chicago. Branches near Terre Haute and Bedford offered passenger service until the 1920s.

The Milwaukee Road's earliest Indiana predecessor, the Evansville & Richmond Railroad, began passenger service July 6, 1890, with one round trip between Elnora in northwest Daviess County and Seymour. The E&R faltered and went into receivership in 1894, purchased 3 years later by Chicago banker John R. Walsh. Renamed the Southern Indiana Railway, Walsh expected the railroad to be a ticket to a fortune built on coal, limestone, and mineral springs.

He discarded plans to build to Richmond and instead extended the railroad to Terre Haute in 1900 to tap the coal reserves of Sullivan and Greene Counties. Walsh negotiated trackage rights between Westport and Greensburg over the Big Four (later New York Central) and eyed through passenger service to Chicago, Indianapolis, Louisville, Benton Harbor, Mich., and Columbus, Ind. Hoping to emulate the success of resort hotels in French Lick and West Baden, Walsh built hotels at Trinity Springs 19 miles west of Bedford and at Indian Springs in Martin County.

After failing to negotiate traffic agreements with railroads operating north of Terre Haute, Walsh built his own line, reaching Humrick, Ill., in 1903, and Chicago Heights, Ill., in 1907. However, Walsh had stretched his finances too thin and began missing payrolls and bond payments. After his Chicago National and Home Savings Bank failed in 1905, Walsh was convicted of violating federal banking laws.

The Southern Indiana went into receivership in 1908 and was reorganized on November 26, 1910, as the Chicago, Terre Haute & Southeastern Railway. The line continued to struggle, and over the next 10 years it paid an average of 1.5 percent in interest on its bonds. The CTH&SE had lost a half million dollars by May 1921 and could not pay interest on

Milwaukee Road

its bonds. The Interstate Commerce Commission declared it a distressed property that its owners wanted to liquidate. Already they had written the securities off as losses.

Milwaukee Road president Harry E. Bryan never had forgotten what it had been like to be at the mercy of other railroads for locomotive fuel during World War I. He hoped the coal mines served by the CTH&SE would be a reliable fuel supply and the Milwaukee Road could develop interchange traffic with railroads crossing the CTH&SE.

The Milwaukee Road began as the Milwaukee & Waukesha Rail Road, which on November 11, 1850, operated Wisconsin's first passenger train. It expanded to St. Paul, Minn., in 1867 and to Chicago in 1873 and in 1874 became the Chicago, Milwaukee & St. Paul. It leased the CTH&SE on July 1, 1921, on terms that must have seemed like a gift to the Chicago bankers stuck with the woebegone railroad. The Milwaukee Road paid $10 a share for 43,000 shares of CTH&SE stock that recently had sold for $1 a share. The Milwaukee Road guaranteed CTH&SE bonds at 100 cents on the dollar, even though the bankers would have accepted 70 cents. The CTH&SE had an indebtedness of $19.5 million.

Management was aware the CTH&SE lease might plunge the Milwaukee Road into receivership, and the ICC questioned the acquisition because of the Milwaukee Road's precarious financial condition. The CTH&SE did turn out to be a good source of locomotive fuel, and the Milwaukee Road was Indiana's dominant coal-hauling railroad until 1945. But the doubts about the CTH&SE lease also proved to be justified. It cost the Milwaukee Road $3.8 million to rebuild the CTH&SE, which through 1925 lost over $4 million. These losses helped nudge the Milwaukee Road into receivership in 1925.

The Milwaukee Road's takeover of the CTH&SE had few tangible effects upon its passenger service. The failure to connect the Indiana passenger trains with the rest of the Milwaukee Road system probably reflected the view that the Indiana lines were an adjunct branch line whose principal business was coal and limestone.

The Milwaukee Road's passenger business declined during the 1920s, particularly on branch lines. To stem the losses, the Milwaukee Road replaced steam engines with gas-electric cars and downgraded some passenger trains to mixed trains. By the time the Milwaukee Road ended service, the branch's passenger revenue had declined to virtually nothing. The Milwaukee Road often told state regulatory authorities that changes in passenger operations would improve freight service.

Service North of Terre Haute

The Southern Indiana Railway built to the Indiana-Illinois border in 1903, but scheduled passenger service did not begin until December 20, 1906, with a round trip between Terre Haute and Humrick, Ill. No passenger train ever operated north of Humrick, a connecting point with the Clover Leaf (later Nickel Plate) between St. Louis and Toledo, Ohio.

The northern terminus became West Dana in Vermillion County near the Illinois border, on November 20, 1912, a connecting point with the Cincinnati, Hamilton & Dayton (later Baltimore & Ohio) between Hamilton, Ohio, and Springfield, Ill. The CTH&SE had two Terre Haute–West Dana round trips and a West Dana–West Clinton round trip. The latter used a motor car powered by batteries, which often ran down before the end of the run, and a steam engine had to tow the train to the station. The West Dana–West Clinton service ended on May 19, 1918.

CTH&SE trains used different stations in Terre Haute: Hulman Street and Maple Avenue. The northern terminus became St. Bernice in Vermillion County on May 22, 1921. At the same time, the CTH&SE began a short-lived pair of trains between Windsor Junction, near the Vigo-Vermillion county line, and Grover, located a mile north of Maple Avenue on Terre Haute's north side. These trains lasted through March 1922.

The St. Bernice trains continued until December 2, 1923, when one pair was discontinued and the other began terminating at West Clinton. Service reverted to four trains between St. Bernice and Maple Avenue in January 1924. On January 8, 1928, one pair of trains was discontinued and the other began terminating at Tighe, 6 miles south of St. Bernice. By July 1929, these trains had begun terminating at Clinton yard.

The trains began terminating at Talleydale, the site of a large coal mine, on April 30, 1939. By October 1941, they were operating to Bridge Junction north of Terre Haute. This continued through December 1, 1945, when Fayette became the terminus.

This service was last shown in *The Official Guide of the Railways* in January 1953. As was the case with most Milwaukee Road passenger trains operating north of Terre Haute, these trains primarily benefited coal miners. Although gone from the *Official Guide*, the trains continued to take miners to work during the 1950s. For 25 years the Milwaukee Road unsuccessfully attempted to gain regulatory permission to discontinue these trains, its last passenger operation in Indiana. A state appeals court finally gave the trains a highball into oblivion in 1959 after the closing of the mine that they had served.

Service South of Terre Haute

The Evansville & Richmond had no rolling stock or locomotives when it began operations with equipment borrowed from the Evansville & Terre Haute (later New York Central). Five years after opening, the E&R offered three pairs of trains: Elnora–Westport, Elnora–Bedford, and Bedford–Seymour. Service to Westport temporarily ended following a March 1897 washout, and the trains temporarily terminated at Kurtz in northwestern Jackson County. By late February 1898, service had been restored the length of the line with two round trips between Elnora and Westport.

Service between Elnora and Greensburg began in April 1898 using trackage rights on the Big Four east of Westport. Service began to Washington via the Evansville & Terre Haute on June 26, 1898. The Southern Indiana Railway had five pairs of passenger trains, two between Elnora and Greensburg, two between Seymour and Washington, and one between Elnora and Westport. An Elnora–Greensburg pair and a Washington–Seymour pair were named *Indian Springs Express*. The Washington–Seymour trains were named *Indianapolis Express*. These names, gone by January 1900, were the only named trains ever to ply the route.

Prior to expansion to Terre Haute, the Southern Indiana Railway operated three pairs of trains between Greensburg and Linton and one pair between Linton and Westport. Service to Terre Haute began July 17, 1900, with a Terre Haute–Greensburg round trip, two Terre Haute–Seymour round trips, and one Westport–Seymour round trip. Service to Greensburg ended on October 7, 1900. The new schedule had three Terre Haute–Seymour round trips and one Seymour–Westport round trip. The Westport passenger train rarely operated west of Seymour.

Passenger service in Sullivan County between Shelburn and Sullivan began August 20, 1905, with three round trips. Within a year, the service had been extended to Terre Haute and increased to four round trips. Service fell to two round trips on November 4, 1906, and one round trip between 1908 and 1910 before reverting to two round trips on September 5, 1910. The CTH&SE discontinued one pair of Sullivan trains on February 27, 1916. The train from Sullivan to Terre Haute began terminating at Blackhawk in southeast Vigo County on June 29, 1924. Otherwise, service remained unchanged until the Milwaukee Road ended passenger service to Sullivan on March 14, 1925.

Through the early 1920s, the Milwaukee Road operated three round trips between Terre Haute and Seymour. Trips were leisurely with a top speed of 40 mph between Terre Haute and Odon and 35 mph between Odon and Seymour. The Southern Indiana Railway, CTH&SE, and Milwaukee Road offered various intermediate pairings, including Terre Haute–Odon (1906–7, 1916–21, and 1923), Terre Haute–Bedford (1909), Terre Haute–Blackhawk (1916–19), and Jasonville–Beehunter in Greene County (1935–39).

Many railroads used motor cars in the 1920s and 1930s to reduce the cost of passenger service on lightly used branch lines. Gas-electric car No. 5938, built by Pullman in 1928, offered the last scheduled passenger service on the Milwaukee Road in Indiana. Indiana Historical Society, negative C8881.

The Milwaukee Road began service between Bedford and Blankenship on October 9, 1941, to serve workers at the Crane Naval Ammunition Depot. This train was extended to Crane on November 6, 1944, and discontinued on February 18, 1946.

The Southern Indiana Railway briefly offered service in 1905 between Jasonville and Hymera in Sullivan County. Miners' trains also operated between Jasonville and Latta and between Linton and Hawton.

By early 1921, the Milwaukee Road had restored Terre Haute–Seymour service to three daily round trips, but in July 1922 one pair was discontinued and another shortened to Terre Haute–Bedford. The latter was extended to Seymour on March 25, 1923, but its discontinuance on June 29, 1924, left Nos. 1/4 as the last passenger trains between Terre Haute and Seymour. These trains were permanently shortened to Terre Haute–Bedford on August 10, 1930. At the same time, the Milwaukee Road established a pair of Bedford–Seymour mixed trains. The Seymour–Westport trains were downgraded to mixed trains on January 8, 1928. The Bedford–Seymour mixed trains became freight trains in February 1939. The Seymour–Westport mixed trains became freight trains on April 30, 1939. Both carried passengers until early 1950.

The Milwaukee Road's last scheduled passenger train south of Terre Haute departed Hulman Station in early morning and arrived in Bedford at midmorning. It left for Terre Haute after an hour's layover. The schedule listed 21 intermediate stops, of which 11 were flag stops. Travel time between stations was as little as two minutes (Beehunter and Ilene in Greene County).

Nos. 1/4 were assigned a motor car in spring 1948, the second time a motor car had served the run, the first having been from about 1929 until World War II, when the train became steam-powered. Nos. 1/4 were the second-to-last motor car train in Indiana. The per-mile fares were approximately the same as they had been in the early 1900s. A ticket for the 5-mile trip from Bedford to Coxton was 16 cents.

The trains made their final runs on July 15, 1950, using gas-electric car No. 5938, built by Pullman in 1928. Engineer H. E. Barnes had worked the run since

Mr. and Mrs. Areli Jones of Bedford had ridden the first Evansville & Richmond passenger train from Bedford in 1890. They purchased tickets for the last passenger train on July 15, 1950. Photo by Richard S. Simons.

The trains are long gone, but Indiana still has many railroad stations. Many, like the former Milwaukee Road station in Bedford photographed in August 2001, have long since outlived their usefulness and stand alone and unwanted, relics of another century's transportation network. Author's photo.

1910. Among those boarding at Bedford were Mr. and Mrs. Areli Jones of Bedford. They had ridden the first Evansville & Richmond passenger train from Bedford in 1890.

Bedford Belt

Chartered March 20, 1892, the 6-mile Bedford Belt Railway between Bedford and Buff Ridge was built by a limestone quarry intent on breaking the Monon's monopoly on hauling Lawrence County oolitic limestone. Passenger service began in August 1892.

The Southern Indiana Railway leased the branch in 1898 after the Bedford Belt defaulted on a loan. Scheduled passenger service did not resume until August 20, 1905, with three round trips between Bedford and Oolitic. A year later, this was trimmed to two round trips. Service was suspended for nearly three months before resuming October 15, 1906, between Bedford and Buff Ridge. The terminal points reverted to Bedford–Oolitic in December 1908. Operations remained largely unchanged until scheduled service ended in late 1928.

CHAPTER 15

SOUTHERN

The Southern Railway is an object lesson in how the railroad with the shortest and fastest route became the first road to drop out of the St. Louis–Louisville passenger market. In the process, the St. Louis line became one of the Southern's first mainlines to lose passenger service. The St. Louis line traversed 234 miles of some of Indiana's most rugged terrain, and its eight tunnels were half of the state's total. Although serving a sparsely populated region, the Southern operated an impressive brace of locals over 93 miles on four branch lines radiating from Huntingburg.

The Southern Railway System was created on July 1, 1894, by a merger of several southern railroads, one of which, the South Carolina Canal & Rail Road, began in 1828. On Christmas Day 1830, that road's *Best Friend of Charleston* carried passengers and freight on a 6-mile trip, America's first scheduled steam railroad. The Southern eventually consisted of more than 100 railroads, covering 6,376 miles in 11 states.

One of the few components of the Southern not born below the Mason-Dixon Line was the Louisville, Evansville & St. Louis Consolidated Railroad, which the Southern acquired in 1900 to gain a foothold north of the Ohio River. This profitable source of freight and passengers enabled the Southern to keep pace with rival Louisville & Nashville. Organized in 1869 as the New Albany & St. Louis Air Line, and renamed the Louisville, New Albany & St. Louis Air Line in 1870, the first segment was built in 1872 between the Gibson County seat of Princeton and Albion, Ill. The line expanded in 1880 from Princeton to Ingleton in Gibson County. Reorganized in 1881 as the Louisville, Evansville & St. Louis, the road expanded eastward to Oakland City in eastern Gibson County in 1882 and westward to Mount Vernon, Ill. The LE&StL reached New Albany the next year.

Although St. Louis appeared in the names of all predecessor companies that operated the St. Louis line, the road did not reach there until 1888. Trains used the L&N west of Mount Vernon, Ill., until the LE&StL finished its own line to East St. Louis, Ill., in 1890. The LE&StL entered receivership in 1894. When purchased in 1900, it was one of the Southern's largest acquisitions.

Scheduled passenger service began March 17, 1873, with a pair of trains between Princeton and Albion, Ill., and a pair between Princeton and Mount Carmel, Ill. Over the next 7 years, service usually was a Princeton–Albion round trip. By the time that train began terminating at Ingleton on October 25, 1880, service had expanded to two pairs, one to Albion and one to Princeton. Service expanded on February 26, 1882, to Fairfield, Ill. Two round trips began operating between Fairfield and Oakland City, Ind., on April 2. Later that year the western terminus became Mount Vernon, Ill.

Southern

When the LE&StL opened to New Albany on July 31, 1882, passenger service expanded to three pairs of trains: New Albany–Mt. Vernon, New Albany–Princeton, and Princeton–Mt. Vernon. Passengers reached Louisville by boat. By mid-1883, all LE&StL passenger trains in Indiana terminated at New Albany and Mount Vernon or Huntingburg.

The road entered Louisville in 1886 with the opening of the Kentucky & Indiana Terminal Bridge. Service between Louisville and St. Louis began August 12, 1888. Nos. 1/2 had coaches and parlor cars; Nos. 3/4 had coaches and sleepers. Trains used the future L&N west of Mount Vernon. An accommodation train operated between Louisville and Huntingburg.

When the LE&StL opened its own line to St. Louis on July 1, 1890, it placed in service new equipment that it advertised as "the finest vestibuled cars in the world." The LE&StL claimed to have the only parlor and dining cars between St. Louis and Louisville and the only cars with vestibules. Night trains Nos. 3/4 carried Pullmans. Daylight trains Nos. 1/2 operated nonstop between New Albany and Huntingburg. By now the Huntingburg accommodation train had become a Louisville–Evansville express train. A Huntingburg–Mount Vernon local operated in the early 1890s.

At the dawn of the 20th century, the LE&StL operated four trains between Louisville and St. Louis. Nos. 1/2 were day trains with vestibule coaches, parlors, and diners. Nos. 3/4, the overnight trains, carried coaches and sleepers. Locals operated between Princeton and Huntingburg and between Princeton and Milltown. A fleet of American-type 4-4-0 locomotives, many of which remained on the Southern roster through 1921, pulled the trains. Ten-Wheelers eventually began pulling the trains, but these locomotives were gone by the 1930s.

Reaching Southward

The Southern instituted a St. Louis–Charleston, S.C., sleeper on October 27, 1901. Local service increased on September 14, 1902, with the addition of a Princeton–Mt. Vernon round trip. The dining cars on Nos. 1/2 were replaced by café-parlor cars. The Charleston sleepers lasted less than a year, but by May 1904 sleepers were operating between St. Louis and Greensboro, N.C., Asheville, N.C., Macon, Ga., Jacksonville, Fla., Lexington, Ky., and Atlanta. Operation of the café-parlor cars was extended to Lexington, and the Princeton–Mount Vernon local was extended to St. Louis.

The Jacksonville, Asheville, and Macon cars were conveyed by the overnight trains, which were renumbered 23/24, and placed on an expedited schedule, stopping only at New Albany, Huntingburg, Princeton, Mount Carmel, Fairfield, Mount Vernon, Centralia, Ill., and East St. Louis. The Atlanta, Greensboro, and Lexington sleepers were gone by July 1904. The Asheville, Macon, and Jacksonville sleepers ended in 1905 in favor of sleepers between St. Louis and Danville, Ky., Lexington, and Knoxville, Tenn. The Southern also began operating St. Louis–Knoxville coaches. The café-parlor cars operated to Danville.

The Knoxville sleepers ran until late 1905, the Knoxville coaches until 1907. The Southern added a Louisville–Princeton local on April 29, 1905, to supplement the St. Louis local and an existing Princeton–Huntingburg local. The Louisville–Princeton local was shortened to Louisville–Huntingburg operation on July 2, 1907. Between 1906 and 1911, the only through cars assigned to the route operated to Danville, a connecting point with Southern expresses between Cincinnati and Chattanooga, Tenn. Beginning in 1909, Nos. 1/2 and Nos. 23/24 began operating to Danville.

The St. Louis–Asheville sleepers resumed in July 1911 after a 6-year hiatus. Louisville–Huntingburg Nos. 3/4 were extended to St. Louis on April 29, 1911, creating three St. Louis–Louisville round trips. The Southern named its St. Louis–Asheville service the *St. Louis Special* in November 1912, the only named Southern passenger train in Indiana. For the 1913 winter travel season, the Southern offered a St. Louis–Jacksonville sleeper. The Jacksonville sleepers operated for the last time during the 1914 winter travel season. The *St.*

The Southern had a cluster of branch lines in southwest Indiana that hosted passenger service into the 1930s. The Southern station at Boonville was a typical small town depot in the early 20th century. Author's collection.

Louis Special had St. Louis–Asheville coaches between June and November 1914. The café-parlor cars were replaced by dining cars that fall.

Further retrenchment occurred on May 2, 1915, with the discontinuance of Nos. 3/4. The St. Louis–Knoxville sleepers reappeared in 1916–17, but by August 1917 the *St. Louis Special* name had vanished and the Asheville and Knoxville sleepers along with it. The St. Louis–Asheville sleepers that were reinstated in November 1919 would be the final through car for the South on the St. Louis line. The Asheville cars were conveyed by Nos. 23/24 and interchanged at Danville with the *Carolina Special*. St. Louis–Danville sleepers operated on Nos. 1/2, which had become overnight trains in 1905 and carried a Louisville setout sleeper until 1917.

Through early 1908, the Southern operated four pairs of locals in Indiana: Princeton–St. Louis Nos. 7/8, Princeton–Huntingburg Nos. 5/6, Louisville–Huntingburg Nos. 3/4, and Louisville–Evansville Nos. 9/10. Nos. 7/8 were shortened to St. Louis–Mount Vernon on March 8, 1908. On August 15, 1909, No. 6 was consolidated with Louisville to Evansville No. 10 to form a Louisville–Princeton train with an Evansville section. The Southern instituted a Princeton–Mount Vernon local on August 16, 1914, which operated through July 1917. Princeton to Huntingburg No. 5 was the next discontinuance. Its counterpart, No. 6, was discontinued west of Huntingburg on June 14, 1925. This left three Southern trains in Indiana: St. Louis–Louisville Nos. 1/2 and 23/24 and Louisville–Evansville Nos. 9/10. This serviced remained unchanged for the remainder of the 1920s.

In the early 1930s, the Southern assigned observation sleepers to St. Louis–Louisville and St. Louis–Danville service. Nos. 23/24 carried a café-parlor car, the dining car having ended when the *St. Louis Special* was downgraded in 1917. The removal of the café-parlor car in January 1932 ended food service on the St. Louis line. The St. Louis–Asheville sleepers were cut back to Louisville–Asheville operation in February 1936. The St. Louis–Danville sleepers operated until August 1936.

The Southern won approval from Illinois and Kentucky regulatory officials in 1941 to discontinue Nos. 1/2, which on August 12, 1941, were shortened to Princeton–Louisville. More than a month later, on September 28, 1941, the train began terminating at New Albany. Nos. 1/2 ended on December 10, 1942.

The Southern shared Louisville's Central Station with the Illinois Central, Baltimore & Ohio, Chesapeake & Ohio, and New York Central. Reaching Central Station was time-consuming for the Southern due to a circuitous route that involved a mile-long backup. To cut the travel time through Louisville, the Southern in 1948 opened a station on Fourth Street near the University of Louisville.

How the Trains Were Lost

Southern president Ernest E. Norris was optimistic that the World War II passenger boom would continue. The Southern had one of the nation's largest passenger train fleets, spread out over innumerable backwoods branch lines. The 141 new lightweight cars the Southern ordered in 1946 were barely enough to reequip its premier trains, the *Crescent, Southerner, Royal Palm,* and *Tennessean,* none of which served Indiana, although the *Royal Palm* had Chicago–Florida cars conveyed between Chicago and Cincinnati by the New York Central.

The typical postwar Southern train had half the patronage of the trains of Southern cousins Atlantic Coast Line and Seaboard Air Line. Most Southern passenger equipment dated to the 1930s or earlier. It is doubtful the Southern planned to assign new equipment to St. Louis–Danville Nos. 23/24, which the bean counters at Southern's Washington, D.C., headquarters probably considered just another local whose losses threatened to drag the company into financial ruin.

In 1948, Nos. 23/24 made more than 70 stops, including flag stops, between St. Louis and Danville and needed 14 hours to complete the 367-mile journey. The St. Louis departure (7:40 A.M.) and arrival (6:45 P.M.) times precluded connections with most trains of the western railroads. Timely connections were available at Danville with the *Carolina Special* (Cincinnati–Carolinas), *Queen and Crescent* (Cincinnati–New Orleans), and *Ponce de Leon* (Cincinnati–Florida).

Patronage on the St. Louis line declined sharply after World War II. Nos. 23/24 might have ended earlier had it not been for their railway post office revenue. The Southern had converted nearly all of its passenger trains to diesel power by the end of 1952, but Nos. 23/24 were the last steam-powered passenger trains on the Southern. A typical consist for Nos. 23/24 was a Ps-2 class steam locomotive, the RPO, baggage car, and a coach. At times, the trains were pulled by Pacific-class 4-6-2 locomotives painted in the Southern's classic green and gold passenger livery.

The Southern created a committee in 1947 to plot how to shed as many passenger trains as possible. A 1948 recession added a sense of urgency to the task. Southern's finances were

The Southern's passenger trains between St. Louis and Danville, Ky., were the last steam-powered passenger mainline trains on the railroad. Pacific type No. 1234 patiently waits at Huntingburg. Dave McKay collection.

so precarious that bankruptcy papers were readied in 1949 for filing at a moment's notice. Only a massive cost-cutting campaign kept those papers in the railroad's files.

The Southern had discontinued or shortened the routes of 17 pairs of passenger trains and sidetracked seven mixed trains by 1950. But it still had 26 pairs of mainline trains and 26 pairs of branch line trains. In some places, the efforts to prune passenger service had encountered fierce opposition. The mainline trains generally covered their direct costs and collectively made an $11.8 million profit in 1950. But the locals, including Nos. 23/24, lost a collective $1.1 million.

Tired of being stymied by courts and state regulatory officials, the Southern adopted a strategy it described as "missionary work." Railroad officers, including freight agents and road foremen, met with public officials and business leaders to explain the Southern's perilous financial condition. The plan worked well enough to overcome much of the opposition that the Southern's train-off campaign had generated.

Nos. 23/24 withered away a little at a time. They began terminating at Relay Station in East St. Louis, Ill., on September 19, 1948, which enabled the Southern to avoid costly Eads Bridge use fees and terminal expenses at St. Louis Union Station. The campaign to remove Nos. 23/24 began on December 30, 1949, when the Southern asked the Illinois Commerce Commission for approval to end service between East St. Louis and Mount Carmel, Ill. Southern claimed the trains lost $100,772 in 1948 and had been unprofitable for several years. Illinois regulators denied the request, then agreed to a rehearing and denied the discontinuance again. Two developments, though, worked in the Southern's favor. On April 16, 1952, the Gulf, Mobile & Ohio discontinued the last passenger trains with which Nos. 23/24 still had connections at East St. Louis. Subsequently the Post Office Department removed the RPO from Nos. 23/24.

The Illinois Commerce Commission in May 1952 finally approved removal of Nos. 23/24 in Illinois. The Southern told the commissioners that the trains earned $55,779 in 1950, but had cost $152,077 to operate. The trains made their final runs in Illinois on June 16, 1952. Indiana regulatory officials spoke next and approved discontinuance between Princeton and Louisville. Southern's last Indiana passenger train ended on June 30, 1953.

Evansville Branch

The Evansville branch dated to the August 1873 establishment of the Lake Erie, Evansville & Southwestern. After reaching Boonville in Warrick County in 1875, the company went bankrupt and was succeeded in 1879 by the Evansville Local Trade Railroad, which completed the line in 1880 to Gentryville in Spencer County and a connection with the Cincinnati, Rockport & Eastern. The two companies merged in 1880 to form the Evansville, Rockport & Eastern, which was sold a year later to the Louisville, New Albany & St. Louis. The first passenger schedules of the Lake Erie, Evansville & Southwestern to be published in the *Traveler's Official Railway Guide* appeared in November 1877 and showed two round trips between Evansville and Boonville.

The Evansville, Rockport & Eastern began operating two round trips between Evansville and Jasper on May 15, 1881. An Evansville–Huntingburg accommodation train was added on June 3, 1883. On August 24, 1884, the Huntingburg accommodation train became the third Evansville–Jasper pairing.

Passenger service peaked on May 13, 1888, at seven trains. One Evansville–Jasper train was curtailed to Evansville–Huntingburg. Another pair became a mixed train. Added to the schedule was a train from Evansville to Jasper, but the return train terminated at Huntingburg. This schedule lasted three months. On August 12, 1888, service was trimmed to two pairs of trains between Evansville and Huntingburg, one of which began operating between Evansville and Louisville. Evansville–Huntingburg service increased to three round trips on December 16, 1888, a schedule pattern that remained through the mid-1920s.

Evansville–Huntingburg Nos. 13/14 were discontinued on June 6, 1926. The Southern on January 3, 1932, cut Evansville service to a single pair of trains, Nos. 9/10, which carried Louisville and West Baden cars. Nos. 9/10 were the last Southern branch line passenger trains in southwest Indiana. After a struggle with the Indiana Public Service Commission that saw one denial of discontinuance, Nos. 9/10 were discontinued in April 1939.

It's the last day of Southern passenger service in June 1953, and the last run is in the hole near Princeton waiting for another train. Photo by Ron Stuckey; John Fuller collection.

Other Branches

After the Civil War, Rockport business leaders wanted to build a railroad to enhance their town's role as a center of commerce and trade. The Cincinnati, Rockport & Southwestern was organized in June 1874 with the goal of building to Mitchell in southern Lawrence County and a connection with the Mississippi & Ohio (later Baltimore & Ohio). The road was completed to Ferdinand Station in Dubois County in 1874. Although shown in the *Traveler's Official Railway Guide* in February 1875, no schedules were published until January 1876, a round trip between Rockport and Ferdinand Station.

The line was extended to Jasper in 1878, and Rockport–Jasper service began on March 9, 1879, with one round trip. Reorganized in December 1880 as the Evansville, Rockport & Eastern, the road subsequently merged with the Evansville Local Trade Railroad. The Rockport–Jasper trains were curtailed on October 25, 1880, to Rockport–Gentryville. Service expanded to two round trips on February 26, 1882, three on June 3, 1883, and four on August 24, 1884. The Rockport shuttle was reduced to three round trips on June 26, 1887, a frequency of service that remained through the late 1920s.

The Louisville, Evansville & St. Louis Railroad controlled the Huntingburg, Tell City & Cannelton Railroad, which built in 1887 between Lincoln City in Spencer County and Cannelton, on the Ohio River in Perry County. Tell City was the largest city on the branch. Passenger service between Cannelton and Lincoln City began January 13, 1888, with one round trip. This expanded to three round trips on May 13, 1888, a schedule pattern that remained unchanged through the late 1920s. When the Cannelton line opened, the Rockport–Gentryville trains began operating between Rockport and Lincoln City. Through the late 1920s, the Lincoln City depot hosted 18 passenger trains a day. Three pairings each operated Lincoln City–Cannelton and Lincoln City–Rockport, connecting with Evansville branch trains at Lincoln City.

Southern pared Rockport service to two round trips on March 27, 1927, and another train came off on March 31, 1929. Rockport service was restored to two round trips on May 5, 1929, the same day that service to Cannelton was cut to two round trips. Three of the four trains each to Rockport and Cannelton became mixed trains on January 2, 1930. These trains continued to chug along until May 1935 when service on each line was reduced to one round trip. These trains ended on May 24, 1937.

Because it served the resort hotels in French Lick and West Baden, the Southern's West Baden branch was the only Indiana branch to boast first-class accommodations. Until 1888, most trains on this branch operated between Jasper and Evansville. This changed on August 12, 1888, when one Evansville–Jasper pair began terminating at Huntingburg and another began operating between Evansville and Louisville, leaving one Jasper–Huntingburg train.

Jasper–Huntingburg service increased to three round trips on December 16, 1888. This schedule pattern remained in place until July 2, 1907, when service expanded to five round trips. When the branch opened to West Baden in December 1907, two of the five pairings were extended to West Baden and began carrying St. Louis–West Baden sleepers. Service was slashed in 1909 to three round trips, all operating to West Baden. The St. Louis–West Baden sleepers were replaced in 1911 with Pullman parlor cars, which operated until May 1914. West Baden service remained at three round trips until World War I, when one pairing ended. Those trains were restored on February 20, 1921. During the 1920s, the only through cars on the West Baden branch operated to Evansville.

The ax began falling on June 14, 1925, when Nos. 5/6 were canceled. By the early 1930s, both pairs of West Baden trains were operating to Evansville. One pairing was discontinued on January 3, 1932. This service was curtailed to Huntingburg–French Lick on November 11, 1934. Six months later, French Lick service was downgraded to mixed trains that were discontinued on May 24, 1937.

CHAPTER 16

SHORT-LINE RAILROADS

Eleven Indiana short-line railroads offered passenger service, most of which was gone by 1930 and the last of which ended in 1953. The service tended to be minimal, no more than three round trips a day. Some short-line railroads offered through car service with a trunk line, but this was not common. The same forces that brought the decline of passenger service on trunk lines also buffeted short lines. In some cases passenger service ended when the railroad went out of business.

Bedford Stone Railway

Opened in June 1901, the Bedford Stone Railway extended 2.96 miles from Rivervale on the Baltimore & Ohio (St. Louis line) southward to Stonington in southeast Lawrence County, where the railroad's parent company operated limestone quarries. Scheduled passenger service began in July 1906 with one round trip. The lone intermediate station was Lawrenceport, and the scheduled running time was 15 minutes. The published schedule remained unchanged over the next 11 years. Financial problems beset the railroad after 1914 when a rate division contract with the B&O expired. Service was temporarily suspended in late 1917 but never resumed, and the line was abandoned.

Central Indiana Railway

Around the turn of the 20th century, traveling salesman Homer H. Beals was riding between Noblesville and Anderson. When asked by the conductor why he looked so glum, Beals replied that he had stuck his head out the window to view the scenery and lost his hat. "And it cost me a dollar, too," Beals said. On Beals's next trip the conductor reached into the luggage rack and produced the wayward hat. "Service of the Midland, sir," the conductor told the astonished Beals. Reportedly, the conductor had ordered a passenger train stopped while he searched for a half-hour for the salesman's hat. Retrieving lost hats for its patrons may be one of the few claims to fame of the 127-mile Central Indiana Railway.

Chartered in 1875 as the Anderson, Lebanon & St. Louis, passenger service began August 13, 1877, with two Anderson–Noblesville round trips. The company faltered and was reorganized on December 23, 1883, as the Cleveland, Indiana & St. Louis. The financial

Short-Line Railroads

predicaments continued, and on April 1, 1885, the 19-mile line was sold to Thomas C. Platt, who reorganized it on July 7, 1885, as the Midland Railway. During this period, passenger service was two Noblesville–Anderson round trips.

The Midland expanded westward to Westfield and Eagletown (both in Hamilton County) in October 1885 and September 1886, respectively, and to the Montgomery County communities of Ladoga (1887), Browns Valley Junction (1888), and Waveland (1890). Between Browns Valley and Sand Creek in Parke County, where it owned several coal mines, the Midland used the Terre Haute & Logansport Railroad (later Pennsylvania). Service between Anderson and Westfield began on November 15, 1885, between Anderson and Lebanon on May 1, 1887, and between Anderson and Ladoga on November 3, 1889. The Midland operated two daily round trips.

The Midland began offering three pairs of trains on June 8, 1890, the new pair operating between Ladoga and Browns Valley. Service began to Waveland on October 12, 1890. The Anderson–Ladoga trains then began operating to Waveland while the Browns Valley trains began operating between Anderson and Vandalia Junction (Waveland Junction).

The Midland's objective had been to reach Paris, Ill., but instead it built to Brazil, Ind., to tap that area's coalfields. Henry Crawford, owner of the Chicago & South Eastern, acquired the Midland on October 20, 1891. The C&SE completed the Brazil extension using a patchwork of lines, including 9.4 miles of trackage rights on the TH&L (Waveland Junction–Sand Creek) and leasing 5.3 miles from the Fort Wayne, Terre Haute & Southwestern (Carbon–Bridgeton) in Parke County. The C&SE built 10.7 miles between Sand Creek and Bridgeton in Parke County and 5.7 miles between Carbon and Brazil in Clay County.

The Midland had reduced service to one Anderson–Vandalia Junction round trip in 1890, but by 1895 this had expanded to two round trips. All trains were extended to Brazil on August 19, 1895. This operation continued for more than a year before one round trip was curtailed to Anderson–Waveland. These trains were reduced to Anderson–Ladoga in 1898.

The Chicago & South Eastern extended eastward to Muncie in 1899, but passenger service did not begin until January 15, 1901, with a Muncie–Waveland round trip. At the same time, Anderson–Brazil service was downgraded to mixed trains. As had its predecessors, the Chicago & South Eastern also struggled. Crawford persuaded the Pennsylvania and Big Four railroads to acquire his troubled railroad's securities. The two trunks on March 16, 1903, created the Central Indiana Railway and agreed to operate it as an Indianapolis bypass route.

In the waning years of Chicago & South Eastern control, passenger service had expanded to three pairs of trains: Muncie–Ladoga, Anderson–Ladoga, and Lebanon–Brazil. A year later (November 30, 1902), service expanded to four pairs of trains: Anderson–Brazil, Muncie–Lebanon, Lebanon–Brazil, and Bridgeton–Brazil. The Muncie terminal became Avondale, less than a mile from the previous Muncie station.

One of the Central Indiana's first moves was to slash passenger service on June 14, 1903, to two round trips, Muncie–Brazil and Anderson–Brazil. The Anderson–Brazil trains began operating on December 18, 1904, between Anderson and Lebanon, and a new pair of trains began operating between Anderson and Waveland. Service reached its previous peak of four daily round trips on April 5, 1908, but no scheduled passenger train operated between Muncie and Brazil. Trains operated included Muncie–Anderson, Anderson–Lebanon, Anderson–Waveland, and Waveland–Brazil. The schedules made it impractical to make connections to travel the length of the line.

The Central Indiana promoted its passenger business by offering excursion trains, holiday fares, and connections with interurban railways. Children in Hamilton County rode the Central Indiana to Westfield High School. In Clay County the Central Indiana operated miners' trains.

Passenger operations were relatively stable on the Central Indiana during the first decade of the 20th century. Nos. 50/51 began operating between Avondale (Muncie) and

Waveland on September 5, 1915, but otherwise there were no other significant changes until Nos. 50/51 were shortened to Avondale–Anderson on May 14, 1916. Service to Muncie ended in September 1917, and the Anderson–Lebanon trains ceased in August 1918. This left Nos. 2/3 (Anderson–Waveland) and Nos. 54/55 (Waveland–Brazil) as the Central Indiana's last scheduled passenger trains.

The use of the Central Indiana as an Indianapolis bypass never materialized. The Pennsylvania and Big Four treated the Central Indiana as a poor cousin, assigning it secondhand equipment, some of it ready for the scrap line. Although a marketing study concluded that the Central Indiana had no future, vigorous protests from shippers and others blocked its abandonment. Scheduled passenger service continued until February 9, 1922. Thereafter, Central Indiana schedules in *The Official Guide of the Railways* carried the notation that passengers were accommodated on local freight trains between Anderson and Brazil. This ended in March 1929.

Cincinnati, Bluffton & Chicago

Known as the "Corned Beef and Cabbage," the 52-mile Cincinnati, Bluffton & Chicago had the second shortest existence of any Indiana railroad established in the 20th century. It duplicated existing railroads, served a sparsely populated area, and spent much of its life in financial difficulty. The CB&C was chartered March 9, 1903. Construction began at Bluffton in Wells County, which had two railroads and was indifferent to a third. Some farmers refused to sell land to the CB&C, and those who did sell became angry when they weren't paid and tore up the tracks, burned ties, and damaged construction supplies. Nonetheless, the CB&C persevered and opened between Bluffton and Pennville in northwest Jay County on December 23, 1903. Scheduled passenger service began two days later with two round trips.

To enter Portland in Jay County, the CB&C had to cross the Lake Erie & Western (later Nickel Plate), which had steadfastly refused to allow the crossing and posted watchmen to keep the CB&C at bay. One Sunday when most of the LE&W watchmen were off duty and no trains were running, the CB&C moved in to build the crossing. Anticipating this, the LE&W had parked a string of boxcars at the proposed CB&C crossing. The CB&C crews derailed a boxcar and went to work. The LE&W rounded up its forces, and a fistfight ensued. The LE&W obtained a court order on Monday restraining the CB&C from using the crossing.

The two railroads later settled their differences, and the CB&C opened to Portland on January 1, 1904. The first schedule in the *Official Guide* to show passenger service to Portland (two round trips) was published in August 1904, effective July 1. After Huntington voters offered it a $100,000 subsidy, the CB&C reached Huntington on January 13, 1908, just two days ahead of the deadline the city had set for completion. In return for the subsidy, the CB&C relocated its shops to Huntington.

Misfortune frequently plagued the CB&C. It missed paydays, and when it did pay its employees, the more savvy ones ran to the bank to cash their checks lest the chronically cash-short CB&C ran out of funds. A Cleveland broker whom the CB&C retained to sell $800,000 in bonds absconded in 1907 with the proceeds. The broker was imprisoned in 1910, but the CB&C was on the hook for the liability of the bonds. Consequently, creditors filed suit to force the CB&C into receivership.

John C. Curtis, a former CB&C superintendent, was appointed receiver on March 13, 1908. He gamely struggled over the next 10 years to keep the CB&C on track. One obstacle Curtis faced was a 1910 court order that prohibited the CB&C from being sold. After the Indiana Supreme Court overturned the decree, the CB&C announced plans in 1911 to become an interurban railway. But a court ruled that the CB&C remain a steam railroad.

The CB&C had built on the Erie right-of-way in Huntington and Wells Counties. The Erie had stipulated that the CB&C upgrade its track to create a shared track arrangement with the Erie. When the CB&C didn't fulfill the agreement, the Erie built its own second track and evicted the CB&C, forcing it to seek donations of land for a new right-of-way. The CB&C built through a lumberyard in Markle, on the Huntington–Wells county line, and in a city street in Uniondale, in Wells County.

CB&C passenger trains generally operated between Huntington and Portland. The first schedule published in the *Official Guide* to show this service indicated that it began December 19, 1907, although these trains may have terminated short of Huntington for the first month of operation. Scheduled service peaked at five round trips on December 14, 1913, and fell to four round trips in July 1915 and to three round trips on April 27, 1917.

The CB&C acquired three gasoline-electric cars from Barber Car Company of York, Pa., in 1912. Each 50-foot car seated 40 and was powered by a six-cylinder 100-horsepower engine. The cars were assigned to two of the three daily round trips. In the meantime, the CB&C had extended its track a mile to Jefferson Street in downtown Huntington. The motor cars were prone to breakdowns and troublesome to maintain, making it difficult for the CB&C to follow its schedules. Following a breakdown on a frigid February night in 1917, the 18 passengers sat stranded for several hours before realizing that help was not going to arrive soon. They summoned a Bluffton jitney to take them to Pennville. A rescue locomotive finally arrived at dawn.

Like other railroads faced with imposing financial problems, the CB&C deferred maintenance. Track conditions were so bad that a Bluffton newspaper described a trip on the CB&C as akin to taking an ocean voyage because the train bobbed so much. After a March 1913 flood damaged a bridge over the Wabash River, a replacement section was installed. But the new section gave way on the afternoon of May 22, 1913, beneath the weight of a mixed train. The engineer died after the locomotive fell into the river. A combine car remained on the bridge, although dangling precariously. No passengers were seriously injured.

For a while the CB&C detoured over the LE&W between Bluffton and Kingsland and on the Erie between Kingsland and Markle. The CB&C built a walkway across the river, and passengers walked between trains. This was replaced with a low bridge that sometimes was covered with water. Some must have found it unnerving to cross the river when they could not see the rails beneath them.

Perhaps the most bizarre occurrence in the CB&C's fleeting lifetime was a runaway locomotive that landed in the basement of a Huntington candy store. The saga began on December 13, 1913, when a mixed train arrived from Portland. Locomotive No. 26 was detached and taken to the coal dock, where its fires were banked for the night. Blocks were placed under the wheels and chains fastened into place. But just before midnight the locomotive began moving backwards, ran out onto the main line, and continued to the end of the track where it crashed into Wayne's Confectionery. The official cause of the accident was a leaky throttle, but it was never discovered who had removed the blocks and chain and lined the switch for the mainline. Reportedly a man jumped off the locomotive just before it struck the store. It also was reported that a man in a room above the store slept through the mishap, which drew large crowds to gaze at the improbable sight.

After a decade of trying to keep the CB&C afloat, management gave up. The CB&C was sold in 1917 to a Kansas City salvage company. The last passenger operation was a motor car that ran between Portland and Huntington on September 24, 1917, with few people on board.

Elgin, Joliet & Eastern

Primarily a belt line that interchanged freight with Chicago's major railroads, the Elgin, Joliet & Eastern had a modest passenger operation in northwest Indiana. Organized on

March 22, 1884, as the Joliet, Aurora & Northern, the first trains operated between Joliet and Aurora, Ill., on August 15, 1886. With the backing of banker J. P. Morgan, the Elgin, Joliet & Eastern Railway Company of Illinois was chartered on March 18, 1887, to extend the JA&N to the Indiana border. A separate company was established to build to Porter, Ind., via Dyer, Griffith, and Hobart. Construction began in summer 1888. Crews reached Hobart in late September and McCool, a junction with the B&O, in early November. The Elgin, Joliet & Eastern of Illinois purchased the JA&N on October 29, 1888. The EJ&E of Indiana merged with the EJ&E of Illinois on December 4, 1888.

The EJ&E began passenger service in Indiana on January 13, 1889, with a round trip between McCool and Bridge Junction near East Joliet, Ill. Nearly 2 years later, the service had been extended to East Joliet. Delays in establishing interchange facilities with the Lake Shore & Michigan Southern (later New York Central) at Porter prevented the EJ&E from building the final 4.5 miles between McCool and Porter until June 1893. Passenger service to Porter began on June 25, 1893.

Passenger service in Indiana ended in 1895, but resumed on June 27, 1897, with trains operating from Porter to Waukegan, Ill., and from East Joliet to Porter. Travelers making the 130-mile trip from Porter to Waukegan had plenty of time to read, knit, or nap. No. 17 departed Porter at 8:15 A.M. and arrived in Waukegan at 9:30 P.M. Some who rode the EJ&E probably were connecting with other lines, for the EJ&E connected with every steam railroad serving Chicago, a fact reflected in its slogan, "Chicago Outer Belt Line."

EJ&E passenger service in Indiana expanded slightly on January 25, 1903, with the institution of an East Joliet–Griffith round trip. United States Steel now owned the EJ&E, which had acquired a number of other lines serving Gary, Hammond, and Whiting. However, only the Porter–Joliet–Waukegan mainline hosted scheduled passenger service in Indiana. The East Joliet–Griffith trains were extended to Hobart on November 14, 1904, discontinued on February 15, 1906, and reinstated on a different schedule on January 14, 1907. One train operated from East Joliet to Hobart, the other from Griffith to East Joliet.

Also on November 14, 1904, the East Joliet to Porter train began originating at Waukegan. These trains departed in early morning and arrived at their terminus in late evening. This changed on February 15, 1906, when the train from Waukegan to Porter began departing at 3:40 P.M. and operating on an overnight schedule, arriving at East Joliet at 1:15 A.M. and Porter at 7:40 A.M. The return train left Porter at 8:30 A.M. and arrived in Waukegan at 11:55 P.M.

EJ&E passenger trains were clean and punctual but nondescript. By the early 20th century, interurban railways had taken away much of the EJ&E's passenger business. The EJ&E downgraded its passenger trains to mixed trains that carried passengers in the caboose. EJ&E's scheduled passenger service in Indiana ended on June 1, 1909.

Ferdinand Railroad

Connecting Ferdinand in southern Dubois County with the Southern Railway's St. Louis–Louisville line, the Ferdinand Railway was incorporated October 25, 1905, after another railroad missed Ferdinand by 7 miles. Constructed in 1909, the line extended 6.48 miles from Ferdinand to a junction with the Southern a mile east of Huntingburg. The first passenger train operated on February 21, 1909, and carried 150 people. The first schedule published in the *Official Guide* showed two round trips.

Service expanded to three round trips in November 1921. For much of its history, the Ferdinand carried passengers in a combination baggage-coach built in 1880. The Ferdinand later used an interurban combine once owned by the Interstate Public Service Company. Most Ferdinand passenger trains were mixed trains. In the 1930s the one-way fare was 20 cents and the railroad earned $850 annually in passenger revenue.

Ferdinand Railroad Company

TIME TABLE NO. 32

Effective 12:01 A. M. Sunday Nov. 24, 1935.
All trains daily except Sunday.

1	3			2	4
AM	PM	LV	AR	AM	PM
7:35	2:20	FERDINAND		9:05	3:30
8:05	2:50	HUNTINGBURG		8:35	3:00
AM	PM	AR	LV	AM	PM

Connections At Huntingburg

No. 1 Connects with Southern train No. 9 to Louisville.

No. 3 Connects with Southern train No. 23 to Louisville.

All trains run to and from Southern Railway Depot at Huntingburg.

V. F. GREWE
General Manager
Ferdinand - - - Indiana

FERDINAND
RAILROAD COMPANY
Time Table Number 39

Effective 12:01 A. M. Sunday, June 30, 1946
All trains daily except Sunday.

1	3			2	4
AM	PM	LV	AR	AM	PM
7:00	1:40	Ferdinand		8:15	2:55
7:30	2:10	Huntingburg		7:45	2:25
AM	PM	AR	LV	AM	PM

CONNECTIONS AT HUNTINGBURG

No. 3 connects with Southern train No. 23 to Louisville, Ky.
All trains run to and from Southern Railway Depot at Huntingburg.

S. A. SCHREINER
GENERAL MANAGER
Ferdinand - - - Indiana

Schedules issued a decade apart by the Ferdinand Railroad of southern Indiana show minor schedule changes but the loss of a connection with the Southern to Louisville. When the Southern ended passenger service in 1953, so did the Ferdinand. Richard S. Simons collection.

Service was reduced to two round trips on January 1, 1933. Operations remained largely unchanged until the end of service in 1953. Trains departed Ferdinand at 7 A.M. and 1:55 P.M. and left Huntingburg at 7:40 A.M. and 2:45 P.M. The running time was 20 minutes. The removal of the Southern's last passenger trains in southern Indiana prompted the discontinuance of the Ferdinand's passenger service, which ended in January 1953.

Findlay, Fort Wayne & Western

The natural gas boom of the 1880s sparked the creation of the 78-mile American Midland Railroad between Fort Wayne and Findlay, Ohio, which opened on January 1, 1895, and used the Wabash station at Fort Wayne. Nearly a straight line, the route's only significant curve was near Fort Wayne. The Findlay, Fort Wayne & Western succeeded the American Midland in June 1890. The Cincinnati, Hamilton & Dayton (later B&O) acquired the line on November 1, 1901, but sold it at foreclosure on July 6, 1903, to the Cincinnati, Findlay & Fort Wayne Railway. The CH&D leased the line back on November 1, 1903, but did no better the second time around. The road entered receivership on July 2, 1914.

In early 1900, the line operated a Fort Wayne–Findlay round trip. A pair of mixed trains was added on December 16, 1900, and service expanded to three round trips on February 23, 1902. At about the same time, the FFtW&W began using the Pennsylvania Railroad station in Fort Wayne, and a Chicago–Findlay sleeper was established. This service soon ended and the road's passenger trains returned to the Wabash station in 1903. Service fell to two round trips in 1904, neither of which operated on Sunday. One pair of trains was restricted to adult male passengers.

Following the 1914 receivership, the CH&D lease was cancelled and it became an orphan operated by the Cincinnati, Findlay & Fort Wayne Railway. The financial woes continued, and on March 4, 1918, passenger service was slashed to triweekly operation. The security holders decided to cut their losses and abandoned the railroad in 1919.

Indiana Harbor Belt

The nation's largest belt railroad, the Indiana Harbor Railroad, hosted a commuter train operation in conjunction with the Nickel Plate Road. Its earliest Indiana predecessor was the Hammond & Blue Island Railroad, created in the mid-1890s to link a Standard Oil refinery in Whiting with the Michigan Central at Hammond.

Passenger service on the Harbor began in summer 1904. Trains originated at Indiana Harbor and served the intermediate stations of Michigan Avenue, East Chicago, Grasselli, Gibson, and Osborn, where the trains switched to the Nickel Plate for the remainder of the trip to Chicago La Salle Street Station. The Harbor operated 12 commuter trains. The 22-mile route between Indiana Harbor and La Salle Street Station covered 12 miles on the Harbor. The service was last shown in the *Official Guide* in May 1907.

Louisville, New Albany & Corydon

Opened on December 1, 1883, the Louisville, New Albany & Corydon was the only Indiana railroad built in the 1880s that still operated under its original name more than a century later. Although it once offered passenger service to its namesake cities, the road's focus was serving Corydon, Indiana's capital from 1816 (when statehood began) to 1824.

This combine-coach was the passenger fleet of the Louisville, New Albany & Corydon Railroad. Its expansive name notwithstanding, the short line did not operate directly to Louisville or New Albany. Photo courtesy of the Louisville, New Albany & Corydon Railroad.

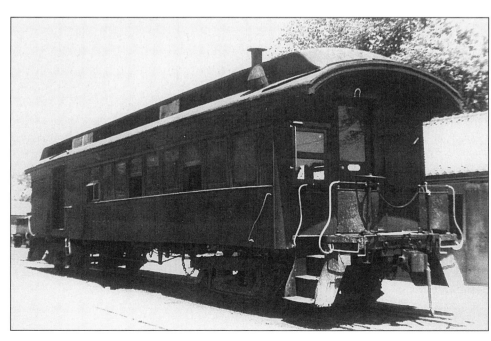

The LNA&C's first passenger schedule showed two Louisville–Corydon round trips, using the LNA&C between Corydon and Corydon Junction, where the LNA&C connected with the Louisville, New Albany & St. Louis Railway (later Southern). The LNA&C added a Corydon–Corydon Junction round trip on August 12, 1888. LNA&C trains began operating solely between Corydon and Corydon Junction on December 3, 1893. Service remained largely unchanged through the early 1940s. Two trains operated in the morning and the third in the afternoon. LNA&C passenger service fell to two round trips on November 16, 1942, but the third round trip was revived on May 17, 1943, and remained in operation until July 1, 1946, when service again fell to two round trips.

The connection with the Southern's train to Louisville was lost on May 23, 1947, when the LNA&C trimmed passenger service to a single morning round trip. The LNA&C continued to connect with the Southern's train to St. Louis. The last LNA&C passenger operation, a mixed train, made its final runs in January 1953. However, the line hosted tourist trains in the 1990s

New Jersey, Indiana & Illinois

The New Jersey, Indiana & Illinois railroad extended 11.4 miles from South Bend to Pine in southern St. Joseph County, where it connected with the Wabash. It was named for the locations of manufacturing facilities operated by its first owner, the Singer Sewing Machine Company. The NJI&I had hoped to begin operations in December 1904, but did not do so until eight months later. Passenger service began August 1, 1905, with two daily-except-Sunday round trips between South Bend and Pine.

The line served three intermediate stations, but most passenger traffic came from South Bend. Service remained two round trips through 1920, when it expanded to three round trips. At the same time, a South Bend–Detroit sleeper began operating via the Wabash. One round trip was discontinued in August 1924. Another pairing ended in January 1925. Although purchased by the Wabash in 1926, the New Jersey, Indiana & Illinois continued to operate independently. The last passenger trains were discontinued on April 2, 1933. Ending with them was the South Bend–Detroit sleeper, which in its final years of service was usually a 12 section, one drawing room car.

St. Joseph Valley

Many men who founded, built, and managed railroads in the 19th century were rugged individualists determined to assemble industrial empires. Although Herbert E. "Doc" Bucklen was cast in that mold, his contribution to railroad history is but a laconic footnote. A wealthy Elkhart manufacturer of patent medicines, Bucklen founded the St. Joseph Valley Railway. Flanked by powerful trunk lines and serving an area of meager population in northeast Indiana, the St. Joseph Valley succumbed after 14 distressed years of operation.

Bucklen got into railroading by establishing the Elkhart & Western, an 11.7-mile line between Elkhart and Mishawaka that opened on September 26, 1893. The E&W offered passenger service in its early years, but its bread and butter was the switching charges and tariff divisions it received that were out of proportion to its size. Bucklen sold the E&W to the Lake Shore & Michigan Southern in 1898.

Bucklen was not out of the railroad business for long. He chartered the St. Joseph Valley Traction Company on March 28, 1903, with the intention of building an interurban railway that would have formed an 84-mile middle link of a Chicago–Toledo interurban route. The line was electrified and operated as an interurban only between Elkhart and Bristol in Elkhart County.

The St. Joseph Valley Railway used various models of motor trains, few of which proved to be satisfactory. One such car is shown at Orland, Ind., in the early 20th century. Richard S. Simons collection.

The St. Joseph Valley Railway never prospered, but it had a colorful and controversial history. A mixed train calls at Mongo in LaGrange County in the early 20th century. Richard S. Simons collection.

Construction of the SJV began in 1903 at LaGrange, the railroad's operating headquarters. It opened in LaGrange County between LaGrange and Shipshewanna on March 13, 1905, and between Shipshewanna and Middlebury in Elkhart County on September 20. Many of these towns welcomed the SJV because they had no rail service. The SJV's bleak future was foreshadowed on the day it began service to Middlebury. More than 100 people greeted the arrival of the first train, but only two purchased tickets for the return trip to LaGrange. At the May 4, 1907, opening of the SJV to Orland in northwest Steuben County, hundreds jammed aboard four special trains, loads more than double the capacity of the cars. Three brass bands played. But late in the day, one of the coaches derailed.

Although Bucklen financed most of the SJV himself, he accepted subsidies and financial inducements from communities that wanted his railroad to serve their town. The SJV had a zigzag profile, changing direction as it was built in order to serve whichever community offered funding. Service to Angola began on August 25, 1907, with three weekday round trips and two round trips on Sunday between Angola and Lake Gage. The trains used a gasoline-electric car built by the Hicks Locomotive Works of Chicago Heights, Ill., reportedly one of the first such cars in the country. But the car contained so much equipment that there was little room for passengers or baggage. The SJV purchased a 48-foot trailer car built by the St. Louis Car Company.

Construction between Bristol and Elkhart was hindered by difficulties in acquiring right-of-way and gaining permission to cross the LS&MS at Bristol, a problem not resolved until 1911. Construction of the 9-mile segment got under way in 1910 and barely finished ahead of a May 31, 1910, deadline to qualify for a subsidy. The first official run between Elkhart and Bristol occurred on July 6, using a Northern Indiana Railway Car. The Northern Indiana later agreed to operate the SJV between Elkhart and Bristol.

The SJV entered Elkhart on East Jackson Street and terminated at Jackson and Main. The Northern Indiana built a connection from there to the Marion Street interurban station in downtown Elkhart served by Northern Indiana Railway interurban lines. The two-year arrangement between the SJV and the Northern Indiana Railway was stormy, with the two unable to agree on much of anything. When the lease expired on July 1, 1912, the Northern Indiana cut the power to the SJV. Undaunted, Bucklen acquired two interurban cars, but they were late in arriving, so the Northern Indiana agreed to continue operating the SJV for another week. The SJV lacked an interurban car repair facility and relied on the Northern Indiana for even minor maintenance.

Bucklen turned his attention to eastward expansion in 1915. In July, the SJV reached Columbia in northwestern Ohio, a city with no railroad connections. SJV passenger trains generally terminated at LaGrange or Angola. In January 1908, the SJV operated two LaGrange–Angola round trips and three LaGrange–Middlebury round trips. The *Official Guide* showed Angola service operated by the St. Joseph Valley Railway and Elkhart–Middlebury service operated by the St. Joseph Valley Traction Company, both controlled by Bucklen. A year later, LaGrange–Angola service had increased to four round trips, a pattern that remained through early 1913. LaGrange–Middlebury service increased to four round trips in 1910.

The SJV's takeover of its Elkhart–Bristol interurban line in 1912 resulted in major schedule changes. The SJV scheduled two Elkhart–Angola round trips, five Elkhart–Bristol round trips, one Elkhart–LaGrange round trip, one train from Angola Junction to Elkhart, and one train from Elkhart to LaGrange. Also on the schedule were a LaGrange–Angola Junction round trip and a train from LaGrange to Angola Junction. Because the Elkhart trains terminated at Main and Jackson Streets, passengers bound for downtown Elkhart had to walk or take a streetcar. The Northern Indiana Railway again leased the SJV interurban line on July 22, 1917.

The SJV had more than its share of mishaps. The Hicks gas-electric car derailed at LaGrange four months after entering service and broke an axle. It took two days to rerail the car and two months to rebuild the damaged track. The Hicks car was destroyed by fire 2 years later when a spark ignited lubricating oil. Bucklen acquired two gasoline-mechanical cars from Stover Motor Car Company of Freeport, Ill., and two more such cars from Sheffield Car Company of Three Rivers, Mich. The cars were merely automobiles with flanged wheels that could carry 25 passengers at a top speed of 20 mph. Passengers dubbed the cars "Bucklen's Arnica Salve Wagon," after his most popular product, and the "tax collector," a reference to the SJV having rushed the cars into service to meet a subsidy deadline.

Eventually replacing this equipment were two chain-driven cars purchased from Fairbanks-Morse that had Brill Car Company bodies and could accommodate 35 passengers at a top speed of 30 mph. A fire in November 1911 destroyed five motor cars and a steam engine. Until it could acquire replacement equipment, the SJV annulled two passenger trains.

In 1913, Bucklen purchased an Edison-Beach storage battery car equipped with four 30-horsepower motors that could carry 45 passengers at a top speed of 40 mph. He described it as a revolutionary leap in transportation technology and boldly predicted that "poles and wires will be things of the past and the costly overhead expenses will be eliminated." But much to Bucklen's consternation, the car could not travel the advertised 150 miles on a single battery charge. It often ran out of power a few miles short of Elkhart and had to be towed by an interurban car. A disillusioned Bucklen sued the manufacturer, but lost.

The Hall-Scott Motor Car Company furnished the SJV with a motor car equipped with a 150-horsepower engine. It had less capacity and was longer, heavier, and wider than the Edison-Beach battery car, but the Hall-Scott car was the most satisfactory motor car the SJV would operate. Not long after the car entered service, however, it was damaged in a collision in a fog with a track car carrying Bucklen's son. The younger Bucklen and another man jumped to safety, but three passengers and a crewman aboard the motor car were injured. Most SJV passenger service was handled by motor cars. Although the motor cars had diminutive capacities, they rarely ran full. The SJV passenger fleet also included a baggage car, combination baggage-coach, and three open-window coaches, all of them secondhand antiques.

At its peak in late 1916, the SJV scheduled seven Elkhart–Bristol round trips. Other scheduled trains included Elkhart to Angola Junction, Elkhart to Angola, Elkhart to Columbia, Columbia to Elkhart (two trains), Angola Junction to Columbia, Columbia to LaGrange, and LaGrange to Elkhart. There was a round trip between LaGrange and Angola Junction.

A December 1916 accident killed a woman and her three-year-old daughter and injured 26 others. No. 7 had departed Columbia 20 minutes late. Departing shortly afterward was Extra 128, a mixed train. No. 7 carried 77 passengers even though the motor car had just 21 seats. The train kept losing time as it plodded westward. At Angola, No. 7 took the track to the downtown station whereas Extra 128 ran on the mainline via Angola Junction. The crew of No. 7 assumed that Extra 128 was now ahead of it and proceeded without checking. While No. 7 was stopped at Inverness, 7 miles west of Angola, Extra 128 struck it from behind. The mixed train was operating at 20 mph, and the impact of the collision pushed the motor car ahead several hundred feet. An Interstate Commerce Commission investigation blamed the accident on the failure of the crew of No. 7 to adequately flag for following traffic.

The ICC determined that Extra 128 had departed Columbia 3 minutes after No. 7 rather than the 5 minutes required by the rules. The engineer of Extra 128 had not shared the train orders with the fireman, who had previously refused to look at train orders. Nor had the fireman kept a watch out his window. The locomotive brakes of Extra 128 were inoperative. The passenger train conductor said he had been busy helping people detrain and was not aware of his duty to protect the rear of a stopped train. Nor did he know that his train carried fusees. A rear marker on No. 7 was missing due to a broken bracket.

Although the SJV had had numerous brushes with the ICC over safety issues, Bucklen insisted on running his railroad his way. "To hell with the Interstate Commerce Commission and its rules," he once said. The fatal accident at Inverness exposed the SJV's slipshod operating practices, but did not bring about the railroad's downfall. The SJV was already on a fast track to extinction. Bucklen lay gravely ill in his Chicago home and never learned of the fatal accident.

After Bucklen's death on January 11, 1917, Herbert E. Bucklen Jr. inherited control of the SJV. The younger Bucklen had never shared his father's passion for railroading. The elder Bucklen's will stipulated that the SJV was to be operated in trust for 10 years, but the trustees quickly realized the SJV could not survive without continued financial support from Bucklen's estate. Eleven months after Bucklen's death, the SJV entered receivership with the younger Bucklen appointed receiver. Service reductions and cost cutting failed to improve the SJV's dismal prospects. Freight and passenger revenue paid just half of operating expenses.

The final SJV schedules published in the *Official Guide* still showed an impressive number of scheduled passenger trains. Six round trips operated weekdays between Elkhart and Bristol. Round trips operated between LaGrange and Angola Junction and between Angola Junction and Columbia. Trains also operated from Elkhart to Angola Junction, Columbia to Angola Junction, and Angola to Columbia.

The SJV was sold on April 3, 1918, to a Chicago salvage company. Service ended between LaGrange and Bristol on April 11, between Elkhart and Bristol on April 17, and between LaGrange and Columbia on April 18. Elkhart Mayor W. H. Foster acquired the SJV tracks within Elkhart and leased them to the Northern Indiana Railway, which operated the Jackson Street line until it discontinued streetcar service in Elkhart on June 2, 1934.

Toledo, Peoria & Western

The TP&W barely touched Indiana, ending at Effner in Newton County on the Illinois border. Peoria civic leaders seeking a rail link to the Mississippi River created the Peoria & Oquawka Railroad in 1849. The charter was amended on June 22, 1852, to authorize building a line between Peoria and the Indiana border.

Construction of the Peoria & Oquawka Eastern Extension got under way in Peoria in 1853. In the meantime, the Toledo, Logansport & Burlington had begun building westward from Logansport. The two railroads met at Effner, then called State Line, on December 10, 1859. The first passenger operation was a December 27 excursion train from Logansport to Peoria. Scheduled service began January 11, 1860.

The P&O was renamed the Logansport, Peoria & Burlington on February 21, 1862. Sold at a foreclosure sale on March 21, 1864, the new owners organized the Toledo, Peoria & Warsaw Railway, which began operations on May 14, 1864. One of the company's first tasks was to rebuild the railroad. Also in 1864 the TP&W merged with the Mississippi & Wabash, which operated between the Mississippi River town of Warsaw, Ill., and Carthage, Ill. The TP&W completed a 105-mile link between the two railroads on October 4, 1868. Ten days later, trains began operating between Effner and Warsaw.

The TP&W was part of the Great Midland Route between Philadelphia and Kearny, Neb. Other railroads making up the Great Midland included the Pennsylvania Central (Philadelphia–Pittsburgh), the Panhandle (later Pennsylvania) (Pittsburgh–Columbus, Ohio), the Columbus, Chicago & Indiana Central (later Pennsylvania) (Columbus–Effner), TP&W (Effner–Warsaw), and the Missouri, Iowa & Nebraska (later the Burlington) (Alexandria, Iowa–Kearny). A through Pullman between Peoria and Columbus, Ohio, began in January 1870. The TP&W took delivery of three new Pullman cars, named *Peoria*, *Logansport*, and *Columbus*, in January 1872 for through service between Burlington, Iowa, and Columbus, Ohio.

In 1868, the TP&W operated one daily round trip between Effner and Warsaw. A year later the TP&W increased Effner–Warsaw service to two round trips, one of them a pair of overnight trains. The Columbus sleepers were gone by early 1874. By early 1875 one of the Effner–Warsaw round trips had begun terminating in Peoria. Later that year, the

TP&W began an alliance with the Cincinnati, Lafayette & Chicago Railroad (later New York Central). Advertised as the "Lafayette Route," TP&W claimed to have the shortest route between Cincinnati and Omaha. However, no through passenger trains operated between those cities via the TP&W. Instead, sleepers operated between Indianapolis and Peoria, the cars interchanging with the TP&W at Sheldon, Ill., 2 miles west of Effner.

The TP&W also named its passenger trains: *Peoria Express/Cincinnati Express, Fast Line/Limited Express,* and *Pacific Express/Atlantic Express.* Service between Effner and Warsaw had increased to two round trips. A year later, Effner–Warsaw service fell to one round trip plus a mixed train operating from Effner to Warsaw. The *Fast Line/Limited Express* were renamed the *Omaha Special/New York Special.* The TP&W discontinued the Effner–Warsaw mixed trains on November 18, 1877, in favor of a second round trip between the two points. The Effner–Peoria trains were downgraded to accommodation trains. The *Peoria Express/Cincinnati Express* names were dropped, and the *Omaha Special* and *Atlantic Express* were renamed the *Through Express/Lightning Express.*

Again in financial difficulties, the Toledo, Peoria & Western was created on December 18, 1879, to take over the Toledo, Peoria & Warsaw. The Wabash, then under the control of Jay Gould, leased the TP&W in May 1880. Gould's dream was the creation of a transcontinental railroad system. The TP&W and the Missouri, Iowa & Nebraska Railroad would make up 300 miles of the Detroit–Omaha leg. During its Wabash years, the TP&W operated through chair cars between Burlington, Iowa, and Lafayette, and parlor day coaches between Toledo, Ohio, and Peoria, interchanged at Sheldon, Ill. Service to Effner during the Wabash era fell to two pairs of trains in late 1880. An Effner–Peoria round trip was reinstated on November 11, 1881, although it became a mixed train in 1882.

The Wabash ceased operating the TP&W on May 31, 1885. The TP&W had deteriorated during Wabash control, so the new trustees launched a rebuilding program. The TP&W opened a bridge across the Mississippi River at Keokuk, Iowa, on June 15, 1871, but Warsaw, Ill., remained the western terminus of TP&W passenger trains originating at Effner. That changed on July 26, 1885, when trains began terminating at Keokuk. One pair of these trains began operating between Effner and Peoria in late 1889. This schedule remained in place until May 28, 1906, when service between Effner and Keokuk increased to two round trips. The TP&W never again operated a through passenger service with an eastern railroad.

In an effort to increase revenue, the TP&W scheduled a series of excursion trips in summer and fall 1887. The first of these left Peoria on August 10 for Niagara Falls, N.Y. The 15-car train had more than 600 passengers aboard when it left Chatsworth, Ill. Just before midnight the crew spotted what it thought was a grass fire. It turned out to be a burning trestle. Unable to stop, the train ran out onto the bridge, which collapsed. The five coaches telescoped. More than 80 people died, and several hundred were injured, many seriously. The cause of the fire was never determined. Some attributed it to a grass fire, but others believed outlaws who planned to rob the passengers had set it. Some passengers reportedly were robbed of jewelry and large sums of money at the accident scene.

In the first decade of the 20th century, the TP&W rehabilitated its track, replaced most wooden bridges with steel ones, and built brick passenger stations at cities where it intersected other railroads. In 1911 the TP&W carried more than a million passengers in a single year for the first time. Patronage remained over a million a year through 1915, when it began to decline. The Pennsylvania Railroad acquired a controlling interest in the TP&W in 1893 with the thought of making it a Chicago bypass route. But that did not happen, and the TP&W entered receivership on July 1, 1917.

Early in the 20th century, TP&W passenger service to Effner was two Keokuk round trips and one Peoria round trip. This changed on July 7, 1907, when one westbound train began terminating at Peoria. Service was trimmed to one Effner–Keokuk round trip and one Effner–Peoria round trip on January 19, 1908. The schedule changed on June 25, 1911, to one Effner–Keokuk train, two Effner–Peoria trains, two Keokuk–Effner trains, and one Peoria–Effner train.

In late 1914, one Keokuk to Effner train began originating at Bushnell, Ill. A service cut imposed on December 26, 1915, reduced overall service to Effner to four trains, an Effner–Peoria round trip, and a pair operating Effner–Peoria and Keokuk–Effner. This schedule remained through the early 1920s. A curious schedule was implemented on September 17, 1922. The two westbound trains terminated at Peoria, but the two eastbound trains both originated at Keokuk. TP&W settled on Effner–Peoria and Effner–Keokuk pairings on November 19, 1922.

By the mid-1920s, the TP&W was back in financial trouble and had lost money on passenger service for years. The TP&W carried 421,629 passengers in 1924, but patronage fell to 260,747 a year later, a decline precipitated by the opening of a number of hard-sur-face highways in the area served by the railroad. Once again in receivership, a foreclosure sale was set for October 28, 1925. But there were no bidders, and the sale was rescheduled for December 9. No one was willing to make the minimum bid of $2.1 million plus assumption of the receiver's liabilities, so a third sale was conducted on June 11, 1926. This time George P. McNear Jr. purchased the TP&W for $1.3 million.

McNear rescued the TP&W from what otherwise might have been abandonment. Under his leadership, the TP&W began to prosper. McNear also did something about the TP&W's passenger problem. Nos. 1/6 were discontinued between Effner and Peoria on April 18, 1926, only to be reinstated on July 25. The trains were discontinued for good on September 26. The Effner–Keokuk trains became mixed trains that October.

The TP&W passenger fleet of 16 coaches, four combination coach-baggage cars, and seven baggage and mail cars was in good condition. For a while, a combine carried the markers on the mixed trains. But eventually the combines were replaced with cabooses. In the early days of mixed service, the trains carried only through freight cars. But this did not last long. TP&W schedules carried the warning "passenger service connection uncertain."

Only the hardiest souls were likely to ride a TP&W mixed train endpoint to endpoint. No. 5 was scheduled to depart Effner at 11:30 A.M. and arrive in Keokuk at 3:30 A.M. the next morning. No. 2 departed Keokuk at 8:30 P.M., trundled through the night, and arrived in Effner at 3:10 P.M. the next afternoon. The TP&W studied the use of motor cars, but shelved the idea because of declining patronage. The TP&W stopped carrying mail on February 17, 1929.

The connection with the Pennsylvania's Effner–Logansport passenger trains ended in December 1928 when the Pennsy rescheduled its Logansport–Effner trains. TP&W Nos. 2/5 were shortened to Effner–Peoria operation on April 12, 1929, and began terminating in the Peoria Yard on November 2, 1930, rather than at Peoria Union Station. The schedule could hardly have been attractive to travelers. The train departed Peoria at 9:15 P.M. and arrived in Effner at 4:14 A.M. The return train departed Effner at 8:30 P.M. and arrived in Peoria at 5:20 A.M.

Nos. 3/4 stopped handling passengers in November 1932 between Effner and Forrest, Ill. TP&W reinstated passenger service to Effner in February 1939 when Nos. 50/51 began carrying passengers. The Effner–Forrest mixed trains began operating to Peoria Yard in September 1942. The TP&W had two mixed trains between Peoria and La Harpe, Ill., that used Peoria Union Station. But the schedules made connections impractical.

McNear was a confident leader but a strong-willed man who seldom listened to suggestions. Relations between McNear and his employees were tense, and the railroad endured two strikes before World War II. During the war, John W. Barriger III, later president of the Monon, was the TP&W's federal manager. But shortly after McNear regained control of his railroad on October 1, 1945, union members walked off the job and McNear hired non-union workers. On February 6, 1946, strikers began following a train traveling from Peoria to Effner and harassing the crew. At Gridley, Ill., the strikers surrounded a switch and refused to let the crew continue their work. A fight broke out, and armed guards hired by the railroad fired into the fray, killing two strikers. A jury concluded the guards had acted in self-defense and acquitted them.

As McNear was returning home on the night of March 10, 1947, after attending a Bradley University basketball game, he was shot and killed near his Peoria home. No arrests were ever made. McNear's murder may have been in retaliation for the incident at Gridley. The federal government took temporary control of the TP&W, and operations resumed in April after 14 months of inactivity. The last TP&W steam engine was retired on October 11, 1950, and the Effner–Peoria Yard mixed trains carried passengers for the final time in February 1952.

REFERENCES

Chapter 1

Bach, Ira J., and Susan Wolfson. *A Guide to Chicago's Train Stations*. Athens: Ohio University Press, 1986.

Beebe, Lucius. *Twentieth Century*. Berkeley, Calif.: Howell-North, 1962.

————. "America's Unremarked and Reluctant but Quite Splendid Innkeepers: The Railroads." *Trains*, October 1965, pp. 26–30.

Bradley, George K. *Northern Indiana Railway*. Chicago: Central Electric Railfans Association, 1998.

"Central Signs Up with an X." *Trains*, July 1956, pp. 6–7.

Dubin, Arthur. "A Pullman Postscript." *Trains*, November 1969, pp. 20–33.

————. *More Classic Trains*. Milwaukee: Kalmbach, 1974.

Edmondson, Harold A. *Journey to Amtrak the Year History Rode the Passenger Train*. Milwaukee: Kalmbach, 1972.

Frailey, Fred W. *Twilight of the Great Trains*. Waukesha, Wis.: Kalmbach, 1998.

"The Great Debate." *Trains*, December 1956, pp. 5, 10.

Hannon, Raymond. "Is Passenger Service Really in the Red?" *Trains and Travel*, October 1951, pp. 18–23.

Hargrave, Frank E. *A Pioneer Indiana Railroad: The Origin and Development of the Monon*. Indianapolis: William D. Burford, 1932.

Harwood, Herbert H., Jr., and Robert S. Korach. *The Lake Shore Electric Railway Story*. Bloomington: Indiana University Press, 2000.

Hetherington, James R. *Indianapolis Union Station Trains, Travelers, and Changing Times*. Carmel, Ind.: Guild Press of Indiana, 2000.

Hilton, George W. "Muckraking in a Day Coach." *Trains*, June 1968, pp. 48–50.

————. *The Transportation Act of 1958*. Bloomington: Indiana University Press, 1969.

————. *Amtrak: The National Railroad Passenger Corporation*. Washington, D.C.: American Enterprise Institute for Public Policy Research, 1980.

Hubbard, Freeman. "Dining Car Blues." *Trains*, September 1951, pp. 36–43.

Itzkoff, Donald M. *Off the Track: The Decline of the Intercity Passenger Train in the United States*. Westport, Conn.: Greenwood Press, 1985.

Lyon, Peter. *To Hell in a Daycoach: An Exasperated Look at American Railroads*. Philadelphia: J. B. Lippincott, 1967.

Madison, James H. *The Indiana Way: A State History*. Bloomington: Indiana University Press, 1986.

Marlette, Jerry. "Trials and Tribulations: The Interurban in Indiana." *Traces of Indiana and Midwestern History*, summer 2001, pp. 12–23.

Martin, Albro. *Railroads Triumphant: The Growth, Rejection, and Rebirth of a Vital American Force*. New York: Oxford University Press, 1992.

Middleton, William D. "Indiana Railroad: The All-American Interurban." *Vintage Rails*, July/August 1998, pp. 62–73.

———. *South Shore: The Last Interurban*. Rev. 2nd ed. Bloomington: Indiana University Press, 1999.

Morgan, David P. "The Day Coach." *Trains*, August 1951, pp. 38–45.

———. "Here's What Went Wrong." *Trains*, April 1959, pp. 16–33.

———. "How Would You Like Your Center of Gravity?" *Trains*, May 1956, pp. 14–20.

———. "Is the Passenger Train Obsolete?" *Trains*, July 1956, pp. 31–37.

———. "No Passenger Trains by 1970." *Trains*, December 1958, pp. 42–44.

———. "Who Shot the Passenger Train?" *Trains*, April 1959, pp. 14–15.

Schafer, Mike. *The American Passenger Train*. St. Paul, Minn.: MBI, 2002.

Shaffer, Frank E. "Pullman Prolificacy." *Trains*, October 1967, pp. 24–28.

Simons, Richard S., and Francis H. Parker. *Railroads of Indiana*. Bloomington: Indiana University Press, 1997.

Southerland, William G., Jr., and William McCleary. *The Way to Go: The Coming Revival of U.S. Passenger Service*. New York: Simon and Schuster, 1973.

Steffee, Donald M. "Those New Trains . . . More Splash than Speed?" *Trains*, May 1956, pp. 40–50.

Stover, John F. *American Railroads*. 2nd ed. Chicago: University of Chicago Press, 1997.

———. *The Life and Decline of the American Railroad*. New York: Oxford University Press, 1970.

Sutton, Robert Mize. *The Illinois Central Railroad in Peace and War*. New York: Arno Press, 1981.

Teaford, Jon C. *Cities of the Heartland: The Rise and Fall of the Industrial Midwest*. Bloomington: Indiana University Press, 1993.

Thompson, Gregory Lee. *The Passenger Train in the Motor Age*. Columbus: Ohio State University Press, 1993.

Watt, William J. *The Pennsylvania Railroad in Indiana*. Bloomington: Indiana University Press, 1999.

Wilner, Frank N. *The Amtrak Story*. Omaha, Neb.: Simmons-Boardman Books, 1994.

"The Wrong Action Taken at the Wrong Time in the Wrong Way." *Trains*, October 1956, pp. 6, 10.

Chapter 2

Barriger, John W. *A Hoosier Centenarian: "The Monon."* New York: Newcomen Society, 1947.

——— "The Monon Is a Guinea Pig." *Trains*, July 1947, pp. 15–19.

"Commission Permits Monon to Discontinue Operation of Last Passenger Train." *Traffic World*, September 16, 1967.

Dolzall, Gary W., and Stephen F. Dolzall. *Monon: The Hoosier Line*. Glendale, Calif.: Interurban Press, 1987.

"End of the Line . . . and an Era." *Indianapolis Star Magazine*, January 14, 1968.

Grabow, Bart. "Monon Is Given 'Half a Cure' for Passenger Loss." *Indianapolis News*, March 31, 1959.

Hilton, George W. *Monon Route*. Forest Park, Ill.: Heimburger House, 1978.

Hungerford, Edward. "The Growth of a Railroad." *Trains*, July 1947, pp. 55–59.

"It's Sad Good-bye on Monon Ride." *Indianapolis News*, September 30, 1967.

Kalmbach, A. C. "Diesels Pull the Monon Trains." *Trains*, July 1947, pp. 43–48.

Lyst, John H. "Monon Asks End to Passenger Trains." *Indianapolis Star*, March 28, 1967.

McCord, Al G. "Last Monon Passenger Train Pulls Heartstrings of Riders." *Indianapolis Star*, October 1, 1967.

———. "Monon's Celebrated Train 'Hoosier' No Longer." *Indianapolis Star*, February 24, 1945.

Maiken, Peter T. *Night Trains: The Pullman System in the Golden Years of American Rail Travel*. Baltimore: Johns Hopkins University Press, 1989.

"Monon Ends Trusteeship." *Indianapolis Star*, May 2, 1946.

"Monon Plans New Train." *New York Times*, August 7, 1911, p. 7.

Monon Railroad Discontinuance of Trains Nos. 5 and 6 between Chicago, Ill. and Louisville, Ky. 330 ICC Reports 882 (May 1967–August 1967).

"Monon Revives 'The Hoosier.'" *Indianapolis Star*, July 13, 1946.

"Monon to Lop Off Passenger Runs Here." *Indianapolis News*, March 31, 1959.

"Monon Won't Act Suddenly." *Indianapolis News*, June 4, 1964.

"Monon's Post–World War II Pullman Cars." *Hoosier Line* 13, no. 1 (1994): 9.

Morgan, David P. "The Railroad Image." *Trains*, December 1959.

"Mrs. Emil Schram Launches Monon Train on 1st Trip." *Indianapolis Star*, August 18, 1947.

"Question and Answer." *Hoosier Line* 16, no. 2 (1997): 5.

Redmond, Pat. "Monon '12' Pulls Out on Last Run." *Indianapolis News*, April 9, 1959.

Scribbins, Jim. "Good Times on the Monon Line." *Passenger Train Journal*, September 1987.

Shull, R. K. "Boss Barriger Puts Brainload of Operating Theory to Practice." *Indianapolis Times*, November 12, 1950.

Simons, Richard S., and Francis H. Parker. *Railroads of Indiana*. Bloomington: Indiana University Press, 1997.

Sulzer, Elmer G. *Ghost Railroads of Indiana*. 1970; rpt., Bloomington: Indiana University Press, 1998.

Ullman, Harrison. "Passenger Run to Be Restored on Hoosier Line." *Indianapolis Star*, February 18, 1964.

Westcott, Linn H. "The Monon System and Its Traffic." *Trains*, July 1947, pp. 21–32.

———. "Today's Monon." *Trains*, March 1951, pp. 18–19.

Chapter 3

"B&O Plans to Curtail Cincinnati–St. Louis Train." *Traffic World*, August 17, 1968, p. 58.

"B&O Seeking to Change Some Passenger Services." *Traffic World*, November 4, 1967, p. 42.

"B&O Starts New Train." *Indianapolis News*, September 27, 1938, p. 8, pt. 2.

"B&O Stops Two Night Expresses." *Indianapolis News*, June 4, 1938, p. 1.

The Baltimore and Ohio Railroad Company Discontinuance of Trains Nos. 7 and 10 between Chicago, Ill., and Akron, Ohio, and Change of Service Train No. 7 between Washington, D.C., and Akron, Ohio, and Train No. 10 between Akron, Ohio, and Pittsburgh, Pa. 336 ICC Reports 340 (October 1969–June 1970).

Bateman, Carroll. *The Baltimore & Ohio: The Story of the Railroad That Grew Up with the United States*. Baltimore: Baltimore & Ohio Railroad, 1951.

Bogart, Stephen. "The Capitol to Chicago." *Trains*, March 1959, pp. 36–39.

"C&O/B&O Trains Drop Movies." *Traffic World*, November 11, 1967, p. 44.

"C&O/B&O to Institute 'Blue' and 'Yellow' Fare System for Coach Passengers." *Traffic World*, April 27, 1968, p. 40.

Dilts, James D. *The Great Road: The Building of the Baltimore and Ohio, the Nation's First Railroad*. Stanford, Calif.: Stanford University Press, 1994.

Dubin, Arthur. *Some Classic Trains*. Milwaukee: Kalmbach, 1964.

"An Exposition of E's." *Passenger Train Journal*, June/July 1986, pp. 17–18.

Frailey, Fred W. *Twilight of the Great Trains*. Waukesha, Wis.: Kalmbach, 1998.

Harwood, Herbert H., Jr. *Royal Blue Line*. Sykesville, Md.: Greenberg, 1990.

Hilton, George W. "The Chicago, Cincinnati & Louisville Railroad." *RLHS Bulletin*, no. 114 (April 1966): 6–14.

The Historical Guide to North American Railroads. 2nd ed. Waukesha, Wis.: Kalmbach, 2000.

Hungerford, Edward. *Daniel Willard Rides the Line: The Story of a Great Railroad Man*. New York: G. P. Putnam's Sons, 1938.

———. *The Story of the Baltimore & Ohio Railroad, 1827–1927*. New York: G. P. Putnam's Sons, 1928.

Ivey, Paul Wesley. *The Pere Marquette Railroad Company*. Grand Rapids, Mich.: Black Letter Press, 1970.

Jacobs, Timothy, ed. *The History of the Baltimore & Ohio: America's First Railroad*. New York: Smithmark, 1994.

"New C&O/B&O Slogan: 'Chessie Loves Passengers.'" *Traffic World*, August 12, 1967, p. 31.

Schafer, Mike. *Classic American Railroads*. Osceola, Wis.: Motorbooks International, 1996.

Schafer, Mike, and Joe Welsh. *Classic American Streamliners*. Osceola, Wis.: Motorbooks International, 1997.

Simons, Richard S., and Francis H. Parker. *Railroads of Indiana*. Bloomington: Indiana University Press, 1997.

Stegmaier, Harry. *Baltimore & Ohio Passenger Service, 1945–1971: Route of the Capitol Limited*. Lynchburg, Va.: TLC, 1997.

———. *Baltimore & Ohio Passenger Service, 1945–1971: Route of the National Limited*. Lynchburg, Va.: TLC, 1993.

Stover, John F. *History of the Baltimore and Ohio Railroad*. West Lafayette, Ind.: Purdue University Press, 1987.

Sulzer, Elmer G. *Ghost Railroads of Indiana*. 1970; rpt., Bloomington: Indiana University Press, 1998.

Welsh, Joseph, and William F. Howes, Jr. "Reflections in Blue and Gray: B&O's Final Years of Passenger Service." *Passenger Train Journal*, May 1995, pp. 22–29.

Zimmerman, Karl. *Domeliners: Yesterday's Trains of Tomorrow*. Waukesha, Wis.: Kalmbach, 1998.

Chapter 4

Agnew, Andy. "Remembering Chicago's Grand Central Station." *Chesapeake & Ohio Historical Magazine*, April 1990, pp. 4–15.

Bostic, Stewart H. "Return to the Chicago Division." *Chesapeake & Ohio Historical Magazine*, July 1992, pp. 6–11.

"C&O and Southern Discontinue Trains." *Trains*, January 1950, p. 4.

"C&O Plans to Discontinue Grand Rapids–Chicago Runs." *Traffic World*, November 9, 1968, p. 76.

Dixon, Thomas W., Jr. "C&O's Brill Gas-Electric Cars." *Chesapeake & Ohio Historical Magazine*, September 1995, pp. 3–16.

———. *Chessie: The Railroad Kitten*. Lynchburg, Va.: TLC, 1988.

Dixon, Tom. "C&O of Indiana Standard Depot." *Chesapeake & Ohio Historical Magazine*, February 1990, pp. 14–18.

Dorin, Patrick. *The Chesapeake & Ohio Railway: George Washington's Railroad*. Seattle: Superior, 1981.

Dubin, Arthur. *More Classic Trains*. Milwaukee: Kalmbach, 1974.

Edmonson, Harold A., ed. *Journey to Amtrak*. Milwaukee: Kalmbach, 1972.

"EMC/EMD E-Unit Delivery Roster, Part II." *Passenger Train Journal*, August 1986, p. 35.

Frailey, Fred W. *Twilight of the Great Trains*. Waukesha, Wis.: Kalmbach, 1998.

Hilton, George W. "The Chicago, Cincinnati & Louisville Railroad." *RLHS Bulletin*, no. 114 (April 1966): 6–14.

The Historical Guide to North American Railroads. 2nd ed. Waukesha: Wis.: Kalmbach, 2000.

Huddleston, Gene. "C&O's 1950 Passenger Car Order: A North-South Controversy." *Chesapeake & Ohio Historical Magazine*, May 1995, pp. 3–6.

"ICC Allows C&O to Halt Two Passenger Trains." *Traffic World*, November 23, 1968, p. 17.

Ivey, Paul Wesley. *The Pere Marquette Railroad Company*. Grand Rapids, Mich.: Black Letter Press, 1970.

McKinney, Kevin. "The Pere Marquette Returns." *Passenger Train Journal*, October 1984, pp. 12–14.

Maiken, Peter T. *Night Trains*. Baltimore: Johns Hopkins University Press, 1989.

Million, Art. "Pere Marquette's Steel Passenger Car Fleet." *Chesapeake & Ohio Historical Magazine*, April 1989, pp. 4–16.

———. "Pere Marquette's Wooden Passenger Car Fleet." *Chesapeake & Ohio Historical Magazine*, October 1988, pp. 3–13.

———. "PM Railcar No. 17." *Chesapeake & Ohio Historical Magazine*, April 1989, p. 17.

"New C&O Dining Service." *Traffic World*, February 9, 1952, p. 76.

Schafer, Mike. "C&O's Mini Marquette." *Passenger Train Journal*, April 1988, pp. 17–23.

Schafer, Mike, and Joe Welsh. *Classic American Streamliners*. Osceola, Wis.: Motorbooks International, 1997.

Simons, Richard S., and Francis H. Parker. *Railroads of Indiana*. Bloomington: Indiana University Press, 1997.

Turner, Charles W., Thomas W. Dixon, Jr., and Eugene L. Huddleston. *Chessie's Road*. 2nd ed. Clifton Forge, Va.: Chesapeake & Ohio Historical Society, 1993.

Zimmerman, Karl. *Domeliners: Yesterday's Trains of Tomorrow*. Waukesha, Wis.: Kalmbach, 1998.

Chapter 5

"*Twentieth Century Limited* to Be 50 Years Old." *Traffic World*, June 14, 1952, pp. 77–78.

Abbey, Wallace W. "New York Central's New England States." *Trains*, September 1951, pp. 20–23.

———. "The Road of Efficiency Plus." *Trains*, February 1953, pp. 24–28.

Aldag, Robert, Jr. "Denting NYC's Last Steam Bastion." *Classic Trains*, spring 2001, pp. 42–47.

Anderson, Williard V. "The Princely New York Central." *Trains*, November 1948, pp. 16–25.

"Arrivals and Departures." *Trains*, July 1956, p. 14.

"Arrivals and Departures." *Trains*, December 1956, p. 10.

"Arrivals and Departures." *Trains*, January 1958, p. 10.

Beebe, Lucius. *Twentieth Century*. Berkeley, Calif.: Howell-North, 1962.

"Big Four in Indiana." *Indiana Magazine of History*, June and September 1925, pp. 109–273.

Bruce, Harry J. "Perlman the Magnificent." *Trains*, March 2002, pp. 38–45.

"Call Made for Seven-City Fight on Train Cuts." *Indianapolis News*, September 1, 1959, p. 11.

"Central Acts to Cut Mid-West Passenger Losses." *New York Central Headlight*, January 1958, p. 15.

"Central Signs Up with an 'X.'" *Trains*, July 1956, pp. 6–7.

Cook, Richard J., Sr. *New York Central's Mercury*. Lynchburg, Va.: TLC, 1991.

————. *The Twentieth Century Limited, 1938–1967*. Lynchburg, Va.: TLC, 1993.

"Diesel Power on NYC." *Traffic World*, May 3, 1952, p. 69.

Doughty, Geoffrey H. *New York Central's Great Steel Fleet*. Rev. ed. Lynchburg, Va.: TLC, 1999.

Dubin, Arthur. "The *Twentieth Century Limited*." *Trains*, August 1962, pp. 16–35.

————. *Some Classic Trains*. Milwaukee: Kalmbach Books, 1964.

Dunbar, Willis Frederick. *All Aboard! A History of Railroads in Michigan*. Grand Rapids, Mich.: William B. Eerdmans, 1969.

"Fast Train to Chicago." *New York Times*, August 25, 1896, p. 10.

Frailey, Fred W. *Twilight of the Great Trains*. Waukesha, Wis.: Kalmbach, 1998.

Hand, Victor. "In Lieu of the Great Steel Fleet." *Trains*, November 1968, pp. 40–43.

Harlow, Alvin F. *The Road of the Century: The Story of the New York Central*. New York: Creative Age Press, 1947.

"Hearings Open on Eight-Train Cut." *Indianapolis News*, July 20, 1959, p. 1.

"ICC Eyes Passenger Deficit Problem." *New York Central Headlight*, July 1957, pp. 14–16.

Klein, Aaron. *New York Central*. New York: Bonanza Books, 1985.

Meints, Graydon M. *Michigan Railroads and Railroad Companies*. East Lansing: Michigan State University Press, 1992.

Morgan, David P. "How Would You Like Your Center of Gravity?" *Trains*, May 1956, pp. 14–20.

"NARP Queries PC on Plan to End NYC Sleepers." *Traffic World*, October 26, 1968, p. 36.

"New York Central Expects Passenger Train Cuts after Loss of U.S. Mail Revenue." *Traffic World*, July 29, 1967, pp. 7–8.

"New York Central Marks Centennial in Chicago." *Traffic World*, February 23, 1952, p. 64.

The New York Central Railroad, 1831–1915. New York: James Kempster Printing Co., 1914.

New York Central Railroad Company Discontinuance of Passenger Train Service between Elkhart, Ind., and Chicago, Ill. 320 ICC Reports 526 (April 1963–October 1964).

New York Central Railroad Company Discontinuance of Trains Nos. 312 and 341 between St. Louis, Mo., and the Indiana–Ohio State Line. 331 ICC Reports 616 (September 1967–April 1968).

New York Central Railroad Company Discontinuance of Trains Nos. 57 and 96 between Chicago, Ill., and the Indiana–Ohio State Line. 331 ICC Reports 627 (September 1967–April 1968).

New York Central Railroad Timetables, various dates.

"NYC Asks End of Passenger Run to Chicago." *Indianapolis Times*, April 12, 1959, p. 1.

"NYC Asks to Quit Trains to St. Louis." *Indianapolis Star*, December 17, 1957, p. 17.

"NYC Plans Restructuring of N.Y. Passenger Services." *Traffic World*, November 11, 1967, pp. 42–43.

"NYC Steps Forward with Aerotrain." *New York Central Headlight*, February 1956, pp. 3, 12.

"NYC to Analyze Its Passenger Operations." *Traffic World*, February 9, 1953, p. 30.

"PC May Curtail Operation of Detroit–Chicago Train." *Traffic World*, October 26, 1968, p. 64.

"PC Train Discontinuance Plan to Be Investigated." *Traffic World*, December 28, 1968, p. 35.

Penn Central Company Discontinuance of Train No. 357 from Detroit, Mich., to Chicago, Ill. 333 ICC Reports 768 (May 1968–November 1968).

Penn Central Company and Illinois Central Railroad Company Discontinuance of Trains Nos. 363 and 304 between Chicago, Ill., and Cincinnati, Ohio. 336 ICC Reports 56 (October 1969–June 1970).

"Penn Central Plans to Halt Chicago-Detroit Train." *Traffic World*, May 25, 1968, p. 74.

Penn Central Transportation Company Discontinuance of 34 Passenger Trains. 338 ICC Reports 380 (July 1970–February 1972).

Pinkepank, Jerry A. "The Kankakee Belt Is Back in Business." *Trains*, February 1969, pp. 20–23.

"PSC Allows 2 Rail Lines to End Runs." *Indianapolis News*, July 25, 1959, p. 13.

"Rail Passenger Service to Cincinnati to Be Cut." *Indianapolis Star*, August 3, 1963, p. 1.

"Railroad Cites Big Loss on Run." *Indianapolis Star*, December 9, 1958, p. 27.

"Railroad Wants to Cut Service." *Indianapolis Star*, March 25, 1959, p. 13.

"The Riley Still Goes Says PSC." *Indianapolis Times*, February 26, 1959, p. 9.

"Riley Will Run One More Year." *Indianapolis News*, November 19, 1969.

Shaffer, Frank E. "Pullman Prolificacy." *Trains*, October 1967, pp. 24–28.

Simons, Richard S., and Francis H. Parker. *Railroads of Indiana*. Bloomington: Indiana University Press, 1997.

"So It Goes—Another Train Retires." *Indianapolis News*, January 10, 1969.

Stegmaier, Harry, Jr. "The Mercury." *Passenger Train Journal*, October 1987, pp. 18–27.

Stefee, Donald M. "How Fast Is New York Central?" *Trains*, February 1957, pp. 19–20.

Stevens, Frank Walker. *The Beginning of the New York Central Railroad*. New York: G. P. Putnam's Sons, 1926.

Stewart, William Benning. "Remembering the Riley." *Passenger Train Journal*, October/November 1976, pp. 15–20.

Sulzer, Elmer G. *Ghost Railroads of Indiana*. 1970; rpt., Bloomington: Indiana University Press, 1998.

"Train Cut Plea Cites 2½ Riders per Trip." *Indianapolis Times*, June 29, 1959, p. 1.

Chapter 6

"*Twentieth Century* and *Broadway* Observe Golden Anniversaries." *Trains*, August 1952, p. 16.

Beebe, Lucius. *Twentieth Century*. Berkeley, Calif.: Howell-North, 1962.

Burgess George H., and Miles C. Kennedy. *Centennial History of the Pennsylvania Railroad Company*. Philadelphia: Pennsylvania Railroad Co., 1949.

Cady, Ron. "Return of the Northern Arrow." *Passenger Train Journal*, April 1983, pp. 11–12.

Davis, Patricia T. *End of the Line: Alexander J. Cassatt and the Pennsylvania Railroad*. New York: Neale Watson, 1978.

Dubin, Arthur. "The Broadway Limited." *Trains*, February 1962, pp. 16–33.

———. *Some Classic Trains*. Milwaukee: Kalmbach, 1964.

Dunbar, Willis Frederick. *All Aboard! A History of Railroads in Michigan*. Grand Rapids, Mich.: William B. Eerdmans, 1969.

"Four-Month Continuation of Two PC Trains Ordered." *Traffic World*, October 5, 1968, p. 50.

Frailey, Fred W. *Twilight of the Great Trains*. Waukesha, Wis.: Kalmbach, 1998.

"ICC Dismisses 'Pennsy' Train Removal Notice." *Traffic World*, February 10, 1968, p. 53.

"ICC Orders PC to Retain Two Passenger Trains." *Traffic World*, August 24, 1968, pp. 38–39.

"ICC Orders Penn Central to Continue Two Trains." *Traffic World*, September 21, 1968, p. 47.

"ICC Reduces Passenger Train Operations Order." *Traffic World*, March 8, 1969, p. 54.

"ICC Rejects Penn Central Train-Removal Notice." *Traffic World*, March 16, 1968, p. 50.

"ICC to Probe PC Proposal to Remove Chicago Trains." *Traffic World*, July 26, 1969, pp. 52–53.

Kutta, Paul. "Advertising the Passenger Train: Pennsy's Last Hurrah." *National Railway Bulletin* 56, no. 6 (1991): 22–25.

Meints, Graydon M. *Michigan Railroads and Railroad Companies*. East Lansing: Michigan State University Press, 1992.

"Patrons Ask Review of ICC 'Train-Off' Rulings." *Traffic World*, March 15, 1969, p. 86.

"PC Authorized to Remove Its Chicago–New York and Pittsburgh-Chicago Trains." *Traffic World*, December 6, 1969, p. 36.

"PC Plans to Consolidate St. Louis–New York Trains." *Traffic World*, May 4, 1968, p. 66.

"PC Plans to Discontinue New York–Chicago Trains." *Traffic World*, July 5, 1969, p. 46.

"PC Plans to Discontinue Two Passenger Trains." *Traffic World*, April 20, 1968, p. 63.

"PC Plans to Discontinue Two Passenger Trains." *Traffic World*, January 3, 1970, p. 11.

"PC Seeks to Halt Trains." *Traffic World*, February 24, 1968, p. 60.

"PC's Petition for Review Denied in 'Train-Off' Case." *Traffic World*, April 19, 1969, p. 85.

"Penn Central Asks Halt of 'Kentuckian' Trains." *Traffic World*, March 23, 1968, p. 55.

Penn Central Company Discontinuance of Trains 3 and 30 between New York, N.Y., and St. Louis, Mo. 333 ICC Reports 736 (May 1968–November 1968).

Penn Central Company Discontinuance of Trains 3 and 30 between St. Louis, Mo., and New York, N.Y. 334 ICC Reports 638 (November 1968–November 1969).

"Penn Central May Remove Kentucky-Indiana Trains." *Traffic World*, April 13, 1968, p. 64.

Penn Central Transportation Company Discontinuance of Trains Nos. 65 and 66 between Chicago. Ill., and Cincinnati, Ohio. 336 ICC Reports 759 (October 1969–June 1970).

Penn Central Transportation Company Discontinuance of Train No. 50 from Chicago, Ill., to New York, N.Y., and Train No. 53 from Pittsburgh, Pa., to Chicago, Ill. 336 ICC Reports 182 (October 1969–June 1970).

Penn Central Transportation Company Discontinuance of 34 Passenger Trains. 338 ICC Reports 380 (July 1970–February 1972).

"Penn Central Would Halt 'Admiral' and 'Fort Pitt.'" *Traffic World*, March 23, 1968, p. 55.

"'Pennsy' Would Withdraw Train-Removal Notice." *Traffic World*, February 3, 1968, p. 68.

Pennsylvania Railroad Company Discontinuance of Trains 30 and 31 between New York, N.Y., and St. Louis, Mo. 328 ICC Reports 921 (August 1966–March 1967).

Pennsylvania Railroad Company Discontinuance of Trains 30 and 31 between St. Louis, Mo., and New York, N.Y. 330 ICC Reports 458 (May 1967–August 1967).

Pennsylvania–New York Central Transportation Company Discontinuance of Trains Nos. 70 and 71 between Chicago, Ill., and Cincinnati, Ohio. 333 ICC Reports 674 (May 1968–November 1968).

Pennsylvania–New York Central Transportation Company Discontinuance of Train No. 50 from Chicago, Ill., to New York, N.Y., and Train No. 53 from Pittsburgh, Pa., to Chicago, Ill. 333 ICC Reports 638 (May 1968–November 1968).

"Plan to Halt Chicago–NYC Passenger Trains Probed." *Traffic World*, April 13, 1964, p. 64.

"Plan to Halt Trains to Be Investigated." *Traffic World*, May 4, 1968, p. 55.

"PRR Intends to Discontinue Two NY–St. Louis Trains." *Traffic World*, December 30, 1967, p. 49.

"Removal of Two PC Trains Seen in Violation of Merger Protective Agreement." *Traffic World*, January 10, 1970, pp. 47–48.

Rosenbaum, Joel, and Tom Gallo. *The Broadway Limited*. Piscataway, N.J.: Railpace Co., 1989.

Schafer, Mike. *Classic American Railroads*. Osceola, Wis.: Motorbooks International, 1996.

Schafer, Mike, and Joe Welsh. *Classic American Streamliners*. Osceola, Wis.: Motorbooks International, 1997.

Seventy Years of America's Greatest Railroad: The Pennsylvania, 1846–1916. New York: Strong, Sturgis, 1916.

Simons, Richard S. "The Eel River and Its Railroads." *National Railway Bulletin* 53, no. 6 (1988): 28–35.

Simons, Richard S., and Francis H. Parker. *Railroads of Indiana*. Bloomington: Indiana University Press, 1997.

Somer, Paul M. *Illinois Central Streamliners, 1936–1946*. Lynchburg, Va.: TLC, 1995.

Sulzer, Elmer G. *Ghost Railroads of Indiana*. 1970; rpt., Bloomington: Indiana University Press, 1998.

Taylor, Jerry. *A Sampling of Penn Central Southern Region on Display*. Bloomington: Indiana University Press, 2000.

"Train-Off Order against ICC Continued by Court." *Traffic World*, March 22, 1969, p. 83.

Trax, Carson. "The Pennsylvania Special." *Bulletin National Railway Historical Society* 39, no. 3 (1974): 36–37.

"Two NY–Chicago Trains Consolidated by 'Pennsy.'" *Traffic World*, December 16, 1967, p. 10.

"U.S. District Court Blocks PC Proposal to Remove Chicago Trains." *Traffic World*, July 26, 1969, p. 74.

Wallis, Richard T. *The Pennsylvania Railroad at Bay*. Bloomington: Indiana University Press, 2001.

Watt, William J. *The Pennsylvania Railroad in Indiana*. Bloomington: Indiana University Press, 1999.

Welsh, Joe. *Pennsy Streamliners: The Blue Ribbon Fleet*. Waukesha, Wis.: Kalmbach, 1999.

Wood, Don, Jr. *The Pennsylvania Railroad, 1940s–1950s*. Chester, Vt.: Elm Tree Books, 1986.

Zimmerman, Karl. "The Broadway Limited Goes Streamlined." *Passenger Train Journal*, June 1988, pp. 16–23.

———. *Domeliners: Yesterday's Trains of Tomorrow*. Waukesha, Wis.: Kalmbach, 1998.

Chapter 7

Carleton, Paul. *The Erie Railroad Story*. Dunnellon, Fla.: D. Carleton Railbooks, 1988.

Cudahy, Brian J. "Last Days of Erie." *National Railway Bulletin*, no. 5 (1994): 5–19.

Erie Railroad: Its Beginnings—and Today. Erie Railroad, 1951.

"EL Authorized to Abandon Chicago–Hoboken Trains." *Traffic World*, January 3, 1970, p. 28.

"EL Plans to Discontinue Through Passenger Runs." *Traffic World*, June 21, 1969, p. 64.

Erie-Lackawanna Railroad Co. Discontinuance of Passenger Trains between Hoboken, N.J., and Chicago, Ill. 330 ICC Reports 234 (1967).

Erie-Lackawanna Railroad Co. Discontinuance of Train No. 1 between Hoboken, N.J. and Chicago, Ill.; Train No. 2 between Chicago, Ill., and Hoboken, N.J.; Train No. 21 between Hoboken, N.J. and Binghamton, N.Y.; Train No. 22 between Binghamton, N.Y., and Hoboken, N.J. 330 ICC Reports 508 (1967).

Grant, H. Roger. *Erie Lackawanna: Death of an American Railroad*. Stanford, Calif.: Stanford University Press, 1994.

Hastings, Phillip R. "Lake Cities Legacy." *Passenger Train Journal*, March 1978, pp. 15–20.

Hungerford, Edward. *Men of Erie*. New York: Random House, 1946.

Mott, Edward Harold. *Between the Ocean and the Lakes: The Story of Erie*. New York: Ticker, 1908.

"Plea by States to Block EL Discontinuance Denied." *Traffic World*, January 10, 1970, p. 63.

Scull, Theodore W. "Hoboken Intermodalism from a Gilded Age." *Passenger Train Journal*, September/October 1982, pp. 28–35.

Simons, Richard S., and Francis H. Parker. *Railroads of Indiana*. Bloomington: Indiana University Press, 1997.

Sulzer, Elmer G. *Ghost Railroads of Indiana*. 1970; rpt., Bloomington: Indiana University Press, 1998.

Welsh, Joe. "A Train Named Phoebe." *Passenger Train Journal*, September 1992, pp. 20–29.

Woodruff, Robert. *Erie Railroad—Its Beginnings*. New York: Newcomen Society, 1945.

Chapter 8

Hampton, Taylor. *The Nickel Plate Road: The History of a Great Railroad*. Cleveland: World, 1947.

Hirsimaki, Eric E. *The Nickel Plate Years*. North Olmsted, Ohio: Mileposts, 1989.

Holland, Kevin J. "Blue Arrows, Blue Darts, and Bluebirds." *Passenger Train Journal*, January 1990, pp. 20–36.

———. *Nickel Plate Passenger Service: The Postwar Years*. Lynchburg, Va.: TLC, 1997.

In the Matter of the Petition of the New York, Chicago and St. Louis Railroad Company for Leave to Discontinue Trains Nos. 15 and 16 Operated by the Company in the State of Indiana from the City of Frankfort to the Indiana-Ohio State Line, Thence to Toledo, Ohio. State of Indiana Public Service Commission, No. 14043, December 27, 1940.

New York, Chicago and St. Louis Railroad Company Discontinuance of Trains Nos. 7 and 8 between Buffalo, N.Y., and Chicago, Ill. 317 ICC Reports 775 (March 1962–June 1963).

Norfolk & Western Railway Co. Discontinuance of Trains Nos. 5 and 6 between Buffalo, N.Y., and Chicago, Ill. 330 ICC Reports 195 (1965).

Rehor, John A. *The Nickel Plate Story*. Milwaukee: Kalmbach, 1965.

Simons, Richard S., "The Clover Leaf Route." *National Railway Bulletin* 43, no. 1 (1978): 16–27.

Simons, Richard S., and Francis H. Parker. *Railroads of Indiana*. Bloomington: Indiana University Press, 1997.

Stephens, Bill. "Hot Times on the Norfolk Southern's Nickel Plate Line." *Trains*, October 1997, pp. 39–48.

White, Lynne L. *The Nickel Plate Road: A Short History of the New York, Chicago & St. Louis Railroad*. New York: Newcomen Society, 1954.

Chapter 9

Dunbar, Frederick. *All Aboard! A History of Railroads in Michigan*. Grand Rapids, Mich.: William B. Eerdmans, 1969.

Heimburger, Donald J. *Wabash*. River Forest, Ill.: Heimburger House, 1984.

The Historical Guide to North American Railroads. 2nd ed. Waukesha: Wis.: Kalmbach, 2000.

"ICC Again Orders N&W to Continue 'Cannonball' for One-Year Period." *Traffic World*, July 5, 1969, p. 13.

"ICC Allows N&W to Halt 'St. Louis Limited' Trains." *Traffic World*, June 15, 1968, p. 43.

Meints, Graydon M. *Michigan Railroads and Railroad Companies*. East Lansing: Michigan State University Press, 1992.

Morgan, David P. "Wabash." *Trains*, July 1950, pp. 12–26.

"N&W Must Continue Two St. Louis–Detroit Trains." *Traffic World*, February 3, 1968, p. 57.

"N&W Ordered to Continue 'Wabash Cannonball,' But It May Halt 'Banner Blue.'" *Traffic World*, September 16, 1967, p. 48.

"N&W Seeks to Halt Two Detroit–St. Louis Trains." *Traffic World*, January 13, 1968, p. 57.

Norfolk & Western Railway Co. *Discontinuance of Trains Nos. 110 and 111 between St. Louis, Mo., and Chicago, Ill., and Trains Nos. 301 and 304 between St. Louis, Mo., and Detroit, Mich.* 331 ICC Reports 415 (1967).

Norfolk & Western Railway Company Discontinuance of Trains Nos. 302/303 between St. Louis, Mo., and Detroit, Mich. 333 ICC Reports 284 (1968).

Norfolk & Western Railway Company Discontinuance of Trains Nos. 301 and 304 between St. Louis, Mo., and Detroit, Mich. 334 ICC Reports 506 (1969).

Norfolk and Western Railway Company v. United States. 316 F. Supp. 1396 (E.D. Mo. 1970).

"Plan to End Cannonball Is Subject to ICC Probe." *Traffic World*, March 1, 1969, p. 47.

Rehor, John A. *The Nickel Plate Story*. Milwaukee: Kalmbach, 1965.

Schafer, Mike. *More Classic American Railroads*. Osceola, Wis.: MBI, 2000.

Simons, Richard S. "The Eel River and Its Railroads." *National Railway Bulletin* 53, no. 6 (1988): 28–35.

———. "Lifeline of the Countryside." *Indianapolis Star Magazine*, April 22, 1955, pp. 26–30.

Simons, Richard S., and Francis H. Parker. *Railroads of Indiana*. Bloomington: Indiana University Press, 1997.

Stephens, Bill. "Automotive Artery." *Trains*, January 1996, pp. 42–55.

Sulzer, Elmer G. *Ghost Railroads of Indiana*. 1970; rpt., Bloomington: Indiana University Press, 1998.

"Wabash Cannonball Again Slated for Extinction." *Traffic World*, February 8, 1969, pp. 55–56.

Wabash Railroad Company Discontinuance of Service between Toledo, Ohio, and Fort Wayne, Ind. 307 ICC Reports 811 (1959).

Chapter 10

Currie, A. W. *The Grand Trunk Railway of Canada*. Toronto: University of Toronto Press, 1957.

Dorin, Patrick C. *The Grand Trunk Western Railroad: A Canadian National Railway*. Seattle: Superior, 1977.

Dubin, Arthur. *Some Classic Trains*. Milwaukee: Kalmbach, 1964.

Edmonson, Harold A., ed. *Journey to Amtrak*. Milwaukee: Kalmbach, 1971.

Grand Trunk Railroad Company Discontinuance of Trains Nos. 155 and 156 between Port Huron, Mich., and Chicago, Ill. 338 ICC Reports 254 (1970).

"GTW to Speed Up 'Mohawk' Detroit-Chicago Timetable." *Traffic World*, November 4, 1967, p. 106.

The Historical Guide to North American Railroads. Waukesha, Wis.: Kalmbach, 2000.

Hofsommer, Don L. *Grand Trunk Corporation: Canadian National Railways in the United States*. East Lansing: Michigan State University Press, 1995.

Lovett, Henry Almon. *Canada and the Grand Trunk*. New York: Arno Press, 1981.

Maiken, Peter T. *Night Trains: The Pullman System in the Golden Years of American Rail Travel*. Baltimore: Johns Hopkins University Press, 1992.

McKinney, Kevin. "Grand What's Its Name Railroad, You're Making Me Smile." *Passenger Train Journal*, spring 1968, pp. 4–8.

———. "Rebirth of Michigan's Corridor." *Passenger Train Journal*, January 1982, pp. 20–31.

Meints, Graydon M. *Michigan Railroads and Railroad Companies*. East Lansing: Michigan State University Press, 1992.

"News Shorts." *Passenger Train Journal*, summer 1968, p. 21.

"News Shorts." *Passenger Train Journal*, fall 1968, p. 20.

"News Shorts." *Passenger Train Journal*, winter 1968, p. 21.

Simons, Richard S., and Francis H. Parker. *Railroads of Indiana*. Bloomington: Indiana University Press, 1997.

Smith, Terry B. "But Nobody Is Listening." *Passenger Train Journal*, summer 1970, pp. 7–8.

Stevens, G. R. *History of the Canadian National Railways*. New York: Macmillan, 1973.

"Train-Offs." *Passenger Train Journal*, winter 1969, p. 27.

"U.S.–Canada Train Drop-off Planned." *Traffic World*, March 26, 1970, p. 104.

Chapter 11

Castner, Charles B., Robert E. Chapman, and Patrick C. Dorin. *Louisville & Nashville Passenger Trains: The Pan American Era, 1921–1971*. Lynchburg, Va.: TLC, 1999.

Chicago and Eastern Illinois Railroad Co. Discontinuance of Trains Nos. 1 and 92 between Danville, Ill., and Evansville, Ind. 328 ICC Reports 427 (1966).

Chicago and Eastern Illinois Railroad Co. Discontinuance of Trains Nos. 3 and 4 between Chicago, Ill., and Danville, Ill. 333 ICC Reports 626 (1968).

Chicago and Eastern Illinois Railroad Co. Discontinuance of Trains Nos. 94 and 54 between Chicago, Ill., and Evansville, Ind. 331 ICC Reports 447 (1968).

Chicago & Eastern Illinois Railroad Company v. United States 308 F. Supp. 645 (N.D. Ill. 1969).

City of Chicago v. United States 294 F. Supp. 1103 (N.D. Ill. 1969)

City of Chicago v. United States 396 U.S. 162 (1969).

City of Chicago v. United States 312 F. Supp. 442 (N.D. Ill. 1970).

Curl, Ray, and Robert McQuown. "The C&EI Railroad and Predecessors: Passenger Train Operations." *C&EI Flyer*, spring–fall 1993, pp. 1–69.

———. "The C&EI Railroad Passenger Train Operations: The Streamline Era Begins." *C&EI Flyer*, spring–fall 1994, pp. 1–62.

Dolzall, Gary W. "The Case for the C&EI." *Trains*, January 1990, pp. 36–43.

Gregory, William W., and Robert St. Clair. "You Can't Keep a Good Railroad Down!" *Trains*, October 1954, pp. 18–30.

The Historical Guide to North American Railroads. Waukesha, Wis.: Kalmbach, 2000.

Illinois Commerce Commission v. United States 346 F. Supp. 910 (N.D. Ill. 1972), *affirmed.* 421 U.S. 956 (1975).

Louisville and Nashville Railroad Co. Discontinuance of Trains Nos. 3 and 4 between Atlanta, Ga. and Evansville, Ind., and Trains Nos. 5 and 10 between Evansville, Ind., and St. Louis, Mo. 336 ICC Reports 81 (1969).

Schafer, Mike, and Joe Welsh. *Classic American Streamliners*. Osceola, Wis.: Motorbooks International, 1977.

Simons, Richard S., and Francis H. Parker. *Railroads of Indiana*. Bloomington: Indiana University Press, 1997.

Somers, Paul M. *Illinois Central Streamliners, 1936–1946*. Lynchburg, Va.: TLC, 1995.

Sulzer, Elmer G. *Ghost Railroads of Indiana*. 1970; rpt., Bloomington: Indiana University Press, 1998.

United States v. City of Chicago 400 U.S. 8 (1970).

"Up and Down the Railroad." *C&EI Flyer* (spring–summer 1992), posted on the website of the Chicago & Eastern Illinois Railroad Historical Society. Found at: http://ww2.justnet.com/cei/cevansv.html.

Chapter 12

"C&EI Seeks Authority to Halt Passenger Trains." *Traffic World*, September 9, 1967, p. 152.

"C&EI Plan to Halt Trains Will Be Probed." *Traffic World*, September 23, 1967, p. 54.

Castner, Charles B., Robert E. Chapman, and Patrick Dorin. *Louisville & Nashville Passenger Trains: The Pan-American Era, 1921–1971*. Lynchburg, Va.: TLC, 1999.

Castner, Charles B., Ronald Flanary, and Patrick Dorin. *Louisville & Nashville Railroad: The Old Reliable*. Lynchburg, Va.: TLC, 1996.

Chicago & Eastern Illinois Railroad Co. Discontinuance of Trains Nos. 1 and 92 between Danville, Ill., and Evansville, Ind. 328 ICC Reports 427 (1966).

Chicago & Eastern Illinois Railroad Company Discontinuance of Trains Nos. 93 and 54 between Chicago, Ill., and Evansville, Ind. 31 ICC Reports 447 (1968).

City of Chicago et al. v. United States et al. 294 F. Supp. 1103 (1969).

Clark, Thomas D. *The Beginning of the L&N*. Louisville, Ky.: Standard Printing, 1933.

Curl, Ray, and Robert McQuown. "The C&EI Railroad and Predecessors: Passenger Train Operations." *C&EI Flyer*, spring–fall 1993, pp. 1–69.

———. "The C&EI Railroad Passenger Train Operations: The Streamline Era Begins." *C&EI Flyer*, spring–fall 1994, pp. 1–62.

"Hartke Assails L&N Plan to Drop Indiana Trains, Seeks 'Full Investigation.'" *Traffic World*, July 26, 1969, p. 38.

Herr, Kincaid. *The Louisville & Nashville Railroad, 1850–1963*. Louisville, Ky.: Louisville & Nashville Railroad, 1964.

"ICC Orders That Six Trains Be Kept Running." *Traffic World*, November 16, 1970, p. 50.

Kerr, John Leeds. *The Story of a Southern Carrier*. New York: Young and Ottley, 1933.

Klein, Maury. *History of the Louisville & Nashville Railroad*. New York: Macmillan, 1972.

"L&N Asks Reconsideration of Train-Off Denial Order." *Traffic World*, January 17, 1970, p. 57.

"L&N Seeks Again to Drop Four Passenger Trains." *Traffic World*, June 13, 1970, pp. 62–63.

Louisville & Nashville Railroad Company Discontinuance of Nos. 53 and 92 between St. Louis, Mo., and Nashville, Tenn. 331 ICC Reports 203 (1967).

Louisville & Nashville Railroad Company Discontinuance of Trains Nos. 3 and 4, between Atlanta, Ga., and Evansville, Ind., and Trains Nos. 5 and 10 between Evansville, Ind., and St. Louis, Mo. 336 ICC Reports 91 (1969).

Prince, Richard E. *Louisville & Nashville Steam Locomotives*. Rev. ed. Green River, Wyo.: self-published, 1968.

Simons, Richard S., and Francis H. Parker. *Railroads of Indiana*. Bloomington: Indiana University Press, 1997.

Stover, John F. *The Railroads of the South, 1865–1900: A Study in Finance and Control*. Chapel Hill: University of North Carolina Press, 1955.

Teaford, Jon C. *Cities of the Heartland: The Rise and Fall of the Industrial Midwest*. Bloomington: Indiana University Press, 1993.

"Train Removal Permitted by ICC Is Held Affecting 'MoPac' Control of C&EI." *Traffic World*, March 9, 1968, p. 67.

Chapter 13

"The Abe Martin Special." *Indianapolis News*, February 17, 1945, p. 6.

Corliss, Carlton J. *Main Line of Mid-America: The Story of the Illinois Central*. New York: Creative Age Press, 1950.

"Court Orders IC Passenger Train Service Restored." *Indianapolis News*, September 5, 1946, p. 8.

"Effingham Run Ordered Resumed." *Indianapolis News*, April 4, 1946.
"Glancing Back." *Mattoon, Ill., Journal Gazette* (Mattoon, Ill.), March 16, 1988, p. 4; June 29, 1988, p. 4; July 10, 1988, p. 4; January 31, 1989, p. 4; February 15, 1989, p. 4.
Grayson, William T. "The Illinois Central Railroad in Evansville, Indiana." *Green Diamond*, June 1999, pp. 21–30.
Holmes, Emmit L. "A Passenger-Minded Railroad." *Illinois Central Magazine*, December 1962, pp. 2–3.
"IC Ordered to Resume Effingham Run." *Indianapolis News*, December 22, 1945, p. 3.
Illinois Central Railroad timetable of June 28, 1934.
Johnston, Wayne A. *The Illinois Central Heritage, 1851–1951*. New York: Newcomen Society, 1951.
"Monon Plans Cuts in Local Train Service." *World Telegraph* (Bloomington, Ind.), February 23, 1945.
Randall, W. David, and Alan R. Lind. *Monarchs of Mid-America*. Park Forest, Ill.: Prototype, 1973.
Simons, Richard S., and Francis H. Parker. *Railroads of Indiana*. Bloomington: Indiana University Press, 1997.
Stover, John F. *History of the Illinois Central*. New York: Macmillan: 1975.
Sulzer, Elmer G. *Ghost Railroads of Indiana*. 1970; rpt., Bloomington: Indiana University Press, 1998.
Sunderland, Edwin S. S. *Illinois Central Railroad: The Simplification of Its Debt Structure, 1938–1952*. Self-published, 1952.
"Train Service Hearings Set." *Indianapolis Star*, November 9, 1945, p. 3.

Chapter 14

Derleth, August. *The Milwaukee Road: Its First Hundred Years*. New York: Creative Age Press, 1948.
Dorin, Patrick C. *The Milwaukee Road East*. Seattle: Superior, 1978.
Lowenthal, Max. *The Investor Pays*. New York: Alfred A. Knopf, 1936.
Ploss, Thomas H. *The Nation Pays Again*. Self-published, 1991.
Scribbins, Jim. *Milwaukee Road Remembered*. Waukesha, Wis.: Kalmbach, 1990.
Simons, Richard. "The Milwaukee Road in Indiana." *National Railway Bulletin* 45, no. 1 (1980): 4–10.
Simons, Richard S., and Francis H. Parker. *Railroads of Indiana*. Bloomington: Indiana University Press, 1997.
Sulzer, Elmer G. *Ghost Railroads of Indiana*. 1970; rpt., Bloomington: Indiana University Press, 1998.

Chapter 15

Davis, Burke. *The Southern Railway Road of Innovators*. Chapel Hill: University of North Carolina Press, 1985.
DeButts, Harry A. *Men of Vision Who Served the South*. New York: Newcomen Society, 1955.
Flippen, Alan. "Louisville and Its Passenger Trains." *Passenger Train Journal*, May 1987, pp. 17–28.
Frailey, Fred W. *Twilight of the Great Trains*. Waukesha, Wis.: Kalmbach, 1998.
The Historical Guide to North American Railroads. 2nd ed. Waukesha, Wis.: Kalmbach, 2000.
Latimer, John. "From a Dispatcher's Notebook." *TRRA of St. Louis Historical and Technical Society*, autumn 1997/winter 1998, pp. 11–14.
"Petition to Abandon Service Evansville–New Albany Denied." *Indianapolis Star*, November 1, 1938, p. 24.
Prince, Richard E. *Southern Railway System: Steam Locomotives and Boats*. Rev. ed. Green River, Wyo.: Self-published, 1970.
Simons, Richard S., and Francis H. Parker. *Railroads of Indiana*. Bloomington: Indiana University Press, 1997.
"Southern to Drop Two Trains." *Traffic World*, May 17, 1952.
Stover, John F. *The Routledge Historical Atlas of the American Railroads*. New York: Routledge, 1998.
Thomas, Lawrence N. "The Southern Serves St. Louis, Too." *TRRA of St. Louis Historical and Technical Society*, autumn 1997/winter 1998, pp. 16–34.

Chapter 16

1913 annual report of the New York Central Railroad System.
Blaszak, Michael W. "Big Steel's Belt Line." *Trains*, August 1989, pp. 26–35.

———. "Change on the Harbor." *Trains*, March 1986, pp. 22–37.

Bradley, George K. *Northern Indiana Railway*. Chicago: Central Electric Railfans Association, 1998.

Heimburger, Donald J. *Wabash*. River Forest, Ill.: Heimburger House, 1984.

Ottesen, Mark. "The New Toledo, Peoria & Western." *Trains*, March 1997, pp. 56–61.

Rehor, John A. *The Nickel Plate Story*. Milwaukee: Kalmbach, 1965.

Simons, Richard S. "St. Joseph Valley Railway." *National Railway Bulletin* 51, no. 1 (1987): 28–36.

Simons, Richard S., and Francis H. Parker. *Railroads of Indiana*. Bloomington: Indiana University Press, 1997.

Stringham, Paul H. *Toledo, Peoria & Western Tried, Proven and Willing*. Peoria, Ill.: Deller Archive, 1993.

Sulzer, Elmer G. *Ghost Railroads of Indiana*. 1970; rpt., Bloomington: Indiana University Press, 1998.

"Toot Toot! Ferdinand Flier's on Line (6.7 miles) for Haul to Huntingburg." *Indianapolis Star*, October 23, 1938.

INDEX

Page numbers in *italics* refer to illustrations.

Craig Sanders teaches journalism and mass media communications at Cleveland State University. He earned a Ph.D. in mass communications and an M.A. in journalism from Indiana University, an M.A. in political studies from Sangamon State University, and a B.A. in history and political science from Eastern Illinois University. His research has focused on the relationship between newspapers and attorneys and the work of newspaper ombudsmen. He worked for 13 years as a newspaper reporter and copy editor. A lifelong railroad enthusiast, he has published articles in *Trains* magazine and *The Observation Car,* the Amtrak Historical Society magazine.